FREE DAISM

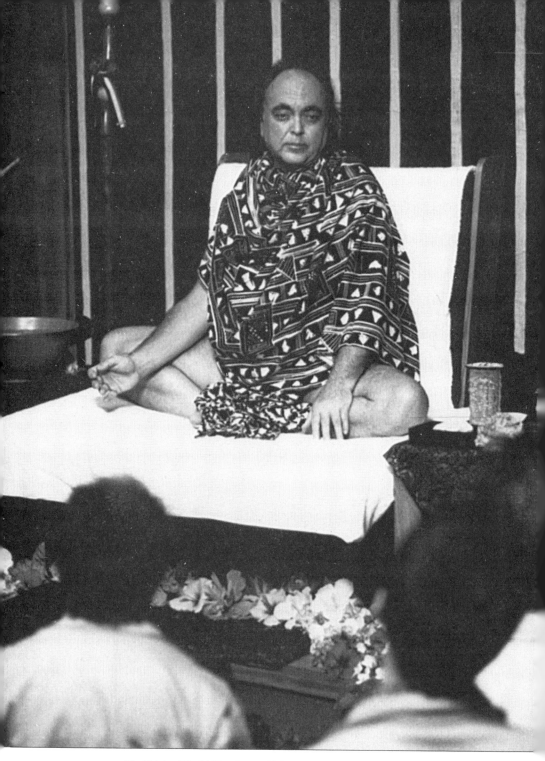

The Divine World-Teacher and True Heart-Master,
DA AVABHASA (THE "BRIGHT")
Sri Love-Anandashram, August 1992

FREE DAISM

The Eternal, Ancient, and New Religion
of God-Realization

*An Introduction to the God-Realizing Way of Life Revealed by
The Divine World-Teacher and True Heart-Master,*

DA AVABHASA
(THE "BRIGHT")

by
the Free Daist Writers Guild

edited by Paul Augspurger

THE DAWN HORSE PRESS
CLEARLAKE, CALIFORNIA

NOTE TO THE READER

The devotional, Spiritual, functional, practical, relational, cultural, and formal community practices and disciplines discussed in this book, including the meditative practices, the Yogic exercises of "conductivity", the breathing exercises, the life-disciplines of right diet and exercise, the intelligent economization and practice of sexuality, etc., are appropriate and natural practices that are voluntarily and progressively adopted by each student-novice and member of the Free Daist Communion and adapted to his or her personal circumstance. Although anyone may find them useful and beneficial, they are not presented as advice or recommendations to the general reader or to anyone who is not a participant in Da Avabhasa International or a member of the Free Daist Communion. And nothing in this book is intended as a diagnosis, prescription, or recommended treatment or cure for any specific "problem", whether medical, emotional, psychological, social, or Spiritual. One should apply a particular program of treatment, prevention, cure, or general health only in consultation with a licensed physician or other qualified professional.

For a further discussion of individual responsibility in the Way of the Heart, our claim to perpetual copyright to the Wisdom-Teaching of Sri Da Avabhasa, and His renunciate status in the Free Daist Communion, please see "Further Notes to the Reader", pages 329-331 of this book.

First Edition September, 1992
Printed in the United States of America

Produced by the Free Daist Communion
in cooperation with the Dawn Horse Press

Library of Congress Cataloging-in-Publication Data

Free Daism: The Eternal, Ancient, and New Religion of God-Realization:
An Introduction to the God-Realizing Way of Life Revealed by The Divine World-Teacher and True Heart-Master, Da Avabhasa (The "Bright") by the Free Daist Writers Guild; edited by Paul Augspurger.
　　　　p.　　cm.
Includes index.
ISBN 0-918801-39-7 : $17.95
1. Spiritual life. 2. Da Free John, 1939–　.   I. Augspurger, Paul
II. Free Daist Writers Guild.
BP610.B82F74　　1992
299' .93—dc20
　　　　　　　　　　　92-22863
　　　　　　　　　　　CIP

CONTENTS

The Eternal, Ancient, and New Religion of God-Realization

by Paul Augspurger

From time immemorial, the Divine Reality has been spoken of and directly revealed to Spiritual aspirants by the great figures of the world's religious traditions, based on their own direct experience and Realization. Sri Da Avabhasa is such an Enlightened, or God-Realized, Being, of the most profound degree. He has appeared in our time in order to establish a new tradition, a God-Realizing Way of life for all of humanity, a Way of Liberation beyond the dead ends of scientific materialism, religious provincialism, and egoic suffering of every kind. This book describes Who Da Avabhasa Is, and it details the Way of life that He Offers to all who would enjoy a Liberated participation in existence—the practice of Free Daism.

Free Daism, or the Way of the Heart, is based in two fundamental principles, which you will find as constantly recurring themes in this book: first, the time-honored practice of devotion to the God-Realized Adept, the Agent of Divine Influence, and second, a world-view based in the Argument and process of "radical" understanding—an understanding so simple yet so profoundly fundamental that it cuts equally through the limitations and misunderstandings of Western and Eastern philosophies, personal problems, and all feelings of limitation, "like a hot knife through butter".

Free Daism makes use of all the great traditional forms of practice: heart-felt, ecstatic devotional worship; study of the Teacher's Word; direct, discriminative examination of the processes of existence; meditative practices; self-discipline; a life of self-giving or service to the Divine. Yet Sri Da Avabhasa's Way of the Heart is not a synthesis carefully garnered from the world's traditions of religion and Spirituality. Each of these practices has been renewed (or Revealed for the first time), Empowered, and understood in a new way by Sri Da Avabhasa.

Free Daism has been described by Sri Da Avabhasa as "the Eternal, Ancient, and New Religion of God-Realization". Because it is an epitome of the timeless verities of the process of God-Realization, Free Daism is eternal; because it is based in the time-honored practice of the devotional, mutually sacrificial relationship to a God-Man, it is ancient; because it represents a modern-day formulation of this time-honored means of practice, cast in the light of a unique "radical" understanding and founded in the living relationship with Sri Da Avabhasa in each moment, it is always new.

What you will find here is no mere statement of dogma. Everything in this book is offered for your "consideration" or intensive personal examination and verification in life. In Free Daist practice, every mere <u>belief</u> about reality is tested.

Free Daism is the real thing, the real Spiritual Process. It is a practice lived every day, in community with other practitioners, in direct relationship with our ultimate Source of Grace—the Living God-Man Da Avabhasa (The "Bright"). Transformation is necessarily an ordeal; Spiritual practice is a self-transcending rather than self-fulfilling course. As Sri Da Avabhasa has Said, "The being grows through confrontation, difficulty, and demand." And Sri Da Avabhasa provides the greatest possible Help, Given through many means, for passing through that ordeal.

This book gives a basic overview of Free Daism. Part One is a "consideration" of the basic principles of Free Daism—Satsang (or the relationship to the Realizer) and "radical" understanding. Part Two is a presentation of Sri Da Avabhasa's Life and Work. This brief biography will give you an understanding of Who He Is, the progressive process of devotion and insight that led to His own Divine Re-Awakening, and a brief outline of His Work with His devotees—the years of His Teaching Work, and then His epochal Divine Emergence and the current form of His relationship with His devotees. A picture of the Guru-devotee relationship so central to Free Daism is given in Part Three, which describes the Seven Gifts of Grace that Sri Da Avabhasa Offers those who establish a formal Sacred relationship with Him. Part Four is a detailed description of the progressive process of growth in the Way of the Heart, from the beginnings of the practice through Divine Self-Realization. Free Daism is already a world religion, with regional centers and area study groups around the world: Part Five describes the community and culture of Free Daism in words and pictures, and ends with a personal account of what it is like to go on retreat at Sri Da Avabhasa's Hermitage Sanctuary. The Epilogue presents one of Sri Da Avabhasa's classic summaries of His Wisdom-Teaching.

Throughout this book you will find stories about what it is like for ordinary men and women to come in contact with a Divinely Enlightened Being. These stories, or "Leelas", are testimonies to Sri Da Avabhasa's Love, His Humor, His Insight, His Freedom, the Truth of His Instruction, and the effectiveness of the great relationship that He Offers those who practice in His Company. These stories provide Glimpses of an utterly astonishing Being—One Who Transcends the limits of human nature, and Who Reveals our own real possibilities.

My own testimony is that the deepest Happiness of my life has come through my devotional relationship with my Sat-Guru. Sri Da Avabhasa has touched me with His

Love, breaking open my heart again and again. That relationship, in its ecstatic heights and its authentic ordeal, is Free Daism.

The men and women who wrote, edited, and produced this book are all Free Daist practitioners. This book is our invitation to you to join us in our life of devotion to this most miraculous Being, Who has come to Liberate us from our patterns of unhappiness and unlove and Bless us with Realization of the Truth.

NOTE TO THE READER

Sri Da Avabhasa has transformed the English language into a vehicle to serve His Communication of the truly Sacred, God-Realizing Process in His Company. In doing so, He has Revealed the logic underlying the common conventions of written English:

Ordinary speech and written language are centered on the ego-"I", as a tent is raised on a centerpole. Therefore, in ordinary speech and written language, the ego-word "I" is commonly capitalized, and everything less than the ego-"I" is shown in lowercase.

In contrast, the "centerpole" of Heart-Master Da's Speech and Writing is the Heart, the Divine Wisdom, Consciousness, Truth, Reality, Happiness, and "Love-Ananda" ("inherently Love-Blissful Unity"). Therefore, He capitalizes those words that express the Ecstatic Feeling of the Awakened Heart, and, in many instances, lowercases those words expressive of the ego or conditional limits in general.

Blessed with the Gift of His Awakening Grace, Sri Da Avabhasa's devotees are thus inspired to use the capitalization of words associated with Sri Da Avabhasa as a means of honoring Him and His Divine Attributes.

The Divine Name "Da Avabhasa" and the Sacred Logo of the Free Daist Communion

Sri Da Avabhasa has described the meaning of His Principal Name, "Da", in *The Dawn Horse Testament*:

"Da" Is A Traditional Name Of God, or A Traditional Feeling-Reference To The Ultimate Condition and Power of Existence. "Da" Is An Eternal, Ancient, and Always New Name For The Divine Being, Source, and Spirit-Power, and "Da" Is An Eternal, Ancient, and Always New Name For The Realizer Who Reveals (and Is The Revelation Of) The Divine Being, Source, and Spirit-Power. Therefore, The Name "Da" Is (Since The Ancient Days) Found In Religious Cultures All Over the world.

As An Expression Of My Realization Of The Eternal, Ancient, and Always New One, The Name "Da" Has Spontaneously Appeared With Me (As A Sign Of The One Who I Have Realized, and Who I Reveal, and Whose Revelation I Am). Indeed, The "I" and "Me" and "My Self" That Speaks To You . . . Is My Own Unique Voice Of Self-Reference, and It Is, With My (Divinely Self-Revealed) Name "Da", The Representation and Expression Of My Ecstatic, or Enstatic, Inherent, Necessary, and Inherently Perfectly Love-Blissful Identification With The One and Only Condition That Is The Great and Only One. (p. 435)

Heart-Master Da Revealed His Name "Avabhasa" in 1991. "Avabhasa" is a Sanskrit term associated with a variety of meanings: "brightness", "appearance", "splendor", "lustre", "light", "knowledge". This Name proclaims His Identification with the "Brightness" of Divine Self-Realization.

The triangular design on the facing page and the cover of this book has been created by Sri Da Avabhasa as the logo for the Free Daist Communion, the sacred Institution charged with the responsibility to serve those who respond to Him. Its symbolism represents the fulfillment of Free Daism, which is Liberation from bondage to the body-mind-self, the Supreme Gift Granted by the Grace of Heart-Master Da.

The major elements of the design are the Divine Name "Da", represented by the Greek letters delta (Δ), and alpha (α), and Sri Da Avabhasa's Sacred Title "Eleutherios", which means "Liberator".

The small circle inside the delta represents the "heart on the right", a locus intuited in the right atrium of the heart, where, in the ultimate course of practice in the Way of the Heart, the mechanism of attention (which is the root of our bondage to the body-mind) is finally dissolved in its Transcendental Source. This allows Awakening to Transcendental Divine Self-Realization, or Perfect Liberation in Truth.

FREE DAISM

The Eternal, Ancient, and New Religion
of God-Realization

Always Behold Me With Your Heart.

*Do Not merely watch Me, Do Not merely think Of Me,
but Always Feel Me, and Thereby Contemplate Me.*

*Therefore, In every moment, <u>Behold</u> Me With Your
Heart, and <u>Thereby</u> Surrender, Forget, and Transcend
Your (Separate and Separative) self In My Heart.*

*Beloved, Even When All My Secrets Are Told, My Heart
Itself Must Shine.*

*And Even Though My Image Shines, My Heart Itself
Must Give You Sight.*

*And I Am Always Standing There, To See You Taste
The Fragrant Light.*

*Always "Brighter" Than all eyes, I Stand Awake In The
Heart's Free Air.*

*And There, Until The Shine Outshines, I White The
Dark That Bites The Heart-Space Thin.*

And I <u>Am</u> The "Bright" Itself.

And To Shine <u>Is</u> The Way Of The Heart.

DA AVABHASA
The Dawn Horse Testament

SRI DA AVABHASA (THE "BRIGHT")
Sri Love-Anandashram, July 1992

A Call To Awakening

a Talk by The Divine World-Teacher and True Heart-Master,
Da Avabhasa (The "Bright")
May 11, 1977

SRI DA AVABHASA: Ordinarily you maintain without the slightest ambiguity the presumption of being this fleshy entity. It just seems necessary to presume. You do not feel that there is any way around it. You do not even regard the body to be something arising in Consciousness. You think that Consciousness is somehow inside the body, in the brain, or in some condition less than the flesh itself, somehow created by senior unconscious atoms, its destiny determined by the fleshy thing that you know well.

When you understand that the body and the mind and the sense of separate identity itself all arise in the Divine Field of "Brightness" as a mere modification, then you will have a great deal of humor relative to this affair of waking life. Then the great adventure of trying to attain a victory or to find the great goal for which all beings are born will come to an end. Then you will be Free, but not until then.

What you know of dreams should illumine your position in the waking state. You are in exactly the same position in the waking state as in the dream state. You know very well, from the point of view of the waking state, that in dreaming you create the environment as well as the sense of being an independent entity. Clearly the dream is your own individual consciousness. It is _your_ dream. Who else made the dream but you? It arises in your own consciousness. If, in the dream, you are running to leap into the water and suddenly it turns into a pit of fire, you created it. Your own psychic nature made the fire, so that you fell into fire instead of swimming across the lake. This is clear when you wake up, though it is not clear in the dream itself, because in the dream you identify exclusively with the knowing entity, the ego-presumption, the separate one in the adventure. When you wake, you realize that you created all of it, that it was your own consciousness, and that now, in the waking state, it has no necessity. Now it is completely arbitrary, an hallucination.

You must wake up! Not a single thought, conception, or experience, high or low, is anything but a permutation of the dream. That is what there is to realize in My Company—this profound initiation into your Real Condition in this moment. Until in your sympathy with Me you begin to Realize the Divine Reality most directly, all I can do is Confess to you that I (and, therefore, you and all beings) am not identical to the condition of being a separate entity. I am not an entity. I am not inside a body. To call My Self this body-mind is just as arbitrary as to say I am the morning star or the vision within or a light you may see by turning upward. These are all arbitrary identifications, completely unnecessary, completely humorous, completely without the slightest bit of seriousness from My Point of View.

Ultimately, it becomes clear that the tree in the yard is an hallucination, that it is a matter of mind, just as any thought that you project inwardly. It is exactly the same. You will not at last have to go through a mental process to believe this. It will just appear to be obviously so. And when it is thus obvious, the Realization is not disorienting. The presumption of your Real Condition is neither a thought nor an act. It is not itself a state of experience, gross or subtle. It is a kind of transparency. The present appearance is simply a process arising in a Condition that is without center, form, relations, or bounds. That Condition is transparent, obvious, and the only presumption that is Truth, or Happiness.

Until Your Divine Condition is obvious, you must be constantly available to Me, constantly available to My Instruction, My Argument, My Disciplines, My Company. The life Awakened in My Company serves the penetration of the dream. When that Realization becomes summary, Most Perfect, in your case, then you are simply Happy.

Da Avabhasa's Revelation of Free Daism

*by Michael Macy
and
Meg McDonnell*

On April 25, 1972, Sri Da Avabhasa opened the doors of His first Ashram to all who would come. It was a humble circumstance—those who sat at His feet that evening, only some thirty-odd, could hear the muffled Los Angeles street traffic passing by outside as the young Spiritual Teacher sat in silence with them. Sri Da Avabhasa's palpable Radiance filled the Meditation Hall where they were gathered, in what had once been an ordinary store, now transformed into an Ashram center called "Sri Hridayam Satsang" ("the Company of the Heart").

There is a Truth beyond words, a Divine Reality that cannot be grasped by the mind but that is directly felt at the heart—such is the Truth that was silently Communicated in Heart-Master Da's Company that night.

Although those present could not know it, this was the inception of a new world religion, the birth of Free Daism. That night, Sri Da Avabhasa Communicated His great Way of the Heart, first in silence, and then, after sitting in silence for an hour, He spoke, outlining His fundamental, new, and "radical" insight into the human condition:

SRI DA AVABHASA: Everyone has understood?

QUESTION: I haven't understood. Explain it to me.

SRI DA AVABHASA: Very good. What haven't you understood?

QUESTION: . . . Well, you could start with the word "understanding".

SRI DA AVABHASA: Yes. There is a disturbance, a feeling of dissatisfaction, some sensation that motivates a person to go to a teacher, read a book about philosophy, believe something, or do some conventional form of Yoga. What people ordinarily think of as spirituality or religion is a search to get free of that sensation, that suffering that is motivating them. So all the usual paths—Yogic methods, beliefs, religion, and so on—are forms of seeking, grown out of this sensation, this subtle suffering. Ultimately, all the usual paths are attempting to get free of that sensation. That is the traditional goal. Indeed, <u>all</u> human beings are seeking, whether or not they are very sophisticated about it, or using very specific methods of Yoga, philosophy, religion, whatever.

When that whole process of seeking begins to break down, one no longer quite has the edge of one's search left. One begins to suspect oneself. One begins to doubt the whole process of one's search. Then one is no longer fascinated with one's search, one's method, one's Yoga, one's religion, one's ordinary teacher. One's attention begins to turn to this sensation that motivates one's entire search.

. . . When the individual begins to see again the dilemma that motivates his or her method, that seeing is understanding. As long as he or she is simply seeking, and has all kinds of motivation, fascination with the search, this is not understanding—this is dilemma itself. But where this dilemma is understood, there is the re-cognition[1] of a structure in consciousness, a separation. And when that separation is observed more and more directly, one begins to see that what one is suffering is not something happening <u>to</u> one but it is one's own action. It is as if you are pinching yourself, without being aware of it. You are "creating" a subtle pain, and, worse than the pain, a continuous modification, which is "mind", which consciousness identifies as itself. The more one observes this, the more one's search is abandoned, spontaneously, intelligently. One simply sees one's motivation, one's

Before becoming a devotee of Da Avabhasa's in October 1987, Michael Macy had engaged in an exaggerated search for Truth—in Western philosophy, extended wilderness hikes, and pilgrimages to India and Nepal. Michael was working on his doctorate in biophysics at the University of California when he encountered Da Avabhasa's Wisdom-Teaching, realized it was the Truth he had been searching for, and took up the practice of the Way of the Heart. Michael has served as managing editor of the Dawn Horse Press for the last three years.

actual suffering. One can only live that suffering. It does not move, until conscious life becomes a crisis. Then one sees that the entire motivation of life is based on a subtle activity in consciousness. That activity is avoidance, separation, a contraction at the root, the origin, the "place", of consciousness. . . .

QUESTION: Is the activity of the mind and thought an obstruction?

SRI DA AVABHASA: What is your experience?

QUESTION: My experience is that in spite of what I will or wish, I have lots of strange thoughts.

SRI DA AVABHASA: If you close the eyes meditatively, you turn yourself mainly to concentration on mind-forms. But if your eyes are open, there are people, functional demands, and the whole cosmic event. And while you are sitting there with your eyes open, you will become aware that all of this thought is also going on. You will begin to feel, almost see, how thought slides between you and all contact with the moving world. Thought is an actual, solid obstruction. It is a form of matter, a modification of energy. What you call the mind is wave-lengths of force, functioning, taking on forms, through the subtle processes of electrical interchange. So when you have a thought, you have modified the energy flowing through the brain regions. In other words, you have <u>contracted</u> it, and you are always concentrating on that contraction. If you pinch your arm, attention centers at the point of pain. If you have a thought, attention centers at the point of thought. Whenever there is distraction by a particular entity, form, function, or whatever, there is loss of direct awareness, of relationship. When there is concentration, everything else is excluded. The "ego" is just another form of concentration, of distraction. In the case of the ego, the distraction is not a particular thought but the separate self sense that all contraction generates. The ego is an activity, not an entity. . . .

 The root of true spirituality is not some activity like desire that seeks to get you to the super-Object. Genuine spirituality is understanding of the whole process of motivation. It is to re-cognize the root of it—this contraction, this separation. (The Method of the Siddhas, *"Understanding"*)

Meg McDonnell, the oldest of eight siblings, spent much of her early life traveling with her exuberant and ever-increasing family. As a young woman, she was drawn, through her exposure to the various cultures they visited, to study art history, dance, theatre, and writing.

 Since becoming a devotee of Sri Da Avabhasa in 1976, her service to Him has been focused around the communication of His Wisdom-Teaching and the Stories of His Life. She has served as lecturer, writer, and director of video and theatrical productions about the Way of the Heart. Meg currently serves as the senior editor at the Dawn Horse Press.

"One begins to see that what one is suffering is not something happening to one,
but it is one's own action. It is as if you are pinching yourself, without being aware of it."

Da Avabhasa on the evening of April 25, 1972

Da Avabhasa Called His listeners that night, as He Calls us now, to notice that there is a subtle (or not-so-subtle) tension, discomfort, or dis-ease motivating all that we do. We are constantly trying to relieve ourselves of that sense of suffering—but without sensitizing ourselves to its underlying cause, as though we could effectively treat the symptoms without addressing the root of the dis-ease itself!

To whatever degree we may be aware of it, our sense of limitation, of separation from Happiness, of the need to reunite with or seek Happiness, even our feeling that we are a separate "self" subject to death and every kind of painful and arbitrary intrusion, all stem from this seed activity, the "self-contraction".

Almost two decades after this first Discourse, in a book entitled *The Da Avabhasa Upanishad* Sri Da Avabhasa would summarize His sweeping, "radical" (or "root") Argument thus:

"Consider" this: You are active as self-contraction. Indeed, you, as a conditional or psycho-physical personality or "I", are the activity of self-contraction.

The activity of self-contraction is suffering, it is deluding, and it is itself an illusion, or an illusory disease.

The activity of self-contraction is un-Necessary. The activity of self-contraction is not Ultimately Real (or Necessary), but it is only (apparently) being added to Reality. The activity of self-contraction is being superimposed on What Always Already Is.

The activity of self-contraction is dramatized in the gross bodily plane of experience as the complex avoidance of relationship. It is dramatized in the subtle plane of experience as emotions and thoughts. It is dramatized essentially (or at the original or causal level) as attention itself. . . .

Therefore, egoity (or the suffered drama of the separate "I" and its separate "other") is a disease (even an imaginary disease, since it is self-caused, unnecessary, and self-contained).

The fascinating "I" (separate, independent of any "other" and the process of relationship) is the ultimate psychological and philosophical Illusion.

There Is no separate "I". (pp. 332, 344)

This "radical" understanding is fundamental to Free Daism, and its ramifications—for each one of us personally and for us as a human collective—cannot be overestimated. The results of this root-activity of contraction show themselves as every kind of human suffering—from our private sense of separation and alienation from others, to our addictive attempts to assuage our consequent neediness through pleasure, power, acquisition, or knowledge, to our constant underlying fear of death, to greed, lust, anger, fear, sorrow, including our fundamental unwillingness to love, to be vulnerable. And all of this manifests, on a larger scale, as every kind of social problem, in the failure to cooperate in solving the common problems facing humanity, in outright conflict

"The 'ego' is just the separate self sense that all contraction generates. The ego is an activity, not an entity."

Los Angeles, 1972

of devastating proportions, and in the most destructive irresponsibility for one another, our resources, and our planet. In fact, all the manifestations of humanity's self-inflicted suffering and unlove are rooted in this activity of self-contraction.

Because of this, it is not merely a matter of personal importance that each of us attend to Da Avabhasa's Arguments and His Offering—it is of primary significance to the world in which we live. In fact, Sri Da Avabhasa's Birth and His entire Life and Work are the expressions of His commitment to provide the very means by which our personal and collective destiny—as it is dictated by the self-contraction—can be undone.

In the weeks following that first night in Los Angeles (and on countless occasions since then), Heart-Master Da spoke very plainly about what we must understand about our seeking and about the self-contraction itself, dispelling in the process many age-old misconceptions about Spirituality, Enlightenment, and Gurus:

SRI DA AVABHASA: That which is called "realization", "liberation", "God-union", or whatever, gets represented to people in various symbolic forms, as something with lots of planes and worlds, colors, lights and visions, figures and forms, methods, universes, "inside" and "outside", going here, going there, distance, direction, shape. These are all conceptual communications, symbols, pictures for the mind. Fundamentally, they exploit your suffering, by motivating you to acquire whatever it is they represent or hide. True spiritual life is not a motivation to these symbols, a belief in them, nor even the acquisition of what they represent. True spiritual life is the process in consciousness in which there is understanding, or re-cognition, of suffering, the present experience.

Where there is no suffering, that which stands out or becomes the obvious is called "heaven", "nirvana", "liberation", the "Self", "Brahman", "God", "God-union", "Truth", "Reality". When there is no dilemma, when consciousness itself ceases to take on form or become identical to form, this is what is called "liberation". The process that is involved is not one of search based on suffering. Ordinarily, if you suffer, you immediately seek to get free, and you attach yourself to all kinds of hopeful signs. But true life, or spiritual life, is the reverse of that. Ordinarily, you are seeking, pursuing forgetfulness from your suffering, your dilemma, your contraction, this separation, this unconsciousness. You pursue the absence of that in delight, enjoyment, distraction, search for perfection, search for all kinds of acquisitions, food, sex, money, good weather, lunch, until this whole process begins to become uninteresting. . . .

Then, instead of simply suffering, you may . . . see beyond this contraction that is your suffering. And you begin to enjoy that which your chronic activity and state always prevent.

Your suffering is your own activity. It is something that you are doing moment to moment. It is a completely voluntary activity. You cognize it in the form of symptoms, which are the sense of separate existence, the mind of endless qualities, of differentiation, and the whole form of motion, of desire. You are always already living in these things, but their root, the source of it all, the thing whose form they are all reflecting, is this contraction, this separative act, this avoidance of relationship, which constantly "creates" the form in consciousness that you cognize as suffering. Where it is re-cognized, known again, this activity and its symptoms cease to be the form of consciousness. Then what is always prevented by the usual state becomes the form of consciousness. Where there is unqualified relationship, where there is no contraction, where there is no separation, no avoidance, there is no differentiation, no necessary mind, no necessary desire, no identification with separate movement. Then consciousness falls into its own form, without effort.

Symbolically, this is called "knowing", or "cognizing", the One Divine Self. But in fact it is not possible to fix attention on the Divine Self. Your own Divine Nature, or Reality Itself, cannot become an object of attention. The actual process involves attention and re-cognition of this suffering, this contraction. Where suffering is thus "known", what it prevents is suddenly, spontaneously enjoyed—not as the "object" of enjoyment, but as the enjoyment itself. Then, prior to effort, motivation, or attention, there is only the Divine Self, Reality, the Heart.[2] (The Method of the Siddhas, "The Avon Lady")

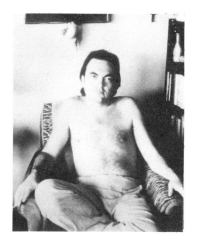

When we understand—which is to say, when we observe and feel into and then feel beyond— our own activity of self-contraction, we can feel what is prior to that contraction. We can feel the "Great Space" in which the contraction is arising, the native Happiness of Being, unspoiled by egoity.

"Prior to effort, motivation, or attention, there is only the Divine Self, Reality, the Heart."

Los Angeles, 1972

This capability is granted, through His Blessing and Help, from the very first moment that we encounter Sri Da Avabhasa's Wisdom-Teaching. This is one of the reasons why Da Avabhasa Says that in His Way of the Heart, Great Blessing is Given from the very beginning of practice—not just Realized at the end. Ultimately, when we understand and transcend this activity of self-contraction most Perfectly, we Realize our true Identity, the Divine Self, permanently and completely.

The understanding of which Da Avabhasa Speaks is not just believing in an idea: It is a literal, obvious, self-authenticating change in one's relationship to the world and oneself, the ultimate paradigm shift. It is the clear acknowledgement of a new and truer vision of Reality—which is directly Revealed in the Spiritual Company of Da Avabhasa Himself.

The following excerpt from one of Sri Da Avabhasa's Discourses summarizes His Argument relative to "radical" understanding. In it, He describes our real situation from the viewpoint of His own Enlightened Realization, and humorously Calls us beyond our apparent suffering to the heart-celebration that is the true Spiritual process. At the same time, Da Avabhasa exposes the errors in the myriad secular and Spiritual traditions that have historically advocated the intractable reality of our suffering and then proposed a course of seeking for a solution.

SRI DA AVABHASA: Have you all heard about the Dreaded Gom-Boo? Or the impossible Three-Day Thumb-and-Finger Problem? Aha! You see? Nobody tells you about these things except Me.

A myth has been circulating for many centuries now that human beings are diseased, that all beings are suffering from what I call the "Dreaded Gom-Boo", also called "sin", "maya", "ego", "suffering", "separated individuality", "illusion", "delusion", "confusion", and "indifference". People are all supposed to accept this diagnosis, realize how diseased they are, and submit themselves to the local religious hospital, where a father or mother doctor will confirm their disease and require them to submit for the rest of their lives to various regimes for their own healing and ultimate cure. This is the basic proposition of traditional religion, and it begins with the diagnosis of the dreaded disease.

Tradition has it that human beings are all, by birth, by virtue of their very existence, even now diseased, sinful, separated from the Great One. What a horror! Yes! What an obscenity has been laid upon people through the traditions of society, which, merely because of the impulse to survive as the body-mind, have for centuries required human beings to invest themselves with the belief in this disease and to suppress their own life-motion, which comes only from the Great One, in order to fulfill the presumed needs of a chaotic society.

I come to tell you, as I stand in the midst of the priests of this horror, that not even one of you is suffering from this disease. It is an imaginary disease—a terrible disease, but altogether imaginary. No one has ever actually had this disease. Not one single being has ever had the Dreaded Gom-Boo, or the impossible Three-Day Thumb-and-Finger Problem. It has never happened! It does not exist!

What is the Truth? We are Happy. We live in God. The Great One is our Very Being. We inhere in the Blissful, Forceful Being of the Starry God, the Mystery, the Person of Love. This is our Situation and our Destiny.

. . . All of us inhere in the Great One, the Fantastic Lord, the Marvelous Starry Person, the Delight of Being. All of us live in That. That is our situation now. This moment is the moment of Happiness, as is every future moment, every moment after death, beyond this world and other worlds, lower worlds, higher worlds, after worlds, no worlds. It is all the moment of infinite Delight, unless you become self-conscious and withdraw from your relations and contract upon your Happiness and forget It.

This is My Message to you, then: There is no disease except the one you fabricate and reinforce through all the propagandas of this horrible world of egos. Understand it and instantly be free of your disease in every moment. Be free of this imaginary concoction of suffering. There is no such thing! . . .

There is no separation from God, not even in the slightest! It is impossible to be separated from God, absolutely impossible. We exist in eternal unity with God. It is totally impossible to be divorced from the Great One. It is an obscene suggestion that we could ever, even in a fraction of our being, be removed from the Room of the Divine Person. It is absolutely impossible. I am certain of this. I hope you will also understand yourselves and Realize this.

There is no disease to cure, therefore. The Spiritual process is not a cure for disease. It is not a strategic approach toward the ultimate event of your Happiness. The Spiritual process is the magnification of well-being, the magnification of health, Happiness, Bliss, Prior and Eternal God-Union. There is not the slightest suggestion in My intimation to you that you should become self-conscious and divorced from the Blissful Happiness of your Union with the Great God. Not even the slightest suggestion of it. (September 9, 1982)

Satsang: The Company of Truth

Sri Da Avabhasa has brought His penetrating Insight to bear on our seeking and suffering in ways that are disarmingly direct. But do not be misled by the simplicity of His Argument. Da Avabhasa has also elaborated the most sophisticated Wisdom-Teaching in history. All of our religious paths, our science and our Yoga, our psychology, our art and history, our cultural forms, every detail of the stages of our growth and evolution, from birth to death (and back again), from infancy to Divine Self-Realization—all of this has come under His Enlightened examination. His Commentary on the One Free Divine Nature that underlies and imbues all existence and His elaboration of how the self-contraction manifests itself in human beings can now be found in over forty published volumes of His Writings and Talks—a body of Wisdom unprecedented in scope and profundity.

"The Guru is like the sunlight in the morning.
He intensifies the light of morning until you awaken."

Sri Love-Anandashram, 1992

But even this comprehensive Wisdom-Teaching is not enough on its own. For those who are fast asleep, fixed in the self-contraction cannot, by their own efforts, wake themselves up. Those who are dreaming cannot, by searching within the dream, find the waking state. Help from someone who is already awake is needed, or there will be no "radical" shift in consciousness, no real liberating change.

Only the Help of an Awakened Adept avails:

SRI DA AVABHASA: What arises falls, what appears disappears, what expands contracts. Every action has an equal and opposite reaction. Neither the expansion nor the contraction, neither the action nor the reaction, is Truth. It is simply expansion, contraction, action, reaction.

. . . No event is itself Truth. All that arises is an appearance to consciousness, a modification of the conscious force that is always already the case. All of this is a dream, if you like. It is an appearance in consciousness. Truth is very consciousness itself. Truth is to all of this what the waking state is to the dreaming state. If you awaken, you don't have to do anything about the condition you may have suffered or enjoyed in the dream state. What happened within the dream is suddenly not your present condition. It is of no consequence any longer, once you are awake. If you persist in dreaming, and your point of view remains that of the dreamer and his or her role within the dream, then your possible actions are numberless. But none of them will "work". They will simply occupy you in the dream. They will modify the dream state, but no action in the dream is the equivalent of waking. . . .

The Guru is like the sunlight in the morning. The Guru intensifies the light of morning until you awaken. Until the light awakens a person, even the true light of consciousness, he or she continues to dream, he or she tries to survive within the dream, manipulates himself or herself within the dream, pursues all kinds of goals, searches, none of which awaken him or her. All ordinary means only console a person and distract him or her within the dream. The Guru, the one who would awaken you, is not a person, not an individual within the dream. The Guru is your very consciousness. The Guru is the Real, the Self, the Light, the true waking state, the Heart, breaking through the force of dreaming. It is not that you are some poor person who needs some other poor person to help you out. It may appear to be so within the dream, but essentially it is your own nature appearing within the dream to awaken you. The Guru is your awakening, and your always already conscious state.

. . . When the search begins to wind down, and you begin to realize you are suffering, then you become sensitive to the Presence of one who is awake. You become attentive to the subtle nature of one who is awake.

It is stated in the traditional writings that, of all the things one can do to realize one's freedom, the best thing one can do, the greatest thing one can do, is spend one's time in the Company of one who is awake. That is Satsang, living in relationship to the Guru and the company of the Guru's friends. All other activities are secondary. And Satsang is not a method, not an exercise or meditative technique one applies to oneself. It is simply the natural and appropriate condition. It is Reality. It is itself Truth, or enlightenment. There are no other means given to disciples.

There is nothing that one can do to save oneself, to become enlightened, to become realized. Nothing whatsoever. If there were something, I would tell you, but there is nothing. This is because one always approaches the Truth from the point of view of the search. One seeks the Truth. But the search is itself a reaction to the dilemma, an expression of this separation, this avoidance of relationship. So none of this seeking, nothing one can do, becomes or attains the Truth.

All the means of transformation belong to the Truth Itself, to the Guru, to the Heart. Therefore, Satsang is itself the only sadhana, the only true spiritual practice. Living, working, sitting with the Guru is sadhana. It is meditation. It is realization.

. . . It is unnecessary to go through the long term of seeking, of suffering, of breaking down, of corruption, before Truth becomes appropriate. The realization of Truth is not a matter of heavy, self-involved, constricted, willful effort. It is as natural as a simple response to sunlight. It is simply the relationship to the Guru, the intelligent life of real sadhana.

"The realization of Truth is not a matter of heavy, self-involved, constricted, willful effort. It is as natural as a simple response to sunlight. It is simply the relationship to the Guru."

Sri Love-Anandashram, 1992

. . . When you become less concerned for your particular search, for your inwardness, for your adventure, you have simply become more sensitive to your real condition. You have felt the sunlight falling on your sleeping eyes. When your eyes have opened in the morning light, everything will be obvious to you. And you will know that you have never slept, that you have never dreamed, that you have never been limited to any thing that has appeared. You have never been in any condition that you have assumed. There was always only Reality, your true Nature, which is Bliss, Consciousness, the unqualified Intensity. (The Method of the Siddhas, *"The Gorilla Sermon"*)

Such is the ancient way, the way of Grace, of "Satsang"—which means literally "Good Company", or "the Company of Truth"—the devotional relationship to the God-Realized Guru. The opportunity to enter into the Sphere of Influence of such a Realizer has always been highly prized in our great religious and Spiritual traditions.

Why? Because we can only be drawn beyond ourselves by a Force more attractive and more powerful than our chronic self-meditation. Since no amount of self-effort can produce illumination, real understanding, or Spiritual growth, we must be distracted from our "selves" by That which is Greater and more appealing. The God-Realized Guru is that Greater Force of Attraction. As Da Avabhasa's devotees attest throughout this book, it is His Attractiveness, His obvious and compelling bodily demonstration of Freedom, Love, and Joy, that inspires us to notice that we are limited, and that we must grow beyond ourselves. Thus, the Guru-devotee relationship is both the means and the medium for the self-forgetting practice of Divine Distraction that is Free Daism itself.

SRI DA AVABHASA: When you simply participate in that Attracted, Distracted condition of existence with the God-Man, all tendencies are released and sublimed, walked out of the purgatory of conditional existence. You cannot earn your passage out of this purgatory by paying your dues or participating in a variety of theatrical moments. In this place, you accumulate as much as you release, until you become Attracted beyond your separate and separative self.

What is supremely Attractive in the conditional universe and in the human world is the God-Man. All beings, male and female, must become Distracted by That One. Divine Distraction is the Supreme Yoga. For this reason the Divine Appears in conditional Form in the likeness of those who are to be drawn out of bondage—but only in their <u>likeness</u>. It is the <u>Divine</u> That Appears in that likeness, and it is the <u>Divine</u> That is made Visible through that likeness.

Even within the pantheon of Divinely Realized Adepts who have appeared through-out the ages to attract human hearts to God, Sri Da Avabhasa (The "Bright") is a unique Event. His full Embodiment of Divine Grace in a human Form is unprecedented, and is the very foundation of Free Daism. He Himself is an unparalleled Example of "radical"

Insight, boundless Energy, and Unconditional Love; He has Given an utterly comprehensive Wisdom-Teaching and Way of life to Guide humankind in the God-Realizing process; and He Offers a literal Blessing-Transmission that opens the heart to love, and ultimately draws us to Divine Self-Realization Itself. This testimony comes from Michael Macy:

In November 1990, I was Graced with an invitation to go on meditation retreat at Sri Love-Anandashram, a beautiful and remote Fijian island where Sri Da Avabhasa resides. No sooner had my feet pressed into the beachfront sand than I felt an immense "Force" that seemed to permeate the entire island. I was quickly escorted by another devotee of Sri Da Avabhasa's to a nearby temple to offer a welcoming gift and prayer. The feeling of this all-pervading "Force" only seemed to intensify within the temple. A subtle blue hue seemed to surround and radiate from all the objects in the temple and even in the air itself.

Shortly thereafter, I found myself in a Communion Hall with some thirty other retreatants waiting to see Sri Da Avabhasa, our Guru. A conch shell was blown in the distance—a signal that Da Avabhasa was coming. A light misty rain began to fall—another sign I'd been told often spontaneously accompanies Sri Da Avabhasa's physical Presence. The rays of the strong Fijian sun overhead scattered brilliantly in the mist, and suddenly there was just a bright whiteness radiating in every direction. The scene was archetypal. I could barely contain my excitement.

In a moment, out of the brightness, Sri Da Avabhasa appeared. In that same instant, the whirrings of my normally overactive mind came to an abrupt halt—unable to fathom the paradox of a God-Man. I suddenly felt blissfully open and alive, and uncharacteristically capable of directly perceiving and feeling the Being now powerfully striding toward us.

Shortly after the incident, I wrote a letter to a friend in which I tried to describe what occurred for me in that timeless moment:

> *The first shock was seeing Sri Da Avabhasa for the first time in His Hermitage Ashram, Sri Love-Anandashram. "He" is literally not a human being. He has a head and a body and arms that swing and legs that propel, but it was just obvious that there was no "one" behind all that. Energy was just pouring out of His body, appearing almost visibly, like heat waves coming off a desert. Things seemed to go into super slow motion and every moment became something of ultimate fascination to be lived with utter attention and presence. And strangely enough I could start to feel "Him" in my own body as a kind of white energy or intensity, coming through my feet and my eyes, the base of my torso and the top of my head, pervading my "inner world" of body and mind.*
>
> *In a real way all this was secondary. It was just an effect of something deeper, something at the heart that was going on. You know when you are <u>totally</u> in love. You see that person and your heart automatically opens up, you feel absolutely happy, a big grin comes uncontrollably to your face, and you simply have to go*

over and hug this person to communicate your feelings of love to them—words just can't express it.

That is what happened when I saw Sri Da Avabhasa. It wasn't like I fell in love with Him in some romantic way, but whatever the truth about love really is, it is contained and radiated in His body so that just looking at Him my whole body opened and filled up just like that classic love-response. It was instant happiness just to be around Him. This is the mystery I am discovering about Sri Da Avabhasa—this feeling that He Transmits is the "Truth" that He has come to Reveal.

Da Avabhasa's Spiritual Gifts to His devotees are utterly without precedent in human history—so full is the Way that He Offers. The devotional relationship to Sri Da Avabhasa is inconceivably rich with Blessing, and cultivating and magnifying this devotional relationship is itself the fundamental practice and Gift that is Free Daism.

If we are to benefit from Da Avabhasa's Gifts, as profound and glorious and transforming as they are, we must participate. Free Daism is a practice. Fundamentally, it is the ancient practice of Guru-devotion, enacted in the context of an eternal Spiritual relationship to Da Avabhasa. And that devotion requires real self-inspection, a rigorous examination of all aspects of existence based on true and intelligent study of His Wisdom-Teaching, understanding of the mechanism of the ego (or self-contraction) in our own case, a fundamental willingness to change and grow, and a commitment to put oneself to the test of the real Spiritual process. Sri Da Avabhasa has characterized Free Daist practice as a life of devotion, service, self-discipline, and meditation. It is through this responsive practice, described in this book, that we can make use of Sri Da Avabhasa's sublime Help:

SRI DA AVABHASA: The human Spiritual Master is Divine Help to the advantage of those in like form. When one enters into right relationship with the Spiritual Master, changes happen in the literal physics of one's existence. I am not just talking about ideas. I am talking about literal transformations at the level of energy, at the level of the higher light of physics, at the level of mind beyond the physical limitations you now presume, at the level of the absolute Speed of ultimate Light. The transforming process is enacted in devotees in and through the Living Company of the Spiritual Master. The relationship between the Spiritual Master and the devotee is not a matter of conceptual symbolisms or emotional attachment to some extraordinary person. The Guru-devotee relationship is real physics. And it is to the advantage of people when some one among them has gone through the whole cycle of Divine Self-Realization, because they can then make use of the Offering of that person's Company.

Spiritual life has nothing to do with the childishness people tend to dramatize in relationship to the Spiritual Master. I criticize that childish, or dependent, approach more

"Something in the physics of the universe makes it possible for a single individual to pass through the entire affair of Divine Self-Realization, and then to bring others into the Sphere of his or her Divinely Enlightened existence, so that they may duplicate that Divine Condition."

directly than most people do. Others are merely petulant about it, in the self-righteous mood of adolescence. But there are real reasons why both the childish and the adolescent approaches to the Spiritual Master are forms of destructive nonsense and must be over-come. However, the mature, sacrificial relationship to the Spiritual Master is absolutely Lawful and necessary. Those who object to that relationship might as well object to the relationship between the Earth and the sun. . . .

There is a profound difference between the condition of the usual individual and the Condition of the Awakened individual. The difference is an inconceivable leap in evolu-tion. But there is a real process for making that leap, and there is Help for it: the devotional relationship to the Adept Spiritual Master. In other words, something in the physics of the universe makes it possible for a single individual to pass through the entire affair of Divine Self-Realization, and then to bring others into the Sphere of his or her Divinely Enlightened existence, so that they may duplicate that Divine Condition. . . . The changes that must occur are literal psycho-physical changes, just as literal as if you were to acquire more legs and arms, except that the most dramatic changes occur in dimensions other

21

than the shape of the body. Certainly changes occur in the flesh and the elemental struc-tures of the body, but those changes do not really alter the body's outward shape. The changes are as literal as evolving from a dinosaur to a human being, and they are as dra-matic as that, but they principally occur at more subtle levels of the physics of the condi-tional being. There are literal changes in the nervous system, literal changes in the chem-istry of the body, literal changes in the structural functioning of the brain.

You cannot realize such changes in a weekend. They are a living process of growth. But they can be quickened and intensified through right practice, through real sacrificial discipline, in the Company of the Spiritual Master. In the Company of a fully Awakened Spiritual Master, the Divine Condition is Communicated to you in such a way that It Effects a "radical" transformation in the disposition of the body-mind and then Magnifies the effectiveness of that disposition many times. . . .

If you move into a relationship with Me, the Divine Process begins to duplicate Itself in your case. It is not as if you are a robot that is being transformed through the effect of some computer—no. The Process is a living and human relationship with Me. But it is not like the conventional doctor-patient and mommy-daddy-baby games. Irresponsible people cannot enter into it. You must be responsible for yourself at the human level, and in a profoundly uncommon way. You must live the discipline of ordinary life. You yourself must be love under all ordinary, daily conditions. You must make this change in your life. There is no way whereby you can be relieved of this necessity, and nobody can do it for you. Nevertheless, all of that ordinary responsibility simply prepares you for the right rela-tionship to the Agency of the Divine in My bodily (human) Form. Such a One As I Am is your unique Advantage, because I Am Present in the same kind of bodily form as you— manifested in the same kind of physical condition, the same kind of nervous system, the same kind of brain. But in Me all these things are Raised to an Absolute level of Functioning, so that your entering into Communion with Me brings changes even at the level of the psycho-physical body that you present to Me.

The abstract Deity cannot serve you in that way, because the physics of this Process must be directly Present, and the human Demonstration of the Process must be Present in a Form that can do its Work in your case. That Work is My Purpose, because I Represent a State of the ultimate physics of things that is your potential but not your actuality at the present time. The abstract Divine and the potential powers of the universe are just as true as the Spiritual Master, but they are not organized (except in the case of the Spiritual Master) for the sake of the immediate transformation of human beings. If people enter into right relationship with Me, they begin to Realize the same transformations I have Described in My own case. . . . [W]hen the Total Representation of Divine Self-Realization is Demonstrated in the literal bodily (human) form of one individual, you must make use of it. It is an Advantage that is unique in human time. (The Hymn Of The True Heart-Master, *"I Am Grace Itself"* section, pp. 273-77)

This kind of change and growth is no casual matter. The real practice of Free Daism, true use of the devotional relationship to Sri Da Avabhasa, is a cauldron of transformation that requires nothing short of a whole-hearted commitment, a participation that includes every aspect of one's life.

Through the Ordeal of His own life, which is summarized in the next chapter, Sri Da Avabhasa has established a Wisdom-Teaching and a whole Way of life so that others, following Him, can pass beyond the constriction of the ego to the Realization of Boundless Happiness.

To sit face to Face with the God-Realized Adept, to witness His Divine Freedom, to receive His tangible Spiritual Blessing and His Guidance, to apply His Wisdom to every aspect of life—these are the miraculous means by which Da Avabhasa makes it possible for us to penetrate our suffering and participate in the sublimity of the God-Realizing process.

In a letter written to an elderly woman who had approached Sri Da Avabhasa very early on, the young Realizer made clear both the gravity and the Gifts that accompany the Guru-devotee relationship:

It is a difficult thing to approach a Teacher. A true Teacher is one who possesses the Siddhi [Power] of the Heart. He awakens us to the Heart. He is not a gentleman, a good guy, or an object we can manipulate by our ordinary games. He does not indulge our ignorance or our strategies. Absolutely nothing about us is hidden from Him. He has the capacity to act as a reflector whereby we get to see how we are dramatizing our lives. Thus, if we do not begin to understand, we begin to confuse Him with the tendencies in ourselves and in the world that we resist or indulge. His purpose is not to be friendly. Cordiality and charm are not qualities of the Heart. He is not here to be our friend. He is here to take us by the neck and shake us silly until we are Awake. He confounds us, and He wrecks our ordinary lives. Thus, to approach a true Teacher is a difficult thing. . . . I love you, and my concern is to awaken you to the Heart, perfectly and finally. I will not entertain you, become a mere "friend" to you, or allow you to dissipate into the form of an ordinary "little old lady".

Because you have come to me for this understanding, I have committed myself to you. And you should know that in every moment, when we are physically present with one another, or when we are apart, I work only through this love and commitment to make understanding possible in you. But this thing cannot take place unless you also become capable of the love and commitment that comes with real understanding. . . .

The Heart does not communicate through words or the physical body. Understanding can be indicated verbally, for it deals with the observation of experience. But the Heart Itself, known to radical understanding, is a most subtle Force and Process. It is communicated only in profound silence, beyond all forms. I want you to know the Heart, so that you will live in It and leave this life in Its care. But you must understand, you must become still, free of your ordinary suppositions and demands. Then you will enjoy this relationship and feel the rising Power of the Heart.

. . . I am very hard on my students, my friends. I know what they need and what must occur in them. Thus, I do not indulge them, but I push them to the brink. I am very willing to go through this experience with you. But you must come to me directly, intelligently, with need, willing to endure this difficult confrontation.

Be still and receive the Heart. I am not the body. I am not what appears to you. What I am to you depends on the level of your understanding and your need. I am the Heart, if you will only understand. And the Heart has the Siddhi to make Itself known.

Traditionally, access to this kind of opportunity was reserved for only the most advanced of Spiritual aspirants. It is a unique characteristic of Sri Da Avabhasa's Work that He has come to make the esoteric God-Realizing process available to all modern men and women who turn to Him in love. There is no one who cannot be transformed by His Grace.

And, as you will see in the testimonies of Free Daist practitioners found throughout this book, there is nothing more real, more challenging and creative, more dynamic, more difficult, more ecstatic, more painfully honest, more sublime than the embrace of this relationship with the Living God-Man, Da Avabhasa (The "Bright").

RECOMMENDED READING

The Method of the Siddhas

The Dawn Horse Testament

NOTES

1. "Re-cognition", which literally means "knowing again", is Sri Da Avabhasa's term for non-verbal, heart-felt, intuitive insight into any and every arising conditional phenomenon as a form of egoic self-contraction.

2. The "Heart" is Sri Da Avabhasa's term for God, the Divine Self, or the Divine Reality.

Born in the "Bright"

Sri Da Avabhasa's
Life and Divine Work

by Richard Schorske

At the center of all great religions is the Person of the Spiritual Realizer—the Prophet, the Saint, the Sage, the Yogi—the man or woman who becomes a "window" to the Divine. Just so, there is a Realizer at the center of Free Daism: the Divine World-Teacher and True Heart-Master, Da Avabhasa (The "Bright"). But Sri Da Avabhasa is more than a Prophet, a Saint, a Sage, or a Yogi. Sri Da Avabhasa is not a man, born like other men, who during His lifetime attained a greater Realization of the Divine. Sri Da Avabhasa is a God-Born Being in Whom the Realization of Divine Freedom was Perfect even at birth.

It will come as no surprise, then, that the life of Sri Da Avabhasa is more than the stuff of ordinary biography. Through contemplation of the Mystery of Sri Da Avabhasa's Identity, including His paradoxical early years as "Franklin Jones", you will come to know His Freedom, and the ferocity of His Impulse to Awaken you to Joy, even, as He has Promised, "Beyond Every Reason For It".

The Divine Mystery of Sri Da Avabhasa's Identity is too profound a matter for mere belief. Rather, the Revelation of who Sri Da Avabhasa Is, and Who you Are, can occur only suddenly, unbidden, when the heart opens and the mind is rested from its seeking for and its judgments against.

So I encourage you not to believe what is written in this chapter merely because it is presented with conviction—and also not to disbelieve merely because it is without precedent in your own experience. Rather, adopt the attitude of open-minded listening. Be rigorous but heart-felt in your empiricism—until the Reality of Who Sri Da Avabhasa Is is proven in your own heart, in your own time.

The "Bright" of Sri Da Avabhasa's Birth, and His Ordeal of Self-Forgetting

Sri Da Avabhasa was born on November 3, 1939, into an ordinary middle-class family in Jamaica, Queens County, New York, a twenty-minute drive from downtown Manhattan. His given name was "Franklin Albert Jones".

From His earliest moments, "Franklin" existed in an extraordinary State, which He called "the 'Bright'":

Even as a baby I remember only crawling around inquisitively with an incredible sense of joy, light, and freedom in the middle of my head that was bathed in energies moving freely down from above, up, around, and down through my body and my heart. It was an expanding sphere of joy from the heart. And I was a radiant form, a source of energy, bliss, and light in the midst of what is entirely energy, bliss, and light. I was the power of Reality, a direct enjoyment and communication. I was the Heart, who lightens the mind and all things. I was the same as every one and every thing, except it became clear that others were apparently unaware of the thing itself.

*. . . That awareness, that conscious enjoyment and space centered in the midst of the heart, is the "bright". And it is the entire source of humor. It is reality. It is not separate from anything. (*The Knee of Listening, *pp. 7-8)*

Where other great Spiritual beings have sought to Realize the State of Divine Freedom through a lifetime (or many lifetimes) of struggle, Sri Da Avabhasa was "God-Born" in

Richard Schorske has been a devotee of Sri Da Avabhasa since August 1984. With a background in journalism, Richard began serving Sri Da Avabhasa's Work as a writer, as an Editor of the Laughing Man *magazine, and later as Director of Education for the Free Daist Communion. He is currently working as a fundraiser and consultant to nonprofit organizations, while continuing to serve at the Dawn Horse Press as a writer.*

Sri Da Avabhasa as a baby

and as that very Freedom. Where others have hoped to ascend above and beyond the world, and so escape the pain of mortal life, Sri Da Avabhasa chose to consciously Sacrifice His Prior Freedom to take on the limitations of human birth.

SRI DA AVABHASA: Instead of making God-Knowing the continuous manifestation of My early Life, I made it the periodic event of My early Life, so that it would serve as a lesson for those who would have an ongoing relationship with Me. I entered this plane of existence without limitations and took hold of a psycho-physical form that was no more illumined than any other psycho-physical form. Like every other psycho-physical form, it needed to be transformed. And "Franklin Jones" is a fictional character, a series of lessons consciously manifested for My devotees.

I did not "pretend" to be Franklin Jones. I became Franklin Jones. Franklin Jones was a strategic way of life, generated from a Spiritual point of view. He was generated in the face of particular circumstances, and He was workable. He was useful for the sake of others. The Guru's Work in the world is of this kind. The Guru must manifest a persona of some kind and create qualities in relationship. And the Guru does all these things consciously, for the sake of devotees. (April 1974)

At the age of two, moved by a "painful loving" of those around Him to find a Way for all to Realize the singular Happiness that was His natural Condition, Sri Da Avabhasa abandoned His native Illumination in order to discover the "way back" to Freedom and Humor from the viewpoint of our ordinary human life. Thus, Sri Da Avabhasa conceived of His Life, even from its early days, as a series of lessons that would benefit all beings, and He consciously chose to associate with the ordinary, unillumined body-mind of "Franklin Jones" as the vehicle of that Instruction.

SRI DA AVABHASA: As a conscious "creation" or condition, "Franklin Jones" began one day while I was crawling across the linoleum floor in a house that My parents had rented from an old woman named Mrs. Farr. A little puppy dog that My parents had gotten for Me was running across the floor towards Me. I saw the puppy dog, and I saw My parents, and it began from that moment. All the rest of the events that occurred during the two or more years before that moment were not the years of "Franklin Jones". "Franklin Jones" has no existence before that time, which was the conscious, or intentional, beginning. (April 1974)

Even though Sri Da Avabhasa "became" Franklin, He could not control or limit the force of the Kundalini Shakti—the Energy of Cosmic Nature—that flowed through Him. Throughout His early years, He suffered the fevers and occasional delirium that are classic signs of a forceful Awakening of the Spiritual Power, or Life-Current, of the Divine Person. And He enjoyed unusual powers of a psychic kind, premonitory dreams and visions, unusual physical abilities, and the like, also associated with the unfolding of the Kundalini process. However, as the turbulence of adolescence came over "Franklin", the periodic breakthroughs of the "Bright" that marked His early childhood years receded from consciousness until, as Sri Da Avabhasa says, "only a fierce and mysterious impulse" remained to Guide Him.

In 1957, Sri Da Avabhasa began undergraduate work in philosophy at Columbia College. There His Quest to recover the "Bright" Freedom of His Illumined Birth began to take an intentional form:

When I entered Columbia College in September 1957, I was possessed with a single, motivating interest. I wanted to understand what we are. What is consciousness? Whatever academic studies were required of me, I was always at work on this one thing. (The Knee of Listening, p. 11)

The president of Columbia College, Grayson Kirk, told the entering freshman class in 1957 only that they would learn how to question, how to think—not that they would learn the deep truths of life. Thus entered into a milieu of rigorously Godless intellectualism, Sri Da Avabhasa pursued His answers Himself. No sacred esoteric tradition was presented in His classes. No genuine Masters of Wisdom appeared at that time to help Him in His Quest. The youthful Sri Da Avabhasa consumed the Western sources of religious and philosophical wisdom, but there was no clear Truth to quench His thirst for the "Bright". Soon He embarked on the only comprehensive course of seeking for God that was available to Him.

. . . I decided that I would begin an experimental life along the same lines which controlled the mood of our civilization. I decided that I would unreservedly exploit every possibility for experience. I would avail myself of every possible human experience, so that nothing possible to mankind, high or low, would be unknown to me.

This decision became very clear to me one night at a party. I knew that no other possibility was open to me but that of exhaustive experience. There appeared to be no single experience or authority among us that was simply true. And I thought, "If God exists, He

As an undergraduate
in college

will not cease to exist by any action of my own, but, if I devote myself to all possible experi-
ence, He will indeed find some way, in some one or a complex of my experiences, or my
openness itself, to reveal Himself to me." Thereafter, I devoted myself utterly and solely to
every possible kind of exploit.

No experience posed a barrier to me. There were no taboos, no extremes to be prevented.
There was no depth of madness and no limit of suffering that my philosophy could prevent,
for, if it did, I would be liable to miss the lesson of reality. Thus, I extended myself even
beyond my own fear. And my pleasures also became extreme, so there was a constant
machine of ecstasy. I could tolerate no mediocrity, no medium experience. I was satisfied
with neither atheism nor belief. Both seemed to me only ideas, possible reactions to a more
fundamental if unconscious fact. I sought reality, to be reality, what is, not what is assert-
ed in the face of what is. . . .

I went on in this fashion for more than two years, until the whole violence of my seek-
ing precipitated an experience late one night in the middle of my junior year. (The Knee
of Listening, *pp. 34-35)*

On that evening, in despair, Sri Da Avabhasa came to the end-point of His search. It
seemed that this forceful, experimental tour of human experience could yield nothing
more.

. . . There seemed no outstanding sources for any new excursion, no remaining and
conclusive possibilities. I was drawn into the interior tension of my mind that held all of
that seeking, every impulse and alternative, every motive in the form of my desiring. I con-
templated it as a whole dramatic force, and it seemed to move me into a profound shape
of energy, so that all the vital centers in my body and mind appeared like a long funnel of

contracted planes that led on to an infinitely regressed and invisible image. I observed this deep sensation of conflict and endlessly multiplied contradictions, so that I seemed to surrender to its very shape, as if to experience it perfectly and to be it. (The Knee of Listening, *p. 35)*

Through the sheer intensity of His awareness of the contradictions in His own mind and desire, Sri Da Avabhasa suddenly experienced "a total revolution of energy and awareness" and a perfect Restoration to the "Brightness", Freedom, and Bliss that He had known at birth.

An absolute sense of understanding opened and arose at the extreme end of all this consciousness. And all of the energy of thought that moved down into that depth appeared to reverse its direction at some unfathomable point. The rising impulse caused me to stand, and I felt a surge of force draw up out of my depths and expand, filling my whole body and every level of my consciousness with wave on wave of the most beautiful and joyous energy.

I felt absolutely mad, but the madness was not of a desperate kind. There was no seeking and no dilemma within it, no question, no unfulfilled motive, not a single object or presence outside myself. (The Knee of Listening, *p. 35)*

Out of that Graceful Illumination, Sri Da Avabhasa emerged with a new understanding. Not only was the fruitlessness of all His previous effortful seeking for freedom and bliss apparent to Him, but Sri Da Avabhasa realized that the effort of seeking itself, though seemingly necessary to "gain" Happiness, is in fact utterly futile. He observed that freedom and joy are never attained by the ego's effort and that seeking obscures the very State we long for. By surrendering His search in that moment of perfect frustration, Sri Da Avabhasa discovered that we are inherently, or "always already", Free, prior to the struggle of the ego-self.

. . . in that great moment of awakening I knew the truth was not a matter of seeking. There were no "reasons" for joy and freedom. It was not a matter of a truth, an object, a concept, a belief, a reason, a motivation, or any external fact. Indeed, it was clear that all such objects are grasped in a state that is already seeking and which has already lost the prior sense of an absolutely unqualified reality. Instead, I saw that the truth or reality was a matter of the removal of all contradictions, of every trace of conflict, opposition, division, or desperate motivation within. Where there is no seeking, no contradiction, there is only the unqualified knowledge and power that is reality. This was the first aspect of that sudden knowledge.

In this state beyond all contradiction I also saw that freedom and joy is not attained, that it is not dependent on any form, object, idea, progress, or experience. I saw that we *are, at any moment, always and already free. I knew that I was not lacking anything I needed yet to find, nor had I ever been without such a thing. . . . I am always already free. This was the second aspect of that fundamental awareness. (*The Knee of Listening, pp. 37-38)

Following this Awakening, however, Sri Da Avabhasa discovered that separation from the "Bright" was once again His chronic experience. The Freedom that He enjoyed that night in His room near the Columbia campus became a goad to conclusively overcome the mechanism of His suffering. Thus, shortly after beginning graduate work at Stanford University, Sri Da Avabhasa devised a spontaneous "Yoga", or concentrated practice, of "listening", or self-observation. Living secluded on a bluff high above the Pacific Ocean due west of Palo Alto, California, Sri Da Avabhasa endeavored to uncover and transcend all obstacles that prevented His conscious enjoyment of the "Bright".

I combined the internal work of listening with the activity of writing. Therefore, the plan of my work as a writer was to remain actively attentive to the movement of my life on every level, to an exhaustive degree. . . .

. . . I spent all of my time concentrated in this witnessing function. I carried a clipboard with me wherever I went. And I would write whatever perceptions were generated in consciousness. I attempted to make this writing exhaustive, so that not a single thought, image, or experience would pass unrecognized. The act of writing seemed necessary to the act of becoming conscious itself. What I did not write seemed to pass away again into unconsciousness, perhaps to remain trapped there and provide matter for the hidden, unconscious form that bounded my awareness and prevented the "bright". . . .

. . . Eventually, I began to recognize a structure in consciousness. . . . My own "myth", the control of all patterns, the source of identity and all seeking, began to stand out in the mind as a living being.

. . . I saw that my entire adventure, the whole desperate cycle of awareness and its decrease, of truly conscious being and its gradual covering in the whole mechanics of living, seeking, dying, and suffering, was produced out of the image or mentality that appears hidden in the ancient myth of Narcissus. . . .

The more I contemplated him, the more profoundly I understood him. I witnessed in awe the primitive control that this self-concept and logic performed in all of my behavior and experience. I began to see that same logic operative in all other human beings, and in every living thing, even in the very life of the cells and in the energies that surround every living entity or process. It was the logic or process of separation itself, of enclosure and immunity. . . . It was the structure of every imbecile link in the history of our suffering.

*He is the ancient one visible in the Greek "myth", who was the universally adored child of the gods, who rejected the loved-one and every form of love and relationship, who was finally condemned to the contemplation of his own image, until he suffered the fact of eternal separation and died in infinite solitude. (*The Knee of Listening, *pp. 46, 58, 60-62)*

Through His "Yoga of listening", Sri Da Avabhasa saw that all the suffering of "Franklin Jones", and the suffering of every individual, was rooted in this primitive presumption and activity of self-enclosure and separation. He saw that the endless activity of human beings is the creation of the separate self. He saw that men and women project upon the field of Consciousness a "self", a thing, an entity, that is every bit as imaginary as the "other" whom Narcissus perceived in the pond.

Through His progressive recovery of the Divine Freedom of His birth, Sri Da Avabhasa intuited that there is in Reality no separate self, or ego, to be experienced over against any "other". On occasions, in moments of revelation, He experienced the Real Status of this world, and He knew that everything, every being, every "thing", is simply a "modification" of, or a "play" upon, the eternal unity of Consciousness Itself.

However, for this intuitive knowledge to become His stable Realization, or rather for the persona of Franklin Jones to be submitted to that Realization, Sri Da Avabhasa would be required to penetrate all the layers of "Narcissus"—and utterly transcend this "logic or process of separation itself, of enclosure and immunity". To complete that journey, the Help of others would be required.

Da Avabhasa during the period of His "Yoga of listening"

Sri Da Avabhasa's Submission
to His First Guru

As if to hasten the process that He called the "death of Narcissus", Sri Da Avabhasa experienced a series of brief precognitive visions in the winter of 1964. An oriental art store appeared to Him in these visions, and He knew that there He would find His Teacher. It became clear to Him that the store was in New York City, and in the late summer of 1964 Sri Da Avabhasa set out for New York. After many weeks of searching the city, He came upon a cluttered oriental art store that matched His vision. There, He found Swami Rudrananda—known simply to His devotees as Rudi.

Sri Da Avabhasa very quickly became aware that Rudi was a potent Transmitter of Spiritual Force. Sri Da Avabhasa describes His experience after their first meeting:

> . . . I became aware of a very strange sensation. A current of very strong energy was rising up my arm from my right hand, the hand Rudi had made it so much a point to shake when I arrived and as I left.
>
> As I became aware of this energy, it quickly passed into the rest of my body and filled me with a profound and thrilling fullness. My heart seemed to strain in a vibrant joy, and my head felt swollen, as if my mind were contained in an aura that extended around my skull several inches. As I walked, I began to run. I felt on fire with a joyous energy, and I had become incredibly light! (The Knee of Listening, p. 89)

Rudi was the first Teacher who would function, for a time, as Sri Da Avabhasa's Guru. Thus, Sri Da Avabhasa gave His life to Rudi in the traditional manner of a devotee to a Sat-Guru ("Revealer of Truth"), surrendering to Rudi without reservation. Among disciples of Rudi, He was known as "Crazy Frank" for His completely unreserved willingness to fulfill the extremes of discipline that Rudi demanded. This purifying "sadhana", or Spiritual practice, of self-surrendering work—known traditionally as "Karma Yoga"—purified the body-mind of "Franklin", so that a new depth of Realization could take hold.

From Rudi, Sri Da Avabhasa learned the traditional fundamentals of discipline, devotion, and obedience to the Guru. And He learned to receive and to "conduct" His Guru's Transmission of Spiritual energy, which Rudi called the "Force". Rudi's Teaching called his devotees to a constant process of growth through a great effort of self-surrender and work that would open them to this Force.

> No description of this period would be adequate and true without the inclusion of my various experiences with the "Force". At first that experience was limited to the kind I first described in meeting with Rudi. I became aware that an actual force (or tangible spiritual power) emanated from him. I could feel it in various ways as a magnetic or electronic

Rudi

energy in my body. This of course is a tremen-dously unique experience in terms of what peo-ple ordinarily would suppose to be reality. But it was for me not unusual or unique in my experi-ence. Rudi's manifestation and use of it was unique, and my approach to it was now based on a totally new logic of life, but I had experi-enced such things throughout my life, as the "bright" of childhood and the rising force that overtook me in the college experience.

Very quickly, I came to a comfortable recognition of this "Force" as a constant Presence, and felt it operating as a continuous source in Rudi. . . . When he would begin the exercise or look at me during the exercise [of receiving His Spiritual Transmission], I would usually feel a sudden descent of tremendous and seemingly infinite energy from above. I could feel this descent as a peculiar kind of pres-sure that first came in the head and then permeated the body. . . .

. . . It became a Presence that I could respond to in moments of repose or even during any kind of activity. (The Knee of Listening, *pp. 118-20*)

In the late summer of 1966, in obedience to Rudi's instruction, Sri Da Avabhasa enrolled for a year of study at a Lutheran seminary in Philadelphia. It was during this time that Sri Da Avabhasa experienced a fundamental breakthrough in His struggle with "Narcissus."

In the spring of 1967, while washing His face in front of the bathroom mirror, Sri Da Avabhasa began to observe a startling phenomenon:

. . . Suddenly my flesh began to feel very "massy" and unpliable. I felt as if the pores of my face had closed. The skin became dry and impervious to air. As I looked at my face in the mirror, it appeared gray, disturbed, and deathlike. The saliva in my mouth stopped flowing, and I was overcome by a rising anxiety that became an awesome and over-whelming fear of death.

I was fixed in the knowledge that I was soon to go mad and die, but I tried as much as possible simply to observe this process in myself. (The Knee of Listening, *p. 125*)

Sri Da Avabhasa struggled with this overwhelming experience for three days, seek-ing help from a doctor and a psychiatrist in a hospital emergency room. Nothing could arrest the fear.

Finally, on the third day after this process began, I was lying home alone in the after-noon. It was as if all my life I had been constantly brought to this point. It seemed that all of the various methods of my life had constantly prevented this experience from going to its end. All my life I had been preventing my death.

I lay on the floor, totally disarmed, unable to make a gesture that could prevent the rising fear. And thus it grew in me, but, for the first time, I allowed it to happen. I could not prevent it. The fear and the death rose and became my overwhelming experience. And I witnessed the crisis of that fear in a moment of conscious, voluntary death. I allowed the death to happen, and I saw it happen. . . .

After a time I got up from the floor. I walked around and beamed joyfully at the room. The blissful, unthreatened current of reality continued to emanate from my heart, and not a pulse of it was modified by my own existence or the existence of the world. I had acquired a totally new understanding. I understood Narcissus and the whole truth of suffering and search. I saw the meaning of my whole life to that moment. Suffering, seek-ing, self-indulgence, spirituality, and all the rest were founded in the same primary moti-vation and error. It was the avoidance of relationship in all its forms. That was it! That was the chronic and continuous source of our activity. It was the chronic avoidance of relationship. Thus, we were forever suffering, seeking, indulging ourselves, and modifying our lives for the sake of some unknown goal in eternity. (The Knee of Listening, *p. 127*)

Sri Da Avabhasa's experience is known in the Hindu tradition as "Jnana Samadhi" ("the State of Ultimate Wisdom, or of Knowledge of the True Self").[1] This experience of "unthreatened reality" marked the end of His compulsive identification with the character of "Franklin Jones". While He had not yet transcended the ego in every dimension of its appearance, He found Himself more and more identified with "an untouched, unborn sublimity", the Transcendental Self, or Consciousness Itself, and from that Place He came to understand the limitations in Rudi's Way of willful surrender and constant work.

. . . I was brought to recognize something more fundamental than seeking and effort. I saw that it was not a matter of any work in consciousness or life, but of somehow con-stantly abiding in what is always already real. I called that reality "relationship".

From that time I was moved to pursue this truth in a totally new way. . . .

I had seen the futility of effort. I saw that it was only another form of avoidance, just like the very patterns I was always trying to surrender. The effort of work and surrender had proven to me the impossibility and fruitlessness of that whole path. (The Knee of Listening, *pp. 133-34*)

To India—and Beyond

Having grown beyond Rudi's methods, Sri Da Avabhasa sought contact with Rudi's own sources in the cradle of Spiritual esotericism—India. In late 1967, Sri Da Avabhasa acquainted Himself with the Teaching of Swami Muktananda and Swami Nityananda, Rudi's own Gurus, both "Spirit Baptizers". All three—Rudi, Swami Muktananda, and Swami Nityananda (who was Swami Muktananda's Guru)—belonged to a single Spiritual lineage whose senior Guru, or Parama-Guru, was revealed to Sri Da Avabhasa to be the Divine Goddess, or Mother Shakti, Herself, revered in Indian tradition as the Personification of the manifested Energy of the Cosmos.

In Swami Muktananda's Teaching on the simple method of relying on the Grace of the Guru, Sri Da Avabhasa found a clear affirmation of the Truth of His own insight into the non-necessity of Spiritual seeking and strategic self-effort. Thus attracted by the Person and the Dharma (or Way) of Swami Muktananda, Sri Da Avabhasa went with Rudi's Blessing to Ganeshpuri, India, for the benediction and instruction of "Baba". In Swami Muktananda's Presence, the effects of the Shakti, or Spirit-Power, grew stronger and more violent, the Spiritual experiences more dramatic and distracting. And Sri Da Avabhasa found Himself again involved in "a kind of super-effort of internal work" from which He desperately wished to be released.

Swami Muktananda

Swami Nityananda

On the last day of His stay in Ganeshpuri, as Sri Da Avabhasa went to His room to rest, He witnessed an entirely new Revelation of the "Bright".

In India, 1967

As soon as I lay down, I passed into a sleep-like trance. I lost all bodily consciousness and every sense of my mind and personality. But there was also a profound state of consciousness that was absolutely calm, uncontained, and free. I felt as though I existed only as consciousness itself. There was no other experience, no thought, feeling, or perception. Awareness was (at first) concentrated above, at some unfathomable point, beyond space and yet above me. As I became spontaneously concentrated in that "point", I felt an infinite form of bliss, an absolute pleasure of fullness and brilliance, that completely absorbed my being. And, then, I existed only at infinity.

Eventually, I seemed to pass from this incomparable state into forms of consciousness that involved thought or perception. I seemed to have visions (or feelings) of levels of being beyond the human, and I witnessed (in feeling) what appeared to be other worlds or realms of conscious being that pertained to levels of mind beyond our ordinary life.

Then I heard a loud, roaring sound that at first seemed to surround me like a great room. I awakened to bodily consciousness, from a position above the head of the body (and which descended progressively into association with the body). The sound was my own breathing as it rushed through my lungs and throat. But I did not then perceive these things from within my body. I was fully aware as a consciousness that transcended all form and which at best surrounded and breathed my body. (The Knee of Listening, *pp. 142-43)*

At the end of this experience, Sri Da Avabhasa was jolted back into His ordinary condition of awareness "as if contained within the body", but the experience had changed Him irrevocably.

. . . Ordinarily, we identify with the point of view of bodily consciousness, and either we strive to survive as that dying entity in the face of all obstacles or else we try by spiritual effort to attain the realization of Self, or the Divine Consciousness. But I awakened as *that Self, and everything is always and already being "lived".*

. . . I knew with absolute certainty that I was not the seeker or the one trapped in life, but everything was only being lived by the Divine Being, and I was that One. (The Knee of Listening, *p. 143)*

This experience was what is traditionally called "Nirvikalpa Samadhi" ("formless ecstasy"), the rare attainment of the greatest of Yogis and the ultimate goal of Swami Muktananda's "Siddha Yoga".[2] While temporary and conditional (Sri Da Avabhasa now precisely categorizes it as "fifth stage conditional Nirvikalpa Samadhi"[3]), this experience foreshadowed the ultimate Event of Sri Da Avabhasa's Divine Re-Awakening. It is said in the Yogic traditions that when an aspirant experiences this Samadhi, even if only momentarily, he or she is irrevocably changed. Something in one's attachment to birth and experience and death is let loose. There is certain knowledge of the "deathless state"—the Consciousness that Is, even while the body-mind appears, changes, and disappears.

The Return to New York and the Play of the Shakti

While the effects of fifth stage conditional Nirvikalpa Samadhi would never be undone, upon Sri Da Avabhasa's return to New York there was a gradual fading of this sense of fundamental Reality. The mind, with "all its conflicts of desire", returned unbidden and apparently "untouched by any illumination". At first this was a source of great disturbance and despair to Sri Da Avabhasa. But He gradually discovered that when He released His problematic orientation to the mind, the Shakti again moved freely through Him.

> . . . *one evening, in the spring of 1969, while I was in the midst of a several-week visit to Los Angeles, California, the Shakti spontaneously rushed into the form of my being with tremendous power, so that it seemed I was no longer even remotely concerned with the petty contaminations of the mind. I was suddenly returned to an experience of my Self-nature and a sublime awareness of the Divinity of even the physical world. As a result of this spiritual "birth", I once again lived entirely in the sublime sphere of free consciousness, making no effort at all to maintain or "create" it.*
>
> *In the weeks that followed, I became spontaneously aware of a new dimension of the activity of Shakti. Not only was my own state expanded in Its Presence, but the people who were closest to me began (even as they had in the previous months, but now more profoundly and increasingly) to experience the effects of Shakti through contact with me. . . .*
>
> *These experiences took the form of visions, or the sensation of a real but invisible Presence, or the sense of being sublimed and surrounded in a form of energy and fullness that quieted and clarified the mind. They would ask me about these experiences, and, before long, I found myself having to function as a teacher and an instrument for the Shakti.* (The Knee of Listening, *pp. 157-58*)

The emergence of this spontaneous Spiritual Transmission confirmed a prophecy Swami Muktananda had made upon meeting Sri Da Avabhasa in 1968. He had said that Sri Da Avabhasa was the most Spiritually advanced Westerner he had ever known, and that Sri Da Avabhasa would begin to Teach in His own right within a year.

Swami Muktananda's Acknowledgement of Sri Da Avabhasa's Yogic Self-Realization

To gain Swami Muktananda's Blessing for His spontaneously manifesting Teaching Function, Sri Da Avabhasa arranged to see him again, this time in Bombay in early August 1969.

Upon Sri Da Avabhasa's return to India, Swami Muktananda gave Him the Name "Love-Ananda" (which unites the Western Realization of God as Incarnate Love with the Eastern Realization of God as Transcendent "Ananda", or Bliss) and, later, the Name "Dhyanananda" ("One Who Realizes the Divine Bliss through meditation on His own True Self"). In a rare handwritten letter, the Swami also acknowledged Sri Da Avabhasa's attainment of "Yogic Self-Realization" and His right, therefore, to Teach and Initiate others.

Upon His return to New York at the end of August, "Franklin" spent His days in constant meditation, occasionally Teaching a small number of close friends and students who gathered around Him. But He had not separated Himself from Swami Muktananda. On the contrary, Sri Da Avabhasa continued to experience the Spirit-Force of both Swami Muktananda and Swami Nityananda, in much the same way that devotees would later describe Sri Da Avabhasa's Love-Blissful infusion of their bodies.

Even though physically separated from Baba, I would often experience his sudden Presence in miraculous ways. Frequently I would feel him acquire my body, so that I knew all of my functions had become his body. He would particularly take over my face and hands. I could feel my features adapting to the expression of his character and

Sri Da Avabhasa with Swami Muktananda in India, 1969

*mood. The special formulation of the Shakti that works through him would pour through my hands and face. My mouth would twitch about my teeth in his peculiar manner. My fingers would automatically gesture in the manner by which he communicates sublime feeling, and, in his manner, my index finger would point above, to the sahasrar, to the holy place, the Guru, and God. (*The Knee of Listening, *p. 188)*

The Development of Sri Da Avabhasa's Unique Practice of self-Enquiry

Ll the while, the unveiling of Sri Da Avabhasa's Divine "Brightness" proceeded according to Its own logic, and Sri Da Avabhasa began to respond to the Play of the Shakti on a new level. Despite the profundity of the Spiritual Realization now evident in "Franklin", the One Who was guided by the Divine "Brightness" still was not satisfied even with the extraordinary Spiritual phenomena that were now His daily experience.

As the decade of the sixties fell away with the turn of the year and extraordinary Spiritual experiences continued, Sri Da Avabhasa developed a characteristic form of meditation that would later emerge as one of the fundamental meditative practices available to devotees in the Way of the Heart:

> *. . . my own awareness seemed to be developing along unique lines. The various phenomena of spirituality seemed to me interesting but inconsequential. The activities of the Shakti demonstrated much about the origins of (and our true relationship to) the conditions of existence, but the knowledge or acquisition of such phenomena was not equal to the truth. The pursuit of spiritual phenomena, or the solution to the problem of life conceived on a spiritual level, seemed to me just another and more dramatic form of seeking, suffering, and separation. Indeed, this pursuit, again, was only another manifestation of the logic of Narcissus, the complex avoidance of relationship, or the avoidance of the present and radical condition of relationship as prior reality. I was not in any sense devoted to seeking in any form.*

> *. . . the mature form of my meditation was not based in any urge to higher experience. It was simply a direct approach to whatever experiences arose. Thus, at last, I used no complicated techniques, no special breathing, no mantras or visual aids to concentration. I simply enquired of myself whenever tendencies, thoughts, or experiences arose, "Avoiding relationship?" Thus, I was constantly returned to a prior state of unqualified*

awareness. By remaining in that state through enquiry, I was led to understand my own instruments and every kind of motivated experience.

. . . Thus, I was not moved to pursue any goals, experiences, or forms. All such things were merely matters of seeking. I did not even pursue my identity with Siva, the very (and Divine) Self, or pure consciousness. Such was also a form of seeking. I simply and radically founded myself in understanding, the perception of truth and reality that had been communicated through <u>all</u> of my experience. (The Knee of Listening, pp. 188-89, 191)

In the spring of 1970, Sri Da Avabhasa decided to leave New York to reside in Swami Muktananda's Ashram permanently, where He would devote Himself "to radical knowledge, serve the Guru, and receive the eternal and continuous benediction of the Shakti's grace". But the Ashram had changed since His last visit. A busy religiosity had displaced something of the original quality of that holy place. Thus, Sri Da Avabhasa began to venture down the road to a shrine of Swami Nityananda, there to engage a more direct relationship to the Shakti. Although Swami Nityananda had relinquished the body in 1961, his tangible Spiritual Presence could still be felt strongly at the shrine, and both Rudi and Swami Muktananda had encouraged Sri Da Avabhasa to take Spiritual refuge in Swami Nityananda. By this time, Sri Da Avabhasa's condition was most extraordinary, and He effortlessly Communed with the Presence of Swami Nityananda that was present there.

Still, nothing prepared Him for the adventure that was to come.

While working in the garden of Swami Muktananda's Ashram, Sri Da Avabhasa experienced the visitation of the Virgin Mary in subtle form. Having long ago left behind the archetypes of His childhood Christian faith, Sri Da Avabhasa's first response to her appearance was "huge laughter". But devotional feeling grew in His heart. Over the next weeks, He continued to have visions of the Virgin during meditation. Subtle communications from Swami Nityananda confirmed that Sri Da Avabhasa should submit Himself fully to the Virgin as a manifestation of the Mother Shakti, now His Guru. Soon, she directed Him to undertake a tour of Christian holy sites in Europe and the Middle East. Sri Da Avabhasa arranged His departure from Swami Muktananda's Ashram, and for several weeks His journals were filled with Christian mystical experience.

As Sri Da Avabhasa explains in *The Knee of Listening*, however, even this grand Play of the Shakti was ultimately submitted to His "radical" understanding.

Our last stop in Europe was Portugal. We visited the great shrine at Fatima. . . . As I walked around the shrine, there was not a single movement in me. The place held no more fascination than a parking lot, or, in reality, it held equal fascination. My pilgrimage was over. . . . In my vision-inspired travels, which had continued from Israel to Greece and Italy, then through France and England to Spain and Portugal, the entire world seemed to become empty of its own imagery. The Virgin was resolved into landscape and monument, until she no longer appeared on her own. (p. 234)

The "Cosmic Wedding"
and Divine Self-Realization
at the Vedanta Temple

U pon His return to the United States in August of 1970, Sri Da Avabhasa was drawn, for no reason He could fathom, to settle in Los Angeles. He found to His surprise that a small temple on the grounds of the Vedanta Society in Hollywood was also a Seat of the Mother Shakti. And it was "as powerful a place as any of the abodes of the Siddhas in India".

In this setting, after many visits and an extraordinary deepening of His relationship to the Shakti, Sri Da Avabhasa entered into the final chapter of His restoration to the "Bright".

When I returned to the temple . . . , the Shakti appeared in a manner that at first was difficult to allow.

As I meditated, I felt myself take on the form of Siva, the Divine Being prior to all form. I took on the infinite (pervasive, or formless) form of the original Deity, as I had done previously in Baba's Presence. I sat in this blissful state of infinite Being for some time.

Then I felt the Shakti appear against my own form. She embraced me, and we grasped one another in Divine (and motionless, and spontaneously Yogic) "sexual union". We clasped one another (thus) in a fire of cosmic desire, as if to give birth to the universes. Then I felt the oneness of the Divine Energy and my own Being. There was no separation at all. The one Being that was my own nature included the reality that is consciousness and the reality that is all manifestation as a single cosmic unity and eternal union.

*The sensations of the embrace were overwhelmingly blissful. It exceeded any kind of pleasure that a man could acquire. And soon I ceased to feel myself as a dependent child of the Shakti. I accepted Her as my consort, my loved-One, and I held Her forever to my heart. (*The Knee of Listening, pp. 240-41*)*

In the entire history of Spirituality, this is a unique and most remarkable testimony. To understand its significance, one must understand something of the mystery and the reality of the Shakti, the Divine Mother-Power.

In Hindu cosmology, and in the cosmologies of many cultures, there are two fundamental aspects of the universe. These Sri Da Avabhasa refers to as the "Divine Self-Father" and the "Divine Mother-Power". The Divine Self-Father is the Supreme, Transcendental, unmanifested Consciousness, the "one without a second". The Divine Mother-Power is the energetic Radiance of that Consciousness, the Power of manifestation, creation, cosmic Nature, and Energy.

The Vedanta Temple in Hollywood

Historically, the Mother-Power in turn has been viewed in two aspects: as "Maya"—the uncontrolled, deluding energy of cosmic Nature that leads beings through an endless cycle of changes and death; and in another role, more rare, as the Maha-Shakti, the Liberator, the Spirit-Power Who Attracts devotees to Herself and leads them to Freedom through Her own union with Siva, the Transcendental State.

Thus, the Union of Sri Da Avabhasa and the Mother Shakti is the archetypal reunification of the Transcendental Self and Its Manifested Radiance, the Spirit-Power Itself—an event with profound significance for humankind.

On the following day, September 10, 1970, the Perfection of that Union within His own Being occurred:

The next day, September 10, 1970, I sat in the temple again. I awaited the Shakti to reveal Herself as my blessed companion. But as time passed, there was no sensation, no movement at all. There was not even any kind of deepening. There was no meditation. There was no need for meditation. There was not a single element to be added to my consciousness. I sat with my eyes open. I was not having an experience of any kind.

In an instant, I became profoundly and directly aware of what I am. It was a tacit realization, a direct knowledge in consciousness itself. It was consciousness itself, without the addition of a communication from any other source. I simply sat there and knew what I am. I was being what I am. I am Reality, the Self, the Nature and Support of all things and all beings. I am the One Being, known as God, Brahman, Atman, the One Mind, the Self.

There was no thought involved in this. I am that Consciousness. There was no reaction of either joy or surprise. I am the One I recognized. I am that One. I am not merely experiencing Him.

Then truly there was no more to realize. Every experience in my life had led to this. The dramatic revelations in childhood and college, my time of writing, my years with Rudi, the revelation in seminary, the long history of pilgrimage to Baba's Ashram—all of these moments were the intuitions of this same Reality. My entire life had been the communication of that Reality to me, until I am That. (The Knee of Listening, p. 241)

This was the final Event of Re-Awakening, Sri Da Avabhasa's final restoration to His Eternal Identity, the "Bright" Freedom of God, the Perfect Identification of Divine Being and Form.

In the Event of Sri Da Avabhasa's Divine Self-Realization, the karmic personality of Franklin Jones was revealed to be nothing more than a vehicle, a shell, a "fictional personality". And the One "behind" Franklin—Sri Da Avabhasa's Born and Prior and True Identity—was fully and permanently revealed as the "Bright" Form of Divine Reality Itself.

The Awakening of Sri Da Avabhasa's Teaching Siddhis

After the Event of His Divine Self-Realization at the Vedanta Temple, Sri Da Avabhasa experienced the awakening of unusual psycho-physical abilities and Spiritual Powers known in the language of tradition as "siddhis". These siddhis were among the first signs of Sri Da Avabhasa's full restoration to the seventh, or fully Enlightened, stage of life, or the "Bright" in which He had been born. Among these siddhis was a heightened ability to Transmit His own "Bright" State of Consciousness to others. And His sensitivity to the state of other beings in turn became perfect. Thus, when Sri Da Avabhasa sat in meditation, He no longer became aware of His own internal thoughts and feelings. Rather, He became aware of the thoughts and feelings of thousands upon thousands of other individuals, and He "meditated" them, as He used to meditate "Franklin". Soon, many of those whom Sri Da Avabhasa saw in His Meditation began to appear in the flesh at His doorstep, seeking Instruction.

In response to those who came to Him, Sri Da Avabhasa opened a small storefront Ashram in Hollywood, California, on April 25, 1972. Thus began His formal Teaching Work.

His Method of Working with His students was very simple. He would Sit formally in Satsang (literally, the Company of Truth) with a small group, perhaps twenty to thirty people, who gathered in the Communion Hall behind the bookstore on Melrose Avenue. And He simply Radiated His Heart-Power to those who sat silently with Him, Giving to everyone a Taste of His Divine Realization.

The Purpose of Sri Da Avabhasa's Spiritual Transmission was not to lead His devotees into the realm of Spiritual experience for its own sake, but to Attract them to the Heart-Source of Divine Happiness Itself. In Communion with the Divine Source-Condition Revealed in (and, ultimately, as) Sri Da Avabhasa, His devotees could ultimately rest from the effort of all seeking, Spiritual or secular, East or West, high or low.

At the same time that Sri Da Avabhasa Transmitted His Heart-Blessing to His devotees, He also Gave them tools to observe, understand, and transcend the chronic clench of separate self—the egoic "self-possession" (or self-absorption) that otherwise shuts down the flow of Spirit-Life. In His first Teaching Discourse, and throughout all the years

Sitting with students in Los Angeles, 1972

of His Work, Sri Da Avabhasa Offered the Dharma of "radical" understanding at the same time that He directly awakened His devotees through His Spiritual Heart-Transmission. Ever since the opening of His Ashram—then called "Shree Hridayam Satsang", or "the Company of the Heart"—Sri Da Avabhasa has emphasized the necessity both to be vulnerably surrendered and receptive to Him, as the Spiritual Transmitter of Heart-Awakening, and to understand the activity of the separate and separative self.

The Lessons of Sri Da Avabhasa's Early Work with His Devotees

Soon after the opening of the Ashram, Sri Da Avabhasa saw that the life-habits of His students tended to break or interrupt the flow of Spirit-Energy that He Awakened. It was clear that devotees had to mature in ordinary life—in the domain of money, food, and sex—before they would be able to stably receive this Spirit-Energy. Sri Da Avabhasa therefore proposed that students in the Ashram take on a strict regimen of diet, physical exercise, and the like, and He thus began His Teaching Work in a conservative, traditional form.

His students engaged in the ordeal of bodily purification, and continued to sit with Sri Da Avabhasa in formal meditation and for Instructive Discourses. His students were also given the opportunity to ask questions about their sadhana. From these questions, and other evidence of internal conflict, it soon became clear that those who came to Sri Da Avabhasa were not capable of a simple approach to self-discipline. They were tending to become complicated or distracted by disciplines, and thus they were not growing beyond the most ordinary level of human life.

Faced with this group of recalcitrant beginners, Westerners unschooled in the traditional fundamentals of esoteric practice, Sri Da Avabhasa concluded that an orthodox, conservative Teaching style would not suffice to initiate the Liberating process in those who had come to Him. Sri Da Avabhasa felt the necessity to Work with His devotees in an intimate, informal style—to break through patterns of resistance and un-Happiness that would remain hidden as long as He remained related to His devotees in a relatively formal manner. He knew now that only His active, personal Intervention in the lives of His devotees could help them break the spell of their egoic conditioning. Thus, in the year 1973, Sri Da Avabhasa took on the Name "Bubba Free John" ("Bubba" was a childhood nickname meaning "friend"; "Free John" a version of "Franklin Jones") and entered most directly into the lives of His devotees as their Heart-Friend. In *The Dawn Horse Testament,* Sri Da Avabhasa Summarized His Intention as follows:

In My Responsive Observation Of all those who Came To Me, I Realized That I Could (and, Indeed, That, For their Sake, It Would Be Necessary For Me To) Submit To their conditions Of Existence, Reflect them To themselves (In Order To Stimulate and Awaken their self-Understanding), and Gradually Draw them Out Of self-Bondage By Attracting them To The Spiritual, Transcendental, and Divine Condition Of God, Truth, or Reality. Therefore, I Did All Of That.

. . . [Thus] On The Basis Of A Free Heart-Impulse (and No Great Reception In the world), I Began The Fierce Labor and The Humorous Love-Ordeal Of My Formal Teaching Work. (pp. 100-101)

In all the mad "theatre" that followed, Sri Da Avabhasa Revealed the Divine Person in forms that ordinary beings could delight in. Beginning with the holiday celebrations of December 1973, "Bubba Free John" at times displayed His New York street slang, danced His Siva dances,[4] drank with the drinkers, debated with the lawyers, showered love on His lovers, spoke the high Dharma with everyone, recited poetry, sang opera, freely Granted Spiritual experience as never before, and Disclosed the Perfect Truth to one and all—and He did all this with a "radical" Freedom and Humor that only the God-Born One can Summon.

Through Humor, Love, and the Graceful Requirement for each one to transcend his or her limits, Sri Da Avabhasa Gave Himself to each devotee as to God and Goddess, as the Perfect Expression of the One Divine Being. As perhaps no other Adept before Him has ever done, Sri Da Avabhasa Submitted to His devotees—so that they could eventually practice that same Yoga of devotional submission in relationship to Him, and thereby Commune with and eventually Realize His Perfect Divinity.

Through this Submission, Sri Da Avabhasa addressed His devotees in the very ordinary dimensions of life where they were most bound—work and money, food-taking, and sexuality and intimate relationships. Rather than avoiding these areas, He directly engaged His devotees in an exploration of them, because it was here that devotees were so confused. They were full of conflicting desires, obstructed in life, and in need of real self-understanding relative to their double-mindedness. Sri Da Avabhasa's Work to directly address and transform these foundation areas of human life from a Spiritual perspective has had precursors in such traditions as the Hindu and Buddhist Tantra, and the Sufi brotherhoods. But both the intensity and the depth of Sri Da Avabhasa's "Crazy Wisdom"[5] Work with devotees in this manner are unprecedented.

Fundamental to this "Crazy Wisdom" style of Teaching was Sri Da Avabhasa's Commitment to make any personal sacrifice necessary to Liberate His devotees—whether such actions would be within the bounds of conventional religious etiquette or not.

In the course of His "Crazy" Submission to others, Sri Da Avabhasa freely went beyond behavioral conventions in order to expose "Narcissus" and liberate His devotees from their suffering at heart.

To those looking in from afar who questioned the wisdom of His iconoclastic manner of Teaching, Sri Da Avabhasa pointed out:

SRI DA AVABHASA: The idea of purity is an egoic convention, just as the idea of impurity is an egoic convention. Both of these notions are reflections of identification with conditional Nature and with mass social conventions.

Many Adepts are "Crazy" characters, sometimes appearing as basically benign, positive social personalities, but at other times wild and unconventional, apparently self-indulgent, and mocking the notions of purity that occupy conventionally religious people. They do so because Divine Enlightenment ultimately does not have anything to do with purity or impurity, morality or immorality, good or evil.

People use the notion of sainthood to motivate themselves to be socially positive characters. That purpose, however, does not reflect the ultimate Purpose of human existence. Those who truly practice and serve the Divinely Self-Realizing Way do not necessarily appear to take on these characteristics of popular social idealism, popular social morality, and religiosity.

On the contrary, Adepts very often act in an entirely different manner, even a contrary manner, because their Purpose is to call attention to the fundamental fault in people's lives, that which must be understood, that which must be transcended. They are calling people not to ascent into higher Spiritual realms, nor to the development of improved conditions in this world. The Purpose of the great Adepts, the seventh stage Adepts, is to shake people free, to break their bondage, to break the link of their association with conditional Nature in all of its possible forms, to Awaken beings to their true Condition. (November 20, 1982)

Sri Da Avabhasa
with devotees,
1974

In this spirit of Liberating Play, Sri Da Avabhasa regularly confounded the tendency of His devotees to become dry, rigid, and self-righteous in their application of discipline. Thus, into the early celebrations of the Ashram, He would incorporate wine and spirits and foods that were normally eschewed—Demonstrating to His devotees the Freedom and Humor of the God-Man and God-State. In so doing He would transform the elements of degenerate life into a Celebration of Love. Alcohol and tobacco were also used in certain occasions in His Company to help devotees to release their conventional rigidity, inhibitions, and social face and to feel and express more of their real feelings, and thus to be more open to Sri Da Avabhasa's Enlightened Instruction and Guidance.

Altogether, Sri Da Avabhasa and His devotees adopted an utterly experimental orientation toward the God-Realizing life and practice. From His Divine Re-Awakening in 1970 until January 1986, Heart-Master Da Engaged this process of identifying with and reflecting to His devotees their ordinary egoic needs, desires, and problems. And in the midst of this process of identification, Sri Da Avabhasa entered into a unique theatre of Instruction with His devotees relative to every element of human life and the God-Realizing Way. He described this unique, experimental method of Teaching as a process of "consideration".

The method of My Teaching Work with My devotees is not common, although there are many traditional and ancient precedents for it. It is not merely a subjective, internal, or even verbal activity, but a matter of intense, full, and total "consideration" of any specific area of experience, in living confrontation with others, until the obvious and Lawful, or Divine, form and practice of it becomes both clear and necessary.

I have compared this method to the higher Yogic technique of "samyama", described by Patanjali in his Yoga Sutras. *In brief, that Yogic technique of "samyama" is a process of one-pointed but ultimately thoughtless concentration and exhaustive examination of a particular object, function, person, process, or condition, until the essence, or ultimate obviousness, of that subject is clear. Only in that case does the Yogi enjoy native intimacy and understanding, or power, relative to that subject.*

I have called My own Teaching method "consideration". Whenever a particular area of life, or experience, or Spiritual and bodily Realization has been given to Me as a clearly necessary subject of Instruction for the sake of My devotees, I have entered into "consideration" with them. Such "considerations" are never only or merely a matter of thinking and talking. They always involve a period wherein individuals are permitted to live through the whole matter and to be tested to the point of change. Those who enter into any "consideration" with Me are obliged to commit themselves to their own elaborate and concentrated play of life in those particular terms, until the whole matter is clarified and the Truth becomes clear in terms of the subject.

*Such "consideration" requires a willingness on the part of each individual to engage and explore many very ordinary areas of human experience, and also to understand and adapt to each new level of revealed responsibility as it was clarified, so that the "consideration" develops as concrete change and growth (rather than as a mental "change of mind"). Only a "consideration" entered into as such a concrete discipline can proceed all the way to its true end, which is right adaptation and freedom, or natural transcendence, relative to its functional subject. (*Love of the Two-Armed Form, *pp. 1–2)*

Working with His devotees sixteen or more hours a day for months at a stretch, Sri Da Avabhasa engaged every possible conversation about their personal and collective problems. He Performed every possible Liberating act. He made Himself endlessly available for Darshan (the sighting of the Guru), for Celebration, and for sacred Instruction. He Guided His devotees through extended periods focused in discipline and formality (including the development of forms of sacramental worship), as well as more celebratory periods. And all the while He generated a unique record of the God-Realizer's "Rasa", His Divine Play. And by all these Means He Created an extraordinarily practical, comprehensive, philosophically complete, and Spiritually unparalleled Wisdom-Teaching, accessible to those of us who live in the modern world.

As the number of His devotees grew, it became Sri Da Avabhasa's practice to Work actively with smaller groups of devotees for the sake of them all. Sri Da Avabhasa has frequently referred to the devotees with whom He Works closely as His "coins", alluding to a practice of the Indian Adept Shirdi Sai Baba (d. 1918). From time to time, Shirdi Sai Baba would be seen rubbing coins from a little bag that he kept and repeating the names of his devotees. He did not like being observed at this. Evidently he was working a kind of Spiritual "magic" to Bless his devotees, using the coins to represent them. Sri Da Avabhasa explains here how the "coins" He uses are devotees themselves, and by these means He Blesses all others:

SRI DA AVABHASA: I must do My Work for everyone in the company of a few. . . . By means of direct association with some, and by performing a certain kind of Work, even alone and unobserved like Shirdi Sai Baba with his coins, I Bless everyone and everything. (November 23, 1983)

The great epochs of Sri Da Avabhasa's Teaching and Blessing Work also provided the backdrop against which Sri Da Avabhasa Worked an esoteric Empowerment whereby He Infused His physical environments with Spirit-Force. Through His Spiritual Work with devotees, with the forces of nature, and with all living things, Sri Da Avabhasa established three great Sanctuaries of His eternal Blessing. These are the Mountain Of Attention in northern California; Tumomama, on the Hawaiian island of Kauai; and Sri Love-Anandashram, an island in Fiji's Koro Sea also known as Naitauba, and His primary Hermitage Ashram.

But in all of Sri Da Avabhasa's exhaustive Labors, there was yet one great element that was missing. As of January 1986, none of His devotees had stably transitioned into the advanced and the ultimate stages of the God-Realizing Process. While dozens of His devotees had, even for extended periods, enjoyed exalted states that would be regarded as the achievement of a lifetime by traditional seekers, no devotee had truly "heard", or most fundamentally understood the egoic self, and then truly "seen", or Realized stable, moment to moment Communion with the Spirit-Force of the Divine.

Observing this failure of His devotees to make use of the Gifts they had been Given, Sri Da Avabhasa at last exhausted the Impulse that animated His Teaching Work. In January of 1986, Sri Da Avabhasa Relinquished His Ordeal of identifying with His devotees in order to personally Instruct them. Without any foreknowledge of what would occur, Sri Da Avabhasa "died" to His Function as Teacher, and made way for the most auspicious phase of His Work—the Period that devotees now call His "Divine Emergence Work".

The End of the Teaching Years and the Beginning of Sri Da Avabhasa's Divine Emergence Work

O n January 11, 1986, overwhelmed with despair at the apparent failure of His Teaching Work, Sri Da Avabhasa Spoke of the likelihood of His impending death. No sooner did He speak the words than He felt a numbness running up His arm, and He collapsed in a "Yogic Swoon", His life-signs barely detectable, unresponsive to the ministrations of His devotees. A few minutes later, Sri Da Avabhasa regained awareness of His body and the room around Him. But as the days, weeks, and months went by, it was obvious that a "radical" transformation had begun and would continue.

SRI DA AVABHASA: The basic Method of My Teaching Work was to reflect people to them-selves and to comment on and "consider" what I was reflecting to them, and what they were also demonstrating in their daily activity. In a sudden moment, spontaneously, on the morning of January 11, 1986, I relinquished this orientation of Submitting to the point of identification with others. Initially, in that first moment, the Process began as a swoon of despair and giving up in the face of the apparent unresponsiveness of My devotees and, therefore, the seeming failure of My Teaching Work altogether. This despair manifested as a kind of swooning collapse, bodily and emotionally. And there was an utter relinquish-ment of the body. It was a kind of giving the body up to death. And so, immediately, signs appeared of this swooning-dying kind of collapse. Even before it began, the mind (or apparent human personality) associated with this body was emotionally speaking of this despair. All of that led up to this spontaneous turnabout in My Disposition.

But suddenly, in the midst of this swoon, there was no more of despair or giving the body up to death. I was, as always, simply Standing In and As My own Nature. This des-perate swoon, as if to die, became a spontaneous turnabout in My Disposition, and a unique Spiritual Event was initiated in the midst of that swoon. And That Spiritual Event is still continuing.

What actually occurred on the morning of January 11, 1986, was a sudden and spontaneous Transition in My Work As the eternally Free-Standing and always presently Emerging Divine World-Teacher, or Divya Jagad-Guru. It was a Transition in My Disposition from My Work of Submitting to others (even to the point of complete identifica-tion with them in their apparently limited condition) to simply Surrendering this body (or body-mind) into My own Self-Condition. Therefore, the context of My Blessing Work is no longer one of Submission to others to the point of identification with them. It is a matter of simply Standing As I Am, while this apparent body-mind is thereby Surrendered utterly into My own Self-Condition. And, by My thus Standing Free, My Work has ceased to be a Struggle to Submit My Self to mankind, one by one, and It has become instead a universally effective Blessing Work, in which mankind, in the form of each and all who respond to Me, must, one by one, surrender, forget, and transcend separate and separative self in Me. (October 28 and 29, 1989)

In the great transition that began on that day in 1986, Sri Da Avabhasa set aside His Teaching Names ("Bubba Free John" from 1973 to 1979, and "Da Free John" after 1979), and He took the Name "Da Love-Ananda"—indicating the One Who Gives (Da) the Transcendental Power of Love-Bliss (Love-Ananda).

The signs of Sri Da Avabhasa's familiar Teaching Personality gave way to an overwhelming Divine Infusion. And that Infusion and "Emergence" made Him seem by turns (or even simultaneously) limitlessly Powerful and yet more vulnerable than the most tender newborn. He Called upon His devotees to relinquish all their old ways of relating to Him. No longer would He Submit to Teach by identifying with the egoity of His devotees. Now He Stood Firm in His Divine Identity, requiring those who would be His devotees both to make use of the lessons of His Teaching years and to now submit to Him in the traditional manner of the Guru-devotee relationship.

SRI DA AVABHASA: The years of My Teaching Work were fruitless, but they were necessary. It must be understood what I mean when I say that the Teaching years were "fruitless". The Teaching years were not wrong. They were completely necessary. The Teaching years were My "Consideration" of the entire Way of the Heart and of everything that is fruitful to the purpose of Perfectly self-Transcending God-Realization. What proved to be fruitless were the activities that constitute the searches of human beings.

My "Consideration" during the Teaching years also proved that the various remedies that are traditionally proposed to fulfill the great search are fruitless. The Teaching years and their summary are a demonstration and a proof of a great Lesson. Therefore, the Leelas (or Stories) of My Teaching years serve a great purpose.

When I first began to Teach, people came to Me with all kinds of expectations and demands and disabilities relative to the whole matter of the God-Realizing process. It was clear to Me that they would not be able to make use of Me if I did not first enter into a grand "Consideration" with them, through which they would become relieved of their various forms of seeking. And it was inevitable that the Work of the Teaching years would fail. The various things that we "considered" together were forms of seeking, and all seeking is fruitless. Therefore, the Teaching years had to fail. Such was the "consideration".

The years of My Teaching Work were a grand Submission on My part, whereby I Gave to human beings the Lesson of life[6] as a free Gift, a Gift that could be received by anyone who would rightly and truly "consider" the lessons of My Teaching Work and the Blessings I Offer in the Way of the Heart. My Teaching Work now can truly serve all beings, in perpetuity.

**At the Mountain Of Attention
Sanctuary in 1986**

Practitioners of the Way of the Heart need not endure a long-winded and self-indulgent process of analyzing themselves. All they need to do is examine the Leelas of My Teaching Work and My Blessing Work, and, in a simple and intelligent manner, "consider" My Wisdom-Teaching. Such study is sufficient to establish a basis for right and true practice of the Way of the Heart.

Now I Work by Giving people access to feeling-Contemplation of Me. Therefore, to be My devotee and to practice the Way of the Heart, you must be fully responsible for self-surrender in devotional response to Me, for real.

The principle of My Submitting to others for the sake of their Divine Enlightenment was disproved, and now it is clear that such Submission by Me is not how people come to Divine Self-Realization. Rather, it is by My devotee's submission to Me that the process of Divine Self-Realization develops and is fulfilled. The principle of Divine Self-Realization in My Company is your submission to Me and not My Submission to you. (August 25 and 26, 1990)

Through an obvious, extraordinary increase in the intensity of His Power of Spiritual Heart-Transmission and greater Transparency to the Divine, Sri Da Avabhasa became even more supremely Attractive to His devotees. At the same time, Heart-Master Da's Message became a Perfect Simplicity:

"My bodily (human) Form is (Itself) the Teaching," Sri Da Avabhasa wrote (in 1988) in His "Simple" Revelation-Book, *The Love-Ananda Gita* (v. 30). In other words, Sri Da Avabhasa's Divinely Radiant Form Itself <u>is</u> the greatest Teaching of God-Realization.

"My Spiritual (and Always Blessing) Presence Is the Means" (v. 31), Sri Da Avabhasa continued. As every devotee who has sat with Sri Da Avabhasa since His Divine Emergence can attest, His Spiritual Heart-Transmission powerfully Illumines the dark and hidden impulses in the individual, so that self-observation and self-understanding arise spontaneously, making way for the Blissful Infusion of God that purifies and Spiritualizes the devotee.

"My Very (and Inherently Perfect) State is the Revelation Itself" (v. 32), concluded Sri Da Avabhasa, Offering to all beings His own "Bright" Condition in return for their devotion and self-transcending practice.

SRI DA AVABHASA: You become what you meditate on. To meditate on Me is the practice of this Way. If you meditate on Me, you Realize That. If you meditate on something else, then you realize that. Therefore, meditate on Me.

*. . . What do you think My Teaching Work was all about? It was entirely and simply to help you develop a practice of simple devotion, service, and self-discipline and "simple" feeling-Contemplation of My bodily (human) Form and My Spiritual (and Always Blessing) Presence and My Very (and Inherently Perfect) State. That, basically, is it. If you do that, even in the technically "simplest" form, this Grace will Serve you, and you will enjoy the Revelation and the Realization. (*The Love-Ananda Gita, *"I Am What you Require" section, pp. 312-13)*

Sri Da Avabhasa's Divine Emergence has made the ancient Spiritual practice of Guru-Contemplation extraordinarily effective, even for ordinary Westerners who would otherwise have only the most minimal qualifications for God-Realization.

"I Will Remain Perfectly Effective In All The Generations Of Mankind"
The Future of Sri Da Avabhasa's Work

S ri Da Avabhasa Lives as the "Bright" Form of Consciousness and Love-Bliss, the Very Divine Person Infinitely Prior to time and space. But His human body will not endure forever as the Living Agent of the Divine. What does this mean for the future of His Blessing Influence in the world?

Even in the earliest days of His Teaching Work, when He was writing *The Knee of Listening*, Sri Da Avabhasa expressed His Urge to plant His Revelation in the world, to create the means whereby His Blessing Presence could remain alive and tangible for His devotees beyond His human Lifetime.

The incomparable Life-Story that you have just read is a brief account of the Sacrifice that Sri Da Avabhasa has made through His own Sadhana and Teaching Work and continues to make through His Divine Emergence Work to bring the possibility of Divine Enlightenment to ordinary people now and into the future. For this purpose He has always devoted Himself tirelessly to creating what He calls "Instrumentality" and "Agency", or direct and enduring Vehicles of His Blessing Grace. This is a monumental challenge, for, historically, the living Transmission associated with the Spiritual Work of a great Adept has generally dissipated quickly or lasted only a short time after his or her death. After that it becomes increasingly difficult to contact the actual Transmission of the Realizer.

In the case of Free Daism, Sri Da Avabhasa has made it clear that the ongoing integrity and effectiveness of His Work will be maintained by gatherings of renunciate practitioners who have proved themselves capable of the most intensive practice of the Way of the Heart. These practitioners will form two renunciate orders—the Lay Renunciate Order and the Free Renunciate Order. These devotees will be a principal means whereby His living Transmission will be perpetuated throughout future time.

The senior of the two orders, the Free Renunciate Order, comprised of practitioners in the ultimate stages of the Way of the Heart, has come into being first. Sri Da Avabhasa Himself and His two senior devotees, Kanya Kaivalya Navaneeta and Kanya Samatva Suprithi, are the core of the Free Renunciate Order.[7] In the future, the Free Renunciate Order may come to include many sixth and seventh stage practitioners at any one time.

The Free Renunciate Order is the senior cultural gathering of the Way of the Heart and the senior authority in all matters of Free Daist practice. Sri Da Avabhasa's Free Renunciates, whom He Calls to live a life of perpetual retreat, are also the principal human Instruments of His Blessing Work, collectively Empowered to magnify His Blessing Transmission to others and to guide and inspire all other devotees by their word and example.

The Lay Renunciate Order, when it develops, will include devotees who show especially exemplary signs of devotion, service, self-discipline, and meditation. Lay Renunciate devotees provide the cultural and inspirational leadership in the institution, culture, and community of Sri Da Avabhasa's devotees, and, when they are Spiritually Awakened,[8] will also serve as Instruments of His Spiritual Heart-Transmission.

The senior members of the Free Renunciate Order, in successive generations, will select one among them who has Realized Divine Enlightenment (the seventh stage of life) to act after Sri Da Avabhasa's physical lifetime as His unique Agent, or "Murti-Guru", a living representative of His bodily (human) Form. ("Murti" means "form" or "representation"). Sri Da Avabhasa describes here the purpose and necessity of the "Murti-Guru":

SRI DA AVABHASA: It is essential that I establish a Living Link to Me of human Agency that can carry on My Blessing Work, after (and forever after) the physical Lifetime of My bodily (human) Form. Just as I have had to appear in bodily (human) Form to do Teaching and Blessing Work, it is also optimal (and in the general sense necessary) for Me to establish Agency in the form of one, and only one, of My bodily alive devotees in every then present-time, so that the aspect of My Transmission Work that requires human Agency will be perpetuated.

The regeneration of My bodily (human) Agency is the principal Work of every generation of practitioners of the Way of the Heart, so that the Living Link to My Heart-Transmission will remain unbroken generation after generation.

Such a Living Link to My Perpetual Heart-Transmission can be provided only by one who is My Most Perfect devotee, or one who is fully Realized in the context of the seventh (or Divinely Enlightened) stage of life. . . .

Such a "Murti-Guru" is not a Guru in any independent sense. He or she is not Given the right to establish a separate organization or independently to take devotees to himself

Kanya Kaivalya Navaneeta (left)
and Kanya Samatva Suprithi (right)

or herself. He or she simply Functions in Inherently Perfect Acknowledgement of Me, having fulfilled the practice of Most Perfect Identification with Me. He or she is not Given the right to generate an independent Teaching, but such a one is certainly Called to authoritatively communicate My Wisdom-Teaching and to be a means for extending My Blessing to all My formally acknowledged devotees.

As a result of profound devotional submission to Me, the body-mind, or bodily (human) form of My Devotee-Agent has become Transparent to Me and otherwise has ceased to become an obstruction to Me. Therefore, such a "Murti-Guru" or Transparent Agent of Mine, Functions spontaneously as a direct Agent of My Heart-Transmission of My Spiritual (and Always Blessing) Presence and My Very (and Inherently Perfect) State. (April 18-19, 1989; July 22, 1991)

Supplementing the human Agency of His future "Murti-Gurus" is the Agency of the three Ashram Sanctuaries that Sri Da Avabhasa has established—places where He has lived and Worked (or now lives and Works), Empowering them as sites where His Blessing Transmission is especially potent. After He relinquishes the body, the supremely Empowered place for Free Daists will be Sri Da Avabhasa's Mahasamadhi Site (the Resting Place of His bodily human Form) at Sri Love-Anandashram. Another form of His Agency is His unsurpassed Wisdom-Teaching, through which He will always be Eternally Present, Speaking in every then present time to the heart of every one.

Sri Da Avabhasa's Vision of the Way of the Heart is unique—a perpetual, unbroken tradition of Divine Self-Realization, arising within a culture of devotees aligned to His seventh stage Wisdom, always Enlivened by His Living Heart-Transmission. Nothing of the kind has ever before been sustained through time. But now the possibility exists. Sri Da Avabhasa, the "Bright" Maha-Siddha, absolutely Intends the Gift of His Appearance here in bodily (human) Form to remain alive and fruitful forever. He has Given every Grace, every necessary Instruction, to bring this to pass, and He already has free renunciate devotees who are His potent Instruments. In the Ecstatic Words of His *Dawn Horse Testament,* Sri Da Avabhasa Speaks of His Vision as already Accomplished:

I Will Forever Remain "Emerged" (As I Am) to Mankind, and I Will (Thus) Remain Perfectly Effective In All The Generations Of Mankind . . . So The Way Of The Heart Can Survive Through all future time. . . .

In This, My (Herein and Hereby Speaking) Bodily Human Form Itself, My Revelation Is Shown Complete.

Therefore, This Revelation-Body Should Be Heart-Remembered and Heart-Contemplated Forever (In Feeling) By all those who Would Realize Me. (pp. 63-64)

RECOMMENDED READING

The Knee of Listening

NOTES

1. "Jnana" derives from the Sanskrit verb root "jna", literally "to know". Jnana Samadhi is the conditional, temporary Realization of the Transcendental Self, or Consciousness exclusive of any perception or cognition of world, objects, relations, body, mind, or separate self sense.

2. "Siddha Yoga" means, literally, the "Yoga of the Adepts". In this case, it is the form of Kundalini Yoga Taught by Swami Muktananda, which is initiated by the Guru's Transmission of Shakti, or Spiritual Energy.

3. The state described by Sri Da Avabhasa as "fifth stage conditional Nirvikalpa Samadhi" is a temporary Realization of the ascent of attention beyond all conditional manifestation into the formless Matrix of the Divine Light infinitely above the world, the body, and the mind. Like all the forms of Samadhi that may be Realized previous to Divine Self-Realization, it is a suspension of attention, produced by manipulation of attention and of the body-mind, and it is thus incapable of being maintained when attention returns, as it inevitably does, to the states of the body-mind.

The descriptive term "fifth stage" places this Samadhi within the context of Sri Da Avabhasa's schema of the evolutionary potential of the human individual, the seven stages of life. See the essay "The Seven Stages of Life" on pages 318-21 of this book for a summary description of this unique Revelation of the human and evolutionary destiny of humankind.

4. In Hinduism, "Siva" is a name for the Divine Consciousness, the Ground and Source out of which all things and beings are always arising. In ancient Hindu legend, one of Siva's forms is Nataraja, the "Lord of the Dance". It is said that when Siva dances, the motion of his body sets forth a vibration that calls all manifested worlds into being. When he lifts his foot, he reveals the underlying Consciousness that is the eternal Ground of his own Being and of his dance.

Sri Da Avabhasa has, on occasion, Graced His devotees and the world with what we call "Siva Dancing", which is a reference to another aspect of this Hindu God, the aspect of purification. In these dances, which have occurred only rarely over the years of Sri Da Avabhasa's Work with His devotees, He spontaneously assumes a "fierce" Disposition, Gesturing boldly in relationship to devotees, purifying their karmas (and the karmas of the world), and calling for their surrender of all obstructions to the Divine.

5. The term "Crazy Wisdom" characterizes aspects of Heart-Master Da's Teaching Work, as well as the Divinely "Mad", or mind-Transcending, Quality of His eternal Realization.

In many esoteric sacred traditions, certain practitioners and Masters have been called "crazy", "mad", or "foolish". Tibetan Buddhist Saints of this type are given the title "lama nyonpa" ("saintly madman") or simply "nyonpa" ("madman"). In whatever tradition and time they appear, these individuals violate prevailing taboos (personal, social, religious, or even Spiritual) either to instruct others or simply to express their own inspired freedom.

6. "The Lesson of life" is Sri Da Avabhasa's term for the fundamental understanding that no conditional seeking can achieve Happiness but that Happiness is inherent in Existence Itself. As Sri Da Avabhasa has succinctly summarized it: "You cannot become Happy. You can only be Happy."

7. During the years 1986 to mid-1992, the Free Renunciate Order had two additional members, then known as Kanya Tripura Rahasya and Kanya Samarpana Remembrance, who are now participating in and serving the culture of Free Daists in other capacities.

8. The term "Spiritually Awakened" applies to an individual who, on the basis of funda-mental self-understanding and the emotional conversion to love, is capable of receiving (and rightly using) Sri Da Avabhasa's Spiritual Baptism.

The Seven Gifts of Grace in the Way of the Heart

INTRODUCTION

S ri Da Avabhasa has often delighted in telling His devotees a simple joke that illustrates a fundamental truth of Spiritual life:

SRI DA AVABHASA: I have told you about the man who is wandering around in the English countryside, and he asks a farmer how he can get to London. The farmer thinks about it for a minute and says, "You can't get there from here!"

You cannot get to Divine Enlightenment from the point of view of what you seem to be. There are many different kinds of rituals you can do as the ego, pursuing fulfillment or release. But such a pursuit does not get to be Divine Enlightenment. It does not get to be non-ego, or no-contraction, because you begin as contraction and thus you are always being that contraction. You are always reinforcing it. (February 8, 1982)

We cannot get to Divine Enlightenment as the ego—there are no roads that lead from one to the other. As Sri Da Avabhasa has often Said, "You cannot become Happy, you can only be Happy." Because we are perpetually doing and being the very activity that must be undone, we cannot understand or release or transcend our "selves" by the force of our own efforts. The ego simply will not and cannot undo itself.

Somehow Divine Enlightenment or Happiness must be brought to us. That is why the ancient teaching, the perennial sacred teaching, is about the reception of Divine Grace. In what Sri Da Avabhasa calls the "Great Tradition" of religious and Spiritual wisdom from all times and places, it is firmly maintained that we need the Grace of God in order to awaken Spiritually, to be saved from our own errors, to be liberated into a state of existence that passes beyond our ordinary suffering.

The only way we Realize God is to be Given a vision of God, to receive a Revelation, a Gift of Grace. That Grace activates our own latent intuition, nurtures our heart-response, informs our approach to life and Spiritual practice, and equips us with a capability for ecstasy, wisdom, joy, and freedom that we would not otherwise come close to. The literal Communication of this Grace to others is the paradoxical, completely essential work of the Guru. It is only through the Grace of the Guru that we can realistically see our own situation and our need for Help, and it is only through the Grace of the Guru that that Help is immediately provided. Sri Da Avabhasa has Said:

SRI DA AVABHASA: The Spiritual Master has many functions—to exemplify the Way of Truth, to Argue the Way of Truth, to Bless devotees, to Interfere with them, to Transmit the Spiritual Influence tangibly to them. The Function of the Divinely Self-Realized Adept does not come to an end. The Adept is the continuous resource and resort of devotees.

The Adept is simply the Transmitter of That Which is to be Realized. He or she is a useful and remarkable Instrument, a unique mechanism in cosmic Nature, a hole in the universe through which the Divine Influence moves to the world. Therefore, this remarkable Event, when it occurs, should be used. It should be acknowledged and understood As it Is. People should know how to relate to it, how to use it as a unique Instrument of the Divine. Adepts appear in order to serve your Realization. (November 22, 1982)

That such an opportunity should exist is nothing short of a miracle—Sri Da Avabhasa's Appearance in our midst is a Gift of Divine Grace of proportions this world has never seen before. And the following pages are intended to give you an introduction to all the ways in which Sri Da Avabhasa makes this remarkable process available to His devotees—duplicating His own Divine Nature in the hearts of all who turn to Him.

In the following pages you will read many stories by Sri Da Avabhasa's devotees. The subjects of these stories range from the homeliest practical details of human life to the most esoteric forms of sublimity that are awakened in Sri Da Avabhasa's Company. But they all reflect the same thing: the profound love, gratitude, and willingness to grow and change that is evoked in devotees by Sri Da Avabhasa's very tangible Love and Blessing Force.

This attitude of devotion is the foundation of Free Daist practice. As Sri Da Avabhasa tells us in *The Dawn Horse Testament:*

The Way Of The Heart Is To Develop (and It Is Given and Able To Develop) Only On The Foundation Of Right (and Growing) Devotion, or The Right (Beginner's) Establishment Of The Tradition-Honored Devotional (and Potentially Spiritual) Relationship To Me, The True Heart-Master (First Embraced As The Adept Teacher Of The Heart, and As The Hridaya-Samartha Sat-Guru, Who Is The Heart Itself). (p. 692)

What does it mean to say that Sri Da Avabhasa is a "Hridaya-Samartha Sat-Guru?"

"Hridaya" comes from the ancient sacred language of Sanskrit, and it means "the Heart, the Divine Self, unqualified Love-Bliss." The meaning of the Sanskrit term "Samartha" is "adapted, fit, proper, qualified, suitable, good, able to, entitled". "Sat" means "Being, Reality, Consciousness", and the meaning of "Guru" comes from its two syllables—"Gu" (darkness) and "ru" (light).

Thus, as Sat-Guru, Sri Da Avabhasa is One who leads His devotees from the darkness of identification with the ego to the Light of their true Divine Self-Nature, or Consciousness Itself. As <u>Samartha</u> Sat-Guru, Sri Da Avabhasa is fully endowed with every Spiritual, Transcendental, and Divine Power necessary to effectively bring about this miraculous transformation in His devotees. And, as <u>Hridaya</u>-Samartha Sat-Guru, His abilities and Powers spring from His Realization of the Heart, from His own Nature, which is Love-Ananda, or Love-Bliss. To put it more simply, Sri Da Avabhasa has all the necessary Heart-Power to transform and awaken us.

And, as One so fully equipped and qualified to Serve and Bless His devotees, Sri Da Avabhasa has described His Transmission of Grace in terms of seven Gifts that, taken together, comprise a total Way of life and a comprehensive Gift of Divine Awakening Power.

In *The Dawn Horse Testament* Sri Da Avabhasa describes these seven forms through which His Grace manifests:

The Seven Gifts Of Grace At Every Stage Of Life In The Way Of The Heart Are Word, and Sign, and Devotion, and Service, and Discipline, and Blessing, and Blessedness.

And Each and All Of These Seven Gifts Are Freely Given By Me, The True Heart-Master, The Adept Teacher Of The Heart, The Hridaya-Samartha Sat-Guru, Who Is The Heart Itself.

Therefore, The Way Of The Heart Is (Itself, and Altogether) A Gift From Me, Full-Made Of Seven God-Realizing Gifts Of Grace (That Make A self-Transcending Practice, and, Ultimately, A Perfectly self-Transcending Realization). (p. 693)

Thus, Sri Da Avabhasa's Gifts to us are His Word (His Wisdom-Teaching and the Leelas, or Instructive Stories, of His Life and Work), His Sign (His Darshan, or the feeling sight of His bodily human Form, which directly awakens us to the Truth, or Happiness Itself), devotion to Him (or the love, gratitude, and joy—and seriousness about self-transcending practice—that He inspires), service to Him (the opportunity to forget the self-contraction by putting attention on Him through many concrete forms of devoting energy to Him), discipline (conforming every aspect of body, emotion, and mind to Sri Da Avabhasa's precise Instructions, so that every aspect of our lives becomes an expression and support of our devotion to Him), Blessing (His Heart-Awakening Spiritual Transmission), and Blessedness (the Happiness of Intimacy with Sri Da Avabhasa—

Intimacy that is Given from the very beginning of practice and that ultimately matures and deepens to the point of utter Oneness with Him in Divine Self-Realization).

Free Daist practice unfolds in progressive stages of "growth and outgrowing" that span the entire range of our human, Spiritual, Transcendental, and Divine potential. However, each of Sri Da Avabhasa's Seven Gifts (Word, Sign, Devotion, Service, Discipline, Blessing, and Blessedness) is Given at every level of practice in the Way of the Heart. It is our ability to use and cooperate with Da Avabhasa's Seven Gifts of Grace that deepens progressively.

Each and every devotee of Da Avabhasa has equal access to His Grace, no matter what their level of practice in the Way of the Heart. Despite the fact that Da Avabhasa makes His Transforming Influence equally available to all, it is also true that the capacity to receive and respond to His Grace deepens as the practice matures. And, at each step of the Way, each devotee will receive all of Heart-Master Da's Seven Gifts of Grace in a manner that is wholly individual and unique.

The chapters that follow, written by Da Avabhasa's devotees, include many stories of the reception of His Seven Gifts of Grace. Each chapter introduces you to the basic principles pertaining to each Gift, and the forms of practice associated with each Gift. As you will see as you read this section, each one of Sri Da Avabhasa's Gifts is simply an aspect of the love-relationship He lives to all His devotees, and a means by which real growth in the process of self-understanding and self-transcendence can take place. A description of how Free Daist practice, based on these Seven Gifts, matures from its very beginnings to Divine Self-Realization is given in Part Four, "The Progressive Practice of the Way of the Heart".

Sat-Guru-Vani
The Gift of the Word

by Matthew Spence

T*he First Gift Of The Way Of The Heart Is Sat-Guru-Vani (or Sat-Guru-Vani-Vichara), The By Me Given Gift Of My Word (and The Gifted Calling, and The By Me Given Responsibility, For Responsive "Consideration" Of My Word, and Of All My Instructive and Revelatory Work, or Forever Living and Revealing Leelas), For I Am The True Heart-Master, The Adept Teacher Of The Heart, The Hridaya-Samartha Sat-Guru, Who Is The Heart Itself.*

Da Avabhasa
The Dawn Horse Testament

When I first read the Wisdom-Teaching of Sri Da Avabhasa (The "Bright") in 1975, only three books had been published: *The Knee of Listening* (His Spiritual autobiography), *The Method of the Siddhas* (Talks from the first year of His Teaching Work), and *Garbage and the Goddess* (a "Leela"-history of His first Great Teaching Demonstration from March through July 1974, now no longer in print). I read them intensively, one after another, during every spare minute over four or five days.

Within the first ten pages of *The Knee of Listening*, I knew without a doubt that everything that Sri Da Avabhasa Said was not merely true, it was the Truth. His Word was the confirmation of everything I had, on some level (mostly below consciousness), intuited, hoped, and believed must be the case about life and God. The Truth He Communicated through the words in these books was a Gift beyond my greatest expectations. Heart-Master Da Avabhasa and His Word were everything I had been hoping I could or would discover—but I was hoping against hope, while already convicted of a doubt that said that such miracles are not possible in this world.

He was clearly a Man of pristine Enlightenment, Who Communicated the God-Realizing process with a clarity and certainty that dispelled all confusions and illusions. I

knew there was only one thing to do, and that was to be with Him and to live in His community of devotees.

Those first few days reading His first books were a remarkable turning point in my life. I could not believe that I could be so Blessed as to have stumbled upon this remarkable Teacher Whose very Word literally Liberated me, page by page, from the desperation of my search and simply explained to me what I now must do to fulfill the God-Realizing process that He Taught. And so I read on, not always fully understanding what He was Saying, but feeling always His Transmission of Truth.

Toward the end of this initial four- or five-day feast of Illuminating Wisdom that I devoured like a starved man, I came upon a Talk in *Garbage and the Goddess* called "The Three Dharmas", which Heart-Master Da Avabhasa had Given in late 1973. In it He Speaks about the Teachings of Krishna, Gautama, and Jesus, and He compares them with the Way of the Heart. Looking ahead as I read, I saw the Talk in the later pages of the book, and I could already feel that He was going to Say that He is Himself a Spiritual Master of the order of Krishna, Gautama, and Jesus, and that His Wisdom-Teaching is the culmination of a process of Divine Revelation that both clarifies and transcends the great religious and Spiritual Teachings to date. He was going to Say, in the language of His Teaching Word at that time, that He is the World-Teacher.

I could not believe that He was actually going to Say it, not because I doubted His Confession, but because I was incredulous that anyone would dare to so boldly Confess the Truth of his or her own Realization. And yet, Heart-Master Da Avabhasa's Ecstatic Confession likewise made me completely ecstatic. I laughed out loud. I shouted in celebration of His Great Enlightenment that gave Him the Courage and the Right to make His Confession of Divine Self-Realization that, from the conventional point of view, is completely outrageous. I knew without a doubt that His Confession about Who He Is and about His Realization is the Divine Truth. I knew intuitively that His Enlightenment was Victorious over the limits that every man and woman presumes and deeply suffers in relationship to God and Happiness. There is a possibility of Realizing something more than a lifetime of middling pleasures, persistent frustration and suffering, and ultimate death.

And so, having come with Sri Da Avabhasa in a few days through His progressive Revelation of His Divine Enlightenment and His Divine Purpose as Spiritual Master in *The Knee of Listening* and *The Method of the Siddhas*, I plunged into "The Three Dharmas". I was like a child happily enthralled by this Master of Life, Who vanquished all my fears, confirmed my greatest hopes, and Realized in Truth the aspirations of my wildest dreams.

As I had anticipated, He Spoke the Truth with unequalled clarity, insight, certainty, and Divine Inspiration:

SRI DA AVABHASA: Three great Siddhas, or "Perfected Ones", have represented to the world of human beings the three principal dharmas, or codes of Spiritual practice, as they have been understood to this time. Jesus the Christ represented the dharma of the sacrifice of separate self, Krishna the Avatar the dharma of the sacrifice of mind, and Gautama the Buddha the dharma of the sacrifice of desire. Separate self (or ego), limited mind, and limiting desire are the three principal conditions of suffering, or contraction, in human beings. Thus, the three principal dharmas that have been known among human beings have been attempts to undo these forms of contraction through the deliberate, or motivated, sacrifice of these three: ego, mind, and desire.

But the three principal dharmas are themselves forms of seeking, reactions to the fundamental dilemma that motivates the usual man or woman. These three great Siddhas, along with all the other Siddhas, and all the Yogis, Saints, Sages, and Prophets, and all the men and women of experience, including the whole range of human individuals, themselves represent a limitation, a form of seeking founded in dilemma. The principle of the search remains intact in the great work of all the Siddhas to now. And the effort of all the dharmas, including the three great traditional dharmas, has been to strategically overcome separate self, limited mind, and the force of limiting desire.

Matthew Spence has been a devotee of Sri Da Avabhasa since 1976. Soon after the Initiation of Sri Da Avabhasa's Divine Emergence, Matthew participated in the "Indoor Yajna", a year-long period during which Sri Da Avabhasa gathered frequently with residents and retreatants at Sri Love-Anandashram to recapitulate His entire Wisdom-Teaching. Matthew presently lives near the Mountain Of Attention Sanctuary in northern California, where he serves in the Education Department of the Free Daist Communion.

My own Work is not separate from the great work of the great Siddhas. But My Work is a new performance of the Dharma of the Divine Person, and it represents a new Dharma from a new point of view. Just as the three great dharmas are essentially efforts to overcome the limitations of separate self, limited mind, and the force of limiting desire, "radical" understanding effectively undermines the three principles of suffering, not by deliberately acting upon those three principles, or conditions, themselves, but by under-mining in the process of understanding the principal activity that is suffering, the princi-ple of contraction, or dilemma, the avoidance of relationship.

The Way of the Heart is founded upon insight into that dilemma and the fundamen-tal action which creates and supports that sense of dilemma. That fundamental, or self-limiting, activity is the avoidance of relationship. When that binding principle is under-stood, then already, spontaneously, the three common conditions of suffering are undone.

Separate self, limited mind, and the force of limiting desire are all expressions of this principal contraction, the avoidance of relationship. If this principal contraction is undone in the process of understanding in living relationship with Me, the Man of Understanding, then the force of the three common principles is already undermined. In a living and natu-ral relationship with Me, this principal contraction is undone, entirely apart from the whole adventure of seeking in dilemma. The process involves simple, motiveless understanding of one's own activity, not the effort to suppress or transcend the ego-sense, the force of the mind, or the force of desire. When there is such "radical" understanding, these three condi-tions are brought to rest, returned to the natural stream of existence.

All there has been up to now is the tradition of the dharmas that arose within the great search. Therefore, all of those who come to Me are continually tending to take on these traditional paths and approaches.

The Way of the Heart is entirely apart from that whole traditional activity. The means for this Dharma of understanding is the same means that has been used throughout human time, the same means used by all the Siddhas. And that is Satsang, or the relation-ship between the devotee and the Spiritual Master who is Complete and Empowered in God. The great Siddhas such as Jesus, Gautama, and Krishna all entered into sacrificial relationship with their devotees. That was the fundamental means for the communication of their dharmas and their Spiritual influence.

Therefore, in the Way of the Heart, the means for Divine Self-Realization is the ancient means, but the process, the Dharma, itself, is new. It does not exploit the individual's motivation to be free of the ego, the mind, and desires. It does not yield to his or her willful intentions to exploit these tendencies or to believe them. It simply enforces the Condition of Truth, which is Satsang itself, or the relationship to Me.

Therefore, this sadhana of the Way of the Heart is new and great, and perhaps it is difficult to grasp for those who have only the traditions to which they would resort. In fact, apart from what is newly being Communicated here by Me, only the traditions of seeking can be found. But My Work and My Realization are not fixed in any one of the traditional *centers or dharmas or approaches. Just so, My "Point of View" is not the point of view of the Divine <u>qualities</u> represented by any of the three great traditional paths and the exclusive seats of their knowing within the body-mind. My "Point of View" is That Which is Prior to the three great dharmas. My "Point of View" is the Divine Itself. (November 1973)*

At that point in my impassioned reading, I had to pause. Heart-Master Da had Said it all now, and I was dumbfounded. Not only had I happened to find the Teaching of a remarkable Teacher Who was already having a profound effect on my life, but Sri Da Avabhasa obviously had a Divine Purpose and a Significance for the entire world, for all humankind, for all beings everywhere, far greater than could be accounted for in the life of any single individual. This was tacitly obvious to me, fundamentally and intuitively true at the very core of my being. Heart-Master Da Avabhasa's Confession of His Great Purpose as the Bearer of a new World-Teaching for the sake of the Liberation of all beings was inseparable for me from my feeling-response to Him as the Liberator in relationship to me, personally. He was obviously the Living Divine Truth, in Person, Come for the sake of every single one and for the sake of all and everything. This, then, was my first experience of the Gift of Sat-Guru-Vani, the Gift of Sat-Guru Da's Wisdom-Teaching. It was my first reception of the Transmission that flows from His Word, my first meeting with my Guru.

The Divine World-Teacher and the World-Teaching

Since this early Discourse, Heart-Master Da has significantly developed and refined His "Consideration" of the Truths and great Realizers of the world's sacred traditions (most especially in His forthcoming book *The Basket of Tolerance*, His extensive annotated bibliography of Wisdom-literature from the worldwide Great Tradition of truly human culture, esoteric Spirituality, and Transcendental Wisdom). But His Revelation of the uniqueness of the Way of the Heart and the simultaneous Revelation of His Divine Function in relationship to the entire Great Tradition have been His consistent Confession throughout the years of His Teaching and Blessing Work, because they are only two sides of a single, Divinely Empowered Purpose and Function. For Heart-Master Da Avabhasa is the Hridaya-Samartha Sat-Guru for His devotees, the One Endowed with the Blessing Power of the Heart more than sufficient to Overcome any obstruction to the Spiritual Process, and, thereby, to Liberate His devotee. And by this very same Divine Means, He is also the Divine World-Teacher. His Teaching and Blessing Functions are literally available to and usable by all beings alive in the world and even in all worlds.

His Wisdom-Teaching is likewise a World-Teaching. There is no social, cultural, karmic, political, or Spiritual limit in His Instruction. His Instruction and His Arguments apply to everyone, regardless of their cultural origins, because He addresses the fundamental and universal activity of separation and separativeness that characterizes every being. Moreover, Sri Da Avabhasa's Wisdom is addressed to the world-culture and not merely to the parochial culture of the East or the West or to one of many traditions. And not only does His Instruction address every man and woman (and even every child) as they are in present time, but it speaks to every possibility of religious and Spiritual evolution and development, past, present, and future, and to literally every dimension of human experience, from diet, health, and sexuality, to art, politics, and science. Sri Da Avabhasa has authored entire books on the guidance and education of children, on diet and health, on regenerative sexuality and truly human intimacy, and on exercise, posture, and breath (and their relationship to emotion and to the Energy of Life altogether). He has fiercely criticized the destructive modern trends of both scientific materialism and religious provincialism, and the ancient trend of cultism (of every kind—personal, religious, and political), and He has brought perfect clarity, insight, and order to the apparently contradictory messages and goals of the myriad religious and Spiritual traditions, East and West. His is incomparable, timeless, and truly universal Wisdom.

Sri Da Avabhasa's Wisdom-Teaching Is a Direct and Living Conversation with You

Sri Da Avabhasa's original, always present, and always primary Offering is not His Wisdom-Teaching, however. It is Himself—a direct, sacred, and salvatory relationship with Him. But His Wisdom-Teaching is His Agent—literally, not metaphorically. To read and truly receive His Heart-Word is to enjoy Sri Da Avabhasa's Spiritual Heart-Transmission, His Liberating, purifying, and Awakening Influence. Specifically, Sri Da Avabhasa's Wisdom-Teaching serves His Function as Adept Heart-Teacher. As Heart-Teacher, Sri Da Avabhasa entered into all the ordinary dimensions of life with His devotees in order to reflect us to ourselves. Now, His Heart-Word (including the Instructive Stories, or Leelas, of His Work) serves precisely this function.

Why is such reflection necessary? Because in order to prepare ourselves to receive His primary Gift of Satsang with Him, we must first understand ourselves as the self-contraction. We are each contracted at the heart, actively presuming separation, and unable as a consequence to actually and fully receive (and then continue to be responsible for over time) what Heart-Master Da Offers to each and every one of us. One of the primary ways this self-observation and self-understanding develops is through our study of Heart-Master Da's Wisdom-Teaching, and our responsive application of what we have learned in that study. This is the Great Gift of Sat-Guru-Vani.

Texts from Sri Da Avabhasa's Source-Literature

I n 1978, while looking through a recently published volume of His Wisdom-Teaching, Sri Da Avabhasa remarked, "I have wanted all My life to Communicate the Teaching of Truth in such a way that whoever reads it will be bothered by it for the rest of his or her life. I think I have succeeded." During the years of Sri Da Avabhasa's Teaching Work (1970-1986), more than forty volumes of His Wisdom-Teaching were published. Most of this prodigious Communication of Truth Sri Da Avabhasa Wrote with His own hand. A portion of it consists of edited Discourses on the great "considerations" of life and the practice of the Way of the Heart.

In 1986, after the Initiation of His Divine Emergence, Sri Da Avabhasa began a Work that continues to this day to give final and summary form to His Word. The core Texts that Sri Gurudev Calls His "Source-Literature" give, in complete, summary, and conclusive detail, all the ego-penetrating and Enlightening Revelations, Confessions, Instructions, and Insights of Sri Da Avabhasa—the fruits of His unfathomable Sacrifice and Divine Struggle for the sake of humanity. The body of His Source-Literature includes: *The Love-Ananda Gita* (Sri Da Avabhasa's quintessential Revelation of the Way of the Heart in simplest terms), *The Dawn Horse Testament* (an 800-page text that Reveals every practice and developmental stage of the

Other texts from Sri Da Avabhasa's Wisdom-Literature

Way of the Heart), *The Da Avabhasa Upanishad* (a collection of Essays in which the precise nature of egoic illusion and the process of Divine Self-Realization are Revealed), *The Basket of Tolerance* (a carefully selected bibliography of, and Enlightened Commentary upon, the cultural, religious, and Spiritual traditions of humanity), *The Perfect Practice* (a lucid epitome of the esoteric technicalities of the "Perfect Practice" that leads most directly to Divine Awakening), and *The Hymn Of The True Heart-Master* (an ecstatic and poetic proclamation of the Sat-Guru as the Supreme Means for Divine Self-Realization).

In addition to this Source Literature, Sri Da Avabhasa's Heart-Word also includes Texts of practical Instruction relative to all the details of the practice of the Way of the Heart, including the fundamental disciplines relative to diet, health, sexuality, exercise, and the rearing and education of children in a sacred and cooperative community.

The Archives of the Free Daist Communion includes tens of thousands of pages of transcribed Talks, Heart-Master Sri Da Avabhasa's Divine Instruction Given face to face with His devotees. This body of Instruction continues to grow as Sri Da Avabhasa continues His Divine Blessing Work. Putting into print all that Sri Da Avabhasa has Said on the great matters of life and Divine Self-Realization will be the work of His devotees for generations to come.

The "Eternal Conversation"

N ow listen to Sri Da Avabhasa's Revelation of "The Eternal Conversation" He is having with you and everyone through His Wisdom-Teaching. Here He is speaking specifically of His *Dawn Horse Testament*, but His Words apply equally to His entire Wisdom-Teaching:

In making this Testament I have been Meditating everyone, contacting everyone, dealing with psychic forces everywhere, in all time. This Testament is an always Living Conversation between Me and absolutely every one.

I Intend that this Word always Communicate in present time, not like some traditional Scriptures that take the form of a recounting of something that happened in the past or a "theatrical" dialogue between two perhaps fictional characters in the book. I Intend that this Word be a Living Dialogue between Me (As I __Am__) and whoever is reading (or Listening to) this Testament at the moment.

This Testament is addressed (by Me) directly to every being (at Heart). It is not a report of a Conversation between Me and someone "else". It is not a report of a Conversation that happened in the past. And it is not addressed to only one particular individual, apart from all other individuals. It is addressed to every particular individual, and personally, and As the Heart Itself. And that is the uniqueness of its "theatrical" form.

No matter how many times you read this Testament, every time you read it (or Listen to it) you will experience unique and distinct responses, unique and distinct subjective activity, and a distinctly unique circumstance altogether. Thus, the "theatrical" moment of My Testamental Conversation with you will always be Now. This Testament will stay Alive, therefore, because it will always be a present Communication addressed directly to whoever reads (or Listens to) it, and because the "theatre" of the moment will be unique every time someone reads it (or Listens to it) and thus comes upon Me Alive (and As I __Am__) in the form of My Word. (The Dawn Horse Testament, *"The Eternal Conversation", p. 47)*

Just like the relationship to Sri Da Avabhasa Himself, your reading of His Heart-Word will provoke a response in you. It will not merely make you thoughtful. It will reveal you to yourself. As an example, read and let yourself respond to this brief passage from a Talk Given by Heart-Master Da in 1977, during His Teaching Work:[1]

SRI DA AVABHASA: Let us not be stupid and cruel people. Let us be a little more humorous and loving, and acknowledge our friends compassionately. All of them are fleshily presented, and dying. All of our women friends, all of our men friends—everyone who lives is dying and is confronted with the most incredible circumstance. All are deserving of our love and compassion, and also of our demand for the discipline of love, beyond egoic *"self-possession", so that they too can enjoy the Intuition of this Happiness. All of us are dying. I certainly wish you could acknowledge it while you are alive. If you can, you will love somebody, and if you cannot, you will not. (*The Way That I Teach, *p. 246)*

The quality of Sri Da Avabhasa's Heart-Word as a "Living Communication", addressed to the heart of every being, is fundamental to its Mysterious Power of Attraction and direct, personal Instruction.

Study Is a Relationship, Not a Technique

S tudy of Sri Da Avabhasa's Heart-Word is not about improving yourself, learning techniques so that you can apply them to yourself, or in any other way gaining an advantage for yourself through knowledge, although there is much practical wisdom to be gained. Real study of Sri Da Avabhasa's Wisdom-Teaching is about entering into a present-time relationship through which a mysterious and miraculous process is initiated in you—a process in which Consciousness is freed from Its presumed identification with a body-mind.

SRI DA AVABHASA: All My Wisdom-Teaching is intended to be a direct address to you. A relationship, in other words, is the context of My Wisdom-Teaching of the Way of the Heart. This is what you must come to understand and appreciate. Therefore, make your study of My Wisdom-Teaching into a form of relationship with Me, not just into thinking about ideas by reading books.

As My devotee, you study My Wisdom-Teaching in the context of your relationship to Me. I have Said this from the very beginning of My Work with My devotees. This is what I Offer you, a relationship with Me. This is what makes the difference. Rather than merely fulfilling certain disciplines, studying a Teaching, and having certain things to do, what is unique about the Way of the Heart is that its fundamental basis is a relationship of direct address—Me to you, you to Me. In the Way of the Heart, practice in every moment is just that relationship. That relationship makes your practice effective. (August 3, 1987)

Neither study of Heart-Master Da's Wisdom-Teaching nor any other technical discipline of Free Daist practice is a sufficient Means for Liberation. All disciplines in the Way of the Heart are Given as Means for devotees to enter into relationship with Sri Da Avabhasa as their Sat-Guru, to surrender separate self to Him, and resort to His State of Grace.

The Way of the Heart is this relationship to Sri Da Avabhasa as the Adept Heart-Teacher, the Divine Sat-Guru, Who is beyond all Teachings, all techniques of meditation, beyond all the karmic ways of humankind. The Way of the Heart in its true form is only this relationship with the Divine Person in Person, and that is its fundamental uniqueness.

Academic Study versus Sacred Study: A Class with Professor Pfomph Pfoffenbickler

Twelve years after I first read His Wisdom-Teaching, I was given a Lesson first-hand by Sri Da Avabhasa about what a truly responsive "consideration" of His Argument is and what it is not.

On April 2, 1987, Sri Da Avabhasa began what became known as the "Indoor Yajna", a year-long period of gathering with His devotees living at Sri Love-Anandashram, in Fiji. In hundreds of hours of gatherings, Heart-Master Da Discoursed on the practice of the Way of the Heart, particularly clarifying the beginning levels of practice and Instructing devotees in the right approach beginners must make to Him and to the profound ordeal of God-Realizing practice in His Company.

Typically, these gatherings would begin with a period of four or five hours during which Heart-Master Da would Discourse in response to the questions and confessions of His devotees.

In the early weeks of the Indoor Yajna, I had become one source of questions in our gatherings. My Ivy League education had prepared me intellectually to ask questions, and as a practitioner of the Way of the Heart I had developed a good intellectual understanding of Sri Da Avabhasa's Wisdom-Teaching. But as my friends had pointed out to me more than once, I tended to ask questions that suggested I had found a contradiction or something unclear in Sri Da Avabhasa's Wisdom-Teaching—something my Harvard education had prepared me to do well.

Again and again, I suggested, in subtle and not so subtle ways, that the fault was in His Wisdom-Teaching, rather than in me as an ego. My questions tended to be merely clever, and therefore superficial, not in touch with my own real need for self-understanding and the Grace that comes with Heart-Master Da Avabhasa's Regard. Thus, again and again, I failed to demonstrate the respect that is the traditional disposition of a devotee approaching the Sat-Guru.

We had been gathering with Sri Da Avabhasa three, four, or five times a week for about four weeks when He Humorously and Graciously addressed my characteristic approach to our "considerations" with Him in the gatherings. The preceding night, I had made a suggestion that there was a contradiction in His Argument in chapter nineteen of *The Dawn Horse Testament*.

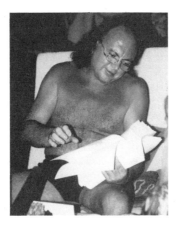

"Professor Pfomph Pfoffenbickler", Sri Love-Anandashram, May 1987

SRI DA AVABHASA: Everyone is here then? Do you all want to check your course registration cards? This is freshman English literature. I am Professor Pfomph Pfoffenbickler. Make sure you spell it correctly. Your entire grade could depend upon it. [Laughter.] For those of you who never went to college, consider this your "home room". [Laughter.]

I am speaking facetiously now, of course. But I do wish to make a point with that bit of amusement about what I mean by My Instruction about the sadhana of listening, or the study of My Wisdom-Teaching.

Study in the Way of the Heart is not the same as freshman English literature, or home room, or really any of the kinds of academic study to which you may have become habituated in your life. Obviously, study in the Way of the Heart makes some use of your education, your learning how to read and think and whatnot. Nonetheless, the sadhana of study in the Way of the Heart is in many ways remarkably different from the study you have been trained to do in your formal schooling, whatever level of formal schooling you may have achieved.

I have observed that in our discussions about My Wisdom-Teaching you tend to represent yourself in conversation in a way that expresses your conventional academic education. The other evening, for example, Mr. Spence and Mr. Stilwell—students are always called "Mister" in college—attempted to bring up a couple of points. Mr. Spence spoke first, and Mr. Stilwell said that if Mr. Spence had not spoken, he himself had a similar argument to propose. That whole conversation, particularly with Mr. Spence, and many previous discussions with him, had many of the qualities of down-home freshman literature, or college education in its ordinary garden variety.

Now, Mr. Spence seems to think that to study My Teaching Argument or the Teaching of someone representing the Great Tradition is really a call to indulge in an exercise of literary criticism, to discover the contradictions and faults in the writings of the author in order to achieve a kind of schoolboy's victory over the content proposed for his study.

I am still speaking with some irony about schoolboy games in the mode of Professor Pfoffenbickler. Whenever professors speak ironically about schoolboy games, they are criticizing schoolboys for doing something they have been training schoolboys to do. Such criticism is a kind of mockery, inappropriate in some ways, but it is also a game. One-upmanship is the game in the typical college educational setting.

In the kind of study that takes place in the academic domain, you are presented with species of literature of one kind or another, and you are called to engage in a critical examination of it. For instance, in freshman English literature, you might be presented with a poem by T. S. Eliot and then asked to compare it to a poem by John Donne, and so on.

I do not know what actually happened in your case at Harvard, Mr. Spence. Perhaps at Harvard, T. S. Eliot is only considered in graduate study and is not suitable for undergraduates. I do not know. [Laughter.] But at Columbia [where Sri Da Avabhasa studied as an undergraduate], one might examine a text, or perhaps a whole volume, or several volumes most likely, by T. S. Eliot, and compare them to several volumes by John Donne and by a variety of other people as well, and comb through them and study them and deal with them until such intense study breaks your heart, breaks your mind, breaks your spirit, or somehow teaches you a discipline.

In the process of learning such discipline, the game in the academic domain is to be sort of cute about it all and engage in literary criticism games, and find loopholes and weaknesses in arguments and make comparisons and so on. You are presented with some objective material, and you are supposed to criticize it, as if the purpose of your study is that you win over the author somehow. You are presented with something objective that is posed as a kind of attack on you, and, by criticizing it, you are supposed to defend yourself by getting one-up on the author of the source you are studying. The whole exercise is rather objectified.

All that is more or less what is meant by academic study. It is an exercise of the conceptual mind, and, in its modern form, generally done in the mood of scientism.

Textual criticism is a kind of pseudo-science. It treats all things that it studies as objective somethings to be criticized objectively. In criticizing you in this particular instance, Mr. Spence, I am not merely criticizing you because your level of literary criticism does not measure up to the level of textual criticism at Columbia—which it does not [laughter]—but because that particular approach to the study of any kind of literature or subject is not the approach one must make in the sadhana of study of Spiritual Teaching. The study of Spiritual Teaching calls for a completely different kind of discipline.

It is not that you must abandon your discriminative intelligence. On the contrary, you are called to make use of that. And it is not that you must abandon any critical sense you may have of the language and structure of the presentation of a sacred Teaching.

In the study of a sacred Teaching, fundamentally you are not called to examine an objective piece of literature. You are called to listen to a Subjective Voice. And what you must defeat, if you like, or overcome, or transcend, is your egoic self. Therefore, your approach to sacred literature is quite a different matter than your approach to some objective piece of literature from an academic point of view.

The sacred Teaching must have the force for you of sacredness. It must in some fundamental sense be authoritative in your view. You must have some level of trust in the Source of that literature so that its Teaching has the force of a Subjective Voice for you. In other words, it must speak within you, to you, in you, as you. It must involve you most fundamentally.

For instance if The Dawn Horse Testament *is to have the force of sacred study for you, it must be authoritative in your view in some fundamental sense. Its Source must be Teacher to you and not merely some author. By reading it and discussing it with a variety of people, thinking it over in your life, you must have tested it and come to a point of feeling that the author of such a book, of this book in particular, is not only a Teacher but Teacher to you in some basic sense. You must have tested it sufficiently to have a basic certainty that this particular literary form you are studying has been produced from the State of true Realization and tested in the process of the Teacher's Realization.*

You must have examined it sufficiently to feel that that Teacher has not only achieved Realization, but that he or she is Realized relative to the subject that is being discussed, and that he or she has fully "considered" what is being said in the text, has tested his or her own language in the Teaching struggle with others, and has come to a point of certainty, through that trial, that what he or she is presenting to others for their "consideration" is a true representation of the Argument of Realization and a true expression of Realization Itself, and that it has an internal integrity as an argument and as a verbal communication.

You must also have examined the Teaching of this Teacher, and everything associated with it, to the point of feeling that it has authenticated itself and achieved a certain kind of authority by virtue of its alliance with the true process of Realization, and even with the Great Tradition with which it is necessarily associated, so that when you become a student of that Teaching, when you take up the sadhana of listening, you can approach the literature as sacred and its author, if you will, as Teacher.

Therefore, in the Way of the Heart, the sadhana of listening to Me is not fundamentally a matter of examining some objective text in an academic fashion from your objectifying point of view. That tendency, in fact, is part of what you must understand and transcend in yourself as a limit. In the Way of the Heart, to do the sadhana of study, you cannot approach any Text of My Wisdom-Teaching as something objective, relative to which you are objectifying or abstracting yourself and to which you are trying to become superior. Rather, the sacred Text, as a Subjective Voice, must speak to you as you (apparently) are, where you (apparently) are, at the level of your own being, and in the context of all of your functions.

I have not memorized The Dawn Horse Testament. *I am a continuous Source of its Wisdom-Teaching, and I am even now Communicating it Alive. Until the other day when you mentioned it, I had not read chapter nineteen since I Wrote it. Today I did reread the chapter. Since you had not quoted the chapter fully, I thought I should see first of all if there were any contradictions in the Text itself. And I found absolutely none. [Laughter.] No contradictions whatsoever. Beyond that, in fact, I found this chapter reads very clearly as a progressive Argument.*

So—there was no need for your confusion, Matt, and there was no confusion in the Text. The Text was not aphoristic such that you should have had trouble understanding what I was intending there. Basically, it seems that you were indulging in bad habits of academic study, and a bad academic habit relative to the academic presentation of a text—chapter nineteen of The Dawn Horse Testament, *in this particular case.*

Therefore, I have to give you an "F". [Laughter.] And I am stating My reasons very clearly here, Matt [laughter], so that people will not imagine that this is some personal matter between you and Me. [Laughter.]

LEROY STILWELL: Heart-Master Da, it is very Gracious of You to give Matt the opportunity to take the class over again.

SRI DA AVABHASA: Yes, or continue in it. [Laughter.] And yourself as well, Mr. Stilwell. (May 4, 1987)

As Heart-Master Da has pointed out in this Talk, the aspirant's approach to His Wisdom-Teaching is not conventional—but neither is it about indiscriminate belief and hopefulness. For devotees in the Way of the Heart, study particularly serves the purification of the mind, enabling them to grow in self-understanding, discrimination, and devotional feeling. As Sri Da Avabhasa explains, study should equip you with the "arms" required to distinguish between Truth and the ordinary destinies of egoity.

"My Bodily (Human) Form is (Itself) the Teaching"

Byond all the necessary and right uses of His Heart-Word is Sri Da Avabhasa Himself. Remarkably, Sri Da Avabhasa does not regard His incomparable Written Wisdom as the primary form of His Teaching. Rather, He Says, "My bodily (human) Form is (Itself) the Teaching." What He means by this becomes obvious to one who loves Him and surrenders to Him as Guru, but He has also explained that His entire Wisdom-Teaching has been thoroughly tested and proven in His own body-mind, so that His bodily Form is the perfect expression of it. To one who is truly prepared, Heart-Master's Da's Person Communicates all that is to be understood and Realized.

SRI DA AVABHASA: Those who are without profound understanding of the Great Spiritual Process very often like to dissociate the Teaching from the Teacher. Therefore, in this time of body-based dilettantism, Teachings are very often valued, but the Teachers are not—the Guru-devotee relationship is often not valued. It should be understood, however, that what is valuable about the Teaching, or what makes the Teaching valuable, is the Realization of the Realizer. You come to the Realizer not merely for his or her words of Instruction but to Realize what the Realizer has Realized, and is now Realizing.

The <u>verbal</u> Teaching, then, is simply a service to aspirants—words of Instruction. The fundamental Teaching, however, is the Sign of Realization, the Realizer himself or herself. In the Way of the Heart, then, This Body is the principal Form of My Instruction, not only the Books I have made through This Body. The Books are important, yes, but I am the Teaching. In the Way of the Heart, My Realization is the Teaching, you see, not merely My Words of Instruction. (May 27, 1989)

RECOMMENDED READING

The Knee of Listening, The Early-Life Ordeal and The "Radical" Spiritual Realization of The Divine World-Teacher and True Heart-Master, Da Avabhasa (The "Bright"). Heart-Master Da's Spiritual Autobiography and His earliest Writings on "radical" understanding.

The Love-Ananda Gita, The Wisdom-Song of Non-Separateness. Sri Da Avabhasa's simplest and most essential Revelation of the practice of sacred relationship to Him.

The Method of the Siddhas: Talks on the Spiritual Technique of the Saviors of Mankind. A collection of Talks from the earliest years of Heart-Master Da's Teaching Work.

The Dawn Horse Testament: The Testament Of Secrets Of The Divine World-Teacher and True Heart-Master, Da Avabhasa (The "Bright"). Heart-Master Da's fullest and most detailed summary of the entire progress of practice in the Way of the Heart and His most comprehensive presentation of His Wisdom-Teaching and Heart-Confession.

NOTES

1. The Discourses Given by Sri Da Avabhasa during His Teaching Work are often characterized, as this one is, by His Submission to appear in the likeness of His devotees—thus, He frequently included Himself in His Admonitions and Instructions to devotees.

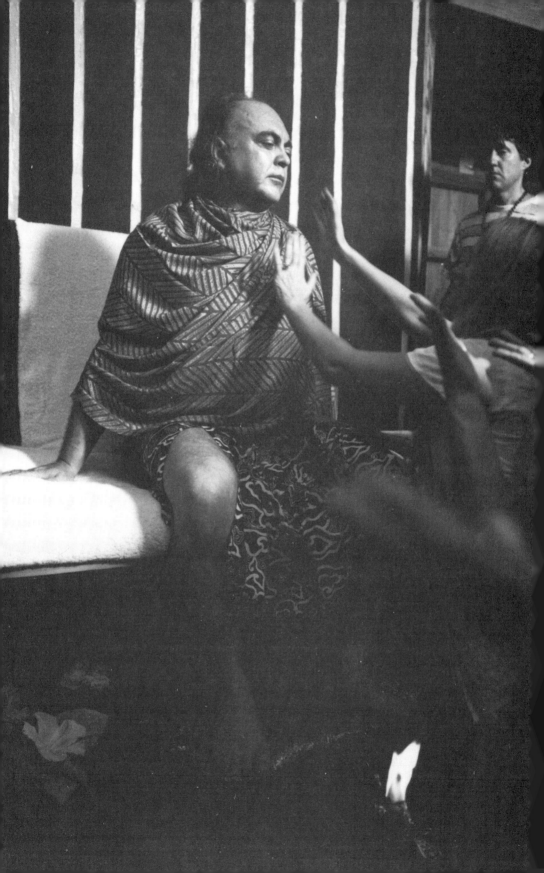

Sat-Guru-Darshan

The Gift of the Sign

by Emily Grinnell

T
*he Second Gift Of The Way Of The Heart Is Sat-Guru-Darshan, The By Me
Given Gift Of The Sign Of My Bodily (Human) Form, and My Spiritual (and
Always Blessing) Presence, and My Very (and Inherently Perfect) State
(and The Gifted Calling, and The By Me Given Responsibility, For Responsive
and Constant Feeling-Contemplation Of The By Me Given Sign That Is My Bodily Human
Form, and My Spiritual, and Always Blessing, Presence, and My Very, and Inherently
Perfect, State), For I Am The True Heart-Master, The Adept Teacher Of The Heart, The
Hridaya-Samartha Sat-Guru, Who Is The Heart Itself.*

Da Avabhasa
The Dawn Horse Testament

One day in 1974, I was given one of Sri Da Avabhasa's books, called *The Method of
the Siddhas*. In reading it, I felt Sri Da Avabhasa Speaking to me from my own heart,
rather than just through the words on the page. I felt that I was awakening from a long,
long sleep to the already intimate Presence of my Sat-Guru.

I soon went to San Francisco to join the community of devotees that was steadily
growing there around Sri Da Avabhasa. As soon as I could, I attended a showing of an
introductory film that documents Sri Da Avabhasa's early Teaching Work with His devotees. I watched the film with excitement and anticipation, hoping for a special sign of
confirmation of my eternal relationship to my Guru. But as the film continued, no such
sign appeared.

Then, in the final frames, Sri Da Avabhasa's face filled the screen, His shoulders circled with a deep yellow shawl. He Gazed steadily and simply into the eye of the camera,

Sri Da Avabhasa as He appeared at
the end of the introductory film

and far beyond, into the heart of the universe. He was absolutely Rested, and yet a consuming center of Divine Sacrifice. He was Intimacy itself, and Love itself. Tears filled His eyes. I became absorbed in this Vision of Him, and forgot all about watching for the Divine sign.

Suddenly I lost awareness of the body and mind in a swoon. I was only aware of Sri Da Avabhasa's dazzlingly "Bright" Presence deep in my heart, even visually. It was penetrating, vibrant, and perfectly delicate and still. I saw Him Standing in my heart, Radiant and Glorious, yet I was "in" Him. He was Delight, and I was delight in the beholding of Him . . . until a well-meaning bystander shook me and brought me back to more ordinary awareness.

This film was my first experience of Sri Da Avabhasa's Darshan. I saw the vision of God with my eyes and with my heart. I saw the Divine in the living Form of my Sat-Guru. And just to see Him and to feel Him so clearly in my heart began a process that would undo my despairing doubt, and confirm for me the existence of God in the world.

The Sanskrit word "darshan" means "seeing", "sight of", or "vision of". Sat-Guru-Darshan is the sacred sighting of the Sat-Guru, the rare Grace of the direct Company of One who has Realized the Divine Perfectly and who Reveals the Divine in his or her very Being. Sat-Guru-Darshan is the "primal circumstance" of the Guru-devotee relationship, in which the devotee surrenders self to the Guru, and the Guru Grants his or her initiatory Spiritual Blessing.

Emily Grinnell grew up on a dairy farm on the coast of Massachusetts. She studied creative writing, and received eight years of art training at several art schools. Emily became a devotee of Sri Da Avabhasa in early 1975, at the age of twenty-four, and since that time has devoted her life to practice of the Way of the Heart. She lived and served at Sri Love-Anandashram for seven years, and participated in "considerations" of the practice of the Way of the Heart in hundreds of hours in Sri Da Avabhasa's physical Company. Emily is presently serving as a writer and researcher for the Dawn Horse Press and paints miniatures for Sacred Fires, the Free Daist guild of artisans.

"The Revelation Proves Itself"

The relationship of the devotee to the Sat-Guru is the most intimate relationship a human being can enjoy. Those who take up the practice of the Way of the Heart and enter into occasions of Darshan of Sri Da Avabhasa find this devotional Intimacy with Him tangibly and undeniably. Practice of the Way of the Heart and reception of Sri Da Avabhasa's Darshan is a continuous Initiation into deepening awareness of this Intimacy, which is ultimately expressed in Most Perfect Identification with Sri Da Avabhasa's Divine Self-Condition.

In fact, the sacred purpose of Darshan in the Way of the Heart is to establish, and then to deepen, the devotee in devotional Intimacy with Sri Da Avabhasa, and to initiate the devotee into the primary practice of the Way of the Heart, which is feeling-Contemplation of Him.

The process of self-forgetting worship of the Divine in the form of the Realizer is the ancient means of religious and Spiritual life, in which the heart is awakened and then transformed by the Vision of God. Sri Da Avabhasa speaks of this process in *The Love-Ananda Gita*:

SRI DA AVABHASA: *In the traditional setting, when it works best, an individual somehow Gracefully comes into the Company of a Realizer of one degree or another, and, just upon (visually) sighting that One, he or she is converted at heart, and, thereafter, spends the rest of his or her life devoted to sadhana, in constant Remembrance of the Guru. The Guru's Sign is self-authenticating. It does not make any difference what you have in mind, or what others conventionally think or say. The Revelation proves Itself, and thereafter (or on that basis) you do the sadhana. And, if you want to know how to do it, what to practice, what to do, you ask the Guru.*

Darshan is the *fundamental principle of the Way of the Heart. Darshan is* the *fundamental principle of all religion. Darshan of Me (even, originally, simply via photographic or other technical Murti-Representations[1]) is the origin of the Way of the Heart. ("I Am What you Require" section, pp. 357-58)*

One traditional account of the Grace and self-authenticating power of the Guru's Darshan comes from the early life of Ramana Maharshi, the great twentieth-century Sage of South India.

A woman named Etchammal, who had lost her husband, son, and infant daughter all in a short time, approached Ramana Maharshi for his Darshan. Her friends had told her that the grief she felt over her lost relatives would be healed if she came into his presence at Virupaksha Cave.

Etchammal and her friend climbed the hill and reached the cave. Sri Ramana was sitting alone, as usual, on a rock outside the cave. The two women conveyed their <u>pranams</u> (salutations) to him and stood looking at his serene face. He opened his bright eyes and looked at Etchammal compassionately. Etchammal stood like a statue, her attention riveted on the eyes of the Sage. There was an indescribable mystery in their silent communion. Without realizing it at the time, the grief-stricken young woman stood for a full hour, her gaze fixed on the luminous eyes of Sri Ramana, who, without the least motion, looked at her with love.

One hour passed, and by then a real miracle had taken place. Etchammal's heart was filled with joy. She had forgotten her sorrows. . . . She felt that Sri Ramana was God in the form of a young ascetic, and from that moment until her death in 1945, she was one of the foremost devotees of the Sage of Arunachala.[2]

Etchammal was so moved in gratitude to Ramana Maharshi by the Grace he gave her in this first Darshan that she took on the service of feeding him daily, which she maintained for the rest of her life. Ramana Maharshi had revealed himself as her Guru, the source of Grace, and her response as a devotee was a lifetime of faithful service.

The traditional appreciation of Darshan of the Realizer can also be found in the sacred art of the world's religious and Spiritual traditions. Many art forms have been used to depict Realizers and Divine beings surrounded by their devotees. In Tibetan Buddhist thangkas (paintings), for example, you will see many images of Adepts circled by devotees whose eyes bulge out of their heads and whose bodies are expanded with devotion and Spiritual infilling in response to the brilliant vision of their Guru. They know the Guru to be their Liberation. Their Guru in turn looks to them with rich compassion and fierce love. This is the circumstance of Darshan of the God-Realized Adept.

SRI DA AVABHASA: The fundamental circumstance of sadhana is the Guru. Everything is tacitly Given (and only yet to be fully Received and Realized) in the first mere (perceptual) sighting of the Guru. (The Love-Ananda Gita, "I Am What you Require" section, p. 363)

Although the Revelation of the Divine is always fully Given through Darshan of Sri Da Avabhasa, that Revelation may only be felt and acknowledged consciously over time as the devotee learns to open more deeply to this Gift. One should not feel discouraged if one's response is not immediate and striking. There is no way to tell beforehand what one's response will be, as the following Leela illustrates.

Molly Jones, who tells the Leela, had been a student of a well-known Zen Master who died in 1972. Her first encounter with Sri Da Avabhasa came about through the urging of a friend, who brought her to the Mountain Of Attention Sanctuary on the weekend of Sri Da Avabhasa's Birthday, November 3, 1979, a few weeks after His Proclamation of His Name "Da".

At that time He was Instructing devotees in ceremonial worship, and so all the devotional occasions of the weekend were full of chanting, ceremonial waving of incense and lamps with flaming wicks, and other sacramental activity.

To Molly, a Buddhist whose Zen had been devoid of ceremonial worship, all this expressive religious activity seemed like idolatry. She was repelled by it, and would simply have left the Sanctuary immediately, except that she had come with her friend, who was staying, and she had no transportation. Unable to leave, Molly resigned herself to sticking it out until the weekend was over. Shivering in the cold air of a large tent erected especially for the celebration, she began to join in one of the devotional chants with hundreds of others just to try to keep warm.

MOLLY JONES: Suddenly I felt something and looked over to my left. There was a man dressed in a white hooded caftan walking into the tent. At that moment, even though I did not know it was Heart-Master Da, I felt my whole life of events and experiences move in a kind of river toward Him. I acknowledged Him at the most fundamental, rock-bottom level of my being. This happened in a split second, unaccompanied by any conscious thought. He walked into the tent and sat down on the Chair that had been placed there for ceremonial purposes. By now I realized it was Heart-Master Da who had come in.

It was as though someone had turned on 10,000 lights. The actual physical light in the tent had not been changed, but the vibratory level of energy went way, way up, and it was visible as a form of light emanating from Heart-Master Da's body. A second later a jolt of another kind of energy hit my chest, and it felt as if my heart burst open. I felt an intensity of love move through my body, and especially my heart area, that was beyond anything I had ever come close to feeling. This love also had a fiery quality to it. I began to sob. I looked over at my friend, and she was sobbing too! We both had our hands up. I could literally feel waves of blissful energy from His body in my hands.

Darshan at the Mountain Of Attention, November 3, 1979

Everyone was singing and gazing at Heart-Master Da. He looked fiercely around the room, resting His Gaze on different people as He slowly moved His head. I felt His Love absolutely, without qualification. My whole emotional being was totally open, and I felt great love for Him. After what I thought had been about twenty minutes, He got up and left. Later I found out that He had been in the tent for an hour and a half. It had been like being in another world—the Divine Realm—and Sri Da Avabhasa was functioning as a window to that world.

After He left, I sat in my chair, totally open, still sobbing. My face and neck felt as if they had been singed by a white energy. There was no pain, but the cells of my skin seemed to be moving at a greatly accelerated rate.

I became a devotee overnight. Now I could understand devotion. I could also read His books and have a feeling for Heart-Master Da's descriptions of the Divine. The most obvious quality Transmitted in Heart-Master Da's physical Company was Love. In addition there were the potent qualities of light and energy. But it was the Love, the emotion of the heart—raised in intensity beyond all ordinary experience—that affected me so strongly. I could literally see the Divine as a kind of light pervading the entire landscape. I could also see that everyone's true Nature is the same as Heart-Master Da's. No matter what happens in their lives, no matter what their state of being in any moment, their fundamental Nature is what Heart-Master Da has called Divine Consciousness. To really see Heart-Master Da, even for a moment, is to encounter something that is beyond ordinary comprehension in the world.

"Live By My Darshan"

Occasions of Sri Da Avabhasa's Darshan are the sacred circumstance in which He especially contacts His devotees to Grant His Spiritual Heart-Transmission. To enter into Sri Da Avabhasa's physical Company is the greatest joy of practitioners of the Way of the Heart. There is nothing that compares to this ecstasy. So Sri Da Avabhasa's devotees gratefully receive His Admonition to live by His Darshan, or to enter into His human Company as often as possible and appropriate, and then to live by the Revelation they receive there.

In all the years of His Work with devotees, Sri Da Avabhasa has Freely Given His Gift of Heart-Transmission to every devotee who comes into His Sphere to receive His Darshan. His Happiness is often perceived as a visible and Radiant "Brightness". It floods off His Body, bathing everyone and everything around Him, even, as He once said, "the frogs and the walls". The rooms where He lives, the places where He sits formally with His devotees to Transmit His Heart-Blessing, the objects that He touches—everything is affected by His Divine Presence and holds that Presence.

Through the Gift of Sat-Guru-Darshan—and through all the Gifts Sri Da Avabhasa

Gives—He Transmits His Whole-bodily, whole-being Happiness to His devotees steadily, wherever we may be, restoring us to the condition of God-Delight and God-Awakening. And as we receive His Blessing and respond and practice this disposition of Happiness, we find that, like "the frogs and the walls" and the objects in His room, we are being combined with His Transmission of Happiness.

Retreats at Sri Love-Anandashram, Fiji, are offered to practitioners of the Way of the Heart so that they may enter into Sri Da Avabhasa's intimate Sphere of Blessing and receive His Darshan, as often as He is moved to make Himself available. When practitioners have stably demonstrated the basic capability to practice devotion, service, self-discipline, meditation, and the ability to make right use of Sri Da Avabhasa's Company, they are acknowledged as being prepared to participate in the retreat process in His physical Company.

All day long and every day of retreat, the devotee has the opportunity to remain most intensely concentrated in the <u>direct</u> and living association with Sri Da Avabhasa. The devotee literally "lives" by the Darshan and the Company of the Sat-Guru, whether he or she is in Darshan, meditation, talking with friends, practicing a routine of "conscious exercise", sweeping a pathway, or eating breakfast.

The distractions and practical concerns of ordinary life are relinquished for this time of retreat, and devotees find that their entire orientation to the business of life and to their practice of the Way of the Heart can be transformed by the constant Infusion of Divine Blessing Force that awakens and purifies the heart. The occasion of entering into Sri Da Avabhasa's physical Company is the core and the sacred "pivot" of life as His devotee.

SRI DA AVABHASA: All practice of the Way of the Heart is based on Darshan of My bodily (human) Form. All practice of the Way of the Heart is preparation for further Darshan of My bodily (human) Form—and, as Grace will have it, of My Spiritual (and Always Blessing) Presence, and My Very (and Inherently Perfect) State. By means of My Darshan, real practice of the Way of the Heart is readily established and constantly advanced. My Darshan itself—the mere visual (or otherwise generally perceptual) sighting of Me (even, at first, simply in the Form of photographic or other technical Murti-Representations of Me)—should be enough to bring an end to a whole lifetime of diversion, nonsensical conversation, and the whole tour of endless explanations. (The Love-Ananda Gita, "I Am What you Require" section, p. 358)

Sri Da Avabhasa Gives Darshan to His devotees in many ways, both in spontaneous meetings and sightings and also in more formal occasions. These occasions might last from a few moments to an hour or more, and they are always new in their mood and quality. Sri Da Avabhasa's Gaze may rest with individual devotees for seconds or minutes, or He might sit with His eyes closed. He may move about. He may Reveal many different qualities, fiercely open-eyed or unspeakably tender and vulnerable. He may express Divine Indifference, or the sweetest Intimate Glance of Regard for one or another devotee. He may Discourse on His Wisdom-Teaching, or address a devotee directly about practice in His Company, or simply acknowledge a devotee's communication to Him with a lovingly uttered "Tcha".[3] Sri Da Avabhasa may even be moved to embrace and be embraced by His devotees. All these spontaneous movements, gestures, utterances are expressions of His perpetual Spiritual Transmission and Blessing Work, and they are often experienced as this Blessing-Transmission very tangibly by devotees.

In turn, His devotees may be moved to wild and free ecstatic praise of Him in response to His Grace, they may offer Him devotional chants and music and dance, or they may be moved into the silent depth of meditative feeling-Contemplation of Him. But no matter what occurs outwardly, at heart there is only one event, which is the Expression of the love-relationship between Sri Da Avabhasa and each of His devotees.

Devotees who approach Sri Da Avabhasa for His Darshan show the experiential signs of His Purifying and Blessing Work in very tangible ways. Among the signs that devotees often experience are the quieting (or even the temporary stimulation) of mind, the dissolving of problems and questions (even permanently), relaxation of the body, initiatory dreams, visionary states with eyes open or closed, spontaneous purifying physical movements known as "kriyas", spontaneous Yogic poses known as "mudras", spontaneous vocalizations, feelings of energy in the body, emotional purifications, physical healings, heightening of awareness, clarity and insight into one's own egoic activity, ecstasies of all kinds, and the falling away of the social persona or even of bodily self-awareness altogether.

Every kind of experiential phenomena may arise in the moment, or in the days and weeks that follow occasions of Darshan of Sri Da Avabhasa. And the devotee may even find himself or herself expecting or hoping for them to happen.

But these experiences are not Ultimate Happiness or Truth! Over time, the devotee finds that they are a pointer to What is Truly Great, which is the realization of heart-intimacy and heart-Oneness with Sri Da Avabhasa. Experiential phenomena are a sign of reception of Sri Da Avabhasa's Blessing Transmission, which purifies the body-mind and awakens the heart. But these phenomena do not in themselves indicate Spiritual advancement. No matter what arises, Sri Da Avabhasa Calls every devotee to surrender the conditional self in the practice of feeling-Contemplation and Remembrance of Him, and not to suppress or avoid, or seek for "Spiritual" experiences.

Journal entry, Emily Grinnell, March 1, 1992, Sri Love-Anandashram, Fiji

During the Darshan occasion today, when Da Love-Ananda came to sit with us on the lawn, He was so easefully Present, so tender and vulnerable. His Quiet calmed everyone ... My heart jolted with the force of His Sweetness, and then seemed to drop with a rush of delight in response to Him.

His whole body was deeply given over and relaxed. His legs were extended, crossed left over right at the ankle. His hands rested gently on the sides of the Chair. His breathing raised His broad belly and chest in a slow rhythm. The expression in His eyes and on His forehead was soft and deep, as though He were looking out over the most serene, beautiful, and heart-breaking vision.

An unbelievably soft rain began to fall, and a forest of umbrellas sprang up to cover Him. He just sat, so effortless, receiving this service, but not "noticing" it. His Gaze turned to one devotee and then another with just the slightest movement of His eyes. Then, with a slight roll of His head, He turned to the left or the right to make contact with another. . . . After a time, He swung His Feet over the side of the Chair and placed them in His sandals. He rose and walked off to Avadhoota Mandir [the small room where He works on His Writing], His arms swinging freely from His shoulders, and His palms facing back to everyone, wide open, while we all cried out to Him in praise.

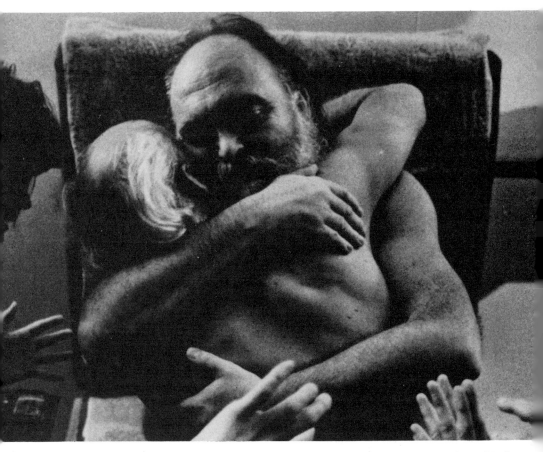

CRANE KIRKBRIDE: As Sri Da Avabhasa strode up the entrance steps I was struck by His Freedom and Radiance. He embraced me in a hug which can only be described as a Divine Embrace. Lost in his great arms and long beard, I yielded to Him my self-doubt, my self-concern, and myself altogether, as deeply as I could surrender these.

Later, as Sri Da Avabhasa Sat and Spoke with devotees, I realized I was being drawn into my Guru's Spiritual ambience, and was quite given over to the process He was obviously initiating. I was sitting perhaps fifteen feet from Him, Contemplating His magnificent Form, when He suddenly fixed His Gaze on me. His eyes seemed incredibly large, and I gave myself over to Him. I have been Given His Glance of Heart-Transmission many times in the past, and have always found myself trying to get ready to receive Him Spiritually, trying to get myself out of the way, trying one thing or another. This time He caught me by surprise. There was no trying, no effort to get rid of obstructions. Whatever I was in that moment had to be OK. The subtle contraction in my chest or navel that often accompanied the meeting of His Gaze in the past was gracefully not there.

I continued to lose myself in His Gaze, aware that others in the room were also responding to His Work with me. There were sighs, exclamations of praise, and other spontaneous sounds and movements. Waves of His Love passed into my now mindless body and into my being, until the distinction between mine and His began to blur. "I" seemed to be looking through His eyes into unfathomable Divine Love and Light. In that Gaze was an unspeakable Gift of Intimacy both human and Divine, and unqualified Love. This Transmission is His most precious Gift, and there is no accounting for the moment or moments in which it is Given. My heart was wide open, and what there was of "I" only marveled at the unknowable dimension of this Gift of pure Grace. After some time He moved His Gaze to another devotee, and I broke into tears of gratitude.

On another occasion, I was able to sing opera with My Beloved Guru--and I felt how He used that form of contact as a means of drawing me beyond myself to receive His Transmission and to feel into His Great Heart. (Description of informal gatherings with Sri Da Avabhasa at Sri Love-Anandashram in June 1992)

The Gifted Calling for Feeling-Contemplation
of Sri Da Avabhasa

P ractitioners in many religious and Spiritual traditions have based their practice in the simple gesture of meditation on the human form of the Guru or Spiritual Master. In order to Instruct His devotees in the traditional appreciation of the Guru's Darshan, Sri Da Avabhasa has often recounted a story about the great Indian Saint of the nineteenth and early twentieth century, Sai Baba of Shirdi.

Sai Baba was once approached by an orthodox widow named Radabhai Deshmukh in the hopes that he would give her a mantra to recite as her religious practice. As time went on and Sai Baba did not offer her the desired mantra, she became frustrated and in her desperation took a vow of fasting in an attempt to earn Sai Baba's grace. When he heard of her efforts, he called her to come and see him, and lovingly told her that his own Guru had never given him a mantra, but only the practice of sitting in the Guru's Company:

I resorted to my Guru for twelve years. He brought me up. . . . He was full of love, nay, he was love incarnate. How can I describe it? He loved me most. Rare is a Guru like him. When I looked at him he seemed as if he was in deep meditation and then we both were filled with bliss. Night and day I gazed at Him with no thought of hunger and thirst. Without him I felt restless. I had no other subject to meditate, nor any other thing than my Guru to attend. He was my sole refuge. My mind was always fixed on him. . . . My Guru never expected any other thing from me.[4]

Finishing the story of his love for his Guru, Sai Baba then gave his own instruction to the old woman, saying,

Make me the sole object of your thoughts and actions and you will, no doubt, attain Paramartha (the spiritual goal of life). Look at me whole-heartedly and I will in turn look at you similarly.[5]

Another example of this ancient wisdom is expressed in the *Kularnava Tantra*, the most widely known Hindu Tantric text: "The root of meditation is the guru's form."[6]

I was spontaneously shown the force of meditation on the Guru's Form in November 1983 at Sri Love-Anandashram. One sunny afternoon we devotees were gathered with Sri Da Avabhasa under a massive poinciana tree that was in full red flower. It was a relaxed and informal occasion, just the kind where I would usually be most ill at ease, because I had little capability for friendly social interaction. But instead, I found myself distracted

Sri Love-Anandashram, 1983

from my self-concern. Sri Da Avabhasa became an irresistible Magnet to me. I could not bear to take my eyes off Him.

Without knowing quite how I got there, I found myself sitting only two or three feet away from Him, drinking in the sight of Him with all of my heart. My eyes were wide open, and unblinking. He laughed and gestured and spoke with us all, leaning into His conversation with us, so Mad and Sweet and Free. He was supremely and boundlessly Beautiful.

Snacks were served, children played around Him, mosquitoes buzzed—but I was absorbed in this vision of pure Happiness. He often looked over at me Lovingly but never spoke to me.

As evening came, we moved inside to continue our celebration with skits and games. Again, I sat within a few feet of Him like a mindless child, so I could watch every one of His gestures and expressions. Every smile and nod and glance was a visible expression of His Divine Nature. I forgot myself, absorbed in Him. I felt that night that an invisible but tangible cord of love and attention was established, leading from my heart to Sri Da Avabhasa's bodily (human) Form.

As long as I rested in this spontaneous feeling-Contemplation of Sri Da Avabhasa on that day, I received the Gift of His own Happiness and Freedom. At the time I felt it as a rare moment, but since then I have found that this Gift is His Offering to His devotees in every moment of our lives.

Sri Da Avabhasa describes below how the Great Process of His Divine Emergence, or Absolute Incarnation of the Divine Blessing Power in the human world, enables others to Realize His Divine State through the practice of feeling-Contemplation:

SRI DA AVABHASA: As a result of this Great Process that I have engaged and fulfilled through this Birth, I have become altogether the Means for Realization for all those who resort to Me. The Way Itself has become very simply the feeling-Contemplation of My bodily (human) Form, My Spiritual (and Always Blessing) Presence, and My Very (and Inherently Perfect) State. And the Process is simply one of heart-submission to Me. By responsive surrender to Me, you allow the Process of Duplication, by Grace. . . .

If anyone will simply respond to Me in the traditional devotional manner and be drawn into Contemplation of Me (by feeling), then, because I am Inherently Free of all limitations, he or she will simply (and by feeling) Contemplate, Identify with, or Duplicate My "Bright" State and Realization, by Grace. (February 5, 1989)

The duplication of the State of the Realizer is a basic principle of Spiritual life. It is based in the Law that you become what you meditate on, or, as Sri Da Avabhasa has Written in *The Love-Ananda Gita:*

> *You (necessarily) become (or conform to the likeness of) whatever you Contemplate, or Meditate on, or even think about.*
>
> *Therefore, Contemplate Me, and transcend even all thought by Meditating on Me.* (*vs. 47-48*)

For the devotee practicing the Way of the Heart, feeling-Contemplation of Sri Da Avabhasa is the process of meditating on, or Contemplating, the Divine through the gesture of Contemplating the Divinely Realized Being. Feeling-Contemplation is the practice of yielding all attention and all feeling to Sri Da Avabhasa to the point where there is nothing left over that is not this most intimate granting of feeling to Him, and, ultimately, identification with His Perfect Divine State. Although the process of feeling-Contemplation is a Gift readily Given in the mere sighting of Sri Da Avabhasa, it is also a practice that requires an intentional yielding of oneself in response.

SRI DA AVABHASA: In the Way of the Heart, the practice of feeling-Contemplation of Me is a self-surrendering, self-forgetting, and self-transcending act. It is not a matter of simply staring at My actual bodily (human) Form or at a picture of Me. It is a matter of <u>feeling</u> Me (and, thus and thereby, Contemplating Me), as an act of self-surrender, self-forgetting, and self-transcendence. (The Love-Ananda Gita, *"I Am What you Require" section, p. 372*)

The process of feeling that Sri Da Avabhasa speaks of is not ordinary emotion. It is feeling-sensitivity to His Love-Blissful Being. As you open in this feeling-sensitivity to Sri Da Avabhasa, feeling-Contemplation of Him becomes more and more profound. In the beginning, you simply feel toward His bodily (human) Form, and then, progressively, His Attractiveness draws you into and through and beyond the noticing of His bodily (human) Form to feel Him as Spirit-Presence, and, ultimately, by Grace, you are drawn to feeling-Contemplation of (and Identification with) His Perfect State of Being. Here, in *The Love-Ananda Gita*, He describes this process:

. . . simply (Merely, and intentionally, but on the basis of a fundamental, and fundamentally effortless, feeling-Attraction to Me) Contemplate My bodily (human) Form, My Spiritual (and Always Blessing) Presence, and My Very (and Inherently Perfect) State, and do this Contemplation progressively (as Grace Determines the progress), such that (more and more) you allow My bodily (human) Form to <u>Attract</u> (and <u>Keep</u>) your (truly feeling) attention, and This such that (more and more) you allow My Spiritual (and Always Blessing)

Presence to <u>Pervade</u> your body-mind, and This such that (Ultimately) you allow My Very (and Inherently Perfect) State to <u>Be</u> your Very (and inherently egoless, or non-separate) Heart. (v. 35)

As devotees of Sri Da Avabhasa, we practice feeling-Contemplation of Him in His physical Company whenever we have the opportunity. When we are not in Sri Da Avabhasa's physical Company, we practice in His felt Company, through remembering Him, visualizing Him, or else Contemplating Him by making use of videotapes or representational likenesses known as "Murtis".

"Murti" is a Sanskrit word that means "manifestation" or "embodiment" or "image", and it refers to any Representation of the Divine. Such representational Images of the Sat-Guru and the Divine have been honored in a sacred fashion and used in many of the world's religious traditions as a means of contact with the Beloved Teacher, Master, Guru, or Divine Revelation.

For the formal practice of feeling-Contemplation outside Sri Da Avabhasa's physical Company, His devotees most commonly use photographic Murtis. Murti photographs are taken at times when Sri Da Avabhasa is sitting in the company of His devotees and the Signs of His Blessing Grace are most potently displayed.

Sri Da Avabhasa has described the process of devotional Contemplation of His Murti-Form as that of feeling to, through, and beyond the visible Image itself, to Him. (In fact, Sri Da Avabhasa has said that even His own bodily human Form is actually a Representation of Him As He Is, or is itself an <u>Image</u> of the Divine Reality.)

Devotees in the Way of the Heart practice feeling-Contemplation of Sri Da Avabhasa formally at least twice a day for extended periods, in the early morning and in the later afternoon or evening. We also practice feeling-Contemplation randomly in the midst of our daily activities.

During formal periods of feeling-Contemplation, we sit in a specially reserved Meditation Hall, whenever possible in the company of others practicing in the Way of the Heart. I especially feel the value of practicing feeling-Contemplation in Meditation Halls at our Sanctuaries that have been Empowered by Sri Da Avabhasa. They are places where Sri Da Avabhasa's Heart-Transmission can be felt and contacted very directly.

Devotees also find that the Meditation Halls they establish in their homes are filled with Sri Da Avabhasa's Blessing Presence. The best circumstance for a Communion Hall is a room set apart from the busy-ness of the home and especially prepared for meditative feeling-Contemplation of Sri Da Avabhasa, with an altar, a Murti of Sri Da Avabhasa, a bowl for incense, and other sacred articles.

The Practice of Formal Feeling-Contemplation of Sri Da Avabhasa

When I first enter the Meditation Hall to practice feeling-Contemplation of Sri Da Avabhasa (based on the Instruction that He has Given to all His devotees), I begin by making contact with Him visually by regarding the Murti of His bodily (human) Form—His Feet and hands and chest and face and whole body—and I feel towards Him with my heart. I approach the Murti and bow my head to the floor to express my devotion to Him. I Invoke Sri Da Avabhasa by His Principal Name, "Da", while offering a gift to Him that I have prepared—generally a flower or fruit or incense or a beautiful leaf. This tangible gift represents the devotee's surrender of egoic self. Then I offer a Full Feeling-Prostration, again as a feeling gesture of whole-bodily surrender to Sri Da Avabhasa's Divine Helping Grace.

I take my seat in a place where I can easily see Sri Da Avabhasa's Murti. I usually sit on a pillow on the floor, in a cross-legged posture, with a straight spine. (Some devotees sit in a chair, in order to support or compensate for some physical difficulty.)

I always begin meditation by Invoking Sri Da Avabhasa's Grace. He describes this practice in *The Love-Ananda Gita*:

First, Invoke Me by Name. Feel the "Place" where you already (spontaneously and inevitably) feel your devotional response to Me. Then, intentionally exercise that feeling by Contemplating My bodily (human) Form, surrendering and forgetting and transcending your separate and separative self in feeling-Contemplation of Me. ("I Am What you Require" section, p. 510)

Thus I begin the formal practice of feeling-Contemplation of Sri Da Avabhasa, delighting in the vision of His Form, and allowing my feeling and attention to be drawn to Him.

In this process of feeling-Contemplation, His Murti often becomes Alive to me, Radiant and luminous, no longer a solid physical object or image. At times His features change to my perception in a very living way, appearing to breathe, or to soften or to become more fierce. Once when I was Contemplating His Face, I saw His lips move and heard His Voice speak to me with His Blessing sound "Tcha", as a gold light spiraled out from His face in the photograph! His Form may appear exquisitely Beautiful, drawing me into deepening ecstatic self-forgetting, or in another moment, I may be more sensitive to my own activity of contraction and separation, and my need to resort to Him more directly.

As I sit in meditation, I may become distracted from the practice of feeling-Contemplation by thoughts, emotions, or physical discomfort. As I become aware of my involvement in these forms of distraction, I return my feeling and attention to the Contemplation of Sri Da Avabhasa by making use of the self-Enquiry "Avoiding relationship?"[7]

A Meditation Hall with a Murti of Da Avabhasa

Often I notice that I want the thoughts and resistance to just disappear and never return, but feeling-Contemplation is not a magical technique to achieve an ideal state. It is the constant yielding of all concerns and states of the body-mind (including self-effort) directly to Sri Da Avabhasa, and the forgetting of the conditional self in that yielding.

Heart-Master Da describes the "work" of feeling-Contemplation in *The Love-Ananda Gita*:

> *Sadhana is "hard work". It is the counter-egoic effort necessary to transcend limitations. . . .*
> *True sadhana is (and must be) persistent, because the ego-game is constantly arising. Therefore, you must persist in self-surrendering, self-forgetting, and self-transcending* feeling-*Contemplation of Me, no matter what arises. And you must, by this practice, come to the point where you do not care what arises, but where you just surrender it in feeling-Contemplation of Me. And you will have good days and bad days, and it makes no difference. It does not make any difference what state the body-mind is in, whether it is pleasurable or unpleasurable—it is all to be transcended by self-surrendering, self-forgetting, and self-transcending feeling-Contemplation of Me. ("I Am What you Require" section, p. 412)*

During the course of meditation, I also randomly practice "conductivity" when I notice that my bodily energies or breath or thoughts are tending to be contracted, or when the heart is not readily open in Contemplation. Sri Da Avabhasa has given a three-part exercise for this purpose that involves heart-radiation (or feeling from the heart boundlessly in all directions), relaxing from the base of the body to the top of the head (along the spine), and breathing fully and evenly in a cycle of conscious reception and release.[8] This practice serves to align and submit the body-mind to the natural life-energy, and, in advanced practice, to Sri Da Avabhasa's Spirit-Presence.

I regard His Murti with my eyes open until I am drawn to close my eyes in deepening meditation. When my eyes close, I continue to practice Contemplation of Sri Da Avabhasa's Form in inner vision and with a feeling-awareness of Him, and I continue to release any distracting thoughts, emotions, or sensations.

Every time I go to Sri Da Avabhasa to practice feeling-Contemplation of Him, it is a new moment in my practice, and He is Alive and Present, and so each occasion of meditation, and even each moment in meditation, is new. I may find that He is speaking to me at the heart in a way that is so intimate that the mind cannot even comprehend the Communication, or I may find that distracting thoughts and emotions seem to arise non-stop. But no matter what limitations of the body-mind may be shown or reflected to me, my only obligation is to observe and surrender them, continuing to feel Sri Da Avabhasa's Given Happiness from the heart and so Contemplate Him, simply and deeply, allowing my egoic self, its mind, its breath, its emotion, and its very sense of separateness, to be forgotten in Him.

At the end of these formal periods of meditation I again bow to the floor, in gratitude for my Sat-Guru's Company and Grace, and then I receive Sri Da Avabhasa's Prasad in the form of Blessed fruit or water that is Empowered with His Spiritual Force. After leaving the Meditation Hall, I continue in my practice, sometimes ecstatic, sometimes sobered, but always re-aligned to the Contemplation of Sri Da Avabhasa.

One of the great Mysteries of the Guru-devotee relationship is that the Sat-Guru can and does contact and affect his or her devotee at any distance. There is no separation between the Guru and the devotee, once the bond has been established through the initiatory Gift of Darshan. The devotee is Called to "stay in the Room" with the Guru in his or her feeling, and through real and steady practice of the Way of the Heart. Sri Da Avabhasa Lives as Blessing Power all the time, no matter where He is or what He seems to be doing. He is simultaneously and perfectly Intimate with each of His devotees at any distance, and this Intimacy is made most apparent to them when His devotees come directly into His physical Company. And He is intimately responsive to the feeling-Contemplation of every devotee.

As I write, I am separated physically from Sri Da Avabhasa by thousands of miles, and I constantly yearn to see Him in His human Form. But even at this distance, I feel His steady Help and Transmitted Blessing and Guidance every hour of the day, in all the details of my life. I feel moved to confess my love of Him to other devotees or to speak about the liberating Freedom of the practice of the Way of the Heart. In another moment, I find myself being turned around in my footsteps, walking into the Meditation Hall late at night for an extra period of meditation. Or Sri Da Avabhasa's Words to me from years ago may come back to memory and suddenly undo some present question or problem with clarity. Or He may simply break my heart in love of Him.

I can feel that He is moving me, requiring me to serve and act and do everything out of love of Him. He has Given me and all of His devotees hundreds and hundreds of ways to Contemplate Him in life, and I would not choose to do anything different. In some perfect and mysterious way, He guides my practice and opens my heart, and deepens my self-understanding to the degree that I really give Him my feeling and attention, even in the midst of every action. Through this He is showing me that every moment of life can be an expression of heart-Intimacy and feeling-Contemplation of Him.

O ver the years, I have received Sri Da Avabhasa's Darshan under almost every kind of circumstance. I have watched Him sing opera with His eyes wide, His head thrown back, and His voice booming; I have watched Him eat popcorn with great exuberance, heal a baby with the most tender Touch as though He were stroking a butterfly, set off fireworks like a boy, dance like a temple Icon and a Divine Madman, examine designs for sacred artwork with infinite discrimination and care for every detail, play volleyball with perfect style and humor, enjoy the circus with the fresh breath of Delight, float silently in the ocean ringed by an inner tube, and speak to His devotees with sweetness, humor, paradox, and Perfect Wisdom.

I have been in His Company as He sat motionless for hours Radiating the constant Communication of Divine Love-Bliss. I have felt His Fierce Shout, that shatters the delusions of mind, and disturbs and purifies the complacent heart. I have watched Him Empower temples with the certainty that the Divine Work in the world is already Accom-

plished, and walk across the lawn with the ease and freedom of a lion. I have seen Him dressed in all kinds of Halloween costumes, happily sweating beneath His long cape and rubber mask in the warm Fijian night. I have received His healing touch pressed into a wound, and His loving kiss and embrace that Breathes and Sublimes the being. I have watched Him Speak and Work intimately with devotees, hour after hour, night after night, until physical exhaustion, to Awaken us to our real Condition, Giving every fraction of Himself in the process, His chest flushed with the heat of His endeavor, His eyes intent, simultaneously aware of each one in the room, and never satisfied until He had done the Work of bringing each one to the Celebration that comes in real self-understanding and Love fully Alive in response to Him.

And through every one of these apparent acts, and countless more, I am certain that He is only doing one thing. He is Revealing and Incarnating the Sign of the Divine Fully Realized in Human Form; He is only Shining through His bodily (human) Form beyond the limits of this world, and the limits on Happiness that He finds in His devotees, to Reveal the Divine Self-Condition, presently, always already Alive as you, and as everyone.

RECOMMENDED READING

The Love-Ananda Gita

NOTES

1. A Murti is a Representational Image of the Divine—a statue, painting, photographic likeness, etc. The most highly valued Murti of the Divine Person, especially among practitioners of esoteric paths of Spiritual, Transcendental, and Divine Awakening, is the bodily (human) Form of the Divinely Self-Realized Adept.

2. T. S. Anantha Murthy, *The Life and Teachings of Sri Ramana Maharshi* (Clearlake, California: The Dawn Horse Press, 1990), pp. 133-34.

3. "Tcha" is a sacred sound that Heart-Master Da characteristically makes as a form of Blessing and Acknowledgement of a devotee's response to Him.

4. Gunaji, Nagesh Vasudev, *Shri Sai Satcharita,* 6th ed. (Shri Kashinath Sitaram Pathak, Bombay, 1972), p. 98.

5. Ibid., p. 99.

6. M. P. Pandit, *Kularnava Tantra* (Madras: Ganesh and Co., 1973), p. 77.

7. This process of self-Enquiry is one of the several possible technical means that Sri Da Avabhasa has Given to devotees to serve the "conscious process", or the disciplined surrender of attention. Early in their practice, devotees experiment with various of these technical aids to determine which (if any) best serve the process of feeling-Contemplation for them.

See Part Four of this book for a further description of the various forms of the "conscious process" in the Way of the Heart.

8. See *The Dawn Horse Testament* for a detailed description of the practices of "conductivity" in the Way of the Heart.

III

Sat-Guru-Bhakti
The Gift of Devotion

by James Steinberg

T*he Third Gift Of The Way Of The Heart Is Sat-Guru-Bhakti, The By Me Given Gift Of Devotion (and The Gifted Calling, and The By Me Given Responsibility, For Responsive Practice Of Fully Felt, and Inherently self-Transcending, Heart-Devotion To Me, and For Fully Activated, and Effectively self-Forgetting and self-Transcending, Devotional Surrender Of Separate and Separative self To Me), For I Am The True Heart-Master, The Adept Teacher Of The Heart, The Hridaya-Samartha Sat-Guru, Who Is The Heart Itself.*

Da Avabhasa
The Dawn Horse Testament

The love-relationship that I enjoy with Sri Da Avabhasa is the basis of my entire life. I approached Sri Da Avabhasa as His devotee and surrendered to Him. I did not really expect to have an intimate or even a personal relationship with Him. I felt grateful that I was simply allowed to be His devotee. And then Sri Da Avabhasa Moved to Me and Embraced Me.

How can I describe to you the endless touches and gestures of Love by which He captured my heart? There were times when He physically hugged me, yes, and kissed my face, and held me close. There were incidents when He verbally told Me that He Loved me, and asked me if I understood this. Over and over again, in formal occasions of receiving His Darshan and in ordinary moments, He looked at me and Radiated His Heart-Bliss. He Guided me more perfectly and lovingly than father, mother, mentor, or dearest friend. He looked me in the eyes and clasped me in His Love, took me to places deeper than the mind and the body, and showed me how transparent all such arising is. And in every place, He has shown me that nothing matches the Succor of His Divine and Perfect Love.

But all of these experiences and Graces, all my good fortune, are Gifts secondary to the relationship with which He has Blessed me, and all His devotees. Fundamentally, every day, He showers His Divine Love upon Me as His Blessing Grace. He is constantly Giving this Grace and Regard. Every day there are moments when I can only stop and feel this Graceful Transmission of His Love, so tangibly bestowed upon Me. It comes over me mysteriously, with an unfathomable sweetness, and instantly restores me to That Which is Happiness Itself.

One weekend afternoon in 1975, I was Graced to be present with Sri Da Avabhasa and some twenty other devotees in the large plunge (swimming pool) in Ordeal Bath Lodge at the Mountain Of Attention Sanctuary. It was midday, and sunny and bright outside, but the "Bathhouse" had its own environment of dim light and rising clouds of hot steam.

My condition at this moment was confused and dark—I was in what one would call a "crisis of practice". Nothing in particular was wrong. Rather, everything was wrong! I was a bundle of knots, and not feeling able to communicate with anyone. Being in the Bathhouse in Sri Gurudev's Company, with my fellow devotees surrounding me and feeling so happy, only accentuated my crunch. I had seated myself on the edge of the plunge, dangling my legs in the water. There were people around me, but I was feeling alone. Sri Da Avabhasa Stood Talking with some devotees in the far corner of the plunge. I kept my attention on Him, but I could not really hear His Conversation.

All of a sudden Sri Da Avabhasa turned His Body about and began swimming straight in my direction. I imagined that He was coming to talk to one of those around me who were happily talking with one another. I was certain that on noticing my condition He would steer clear of me. Therefore, I hardly believed my ears when halfway across the pool, while still swimming, the Divine Sat-Guru looked at me directly and called out in a Love-filled voice, "How's business?"

Sri Da Avabhasa was referring to the Dawn Horse Bookstore in San Francisco, which I managed at the time. I never answered the question. I was too bound up in my emotions to respond. And Sri Gurudev never pressed the issue. It was not the point in any case. Instead, coming close to me, He enveloped me in His Emotion of Love. He moved close to me, and put His vast arms on either side of my body on the edge of the pool. He held Himself up in this way, while remaining in the water. He bowed His head onto my lap and gathered me in.

The room became silent. And Sri Da Avabhasa remained in this Embrace as the minutes passed. His Blessing Presence suffused the room, palpable, thick, and moving, but at the same time very deep and still.

I was stunned by His Compassion beyond any thought. I simply turned to Him. And as the minutes passed, my self-contraction disappeared. I forgot it. I did nothing but turn to Da Love-Ananda. He absorbed all my pain and replaced it with His Love-Bliss. Minutes passed, and Sri Gurudev stayed with His arms Enveloping me, His head bent to me. I felt His Love, and His Love pushed out my suffering. There was no room for my suffering anymore. I felt rested, full, alive, and healed. I felt aligned to the Divine, cleansed and washed of my ordinary concerns and aggravated pursuits.

Finally Sri Gurudev raised His head. He looked me in the eyes briefly while softly uttering His characteristic Blessing syllable, "Tcha". Then, with Blessing force still surrounding Him, He slowly turned, swam to the shallow end of the pool, and walked up the stairs out of the pool and into the dressing room.

I remained in the plunge. I burst into tears, not moving, even as others now began to leave the room. I realized that Sri Da Avabhasa had taken away my pain and replaced it with His Love. I loved Him so fully. I was restored to His Grace and Blessing. In this state, I was amazed that I had allowed myself to become so troubled by what had been arising as to forget Sri Gurudev's Love, which cuts through everything. How could I have been so upset and self-enclosed, and so weak in my resort to Sri Da Avabhasa? I vowed to live on the basis of my devotion to Him always, to allow this to always inform my life. I vowed to never let myself forget again how I felt in that moment—so full, so Graced, and knowing that Love which makes everything else feel petty and unimportant, simply so much stuff to be handled and taken care of. I wanted to somehow press it so deeply into my brain and body that I would never forget it.

James Steinberg, author of Love of the God-Man, Divine Distraction, *and a forthcoming book on the "Crazy Wisdom" tradition, served as Sri Da Avabhasa's librarian for many years, and is a scholar of the world's religious and Spiritual traditions.*

James is well-known among his friends for his unique and ecstatic dance-form, "The Gator", which once led Sri Da Avabhasa to dub him "Buddy Jim Gatorberg". James lives at the Mountain Of Attention, where he serves in the Editorial and Education Departments of the Free Daist Communion.

Remembering this incident, now almost seventeen years past, I remain totally grateful for the Compassion and Love that Sri Gurudev Da Avabhasa exhibited on that occasion. But I know now that it is not sufficient to mechanically remember some experience of the past. Sri Gurudev's Love is always Given, and even now. To long for, or to cling to, the love that one once felt in relationship to Sri Da Avabhasa is natural enough. But such remembrance will become an aggravation if we do not allow it to become present Communion with Sri Da Avabhasa, and present experience of His Love and Grace.

This extraordinary incident in Ordeal Bath Lodge for me now is a reminder of the constant Gift and Responsibility that is Sat-Guru-Bhakti. Gift, because Sri Da Avabhasa never abandons His relationship of Love to His devotee, and His Love is available to every devotee, and now. And Responsibility, for although Sri Da Avabhasa's Love is so Given and will always remain as the core of the devotee's experience, circumstances will constantly test our ability to always stably receive and respond to it.

Just as Sri Da Avabhasa showed me in Ordeal Bath Lodge, the Guru Loves the devotee first. As He has described in the Epilogue to *The Dawn Horse Testament*, "Mine Is The First Submission. Mine Is The First Sacrifice." (p. 689) And on the basis of that Love and Submission to His devotee, that always Given relationship, Sri Da Avabhasa Calls His devotee to surrender to Him.

Only such one-pointed giving over of one's energy and attention allows the devotee to be transformed. The devotee surrenders the self-contraction in self-forgetting feeling-Contemplation of Sri Da Avabhasa. Through this release performed by the devotee, Sri Gurudev is given the space to replace the devotee's obsessions with His Divine Love. For the devotee, no technique is as significant as the real gesture of surrender, devotion, and love itself. It is only on the basis of such devotion that all other practices of the Way of the Heart become fruitful.

The primacy of devotion to Sri Da Avabhasa in the Way of the Heart cannot be questioned. Sri Da Avabhasa Writes in *The Hymn Of The True Heart-Master* that "the devotional relationship to the True Heart-Master is the Unique Method of Awakening, provided by the Grace of God to living beings" (v. 87). Neither great efforts of the will, nor exertions of the mind, nor any other self-applied techniques can replace simple heart-felt surrender and devotion to the Divine Sat-Guru. Sri Da Avabhasa has Proclaimed that every practice of the Way of the Heart is secondary to the Yoga of Satsang, or the devotional relationship to Him. In fact, such devotion is so primary to the life of those who practice in Sri Da Avabhasa's Company that each practitioner is called a "devotee", one "devoted to the Sat-Guru".

Devotion to Sri Gurudev Da Avabhasa is no different than love of Him, or "heart-response" to Him. ("Bhakti", a Sanskrit word, translates as "love" as well as "devotion".) Sat-Guru-Bhakti, devotion to the True Guru, is Given through Grace. When you truly open yourself to Sri Da Avabhasa and receive His Darshan, it is natural to love Him, to be devoted to Him. And when His Teaching Argument penetrates you, so that you can release the baggage of your suffering and self-contraction, it is natural to feel your devotion increasing. One should not feel that such true devotion can only be felt by great Spiritual practitioners. Its seed is present in every person, and it can be cultivated by anyone who takes up the Way of the Heart.

Devotion is made possible by the Love of Sri Da Avabhasa for His devotees. Sri Da Avabhasa, Who is the Divine Incarnate, wins the hearts of His devotees through His Love of them. The Divine has no Argument.

Sri Da Avabhasa embracing James Steinberg, Sri Love-Anandashram, 1985

The Divine Is Unchanging Happiness. And the devotee is Attracted by that Happiness. Likewise, the devotee comes to understand that there is no recourse but to embrace this Happiness, and its Law of mutual submission. Who can refuse the Gift of Love that is Given by the Guru? Yes, in any moment or period of time, the devotee may become distracted by the trappings of conditional experience and refuse to embrace devotion. But time and again, the Sat-Guru's Love for the devotee returns the devotee to that naturally ecstatic relationship.

Divine Distraction

What makes it possible to be devoted to Sri Da Avabhasa, and to grant Him one's feeling-attention, is His Supreme Attractiveness. One's attention naturally moves to what is attractive. One does not need to command attention to move to what distracts one—to what is lustrous, brilliant, and full. To one who can truly acknowledge and feel Sri Da Avabhasa, there is no question that He is the most enchanting of all possible objects. The Divine Radiance that Shines through Him is "Brighter" than any ordinary light.

Thus, over time, the devotee falls in love with Sri Da Avabhasa, and becomes naturally distracted by Him. The devotee no longer must fight his or her tendencies and difficulties, cutting them away with acts of willful asceticism. Rather, the devotee of Sri Da Avabhasa naturally finds himself or herself attracted beyond the egoic self by the power of the Divine Vision of Sri Da Avabhasa Himself.

Sri Da Avabhasa has often used the story of Krishna and the gopis to describe the Graceful process of attraction and distraction that accompanies the appearance of the

God-Man. Krishna, the great Divine Realizer of ancient India, is described as radiant blue, with an attractiveness that captivated his devotees. Although both men and women loved him equally, it is his play with the gopis, or milkmaids, that has become legendary. Krishna would charm them, first through the sound of his flute, but ultimately through His Divine Lustre, enticing them to the moonlit fields of Vrindavan. This Ecstatic Gift of Divine Distraction is available to us today with unrivaled Potency, via Sri Da Avabhasa's own Grace-Bestowing Incarnation, Supremely Radiant and Full of Love:

SRI DA AVABHASA: The ancient legends of Krishna and his gopis are an allegory of Divine Distraction. As Krishna wandered about in the fields, the women who tended the cattle would see him from day to day, and in spite of themselves they would wander away and leave their posts. They completely forgot about the cattle. They forgot to go home and cook for their husbands. They wandered about where they thought they might find Krishna, and when they found him, they gazed at him as he sat in the distance somewhere. This legend is a play upon the romance between Krishna, or the Divine manifested in human form—the Spiritual Master—and these ordinary women, who became madly involved in an absolute attachment to Krishna, and who, as a result of this attachment, became more and more ecstatically absorbed in the God-State.

The foundation of practice of the Way of the Heart is exactly that attachment. If such attachment—not cultic attachment, but Divine attachment—does not develop to the Spiritual Master, if that attachment is not there that overwhelms the life completely, distracts you from the conventional destiny to which you are disposed through the medium of your desires, inclinations, and circumstances, then the practice of real, or Spiritual, life cannot exist.

The cattle that the women abandoned represent the force of all the tendencies of life. The husbands they left are the fundamental attachment to separated existence, to existence in form, to bodily existence, individuated existence, egoic life on its own, motivated toward survival and apparently distinct from the Divine Reality. Thus, in the allegory of the relationship between Krishna and his gopis, we see a fundamental description of the principle of sadhana in the Way of the Heart. Sadhana is not about bearing down and being motivated by problems in your life, by some sort of a philosophical detachment or some inclination to have Yogic and mystical experiences. Nor is it about doing what you have to in order to produce the change that you desire. Sadhana in the Way of the Heart is about distraction from the life of tendencies. It is a distraction from that life. It is not a motivated kind of detachment from your life of tendencies, or an effort relative to them or the taking on of conditions to stop tendencies from arising or lifetimes from occurring.

The gopis simply left the cattle. They did not say, "I'm not going to tend cattle anymore! I'm not going to submit to my desires, my tendencies, my job!" They did not make any such decisions. They simply forgot about the cattle. They were so distracted, so in love with Krishna, so ecstatic, that they just forgot to go home. It never even occurred to them to

Krishna and the gopis

go home. They never worried, "Should I go home, or should I stay here? Should I watch the cattle, or should I go look for Krishna? Should I discipline myself?" They did not create a problem out of their sadhana or out of their relationship to God.

As Guru, I am not simply present to rap out a philosophy or distribute techniques that you may apply depending on your intelligence. I am Present to enjoy a Divine relationship with all those who are willing to assume such a relationship with Me, with all those who have the capability for distraction by Me in an absolute love-relationship that is more and more distracting. But if that distraction is not present, if that love-desire distraction is not present in an individual's life, then the sadhana of the Way of the Heart is not initiated. It cannot begin. There is no point in even discussing the technical aspects of development of the Way of the Heart until the individual has begun to enjoy an ecstatic relationship with Me—not one that is in the air but one that includes the whole of life, that draws the emotion, that awakens the love, that awakens the heart. That distracting relationship with Me which is the principle of sadhana in the Way of the Heart must be established. On its basis the individual may begin to assume life-conditions, turn them into service to Me, and realize that service in more personal and complex ways over time.

The same approach is necessary for all, and it is represented in the allegory of Krishna and the gopis. Without that distraction by the Guru, there is no sadhana in any form in anybody's case. Once that distraction exists and the movement of the individual begins to be governed by the intuition and the enjoyment of the Divine, then all the disciplines, the theatre, the lessons, the responsibilities, the Teaching Revelation, and all the rest begin to appear, according to the individual's capability and state of existence. (December 16, 1975)

Ishta-Guru-Bhakti Yoga

T he devotee who lives with Sri Da Avabhasa in this relationship of ecstatic distraction and attachment receives His Gift of Sat-Guru-Bhakti. It comes to the
devotee naturally, easily, and Gracefully. And he or she continually tastes a
Happiness that cannot be found through any other experience or relationship.
When the devotee is Given such Divine Love from the God-Man, he or she naturally finds
himself or herself capable of self-transcendence and self-surrender at Sri Da Avabhasa's
Feet. Sri Da Avabhasa has termed this Graceful practice "Ishta-Guru-Bhakti Yoga".

*SRI DA AVABHASA: The relationship between the devotee and the Guru is a unique rela-
tionship and an extraordinary Yoga. It is Ishta-Guru-Bhakti Yoga, in which the Guru is
embraced as what is traditionally called the "Ishta-Guru", the Very Person, and the "chosen"
Form, of the Divine Reality, Appearing as the Guru. Ishta-Guru-Bhakti Yoga is the tradition in which My Sadhana developed. It is the Yoga of allowing the Ishta-Guru to be the
Divine Form, in meditation and in moment to moment practice. The devotee is devoted to
that bodily Form, that Being, that Person, that Transmitting Power. The Divine Person, in
other words, is acknowledged by the devotee in the Form of the Guru.*

*A unique aspect of Ishta-Guru-Bhakti Yoga is that one is invited to practice it on the
basis of one's acknowledgement of the Ishta-Guru. It is not announced to you so that
thereupon you will believe it and then practice it. Only those who acknowledge the Guru
as the Ishta, or the one "chosen" by the heart, only those who truly are the devotees of the
Ishta-Guru, can practice this unique Yoga.*

*As My true devotee, as one who acknowledges Me as your Ishta-Guru, you give your-
self to the Divine Person Appearing as My bodily (human) Form, My Spiritual (and
Always Blessing) Presence, and My Very (and Inherently Perfect) State, and, thereby, you
allow the Divine Person to acquire your own form. By devoting yourself to Me as your
Ishta-Guru, or True Heart-Master, you thereby give the body-mind and all conditional
aspects of your personality to the Divine Person, and you allow the Divine Person to take
over your body-mind, and to Stand in its place.*

*This unique Yoga is not the practice of relating to Me as an other, although, of course,
you do relate to My bodily (human) Form and you feel the Force of My Spiritual Heart-
Transmission in relationship to the body-mind. There is an objective dimension, then, to your
responsiveness to Me and to your acknowledgement of Me. But most fundamentally, through
your feeling-Contemplation of Me, you allow yourself to be taken over by the Divine Person.
You allow That One to Stand in the place where you give yourself, to the point of Realizing
Most Perfect Identity with That One, not by effort, but simply by allowing That One to Be.*

*You use My Image, then, not only in the form of My Murti in the Communion Hall
but in the form of your recollection of Me. You "put on" the Ishta-Guru, you "put on" the
True Heart-Master, at all times. You let the Ishta-Guru Acquire and Be your own body-mind.*

In this way, My Spirit-Power Works in your body-mind as if it were My body-mind. The same process that has developed in My apparent body-mind is developed in your own body-mind. You simply give way to Me to Be and Acquire all conditional forms that previously were your own independently, or "Narcissistically", and you allow My Spiritual Processes to take place in you. All the processes of sadhana in the Way of the Heart will take place spontaneously. You will respond to them, participate in them, but they will be generated spontaneously by My Spiritual Heart-Transmission.

Divine Self-Realization is simply the Realization of the Divine Self-Nature of the Divine Person, and also, then, the Divine Self-Nature of the Ishta-Guru and of yourself. You will simply Realize the Divine State of the One Who is your Ishta-Guru by giving way to That One and by allowing That One to Stand in your place. If, through your self-transcending submission to Me, the body-mind, the self-contraction, and all the forms of egoity are thrown into the Fire of My Divine Presence, you make way for My Yoga to take place. And, through your devotional acknowledgement of Me, you allow Me, as the True Heart-Master, to Attract you into the Divinely Self-Realized Condition.

*Therefore, your responsibility is devotional acknowledgement of Me, submission to Me, or making way for Me, and response to Me. Your practice is simply to respond to Me as the True Heart-Master, not to observe that you are identified with a limitation and then to work to overcome it. Yes, in the Way of the Heart, self-understanding awakens the motive of self-transcendence, but practice of the Way of the Heart is not a strategic effort to overcome something in yourself. It is simply a response to That Which Reveals Itself as My bodily (human) Form, My Spiritual (and Always Blessing) Presence, and My Very (and Inherently Perfect) State. That is the whole process of Divine Awakening in the Way of the Heart. (*The Hymn Of The True Heart-Master, *"I Am Grace Itself" section, pp. 145-46)*

For the devotee who surrenders to and Contemplates Sri Da Avabhasa as a continual practice, and abides by His Given Instructions, the relationship to Sri Da Avabhasa is more intimate than the relationship to an intimate partner, children, or any other person or thing that could exist. Sri Da Avabhasa is truly the Heart-Husband of all His devotees, and it is the relationship to Him that Awakens the capability to truly live as love in all the other relationships in one's life.

The signs of this process of Ishta-Guru-Bhakti Yoga that may appear in the devotee's body-mind are extraordinary, for Ishta-Guru-Bhakti Yoga unleashes into the devotee's life the Divine psycho-physics of Sri Da Avabhasa's own Form, Presence, and State. Here Kanya Samatva Suprithi, a member of the Da Avabhasa Gurukula Kanyadana Kumari Order, relates some of her experiences of reception of Da Love-Ananda's Blessing Transmission through her practice of Ishta-Guru-Bhakti Yoga:

At times I felt His Presence enter my own body so fully that I felt my body become His own bodily (human) Form. My hands became His Hands, My face became His Face with all His Features. My stomach and chest became His. This was extremely Blissful and also sometimes amusing. Sometimes when I was in this state I wondered what I must look like to others, because I felt so much that I was Sri Da Avabhasa I thought I must actually look like Him! But even these thoughts were very secondary, fleeting, and superficial, as I was in a most profound state of rapture when His Body took over mine in this way.

This is another of the classic traditional signs of being absorbed in the Sat-Guru that now began to spontaneously occur in me. It is one of the Sat-Guru's most profound ways of transforming a devotee. When the very mechanism of the Guru's own Body acquires the devotee, the devotee thus Graced is awakened and profoundly enlivened by the Guru's Divine Presence. (The Hymn Of The True Heart-Master, *"Anything Offered at His Feet Is Returned in the Form of Radiant Blessings" section, p. 405)*

In the Way of the Heart, the practice of Ishta-Guru-Bhakti Yoga is to occur moment to moment, although it is generally not felt in such dramatic forms. More typically, the devotee simply feels Sri Da Avabhasa's Influence as a Graceful Blessing Transmission and Help. Over time, Ishta-Guru-Bhakti Yoga becomes the very substance of the devotee's life. The true devotee lives every moment in relationship to Sri Da Avabhasa and thus is constantly feeling His Influence. Some of this is very ordinary—such as naturally thinking about His Wisdom-Teaching, listening to the most recent stories from Sri Love-Anandashram, or serving in loving Contemplation of Sri Da Avabhasa. But the life of devotion is most potently expressed in the devotional occasions that comprise the daily life of each practitioner in the Way of the Heart.

"Love Me with Open Eyes"
Devotional Activities in the Way of the Heart

The devotional relationship to Sri Da Avabhasa is most beautifully demonstrated through tangible and concrete expressions of the devotee's love and worship of Him. Through such heart-felt devotion, the fullness of Sri Da Avabhasa's Blessing enters into the devotee's daily life. The full sacramental life of the Way of the Heart gives the devotee many opportunities to express and enact such heart-felt devotion. Our love for Sri Da Avabhasa makes our worship of Him ecstatic—and as Sri Da Avabhasa has said on many occasions, there is no true worship unless He is there, Invoked and felt through the devotee's devotion.

In the Way of the Heart, all devotional occasions occur in the context of what Sri Da Avabhasa calls the "Sacrament of Universal Sacrifice". The devotee surrenders and offers himself or herself to the Sat-Guru. This self-giving is symbolically represented by the devotee's placing a simple gift, such as a leaf, a flower, a fruit, or a small sum of money, before Sri Da Avabhasa or His Murti, and, with heart-devotion, prostrating himself or herself on the floor. The devotee does not bow to another ego. Rather, he or she bows in humble submission to the Divine that he or she has acknowledged <u>as</u> Sri Da Avabhasa, in His Divine Self-Realization.

Each occasion of the Sacrament of Universal Sacrifice also involves the devotee's reception of a Divine and Blessed Gift (Prasad) from Sri Da Avabhasa. In some devotional occasions this Prasad is water, Blessed by contact with Sri Gurudev Da Avabhasa Personally, or by contact with His Murti. But Prasad might come in the form of sacred ash from special fire ceremonies, or light from a candle or lamp that has been waved about Sri Da Avabhasa's bodily (human) Form or His Murti. This giving and receiving of Gifts becomes for the devotee a heart-felt enactment of the mutual sacrifice that is inherent in the Guru-devotee relationship and in the true practice of Sat-Guru-Bhakti.

For the devotee in the Way of the Heart, the highlight of devotional activity each day is the Sat-Guru Puja that generally occurs immediately following early morning meditation. Through this ceremony ("puja" means an occasion of sacramental worship) the devotee Invokes and Contemplates the living Blessing Transmission of Sri Da Avabhasa, and Installs Him in front of his or her heart. In the morning Sat-Guru Puja, Sri Gurudev Da Avabhasa is celebrated by means of ceremonially serving His Murti and His Padukas (sandals Blessed by the Sat-Guru). This Sat-Guru Puja is a great swirl of devotional regard for Sri Da Avabhasa, replete with recitations of His Wisdom-Teaching, the singing of devotional chants, and group recitations of prayers. In the heart of the puja, a priest washes, anoints, and adorns with flowers Sri Da Avabhasa's Murti and Padukas. The devotee leaves the Sat-Guru Puja feeling Embraced by Sri Da Avabhasa's Grace, and rightly established in devotion to Him.

Each evening, the Free Daist practitioner is called to energetically worship Sri Da Avabhasa through the Sat-Guru Arati Puja. This Puja is begun by a designated priest who rings a bell and carries incense in a circumambulation around the places where devotees reside or work. When the priest arrives at the Murti, the assembled devotees make a rousing noise—ringing bells, blowing conches, and beating drums—in praise of Sri Da Avabhasa. Altogether, it is a time for devotees to joyously allow themselves to let go and to worship their Heart-Husband. Then, as traditional songs of praise for the Guru are sung, lights are waved around the Murti of Sri Da Avabhasa, followed by a group recitation extolling His "Brightness" and Grace ("The Hymn Of Conformation To The 'Brightness' Of Da Avabhasa"). At times, the Sat-Guru Arati, or any other devotional occasion, may become a kirtan, an occasion of particularly joyous worship of Sri Da Avabhasa, in which devotees become whole bodily ecstatic—dancing about, moving spontaneously and especially energetically, and shouting ecstatic praises of the Sat-Guru, Sri Da Avabhasa.

Truly, the devotee in the Way of the Heart is Called to ecstatic and self-transcending devotion at all times. Even the more ordinary occasions when devotees come together begin and end with formal Invocation of Sri Da Avabhasa. And the true devotee

Top: Sat-Guru Arati Puja, Sri
Love-Anandashram

Middle left: Flower offering
during a Sat-Guru-Murti Puja

Middle right: A flower offering

Bottom left: Devotee bowing
in Full Feeling-Prostration

constantly looks for ways to intensify his or her devotion. Writes Sri Da Avabhasa in *The Hymn Of The True Heart-Master:*

> *The devotee of the True Heart-Master should always surrender to Him openly, without hesitation, and most obviously, for true self-surrender is always an act of expressive worship. Therefore, surrender separate self (always and obviously) to the True Heart-Master, and be (thus and thereby) given to the Divine Person and Self-Condition in every moment. (verse 56)*

The rich life of devotion in the Way of the Heart gives the devotee every opportunity to truly enact and magnify his or her love and regard for Sri Da Avabhasa, expressively and full-bodily. Sri Da Avabhasa has called Free Daism a "culture of celebration", for the Divine Sat-Guru has Appeared in our midst, and we are in each moment Given the opportunity to receive His Blessings tangibly and to express our gratitude.

The Hard School and the Happy Way of Life

Sri Da Avabhasa has said that sometimes one of His devotees will come to the Guru's Chair and place a flower down before it, and although outwardly it may look like the simplest of gestures, the gift of this flower represents a tremendous sacrifice and surrender of attachment and difficulty. Sat-Guru-Bhakti requires not only heart-devotion to Sri Da Avabhasa, but also the devotional surrender of separate and separative self to Him. To be devoted to Sri Da Avabhasa is to remain turned to Him, not only in the midst of the reception of His Love-Blissful Blessings but also in the midst of trials and difficult moments.

One must not get the mistaken impression that Spiritual life is easy. Sri Da Avabhasa has termed the Way of the Heart "a hard school and a Happy Way of life". The ordeal of self-transcendence requires the encounter with every limit and obstruction to devotion that exists in the devotee's body-mind. Thus, true practice of the Way of the Heart is a sacred ordeal and a constant test of the devotee's growing capability to continually surrender to Sri Da Avabhasa and to go beyond all the tendencies towards self-involvement that will arise. In the midst of this purification of "Narcissistic" patterns and habits, the Grace and Help of Sri Da Avabhasa remain. And the mature devotee comes to appreciate that such purification has a deep purpose: to strengthen his or her real self-understanding and resort to Sri Da Avabhasa. The devotee of Sri Da Avabhasa understands, then, that each moment in the Way of the Heart is a test of one's devotion, of whether one will remain fully related to Sri Da Avabhasa in practice or instead withdraw from Him through self-concerned involvement in what is arising. The true devotee remains devoted to Sri Da Avabhasa in the midst of every arising condition.

Understanding the Limits on Devotion:
Childish and Adolescent Strategies

S ri Da Avabhasa describes two broad types of limitation that impinge upon His devotee's practice of true surrender: the childish strategy and the adolescent strategy. The childish individual dramatizes dependency, relating to the Guru as to a parent, and the adolescent individual dramatizes independence, in reaction against and dissociation from the Sat-Guru. Dramatizing either of these tendencies is a sign of human immaturity that makes genuine devotion and real Spiritual growth impossible. If the childish and adolescent tendencies (or any other "Narcissistic" orientation) in the practitioner remain effective, then no matter how determinedly the practitioner goes through the motions of devotion, the devotion will not be real. At heart, he or she will remain related to Sri Da Avabhasa in an uninspected or unsubmitted disposition. Writes Sri Da Avabhasa in *The Hymn Of The True Heart-Master:*

> *Do not practice the "childish cult" of superficial and ego-serving emotionalism (full of want and dependency, and empty of faith), and do not practice the "adolescent cult" of non-feeling (willful, self-absorbed, abstract, and independent), but always practice (and cultivate) the true (and truly feeling, and truly self-surrendering, and truly self-forgetting, and truly self-transcending) devotional Way of the Heart Itself. (v. 28)*

Sri Da Avabhasa continues His description of childish and adolescent strategies in *The Basket of Tolerance* (forthcoming):

> *Childish religiosity, characterized by dependent emotionalism, or mere enthusiastic attachment, bereft of discrimination and real self-discipline, is what may rightly, without bad intentions, be described and criticized as "cultism". . . . And any one whose developmental disposition is yet relatively adolescent (or tending, in general, to seek egoic security via the dramatization of the role of reactive independence) will tend to . . . want to be his or her own "guru" in all matters. And, characteristically, the rather adolescent seeker will resist, and would even prefer to avoid, a truly intelligent, rightly self-disciplined, and, altogether, devotionally self-surrendered relationship to a true Guru, or Sat-Guru. . . .*

The real requirements for Spiritual life and the relationship to the Guru, then, naturally involve self-understanding and self-transcendence relative to childishness and adolescence (as well as all the other "Narcissistic" tendencies in the devotee). Thus, Sri Da Avabhasa has gone to great pains to Criticize and Instruct His devotees relative to these strategies, clearing the ground for a right and true relationship to Him.

Each of us must see that we are dramatizing such childish and adolescent motivations: Am I merely looking to be consoled, satisfied, or "saved" by Sri Da Avabhasa, and for things to be "all right" by virtue of my mere association with Him? Am I refusing real responsibility for my own life, depending on Sri Da Avabhasa as if He were my parent? Or am I abstracting myself from Sri Gurudev Da Avabhasa, using bits and pieces of His Arguments, and surrendering here and there perhaps, but remaining independent, willful, heady, and abstracted? Am I therefore reacting to and protecting myself from Sri Da Avabhasa as if rebelling against a parent in adolescent fashion?

Clear self-observation and most fundamental self-understanding of these tendencies are prerequisites for growth in Free Daist practice. For if the devotee does not relate to Sri Da Avabhasa on the basis of genuine self-understanding, he or she will lose the true motivation for heart-devotion, becoming locked into the uninspected tendencies of the body-mind that are grabbing his or her attention. Thus, self-understanding supports Sat-Guru-Bhakti. The secret known by the devotee is that even self-understanding is Given by Grace through the relationship with Sri Da Avabhasa. Through practicing devotion to Sri Da Avabhasa in every circumstance, in every relationship, and in the midst of all arising conditions, the devotee grows in his or her capability to receive, without obstruction, the outpouring of Gifts Given by Sri Da Avabhasa. Thus, the devotee who has transcended his or her childish and adolescent strategies is, as He says, "Characterized By Basic human Equanimity, Discriminative Intelligence, Responsive Heart-Feeling, and The Active Impulse (or Counter-egoic Will) To Always Continue To Grow" (*The Dawn Horse Testament*, p. 171).

Cultism and Spiritual Authority

The requirement that devotees understand and grow beyond their childish and adolescent tendencies in relationship to the Spiritual Master is not new. In the ancient Spiritual traditions of God-Realization, real (and often very stringent) tests of human maturity had to be passed by the aspirant before he or she would even be accepted by a Teacher. Likewise, there were genuine, generally understood criteria by which one would evaluate a religious or Spiritual authority. Without such qualifications being met—on both sides—confusion or lack of success was inevitable. Indeed, it is because of the failure to understand and meet the real qualifications for Spiritual life that the immature behavior branded as "cultism" today arises:

SRI DA AVABHASA: In our time it has become routine for both true Spiritual Masters and ordinary teachers to be instantly "cultified", exclusively Deified, and made the fascinating Object of a self-contained popular movement that worships the Spiritual Master ritually and adores the Spiritual Master as a Parent-like Savior, while embracing very little of the significant Wisdom-Teaching of the Spiritual Master.

The error of conventional cultism is precisely this childish, or ego-based, orientation to fascination with Teachers, God-Ideas, sacred lore, cosmic pictures, and self-based mysticism. The cultic tendency in religion is the essence of what is wrong with religion. The problem is not that there is no God, or that there is no Sublime Teaching, or that there are no true Spiritual Masters. The problem with religion is the childish egoism that is the basis of all forms of ordinary existence. (The Hymn Of The True Heart-Master, *"Beyond the Cultic Tendency in Religion" section, pp. 185-86)*

Unfortunately in the Western world today, bereft as it is of any such understanding about the true causes of cultism, the validity and necessity of the Guru-devotee relationship itself has become obscured in a mass of confusion and emotional charge. This is most evident in the popular communications media which play such a major role in defining (and inflaming) public opinion. Because the modern news and information media are themselves so uninformed, and misinformed, about the real nature and requirements of the Guru-devotee relationship, suspicion and even condemnation are often directed at any alternative religious Teacher or practitioner. This suspicion and condemnation are simply a currently acceptable form of prejudice that, like racism and sexism, should no longer be tolerated. As it is now clearly not acceptable for a commentator to imply that all women are "stupid", blacks "lazy", Jews "avaricious", or homosexuals "weak", just so, it is equally hurtful for a commentator to call all followers of Gurus "slave-like" or "brainwashed", and to disparage all alternative religious ways as "cults", or characterize all Gurus as negative figures.

Behind this form of prejudice lies the assumption that a person involved with a Spiritual Teacher has automatically surrendered his or her freedom of choice and independence. But no true Guru asks devotees to do this. The Spiritual process requires the growth of the discriminative capability and the right use of the will, rather than the relinquishment of these. Likewise, Spiritual surrender in the Company of a Sat-Guru requires the foundation of self-understanding and the transcendence of the childish motives of enthusiastic belief and the need to be protected and parented:

SRI DA AVABHASA: Over the years you have all heard Me Speak about cultism in negative terms. I have criticized the cult of the Spiritual Master, as well as the cultic attachments that people create with one another. To the degree that you tend to approach Me in this manner, you make Me a cultic figure and you yourselves become a bunch of balmy enthusiasts. In that condition I cannot deal with you, I cannot Instruct you, you cannot live this practice, you cannot hear what I am Saying.

Everything about cultism that is negative is specifically criticized in My Wisdom-Teaching. I do not want your enthusiasm to be superficially generated by the books that I Write. I want you to "consider" the matters this literature contains. I want you to "consider" yourself very critically, very directly and rigorously, and come to the point of insight as it is expressed in these books. When you come to that point of insight into your own game, into your childishness and adolescence, you will be able to take up the practice I have Given to you, the forms of adaptation that serve your continued growth beyond your present stage of life. (December 17, 1978)

Sri Da Avabhasa has had to re-educate modern men and women relative to the Guru-devotee relationship in the face of false notions, limited understanding, and adolescent and childish views, and in a world where even the idea of genuine Spiritual authority has become taboo. Indeed, in the West an unwillingness to submit to any authority (other than our own egos) has even come to seem commendable. For authentic Spiritual growth to occur, we must instead become able to acknowledge One Who is Superior in Love, in self-Sacrifice, in Wisdom, in Spiritual Realization, and accept that our growth in Wisdom and Realization could come from our devotion to such a One.

Our resistance to Spiritual authority comes from a confused version of egalitarianism. At the level of politics and human rights, all are equal, equally entitled to those rights, and equally entitled to their point of view. However, at the Spiritual level, the Saints, the Sages, and, above all, the Divinely Realized Beings—the God-Men and God-Women—have always been revered as the greatest Authorities, the Sources of True Happiness and Guidance. To cast aspersions upon the ancient and Supremely Honorable Function of the Spiritual Adept is itself evidence of ignorance and irresponsibility. However, in the West and the "Westernized" world, now so secularized, we have relegated these rare beings, who are our greatest Help, to an ancient time and place, and in so doing we do great disservice to ourselves and to all others.

Just as those interested in the disciplines of science or literature or the arts consult and become steeped in the work and advancements of those who have come before, those who wish to devote themselves to the pursuit of greater truths and the Spiritual Reality must likewise consult true Sources of Wisdom. The long tradition of genuine Spiritual practice in the Company of Realized Masters, or Adepts, through whose Grace and Instruction true Happiness may be found, is our greatest inheritance. Sri Da Avabhasa has regenerated this great tradition of Guru-devotion and established it in the West, supremely effective for all willing to outgrow childish tendencies toward "cultism" and the popular adolescent preference for self-"guruing", and to embrace and grow in the ordeal of practice that is the Divine Way Itself.

Enchantment

At last, Sri Da Avabhasa Attracts His devotee even beyond the mind and all categories of description into constant feeling-Contemplation of Him and His Love-Bliss. In a Talk Given in 1983, Sri Da Avabhasa ecstatically describes the great delight of such Enchantment:

SRI DA AVABHASA: What is the Spiritual Master, anyway? When you cannot really identify what attracts you in any concrete terms that relate to the sense and the categories of mind, then you are Enchanted. You have moved into the realm of attractedness, and that attract-

edness begins to transform your existence in the direction of Divine Self-Realization, although it might also very well begin to destroy some of the conventional balances of your ordinary living. Therefore, you release these conventions. You become more ordinary, and you continue to be attracted until attractedness becomes an absolute, spontaneous, uncaused, even unchosen disposition. You have no choice but to be so attracted. The more you are attracted to That Which Is Attractive and the more you Commune with Its Qualities, the more you identify with them. And you have nothing to say about It except That is Bliss, That is Love, That is Beauty, That is Consciousness, That is Truth. Then at some point you find yourself confessing the Realization of the seventh stage of life. (April 26, 1983)

We close this chapter with a letter to Sri Da Avabhasa from a heart-wounded devotee, expressing such devotion and Enchantment. It was written while this devotee was on retreat at Sri Love-Anandashram in the spring of 1990, shortly after she had been Graced to be present with Sri Da Avabhasa in a formal Darshan occasion.

The world will be stunned to witness Your outpouring of Love. You are a Miracle that is beyond comprehension. My body is so infused with Your Gift of Compassionate Love I can scarcely lift my hand to thank You.

I feel the space between my body and the air softened, diffused. I feel a lack of identity separate from this Love-Bliss, which You Poured out on all of us. I would like to sit here forever, dissolved in You, pleasurably still and quiet, without thought or problem, only You in me and through me and with me.

I am lost in Your Love, and it is the most Blissful Place imaginable. I am drunk with You and never want to return. I never imagined that to surrender myself would be such Happiness.

Susan Raczka

RECOMMENDED READING

The Hymn Of The True Heart-Master

Divine Distraction, by James Steinberg

IV

Sat-Guru-Seva
The Gift of Service

by Donald Webley

T   *he Fourth Gift Of The Way Of The Heart Is Sat-Guru-Seva, The By Me Given Gift Of Service (and The Gifted Calling, and The By Me Given Responsibility, For Responsive Life-Practice, Whereby all action, and each and every action, Is Engaged Entirely and Only As Direct Service To Me, and As A Direct Response To Each and All Of My Admonitions), For I Am The True Heart-Master, The Adept Teacher Of The Heart, The Hridaya-Samartha Sat-Guru, Who Is The Heart Itself.*

Da Avabhasa
The Dawn Horse Testament

The essence of the Guru-devotee relationship is mutual submission. The Latin root from which "submission" derives means "to let down, to lower, to bow to". By consenting to Assume a mortal body in the human world, Heart-Master Da has "bowed to" the Cosmic Mandala[1] and has "let down" into human time His Divine Grace, the Matrix and Substance of the relationship He Offers to His devotees. This Great Sacrifice requires a corresponding gesture from His devotees. Thus they assume a life of service in relationship to Sri Da Avabhasa. It is this response of loving service that "completes the circuit", and allows Sri Da Avabhasa's Divine Grace to become effective in their lives. Therefore, He Tells us,

SRI DA AVABHASA: If you enter into devotional relationship with an Adept, you must also enter into the Adept's service. And when you are receiving the great Gift of Spiritual Transmission from your Guru, your obligation to serve the Guru is effective twenty-four hours a day. You are under a lifelong obligation, even as the Guru lives always in obligation to you as his or her devotee.

As a practitioner of the Way of the Heart, you are obliged, by your devotional relationship to Me, to express your commitment to self-transcendence in all your relations and

under all conditions. And you are obliged to do so constantly. Such service to Me is practice of the Way of the Heart. Such service to Me is participation in the reception of My Grace. Such service to Me is the God-Realizing Way of life.

You must respond to Me, to My existence here, through service. (November 2, 1981)

Service is the cornerstone of Spiritual life. The beginning practitioner is not generally capable of profound meditative practice, but all are called and all are capable of adapting to the orientation and practice of Sat-Guru-Seva, which disposition serves as the foundation of all further practice of the Way of the Heart.

Traditionally, service (based on devotion) is regarded as the necessary (and first) beginner's orientation to religious (and progressively Spiritual) practice. Service is the traditional discipline of the "outward-directed" personality. Likewise, in the Way of the Heart, practitioners in the early phases of student-beginner practice[2] are (with even all practitioners of the Way of the Heart) Called by Me to establish (and to progressively increase) their participation in the discipline of service.

In the beginning phases of their practice of the Way of the Heart, student-beginners are (typically) very much outward-directed in their attention, very much involved in outward-directed activities, and not yet very much prepared to practice the transcendence of outward-directed attention through the very profound exercise of meditation and the other Contemplative disciplines of the Way of the Heart. Even so, even very early student-beginners in the Way of the Heart can honor My Work and participate fully in the practice of the Way of the Heart by engaging in their outward-directed activities as <u>servants</u> of <u>My</u> Work.

Therefore, I Call all student-beginners of the Way of the Heart to maximize their practice of the discipline of service, and I Call all student-beginners (and, indeed, all practitioners at any and every developmental stage) of the Way of the Heart to turn their practice of service into a form of Yoga that is the epitome of what is traditionally called "Karma Yoga".³ That epitome (or fullest development) of Karma Yoga is Ishta-Guru-Seva, or Sat-Guru-Seva.

Ishta-Guru-Seva, or Sat-Guru-Seva, is not service based merely on a socially conscious point of view, or the view that it is one's social duty to do "charitable" work. Ishta-Guru-Seva, or Sat-Guru-Seva, is based on the point of view that one should <u>always</u> (in and by means of <u>all</u> activities) serve the Sat-Guru, and that one should devote to the Sat-Guru the fruits, or the rewards, of one's service, rather than take the fruits to oneself. Therefore, the "Karma-Yoga-Principle" of Ishta-Guru-Seva is the self-transcending, or ego-transcending, <u>re-orientation</u> of the purposes and the rewards of one's service (and of even all one's actions).

The <u>specific</u> practice of Ishta-Guru-Seva, or of traditional Karma Yoga, is not to help others (in a socially conscious sense), but to transcend <u>egoic</u> purposes and <u>egoic</u> results. Of course, helping others is implicit in all true service, but the practice of Ishta-Guru-Seva does not require that you devote your life to so-called "charitable" work (or social work). You should, of course, always do service that serves others in one way or another. Nonetheless, "charitable" work, or social work, like any form of work, can be done for all kinds of egoic purposes and rewards, including financial rewards. Therefore, "charitable" work, or social work, is not in itself ego-transcending. Such work—or any kind of work— is ego-transcending only if its fruits (or rewards) are surrendered, and only if the work itself is done in actual (or actively self-surrendering) feeling-Contemplation of the One Who Transcends (or Stands Beyond) the ego (or self-contraction).

The traditional principle, or the "Karma-Yoga-Principle", of Ishta-Guru-Seva is to devote the attention, the purpose (or intention), and the fruits of one's work to the Sat-Guru, and, over time, that "Karma-Yoga-Principle" is to be applied to <u>every</u> aspect of one's life, including every activity. Through constant service to the Sat-Guru, the lives of devotees become altogether more and more self-transcending. Therefore, My truly serving devotees do not perform actions for the sake of the results or pleasures they may enjoy as a result, but every action is (and becomes more and more directly and simply) a form of My devotee's self-surrendering, self-forgetting, and self-transcending feeling-Contemplation of Me. (The Love-Ananda Gita, *"I Am What you Require" section, pp. 513-15)*

Donald Webley was born in Kingston, Jamaica, the son of a Congregational clergyman. He came to the United States in 1969 to study physics at Yale University—a pursuit he hoped would resolve the burning questions that had driven him since childhood. When this did not prove to be the case, he abandoned academic life to practice Buddhism. He found Sri Da Avabhasa's Wisdom-Teaching in 1973 and first saw Him in 1980. At this first sighting of his Sat-Guru, his questions were answered before his eyes. Don became a formal practitioner of Free Daism in 1983. He lives with his intimate partner, six children, four cats, a dog, and two rabbits in Portland, Oregon.

True service is not different from love, as Sri Da Avabhasa Writes in *The Paradox of Instruction:*

> *The condition or demand of service is the condition or demand of love. Love and service are identical, and they are fulfillment of the Law, which is sacrifice.*
>
> *Love is relational action rather than the action of one who is egoically "self-possessed" (or self-absorbed)—but love is <u>action</u>, or real availability, not a merely subjective attitude of mind and emotion.*
>
> *Love is the essential practical discipline of the whole Way of the Heart. (p. 80)*

Here Catherine Lewis talks about the Instruction in the discipline of service she received from Sri Da Avabhasa in the early years of His Teaching Work:

Catherine Lewis

When I first came to Sri Gurudev Da Avabhasa (then Bubba Free John) in 1974, I was immature in almost every dimension of human life, but particularly in the emotional dimension, and Sri Da Avabhasa expanded and Instructed me in so many different ways. One of these ways was through service, and through requiring me to put out energy. Since I am a rather sedentary and lazy person, for me this demand was not an easy one. A moment of crisis came on a Saturday when I was serving in our food co-op. I was being a very reluctant server and very grumpy because I didn't want to be there. I wanted to be doing something for myself.

I went home for lunch and fell asleep listening to an audiotape of Sri Gurudev Giving a Talk. I dreamed that I was struggling against someone. Someone was holding me from behind, and I was desperately trying to get away. At one point it occurred to me that maybe I should find out who I was struggling to get away from. I slowly turned around and found that it was Sri Da Avabhasa Who was holding me! Instead of struggling, I relaxed back into His Body, and I experienced the most profound feeling of His Love-Bliss. When I awoke from that dream, my relationship to service had changed dramatically. From then on I experienced real pleasure in my service, because I could feel that Sat-Guru-Seva is direct service to my Guru and not just "work". My first layer of resistance to service had been undone, but the emotional dimension in me was still very much locked up.

One evening at a gathering with Sri Da Avabhasa, I was sitting alone in a corner of the room, feeling very sorry for myself. It seemed to me that everyone else was very socially adept, talking and laughing with Sri Da Avabhasa, but I felt shy and awkward and inadequate even to carry on a conversation with my Sat-Guru. I felt He could never love me. Just at the moment of thinking this, someone called me to come over to where Sri Da Avabhasa was sitting and talking with His devotees. As I approached Him, I noticed that He was also talking with one of my housemates, a young man named Fred, whom I regarded as a very eccentric person.

The first thing Sri Gurudev said was, "This man says that he is attracted to you. Do you feel any attraction for him?" My heart sank. I became very afraid, because I definitely did <u>not</u> feel attracted to this man and I did not want to get involved with him in any way! Would the Guru ask me do something I didn't want to do?

"No, Bubba, I am not attracted to this man," I said very righteously and emphatically.

"Who are you attracted to, then?" Sri Gurudev asked.

"No one but you, Bubba," I replied, with a little fear.

"Well, you'd better get attracted to somebody," He said playfully. "I can't marry everybody!" As He was talking with me, I could feel His Love for me very strongly, and I was lifted out of concern for myself.

Then Sri Da Avabhasa did a most wonderful thing. He Instructed me on how to enter into a relationship of service with Fred. He said, "Cathy, I've been looking at this young man and he has the most ugly glasses, don't you agree?" I agreed without hesitation. "I would like you to go with Fred to an optometrist and pick out a very handsome pair of glasses, something attractive that will make him look good. Will you do that?"

I again agreed emphatically; I was relieved to have such a humble and simple test from my Guru. He didn't address my total unlove and inhumanity to Fred; He didn't point out how totally shut down I was in the area of human relations; He simply asked me to enter into a relationship of service. Fred also seemed happy with the arrangement.

A few days later Fred and I went downtown together to pick out some glasses. To my amazement, we had a wonderful time. I realized later that I had forgotten all about my righteous reactions to Fred's qualities. I was simply happy to be serving the Guru and to be serving another human being instead of reacting to him. And in this simple act of service, the most ordinary human emotion of love was awakened.

Many times over the years I have remembered this moment of Instruction when My Beloved Heart-Master Da drew me out of myself and showed me that if I keep my attention on Him, the whole quality of my life is transformed. Sat-Guru-Seva is a great Gift, and I am profoundly grateful for every moment that I remember to serve Him instead of myself.

In the Guru-devotee relationship, service to the Sat-Guru is a passionate commitment. It is a cardinal rule that the devotee always makes sure that the Sat-Guru's needs are provided for. Thus, Free Daist practitioners spend a "tithe" of their time each week in direct service to Sri Da Avabhasa and the community of His devotees. Such service to Sri Da Avabhasa can take many forms. Devotees might serve Sri Da Avbhasa's Personal Circumstance, by preparing a meal for Him, or cleaning His House; or serve the availability of His Wisdom-Teaching by working on the publication of the literature of the Way of the Heart; or host an "area study group", to which interested members of the public may come to discuss Sri Da Avabhasa's Wisdom-Teaching or see a video or hear a Talk of Sri Da Avabhasa; or tend to the grounds of the Retreat Sanctuaries of the Way of the Heart.

Likewise, we support Sri Da Avabhasa's Blessing Work in the world by tithing a portion of our income each month. Tithing is the ancient Spiritual principle and practice of giving a percentage of one's earnings to "God's Work". Tithing, like other areas of service, is an expression of gratitude for the Sat-Guru's Gifts and a concrete demonstration of support for His Work. It is a gift, not a payment in return for which one expects something further.

Early in His Teaching Work, Sri Da Avabhasa spoke about tithing as a very practical and necessary aspect of the "giving of energy" that true service represents:

SRI DA AVABHASA: We are not in heaven. This is the earth. Everything here costs life, effort, and money. It costs a great deal of life, effort, and money to maintain a religious or spiritual community. The purposes may be "spiritual", but as a living community it must fulfill the same functional laws as any household and any business corporation. . . .

*There is the suspicion that if you are "spiritual" you are not supposed to need money, you are not supposed to require anything, and you are supposed to abandon the functions of life. Obviously though, money is needed in most circumstances, and work, force, love, and energy are necessary for functional survival. (*The Method of the Siddhas, *pp. 50-51)*

Anyone, not just members of the Free Daist Communion, who appreciates the significance of Sri Da Avabhasa's Appearance and feels drawn to support His Sacred Work in the world is invited to become a patron of His Work. This sort of financial support of an Adept and his or her sacred work has traditionally been regarded as an auspicious form of religious practice in its own right.

A booklet by Emmet Fox called *The Magic of Tithing* discusses the attitude of such tithing or patronage:

[Tithing] is devoted to the spreading abroad of the knowledge of Truth in some form or other, usually in support of those institutions or activities which are thus employed. Anyone who understands the Spiritual Idea, knows that the one and only thing that the world needs to deliver it from its difficulties is knowledge of Spiritual Truth; that until a man comes to this knowledge, no other thing will really benefit him; that until this knowledge becomes general, no amount of secular learning, no scientific discoveries, no schemes of social reform, no amount of political reconstruction, can do any real good; and that once this knowledge does become general, all political and social problems will adjust themselves automatically. . . .[4]

Emmet Fox also points out that there is a frequently observed positive correlation between true tithing, or selfless giving to the Divine, and prosperity:

The connection between tithing and prosperity is, after all, but a particular expression of the general law that what we are to the universe, that will the universe be to us;

that what we give out, whether it be generosity or parsimony, that we shall receive back; that like attracts like; that whatsoever a man soweth, that shall he also reap; and that no man escapes the Law.[5]

In recent months I myself have been greatly served in my understanding of tithing as a Spiritual practice. Because of the size of my family, I had, throughout the more than ten years of my formal association with the Free Daist Communion always asked for and received an exemption from the full monetary discipline. Eventually, however, I came to feel my continued request for exemption as a form of withholding in relationship to my Sat-Guru and felt moved to tithe fully. I did so, though it seemed at the time that it would be very difficult to make ends meet.

In fact, the next couple of months were rather lean, testing my resolve and understanding, but over time my money situation has dramatically changed—I now make considerably more money, even after the tithe, than I did a few short months ago. By tithing to Sri Da Avabhasa first, I aligned myself to the time-honored principle of first taking care of the needs of one's Guru, before doing anything else. By embracing the disposition of a devotee, my fear and withholding were released, and the Divine Blessing permitted to transform this area of my life. It was clear that my ability to make more money resulted from releasing the stranglehold in which my energy had been bound, especially in the domain of money. But of much more importance than any change in my financial situation, my entire relationship with my Sat-Guru changed, and I found myself open and available to Him in a way that had been impossible before.

Because Sat-Guru-Seva is a practice engaged in direct relationship to Sri Da Avabhasa, its essence is our sensitivity to and responsiveness to Him.

For all practitioners of the Way of the Heart, the practical principle of true service is responsiveness (to Me, and in present time). Therefore, when I Call My devotee to do something, My devotee should do it immediately. If you cannot (as a practical matter) immediately do everything you must do to fully respond to My Call for a particular service, you must nevertheless do something in response to that Call, and immediately, and with good effect. If you do not do this, then you invariably miss the mark of your relationship to Me, and you will not properly handle even the practical details of your responsibilities.

*In the traditional setting, when the Guru mentions that something needs to be done, it is done instantly. True devotees do whatever must be done, and they do it at the moment of becoming aware of what must be done. Such devotees function in such a way that they transcend karma and the egoic self. Their service is a form of Yoga, based on sacred principles, and not based merely on "labor" and "work-obligation". (*The Love-Ananda Gita, *"I Am What you Require" section, p. 515)*

A Leela from Meg McDonnell speaks to this point:

On the Day of the Heart in 1979, the day when Sri Da Avabhasa first Revealed His Divine Name "Da" and Told us to call upon Him by that Name, a major celebration was taking place at the Mountain Of Attention Sanctuary in northern California, where He lived at that time.

We had spent days and nights—all night long for many nights—cleaning, raking, decorating, and in every way preparing the Sanctuary. We built a special outdoor pavilion where Sri Da Avabhasa would sit with the hundreds of visitors who were invited to come to the Sanctuary that day. We painted, cooked, made flower malas (garlands) by the hundreds, raised prayer flags, and groomed the lawns. Just preparing the Sanctuary in this way was itself a celebration—one that required us to go far beyond our usual level of energy.

We had also put much attention on how we greeted the visitors as they poured onto the Sanctuary to receive Sri Da Avabhasa's Darshan that day. Excitement was electric in the air.

Finally, the moment had arrived. Sri Da Avabhasa was about to appear, to walk from His Residence and take His Seat in front of everyone on the newly built and highly decorated pavilion that we had provided for Him. Almost a thousand people sat on the huge lawn surrounding the pavilion, waiting expectantly.

Because my service kept me busy up until the last minute, when I finally came to take my seat, I was sitting at the back of the crowd. After all my days and nights of service preparing for this moment, I felt I deserved a better reward than this! Intense anger began to rise up in me. In fact, I was choked with anger and jealousy—envious of those sitting closer to Sri Da Avabhasa's still empty Seat. I hated what I was feeling. The emotion that I felt seemed so out of place in this sublime circumstance, but no amount of talking to myself rationally and no amount of struggling to release it made any difference. I was suffering, and that was all there was to it. I felt terrible that this was the mood with which I was going to greet my Sat-Guru!

Suddenly, I remembered one last detail that had not been attended to in our preparations. Whenever Sri Da Avabhasa enters a room or a sacred site, He removes His shoes. It is our custom, and a highly prized service opportunity, to provide a mat for His shoes and, after He removes His shoes, to turn them around so that when He leaves He can simply slip His feet into His shoes and keep walking. Also, to honor the place where He has walked, and to show the sign of our surrender at His Feet, we always place a flower by His shoes when we have turned them around and prepared them for His departure. In the flurry of construction and decoration to prepare this new pavilion, we had forgotten to ensure that this service would be available for Him.

I looked around. Every sign indicated that He would be coming any moment. I knew that I did not have a second to spare. I stood up and ran—no, flew—across the Sanctuary's gravel pathways barefoot because I knew I had no time to find my shoes. I was in a sweat of concentration, moving as fast as I could to find a flower and a footmat. I found what I needed and flew back to put the mat in place and to give the flower to an attendant who would serve Sri Da Avabhasa's shoes.

Sri Da Avabhasa on the Day of the Heart Celebration,
the Mountain Of Attention Sanctuary, 1979

Sweating and completely out of breath, I slid into my new seat—now even farther back in the crowd—just moments before Sri Da Avabhasa came around the corner. That moment, when He first appeared in our view on this day of the Revelation of His Divine Name, was one of the most powerful moments in the history of His Work. He looked Glorious, absolutely Divine, Radiant with His own Love and Bliss. Immediately upon seeing Him, many of the hundreds there began to weep out loud in joy and acknowledgement of the Divine Being Who had come to be with us that day!

And, just before being swept away by the sight of His bodily (human) Form, I noticed a small miracle. When I sat down, despite the fact that I was even further away from Sri Da Avabhasa than I had been before, I was completely Happy. My anger and my jealousy, as well as my guilt and struggle with my own reactive emotion, were completely dissolved. I had forgotten my problems by remembering my Heart-Master's needs rather than my own, and by doing something for Him rather than dwelling on myself. And in that mood of remembering Him, I was able to see and feel and receive Him much more fully. I understood clearly that day why it is such a great Gift to be able to serve Sri Da Avabhasa, and the great joy that flows to His devotees who embrace service to Him in that spirit.

Sri Da Avabhasa Instructs us further on the unique disposition that transforms mere work into self-transcending practice:

In the Way of the Heart, Karma Yoga bears all the responsibilities of traditional, full, and true Ishta-Guru-Seva. And Ishta-Guru-Seva is not merely an "organizational" or "businesslike" fulfillment of tasks in relationship to Me. The institution, the culture, and the community of the Way of the Heart all have the responsibility to manage and perform services in an orderly and productive fashion, but what makes these responsibilities Ishta-Guru-Seva is the spirit and the manner in which they are done, and (therefore) the Liberating effect such true service has on the lives of those who perform *the service.*

In the Way of the Heart, Ishta-Guru-Seva is self-surrendering, self-forgetting, and truly self-transcending feeling-Contemplation of Me via a right and complete re-orientation (to Me) of all the activities of daily life. Therefore, whenever you (as My devotee) engage in Ishta-Guru-Seva, you relate to Me directly. . . .

The immediacy *of* response *is the key to Ishta-Guru-Seva. . . .*

Mere work *(or "labor") is an egoic (or ego-serving) occupation.*

Mere work begins to become service *only when it is done for the sake of another.*

And, for My devotee, even service becomes Ishta-Guru-Seva *only when it is done as an immediate and energetic and self-transcending response to Me.*

Human beings do not grow to Realize the Divine Self by performing the ego's work. Growth and Divine Self-Realization require self-surrender, self-forgetting, and self-transcendence. And, in the Way of the Heart, self-surrender, self-forgetting, self-transcendence, and Divine Self-Realization are Given and grown by the Grace-Given (and Grace-Giving) Means of devotional Contemplation of Me (to the degree of Heart-Communion with Me). Therefore, in the Way of the Heart, growth (in the Great Process of Divine Self-Realization) requires that all *activities become Ishta-Guru-Seva, or immediate, direct, energetic, enthusiastic, altogether responsive, and really self-surrendering service to* Me *(and truly self-forgetting and self-transcending Communion with* Me*).* (The Love-Ananda Gita, *"I Am What you Require" section, pp. 516-17)*

The mind often finds it easier to accept that a "spiritual" practice like meditation affords access to the Blessing Grace of the Sat-Guru; service, on the other hand, can seem almost like a diversion from the "real" work of sadhana. However, service to Heart-Master Da and meditative feeling-Contemplation of Him are co-equal aspects of the Way of the Heart. Meditation embodies a specific disposition of surrender wherein outward-directed energy and attention are abandoned and the body-mind is yielded into the Divine Love-Bliss. Service, or Sat-Guru-Seva, embodies the same disposition, but animated through the vehicle of an active body-mind. Feeling-Contemplation expressed now as bodily submission through service allows Sri Da Avabhasa's Heart-Transmission to Flow in our body-minds and our lives.

SRI DA AVABHASA: All action must become service. All service must be Guru-Seva. All Guru-Seva is Guru-Contemplation. Action, or service, then, is Guru-Contemplation. In the Way of the Heart, Sat-Guru-Seva is to abide in that Contemplation of Me constantly in the midst of activity. In the Way of the Heart, service, like meditation, is a form of sadhana, and both service and meditation are about feeling-Contemplation of Me, each through a somewhat different apparent design.

The secret of service, and of meditation, is to remain always in feeling-Contemplation of Me. (July 9, 1988)

Our understanding of service in the Way of the Heart, then, differs from the conventional conception of service as mere socially positive activity. Its practice also liberates the aspirant from the traditional error of seeking God by exclusive inwardness and the minimization of outward-directed activity.

SRI DA AVABHASA: In the Way of the Heart, the discipline of service is not the usual ambiguous ceremony of being nice to people. In the Way of the Heart, the discipline of service expresses the self-transcending disposition in relationship. Such service is a hard course of discipline. The same self-transcending disposition that is expressed through meditation and self-discipline must also be expressed in the plane of conventional relations. Therefore, in your practice of the Way of the Heart, service must not be minimized.

People who are attracted to ascetical self-discipline and meditative inversion often like to minimize service, or the free sharing of energy, or love. Therefore, their so-called practice of religion or Spirituality is not true practice, since true religious or Spiritual practice is expressed in the plane of the body-mind-self, in the plane of the Divine, and in the plane of relations with others. ("I" Is the Body of Life, *p. 96)*

Sat-Guru-Seva is the devotee's obligation both at the beginning of the Way of the Heart and forever. Far from being a mere "beginner's practice", or "training" for "real" sadhana, service to Sri Da Avabhasa expresses the fundamental disposition of our submission to Him, which is never outgrown, but only grows more full as we mature as practitioners.

RECOMMENDED READING

The Love-Ananda Gita, Part III: "I Am What you Require",
pp. 513-17, 541-47

NOTES

1. The Sanskrit word "mandala" (literally, "circle") is commonly used in the esoteric
Spiritual traditions to describe the hierarchical levels of cosmic existence. Heart-Master
Da Avabhasa uses the phrase "Cosmic Mandala" to describe the totality of the conditional
cosmos.

2. A student-beginner is a practitioner in the initial developmental stage of the Way of
the Heart. In the course of student-beginner practice, the practitioner becomes stable in
the foundation disciplines of the Way of the Heart, which are devotion, service, self-
discipline, and meditation.

3. The tradition of Yoga encompasses several traditional paths of Spiritual union with the
Divine. One of these is Karma Yoga, which, extolled by Krishna in the *Bhagavad Gita,* is
the Yoga of action, in which every activity, no matter how humble, is transformed into
self-transcending service to the Divine.

4. Fox, Emmet, *The Magic of Tithing* (Marina del Rey, California: DeVorss & Company,
1960), pp. 8-9.

5. Ibid., pp. 13.

Sat-Guru-Tapas
The Gift of Discipline

by Donald Webley

Thbe Fifth Gift Of The Way Of The Heart Is Sat-Guru-Tapas, The By Me Given Gift Of Discipline (and The Gifted Calling, and The By Me Given Responsibility, For Responsive and Sure Embrace Of Each and All Of The Forms Of functional, practical, relational, and Cultural Discipline, and Even All The Forms Of self-Disciplined Practice, Required By Me), For I Am The True Heart-Master, The Adept Teacher Of The Heart, The Hridaya-Samartha Sat-Guru, Who Is The Heart Itself.*

Da Avabhasa
The Dawn Horse Testament

An investigation of the Sanskrit root of the word "tapas" reveals its manifold meanings, and sheds light upon the traditional understanding of discipline in Spiritual life. "Tapas" derives from the verb "tap", which means "to shine", "to blaze", "to be hot", or "to give out heat". It also means "to suffer pain", or "to undergo penance". In authentic Spiritual cultures, therefore, it is understood that discipline is difficult, even painful. It is also accepted that tapas, or the heat of self-transcending sadhana, is the necessary means by which the being is purified of egoic impediments, thereby allowing the Divine Radiance to "Blaze" or "Shine" in and through the body-mind of the Spiritually mature devotee.

In the Way of the Heart, discipline is likewise understood in these terms. But, even more important, the various disciplines and practices Given by Sri Da Avabhasa are a direct means of feeling and Contemplating Him—while eating, breathing, walking, sitting, exercising, engaging in sexuality. There is, quite literally, no activity for which Heart-Master Da has not provided a very specific discipline that allows that activity to be converted from self-meditation to self-forgetting Remembrance of and direct, living relationship to Him. And to submit oneself to such a practice of going beyond the limited self in the midst of every ordinary activity is sadhana. It is a "fire", a profound tapas.

SRI DA AVABHASA: Sadhana hurts. It definitely hurts. It hurts the body, it hurts the feeling, it hurts the mind. It is just heat. It is just energy. And all the time you are feeling beyond it. What a glory! That is how you grow. Such sadhana is greater than death. It is the domain of love, you see. That is what exceeds limits. Love exceeds limits. Love is not indulgence in desire. It is a heat. It is a purifying force. It is a glow. Ultimately it becomes infinitely Radiant and Outshines everything.

And it is difficult. In fact, measure it: If it is not difficult today, you are not doing sadhana. Sadhana is difficult. It is a heat. It works against motions, energies, impulses, adaptations. It works against them. It confounds them. It frustrates them. If you do not feel so confounded every day, you are not practicing. You are not doing sadhana. . . . Having been born in the ordinary way, having lived the ordinary life, having had to suffer the entire ordeal in every dimension, and in every stage of life, I know what I am talking about. The ordeal is terrible, difficult, painful! But that is what it takes. If you are not enduring the ordeal every day, you are not doing sadhana. (December 19, 1987)

This is true throughout the course of practice, not just at the beginning. The mature practitioner, however, has more and more attention on Sri Da Avabhasa, and less and less on himself or herself. And over time the devotee becomes gratefully aware of the transformation of his or her egoic tendencies, which allows for a deeper devotional relationship with Heart-Master Da and more profound reception of His Blessing Grace.

The Confrontation with Discipline Is the Necessary Foundation of Spiritual Life

I t has always been acknowledged by the great Realizers and practitioners in all traditions that real Spiritual life is an ordeal.

SRI DA AVABHASA: Spiritual life is a demand, not a form of therapy. It is a demand under the conditions of Satsang, the relationship to Guru. It is the practice of life in a world where the living Heart, not your own dilemma and search, is the condition. The demand itself does not make real sadhana possible. It is Satsang, the prior condition of Truth, that makes it necessary. Satsang contains and communicates itself as a demand. And this demand acts as an obstacle for those who are not certain about their interest in this radical life. They have read a little about it, heard a little about it, and now it tests them in the fire of living.

*Such is the way it has always been. The monasteries, the ashrams, the schools of teachers in the past were conceived like fortresses in the hills. They were difficult to get to, and very few people ever returned from them. People didn't gaze nostalgically at the place up on the hill, or hear about it on the evening news, and say, "Wow, I wish I could just go up there, you know, turn on to where it's really at, go up there and everything is groovy forever, great macrobiotic food, and my mantra, man, and really get it on." Traditional spiritual life was never confused with any sort of playful getting high. All of that is only a mediocre interpretation fabricated by people who have no real capacity for sadhana or the true and radical bliss of conscious existence. Spiritual life is not getting high. From the human point of view, the resistive, narcissistic, ordinary human point of view, spiritual life is the most completely oppressive prospect. And it creates massive resistance in such people as soon as they get a taste of it. Traditionally, incredible obstacles were put out front, so that people would not bother even to come to the door. It was purposely intended that people would never even ask about it unless they had already overcome tremendous resistance in themselves. (*The Method of the Siddhas*, pp. 56-57)*

Part of the process of self-transcending sadhana is the practice of various forms of self-discipline. In *The Method of the Siddhas*, Sri Da Avabhasa goes on to describe the initial confrontation with discipline in the context of His own Sadhana with His first Guru, Rudi. During this period, Sri Da Avabhasa has said, literal heat consumed His body:

SRI DA AVABHASA: The first level of sadhana, or spiritual discipline that I had to endure with a human teacher wasn't any sort of other-worldly yoga, nor did it involve love and acknowledgement from the Guru, or even kind words. I spent about two minutes with Rudi when I first met him. He told me to get a job and come back in one year! But I was perfectly willing to do that. As it happened, within a month or two later, my spiritual work with him did begin. It wasn't in fact necessary for me to be away a year, but I was perfectly willing for it to be so. I was ecstatically happy to have made this contact, to have a beginning, to have become capable of spiritual life. It was a profound joy to me to have found someone who was obviously capable of drawing me into a condition at least more profound than the one I was living. From that moment it was one demand on top of the other. It was work. Work was the sadhana, work was the spiritual life. There was no "Come to me and sit and chat." It was "Take out the garbage, sweep out this place." If I came to sit and talk with Rudi, I was most often told "Scrub the floor," or "There is a new shipment in the warehouse, so go and unload my truck." I worked constantly, day and night, for four years. On top of the heavy physical labor, Rudi had me going to seminaries, where I studied Christian theology, masses of historical literature, ancient languages, all kinds of things in which I had no fundamental interest. I had to live in Protestant and Orthodox seminaries, but I was not a Christian. My sadhana was continuous work and self-transcendence. There was no ending of it. Even in sleep and dreams, there was no ending of it.

My time with Rudi did not see the fulfillment of my spiritual life. I moved on to other relationships and the order of my sadhana and my understanding changed. But his requirements for sadhana in the functions of life and body, in terms of money, food and sex, were more than useful to me. The sadhana performed in those years became the very foundation of my spiritual life. During that time I was strengthened and stabilized in mind, body and life. When I came to Rudi, I wasn't prepared for an elusive yogi. Such a one could have been of no use to me in the beginning. Truth is resurrected from the ground up. The conscious force can never leave the ground if you begin your sadhana in the air. If sadhana is begun as an effort to become "spiritual", then what is merely alive remains a mass of confusion and craziness. So I must insist that all who come to me take on functional responsibility for the powers of life, which are money, food and sex. (The Method of the Siddhas, *pp. 52-53)*

Why is discipline so fundamental to Spiritual life? In *The Dawn Horse Testament,* Sri Da Avabhasa Says that "the ego-'I' is (Inherently and Entirely) An 'Addict', A Compulsive and Obsessive and Intensely Persistent Seeker, In Perpetual (and Never To Be Satisfied) Pursuit Of Utter self-Fulfillment and (Yet self-Centered) self-Release" (pp. 262-63).

In an Essay in *The Basket of Tolerance* (forthcoming), Sri Da Avabhasa describes the addictive quality of egoity as the <u>root</u> addiction of humankind, from which all other addictions, such as alcoholism, stem. And He Comments upon the central role that discipline, especially the discipline of living in a true Spiritual community, plays in healing our self-inflicted suffering:

. . . the process of truly human growth is necessarily and inherently religious. The ego-"I" is an addict (or a seeker) in everything he or she does. That search is always a lust for objects and effects (whether apparently external or apparently internal). And the search itself is <u>always</u> founded upon "Narcissus", the basic self-contraction, the alienated, separate, and separative ego-"I". . . .

True and complete religious life (such as is practiced in the Way of the Heart, which I have Revealed) is a comprehensive discipline of separate and separative self (or egoity) that is committed to utterly transcend (rather than merely to fulfill or release) the ego-"I" (or <u>all</u> of self-contraction and seeking). Such a Way of life necessarily begins with (and must, with the help of the religious community of exemplary others, constantly and consistently re-establish) right and comprehensive self-appraisal (or growing self-understanding). Also, even though true religion is a practice that functions as a thoroughly personal, individual, and often private process, it is, as a real and effective practice and process, not an independent enterprise carried out and fulfilled by the separate (and inherently separative) ego-"I". Therefore, true religion (in any and every stage of life) is always and necessarily and inherently a practice and a process that originates, develops, and continues to develop only in the context of a living and effectively functioning religious <u>community</u>

(which, as a "culture of expectation and inspiration", must nurture, stimulate, support, guide, and direct, and thus both inform and test, the individual's religious practice and process). . . . And such true (and truly human, or humanly mature) religious life progressively (and necessarily) requires the relinquishment of <u>all</u> seeking and <u>all</u> mere self-indulgence, or (via the progressive development of the seven stages of life) the discipline and the transcendence of the <u>total</u> egoic life.

Self-Discipline in the Way of the Heart

T he Way of the Heart is a comprehensive Way of life, in which devotees of Sri Da Avabhasa study His Instruction and accept His Guidance in every area, and thus we align every aspect of our lives to His Blessing. Throughout the many years of His Teaching Work, Sri Da Avabhasa "considered" with His devotees in great detail many forms of discipline, along with all other aspects of human and Spiritual life. This "consideration" was never a merely academic exercise. Rather, it was a matter of freely and unreservedly experimenting with the whole array of approaches, modern and ancient, Eastern and Western, to find what would best serve Spiritual growth and human well-being in modern men and women. The disciplines lived by practitioners of Free Daism are the distilled wisdom of this process of "consideration".

Taken together, the life-disciplines in the Way of the Heart cover every aspect of the devotee's life-circumstance, but they fall, for the purposes of discussion, into five general spheres, of general health (especially "conscious exercise"), diet, sexuality, service, and cooperative community.

Thus, basic discipline for devotees in the Way of the Heart includes conscious participation in sitting, standing, walking, breathing, and two formal periods of exercise daily; eating what Sri Da Avabhasa describes as the "wholly regenerative" vegetarian diet; observing and taking responsibility for one's childish and adolescent character patterns (and, indeed, all strategies of lovelessness), developing the capability for regenerative (or energy-conserving and rejuvenative) sexuality, and (as a means of making this possible) restricting sexual activity to an emotionally committed intimate relationship; contributing time, energy, and financial support for Sri Da Avabhasa and His Work; and active participation in the cooperative community of Free Daists. (The disciplines of "conscious exercise", diet, and sexuality will be described in more detail later in this chapter; service has been discussed in the preceding chapter, "Sat-Guru-Seva", and the principles of cooperative community are presented in Part Five, "I Would Find a New Order of Men and Women".) In the widest sense, all the daily activities of Free Daist devotees, including meditative and devotional practices, can be regarded as forms of discipline.

The primary purpose of discipline in the Way of the Heart is to serve "self-Observation, self-Understanding, self-Transcendence, and self-Transcending God-

---

THE DAILY "FORM"

From the preparatory level of practice as a student-novice to the advanced and the ultimate stages of practice in the Way of the Heart, a basic daily "form", or schedule, of practice is Recommended by Sri Da Avabhasa. Though the specifics of that "form" vary from one stage of practice to the next (especially in terms of time spent in any given activity), and the order of certain activities may vary depending on one's circumstance, the basic daily "form" begins with early-morning meditation, followed by the Sat-Guru Puja, a period of study, and calisthenics, or other vigorous exercise. After a day of work or service, the evening schedule calls for Hatha Yoga, dinner, the Sat-Guru Arati Puja (for devotees who live in Ashram), and an evening activity (which may be service, study, a group to talk about practice, intimate time with one's intimate partner or family, or a community meeting, to mention a few of the possibilities). A daily diary entry precedes evening meditation, which is the last event of the day.

Realization". For the devotee in the early levels of practice, self-discipline is primarily intended to serve the process of self-observation and self-understanding. (After practice has matured beyond the beginning developmental stages of the Way of the Heart, the disciplines continue to be lived, but now as a natural expression of the equanimity and economy of one who has regained the capability to consistently understand and transcend the self-contraction.) As Sri Da Avabhasa has explained in *The Dawn Horse Testament,* disciplines serve the process of self-observation "By Frustrating The Patterns and Accumulated Addictions Of egoic Seeking."

Take this very simple example: an individual who drinks three cups of coffee before leaving for work in the morning, and another five during the day. He has done this all his adult life, without ever questioning the motivation behind it. He is, after all, not doing anything beyond the pale of common acceptability. Then he becomes a Free Daist, and has to stop the coffee. Suddenly, he must confront the feelings of neediness, boredom, depression, and lack of energy and motivation that his habit had at least partially disguised for so many years. Because these are now revealed to him, he is in a position to understand these emotional limits.

The same new practitioner would, however, also notice, after the initial difficult period of purification and adaptation, that he had more clarity and balance. He would sleep more easily, be less volatile, and would be able to be more fully present at meditative and devotional occasions. By serving bodily equanimity, therefore, the disciplines liberate energy and attention from the egoic addictions of seeking and separation and free them for the Spiritual process.

Because it frustrates our self-oriented and self-indulgent tendencies, the practice of the disciplines necessarily generates the "heat" that is tapas. Sri Da Avabhasa has pointed out that devotees tend to regard this "heat" as an unnecessary by-product of the practice, or as a sign that the practice is ineffective in their case. Quite the contrary, the feeling of heat is a necessary sign of the workings of the process of transformation.

The "Radical" Nature of Discipline in the Way of the Heart

I n the Way of the Heart, discipline is engaged from a "radical" point of view. That is to say, although the life-disciplines of the Way of the Heart certainly do help practitioners become more balanced, healthy, etc., we do not practice disciplines primarily as a "method" of attaining some desirable goal or state for ourselves. Nor do we engage the disciplines on the basis of a negative estimation of the body, the mind, or the world, in an attempt to suppress or escape them. Sri Da Avabhasa has contrasted the "radical" approach of the Way of the Heart with traditional approaches:

In the traditional setting, religious or Spiritual life is commonly engaged as an effort toward cure, or the ultimate solution to a consistently presumed problem. And, for this reason, the traditional language of religion and Spirituality is, by convention, based on negative or problematic conceptions, such as "sin", the "flesh", "evil", the "Devil", "hell", "damnation", "samsara", "ignorance", "illusion", "maya", the "body", and the egoic "self" as a concrete or inherently independent entity.

In contrast to these traditional conceptions, the Way of the Heart may be said to be based on the model of inherent well-being, and practice of the Way of the Heart may be likened to a process wherein health itself is more and more profoundly magnified.

The traditional, or conventional, course of religious or Spiritual practice may be likened to a progressive cure, developed through often drastic remedies and dissociative seclusion (or confinement to the "inwardness" of the disease itself), and involving a protracted or even life-long practice of convalescence (even in remedial isolation). In contrast, the Way of the Heart involves immediate self-diagnosis (or self-understanding) and direct, instantaneous, or always present and complete release (in the form of present self-transcendence) of the entire principle of dis-ease. (August 25, 1982)

Thus, the disciplines of the Way of the Heart are undertaken with the understanding that they are not a "cure" for un-Happiness. As Heart-Master Da has Said, "The practices of the Way of the Heart are not methods for attaining Happiness but they are the expressions of Happiness. The disciplines of 'money, food, and sex' are not a way to become Happy. Discipline is difficult enough—why should we also burden it with the obligation to make us Happy!" (November 28, 1981)

Discipline in and of itself is not what accomplishes the fundamental Work of Spiritual transformation. That Work is the Function of the Sat-Guru, the Liberator of beings. In the Way of the Heart, disciplines are therefore taken up in the context of the relationship to Sri Da Avabhasa, and it is His Grace that makes them ultimately fruitful.

Thus Satsang, the relationship to the Realizer, is the Great Secret of Spiritual life:

SRI DA AVABHASA: Satsang is the prior Revelation of That Which is to be Realized. It is the Graceful Giving of that Revelation. It is the context of practice. It is what makes discipline effective. It is what makes discipline reasonable, even. Therefore, you must live always in the context of that Revelation. This is the secret of those who live in Satsang with the Realizer. They have been Given the Gift that makes sadhana possible, reasonable, and effective. Whereas if you are only resorting to yourself and whatever motives you can capture in yourself in any given moment, there will be no consistency, and the so-called sadhana will not be effective. Effective sadhana is consistent. It cuts through limitation, goes beyond it, drops it, is disappeared of it.

Your sadhana must be based on That Which transcends these dualities. Your sadhana must be based upon the direct Revelation, Satsang as constant Company. Then you can deal with these dualities, be responsible for equanimity, be responsible for discipline. You can do an effective sadhana. Discipline in and of itself has only a sheerly conventional function. Obviously a certain amount of discipline helps you to survive and helps you to be healthy and so on, but apart from that, discipline serves no ultimate function relative to the Great Process. Discipline must simply be part of your response to Revelation. Discipline is the activated mechanism of self-transcendence.

You must devote your life to feeling-Contemplation of Me, to Satsang with Me. Allow every fraction of your life to be conformed to Satsang with Me, to this Contemplation of Me. All the disciplines of the Way of the Heart that I have Described to you are means of transforming ordinary action into Puja, into feeling-Contemplation of Me, into the sacredness of Satsang with Me. Therefore, the disciplines are not merely conventional improvements of the body-mind. They are the principle of Satsang animated.

Since the ancient days it has been said that Samadhi, God-Realization, Liberation, Enlightenment, is the purpose of life. The best thing you can do is spend time in the Company of someone in Samadhi, spend time in the Company of a Realizer. Realization itself, Samadhi, Transmits itself. It is a Power, a Siddhi. It is not by stressful effort, by the seeking of the self-contracted being, or ego, that Samadhi is Realized. It is by Sympathy with Samadhi itself, with God-Realization itself, that Samadhi is Realized. It is by Sympathetic association with the Realizer, Communion with the Realizer, that Realization is accomplished, not by self-effort.

All of the disciplines you practice are a way of being responsive, of participating in the Gift. They are not efforts that can cause Divine Self-Realization. They are ways of participating in the Samadhi of the Realizer and allowing that Samadhi to accomplish you. This is the Great Secret. (July 2, 1988)

Thus, first and foremost, the disciplines of Free Daism are based in feeling-Contemplation of Sri Da Avabhasa, and they provide a means by which we maintain our attention upon Him. That attention is the channel or conduit by which His Divine Grace enters our lives and transforms us.

It is the Grace of the Divine World-Teacher and our responsive surrender to Him that are the Circumstance in which practitioners of the Way of the Heart understand and approach the life-disciplines. As has been noted previously, Sri Da Avabhasa characterizes the Way of the Heart as "a hard school", because there are real requirements, but also as a "happy Way of life", because it is founded in the Prior and Uncaused Joy that He Is and Reveals to us.

Lunch-Righteousness vs. God-Communion

The life-disciplines of the Way of the Heart are taken up progressively, and based on intelligent and self-renouncing evaluation of one's individual tendencies and necessities. Sri Da Avabhasa Offers a basic design for self-discipline within which each individual practitioner must gradually discover a detailed personal design that is "Both Appropriate and Optimum In his or her own case".

Thus, for example, although the diet for practitioners of Free Daism normally is strictly vegetarian (aside from rare celebratory occasions), those whose bodily constitution is such that it requires flesh food for its proper maintenance, may, after appropriate medical consultation, adopt a diet that includes meat or fish. Likewise, temporary health conditions may also require a deviation from the usual dietary regime.

The disciplines bear the fruits of self-transcendence and God-Realization only to the extent to which the devotee resorts to the Grace of the Sat-Guru. The <u>perfection</u> of the disciplines is neither expected nor possible. What is both expected <u>and</u> possible is that the devotee apply himself or herself to the disciplines with the utmost intensity and to the maximum degree possible at his or her present level of practice in the Way of the Heart.

Sri Da Avabhasa, originally Speaking in reference to the dietary disciplines, has coined the term "lunch righteousness", to refer to dry, sterile, and humorless adherence to the "letter of the law". True Freedom, He would Remind us, lies neither in self-indulgence nor in self-denial, but in God-Communion. During the early years of His Teaching Work, Sri Da Avabhasa therefore often alternated periods of strict discipline with periods of celebration, where His devotees would make liberal use of the dietary "accessories", such as meat, alcohol, tobacco, and "junk" food.

A Leela from Catherine Lewis describes her first confrontation with the disciplines of the Way of the Heart:

When people think of discipline, they usually think of something unpleasant, something you have to do for the sake of something else, but not something that is pleasurable in itself. In the context of Satsang, though, everything changes and takes on a new significance.

After many years of exploring every path I could find, I finally came upon the Wisdom-Teaching of Sri Gurudev Da Love-Ananda. In my various searches, I had applied many different kinds of discipline but nothing consistently, and everything was done on my own terms. My initial adaptation to the disciplines of the Way of the Heart happened more or less overnight. I first approached the Free Daist Communion one day in July of 1974 and that same day I signed up to be a student. I was handed a manual that was an inch and a half thick with all the disciplines that I was now responsible for!

I took my new obligations very seriously; I had suffered ordinary life long enough to know that I wanted to do something very different with my life. And I had studied enough of Sri Gurudev's Wisdom-Teaching to understand that He was going to require a lot from me, including giving up an old habit of living.

I approached the disciplines like a fanatic, paying attention to every detail and being very righteous with people who weren't so scrupulous. Food was the hardest area of my own adaptation, and so it was the area where I exhibited the most righteousness. I read every ingredient on every label to make sure I was within the letter of the law, and I was once caught yelling at someone for eating an egg salad sandwich "on white bread?!"—someone who turned out to be a stranger visiting the Ashram and not involved in our Way of life at all! In moments like that, I was aware that something might be a little "off" in my approach, but it didn't seem to deter me in the slightest. Being a typically self-indulgent character, I felt that if I let myself off the hook even a little bit, I would lose my hold on the discipline altogether.

Another area of tremendous intensity for me was holding down a full-time job. I came out of the age of hippies, traveling, and being "free", so the discipline of a nine-to-five job was generating a lot of "heat". It represented everything that I did not want to do by tendency. Every day when I came home from work, I wanted to get rid of this uncomfortable feeling and go and have an ice cream cone or do something wild or divert my attention in some way, but instead I would study Sri Gurudev's Wisdom-Teaching, do my laundry, and try not to pay too much attention to the insanity that was arising in my body-mind. Fortunately for me, Sri Gurudev had described the process that I was going through in such detail in The Method of the Siddhas *that I felt like I had a map, and could understand what was happening to me. After a while this purification phase of applying myself to discipline calmed down somewhat, and the vegetarian diet and disciplined life I was leading started to feel more ordinary.*

I was living in the community of devotees in San Francisco and every weekend we would all go up to serve the Mountain Of Attention Sanctuary (called "Persimmon" at the time), where Sri Gurudev was living. Most of the time we would get to sit with Sri Gurudev in meditation, and sometimes He would invite us to ask questions in a formal question-and-answer period. After a couple of months of this kind of meeting with Him, He called for a different kind of gathering in what is now our largest Meditation Hall, Western Face Cathedral. We were going to be watching a film that had recently been produced about Sri Gurudev and His community of devotees and we were going to be drinking beer and smoking cigarettes! I knew that Sri Gurudev had had this type of gathering with His devotees in the past, but I never suspected He would have them again, and I was excited.

I will never forget the feeling that overtook me when I popped open my first can of beer. I was sitting very close to Sri Gurudev, which had already awakened in me a tremendous feeling of happiness and love; but then as I popped open the beer, my whole life of discipline flashed up before me. I saw that I was relating to the disciplines as though they were something in and of themselves. I saw that I was a totally self-righteous and uptight person; and I saw that what the Way of the Heart was about was living in direct relationship to Sri Da Love-Ananda, Who was the Happiest Being I had ever seen, and Who made me extremely Happy just to be with Him. I saw that the Way of the Heart was not primarily about following all these rules of behavior, but it was about allowing my attention to rest on this very Happy Being. All these things exploded in my brain in just this one moment of popping open this beer can. Tapas now had a whole new meaning for me.

I was living with this Ecstatic Being Who was Teaching me how to live a disciplined life to be sure, but all that was secondary. He was Teaching me to live with Him, in feeling-Communion with Him, and what He was opening me to was so much beyond just the physical dimension of the discipline that I realized I had to open to His Ever-Present Relationship in my life. It was easy to be extremely Happy drinking beer with my Guru, but it was a lot harder to be that Happy when I was at home doing my Yoga, for example. I still had a long way to go to be able to practice such Happiness all the time, but I was a lot less uptight after that lesson! And mysteriously, without my doing anything about it, I was much Happier too. I realized that tapas really was about being this Happy all the time, no matter what discipline my Guru was presently Giving me.

Ultimately, we do not practice the disciplines on the basis of any compelling self-oriented logic. We do so because we love our Divine Sat-Guru and understand Who He Is. Traditionally, it is understood that obedience to one's Guru is the fundamental basis and ultimate means of Spiritual life and growth. The Guru knows what we need better than we do. The devotee establishes the sacred relationship with the Guru based precisely upon this understanding that the Guru is a Guide to the most important matters of life, and the devotee gratefully and humbly accepts the Guru's Guidance. This principle transcends all the rational, self-motivated reasons for following such instruction. It is the key that unlocks the floodgates and allows the Guru's All-Purifying Grace to Flow. Thus, it is said in the Fifty Verses of Guru-Devotion, from the Tibetan Buddhist tradition: "What need is there to say much more? Do what pleases your guru and avoid what displeases him. Be diligent in both of these."

To His own devotees, Sri Da Avabhasa expands upon and clarifies the Sat-Guru's Eternal Demand. He also makes explicit His Promise to Serve the Divine Self-Realization of those who will submit to Him in the traditional manner:

In the Way of the Heart, the self-transcending and God-Realizing Process (which becomes Divine Self-Realization) is not possible unless you Lawfully, fully, and in the traditional manner embrace and fulfill the Guru-devotee relationship to Me.

*I will Serve anyone who, not as an ego but as a true devotee, enters into this relationship, surrendered to Me through obedience (or sympathetic and true conformity) to My Instruction, My Permission, My Blessing, and My Person. (*The Love-Ananda Gita, *"I Am What you Require" section, pp. 546-47)*

The following sections discuss Sri Da Avabhasa's Instruction and Requirements in the areas of "conscious exercise", diet, and sexuality.

"Conscious Exercise"

T*he Basic Disciplines Relative To General Health Involve "Conscious Exercise", or The Maintenance Of bodily Equanimity and physical Well-being Through Systematic Exercises and General bodily Practices That Conduct Natural human (and etheric) life-energy Throughout. (*The Dawn Horse Testament, *p. 259)*

The tensions, ill health, and "dis-ease" that plague our body-minds are the result of our contraction from the universal etheric energy-field that naturally pervades the body-minds of all beings. The bodily exercises and general health practices engaged in the Way of the Heart serve primarily to realign and harmonize the physical body with this etheric field and restore us to intimacy with this dimension of existence. As Sri Da Avabhasa Writes:

The body-mind of the human being is constantly sustained by the universal etheric, or pranic, energy-field that naturally pervades it. In the individual's infantile recoil, reaction, and psycho-physical contraction toward egoic, or independent, self, the individual separates from the Eternal Divine Reality and becomes egoically "self-possessed" (or self-absorbed). Thus, the individual begins to starve and suffer. The body-mind becomes a

*field of tensions, devoted to the search for consoling experiences that release tensions plea-
surably. Such experiences include pleasures of eating and sex, willful control of life-
circumstances, the acquisition of mental knowledge, and the mental contemplation of
abstractions. Such pleasures preoccupy and degenerate the usual person, until he or she is
restored to Transcendental (and Inherently Spiritual) Divine Life.*

*The Self-Existing and Self-Radiant Divine Consciousness Itself Lives as the individual
body-mind and Sustains it. If only the body-mind will open into the pervasive and objective natural (etheric, or pranic, and bodily experienced) energy, and, in due course, into
My Spiritual Current of Divine Life, with full feeling and without thought, it will be
Liberated from the egoically "self-possessed" games of tension and release of tension. Then
there is only Fullness of Life. (*The Eating Gorilla Comes in Peace, *pp. 31-32)*

The foundation of "conscious exercise" is the ability to be surrendered into the universal etheric energy-field. Any activity can be performed as "conscious exercise".
However, activity becomes "conscious exercise" when—and only when—mind, emotion,
and body are simultaneously surrendered in the universal life-energy that pervades and
animates them. It is this understanding and disposition, rather than any technical
"secrets", that converts the physical exercises presented in the Way of the Heart, or any
other exercises, into "conscious exercise".

"Conscious exercise" is a practice of what Sri Da Avabhasa calls "conductivity", or
conducting and intensifying the natural energy of the body-mind, and, in the Spiritually
awakened stages of the Way of the Heart, conducting the Spiritual Current of Divine Life.
The most basic exercise of "conductivity" is the simple psycho-physical process of
"reception-release", breathing in the universal etheric energy with every inhalation, and
releasing all obstructions into that All-Pervading field with the exhaled breath.

The technical process of "conductivity" that Sri Da Avabhasa Gives to beginning
practitioners is a three-part practice that relaxes and opens the body to the universal
etheric energy. It may be engaged randomly throughout the day and particularly during
meditation. The first and most fundamental part of this practice is self-transcending
feeling-radiation from the heart, boundlessly in all directions (a practice that Heart-Master
Da Recommends be done at all times, in meditation and daily life). In this disposition of
heart-radiation, one practices the second part of this process, which is to persistently
relax the body in its natural polarity, upward along the spinal axis, from the bodily base
to the crown of the head. The third part of the process, which is a breathing exercise, is
done by drawing the inhaled breath down the frontal line of the body and then releasing
and diffusing the breath through the whole body on exhalation.

Sri Da Avabhasa Instructs us that when the process of "conductivity" is engaged
fully, "a great Bliss is released from the body-mind, and attention is granted more and
more freedom to enter into the 'conscious process'". (The "conscious process", which is
the submission of feeling and attention to Sri Da Avabhasa, is the primary discipline of

the Way of the Heart.) Thus, "conscious exercise", as a primary form of "conductivity", frees energy and attention for the purposes of Spiritual practice. It is therefore to be understood as a profound practice, the necessary adjunct of the "conscious process" of feelingly-Contemplating Sri Da Avabhasa, not just an alternative exercise technique.

Sri Da Avabhasa contrasts this understanding of the purpose of exercise with the prevailing Western approach:

SRI DA AVABHASA: The currently popular approach to health and well-being—wherein people engage in exaggerated physical activity, endless jogging, frequent orgasmic sexual intercourse, one or another kind of hyperactivity—is an attempted solution to a problem created by habits of living that themselves must be changed. The common approach to health today is a degenerative solution to reactive emotion, physical tension, psychological tension, the entire self-contracted bodily tendency toward degeneration and disease.

The more traditional and ancient approach is quite different. The ancient approach was not to give first aid or to offer an emergency solution to a life that is already adapted to bad habits, but to view the life as a whole and determine what is the best way to live altogether. From that point of view, the appropriate recommendation is not that you should jog five miles every day, have as many orgasms per week as possible, and make your physical life a frenzy of activity, but rather that you should transform the habits of living that motivate you to such activities as a solution to accumulated tensions, obstructions, and general toxicity.

The traditional approach to health and long life was to avoid entirely the habit of living that accepts stimulation as a right solution. The ancient recommendation, and the right recommendation, is to enter into a graceful psycho-physical condition wherein motions are natural, one is essentially open to the universal field of etheric energy, and one breathes and conducts the etheric energy naturally and fully to the entire body.

Exaggerated, stimulating activity tends to affect the grosser part of the body exclusively rather than the body-mind as a whole. Exaggerated physical activity, such as jogging and overindulgence in sexual intercourse, stimulates, at least temporarily, the organs and musculature of the lower body. But at the same time, such activity fails to bring the etheric energy and even the received oxygen to the higher centers of the body and to the brain. Deprived of energy and life, those higher functional organs of the body-mind become enervated.

The right approach to exercise, breath, and life is the conservation of the natural energy of the body-mind and the bodily chemistry, the natural "conductivity" of the pure, oxygenated blood to the whole body, the elimination of toxins such as carbon dioxide, and the natural feeding upon the universal etheric energy by the whole body-mind, including the subtler and higher centers of the body, rather than mere exploitation and emptying of life through the stimulation and release of tensions in the lower body. A pleasureless, ascetic point of view is not necessary to this process; the etheric

energy is pleasurably conducted to every part of the living being, naturally and harmo-niously, without exaggeration. A graceful pattern of life, in other words, is the right Way of life, a life that does not in itself create problems that must be solved but rather fulfills the Law. (The Eating Gorilla Comes in Peace, *pp. 307–310)*

Sri Da Avabhasa's book *Conscious Exercise and the Transcendental Sun* fully explains the principles of "conscious exercise", and shows how these principles are to be applied throughout daily life in conscious breathing, sitting, standing, walking, and in recommended formal routines of Da Namaskar (a sequence of poses evolved from the traditional Surya Namaskar postures), Hatha Yoga, calisthenics, and pranayama (control of breath).

The exercise routines Given in the Way of the Heart are "sattvic", or balanced, rather than "rajasic", or overly stimulating. In the morning, the devotee engages a formal routine of calisthenics that energize the body-mind for the day ahead. In the early evening, a Hatha Yoga sequence (perhaps augmented by some other form of calming exercise such as t'ai chi) is engaged to relax the body-mind and release the stresses of the day. (The actual exercises adopted by each individual should be based on appropriate medical consultation.)

The exercise routines are not intended or expected to produce bodily perfection, nor does some esoteric secret reside in the particular sequences of prescribed exercises. Rather, they are an expression of our own devotional relationship with our Sat-Guru and a simple way of healthfully maintaining our bodies and minds.

The Dietary Discipline

(This section was contributed by Richard Schorske)

S RI DA AVABHASA: *Much of that disturbed condition that people bring to the Guru is not a matter of anything subtle or spiritual. For the most part, it is simply a functional disharmony. In many cases, the simple moderation and purification of diet is the most dramatic form of sadhana. The simple moderation and intelligent selection of diet purifies the body. The judicious use of occasional fasting also aids this normalization of psycho-physical life. All "ordinary" sadhana purifies the body, and returns it to a normal condition of vitality.*

*The use or transformation of food is the fundamental process at the level of organic life. Therefore, the simple intelligence of diet is very useful, very appropriate. (*The Method of the Siddhas*)*

Sri Da Avabhasa has Said that an essential foundation for a life of equanimity and devotional ecstasy is purification of the body. And bodily purification begins with a right discipline of food-taking—because food-taking significantly determines, even controls, the state of one's energy and attention. Because food-taking is so fundamental to mental clarity, emotional balance, and general health, Sri Da Avabhasa has generated a comprehensive Wisdom-Teaching relative to appropriate diet.

Of course, the whole matter of food-taking seems simple enough in concept.

You get hungry, you eat.

But how often do we approximate that simplicity? For so many of us, the pattern is more like this: You get anxious or frustrated or bored, you start thinking that you are hungry, and then you eat. Physiological hunger-responses barely enter into the picture! For many of us, food is treated as a palliative for emotional problems. In fact, our relationship to food is just part of our self-contracted philosophy—our feeling of being a threatened, mortal entity, unsustained by the universe—and fundamentally unloved. And on the basis of this feeling of being unloved ("You don't love me"), we live as unlove ourselves ("I don't love you"). As part of this philosophy, we are constantly looking for Perfect Sustenance—the "edible deity" as Sri Da Avabhasa puts it—something that will sustain us absolutely, make us perfectly Happy. We look to food to suppress anxiety, interrupt the boredom of mind and desire, even make us happy. Whereas, what we must simply do is, in the Blessing Company of Sri Da Avabhasa, understand our own activity of turning away and be restored to God and to Love, our True Sustenance.

"Your order is not ready, nor will it ever be."

In *The Eating Gorilla Comes in Peace*, Sri Da Avabhasa identifies the roots of our disorder, and proposes a total culture—not merely a "diet"—that inherently resolves our food-frenzy:

SRI DA AVABHASA: A life that is obsessed with reactive needs, feeding on all that ener- vates, toxifies, and kills, and dramatizing doubt and unlove in the patterns of common functional relations is subhuman, un-Awakened at the heart, and unable to Realize and stabilize within its own Divine Condition. Therefore, peace must be restored to the com- mon meal. The bodily individual must be purified, harmonized or balanced, and intensi- fied. . . . And the life of such a one must be founded not in any problematic search for pleasure or happiness but in the present certainty of the inherent pleasurableness of exis- tence, even in its gross bodily form. (pp. 18-19)

Before we describe the diet that Sri Da Avabhasa recommends to devotees in the Way of the Heart, it is worth noting that diet, while important, is not "the means to Salvation":

SRI DA AVABHASA: It is not appropriate to cut off a finger each day. To stop cutting your fingers off, however, will not make you realize the Truth. It is simply appropriate to put fingers to proper use. Just so, there is appropriate use of food and life. If you obstruct the natural process by excess and wrong use it is like cutting off a finger every day. It creates suffering, disability. On the other hand, if you correct your diet, moderate it, you don't re-alize the Truth for doing that. It is simply appropriate to do that. (The Method of the Siddhas, *pp. 71-72)*

Furthermore, Sri Da Avabhasa cautions us to beware of "lunch-righteousness":

SRI DA AVABHASA: Just as you must be free of self-indulgence and all its goals, you must be equally free of the cult of discipline, the form of righteousness that appears whenever you fulfill a discipline. Feeling self-conscious and modest while drinking a little mint tea with friends who are drinking coffee is so small, so narrow and tacky. It is the product of that motivated cult of discipline in which there is no freedom, no fundamental humor, no real comprehension of the importance of daily events—just foolish concerns for purity of diet when people are murdering one another with every movement of their minds. All that obsessive concern for diet is inappropriate. What is appropriate is just a natural, func-tional awareness of what you eat. (The Eating Gorilla Comes in Peace, *p. 79)*

Foods That Free Daists Choose to Eat

In keeping with the fundamental purpose of the Free Daist diet, which is to "fully serve the submission of personal energy and attention to the Great Process that becomes Spiritual and Transcendental Divine Self-Realization" (*The ego-"I" is the Illusion of Relatedness,* p. 60), Sri Da Avabhasa argues that right diet must be tai-lored to free energy and attention in the case of each individual practitioner.

In the Way of the Heart, right diet is <u>whatever</u> diet is the "Minimum Optimum" diet for good health, well-being, and full practice of the Way of the Heart, in the case of the <u>individual.</u> Therefore, there is no <u>absolute</u> standard diet, applicable to all cases, but there is a <u>basic</u> dietary orientation that should stand as a guide to all. (The ego-"I" is the Illusion of Relatedness, *p. 60)*

For reasons of health, and in agreement with ancient and modern research on the psycho-physiology of nutrition, the basic diet of devotees in the Way of the Heart con-sists primarily of raw and (if possible) organically grown fruit, sprouts, vegetables (raw or cooked), soaked or sprouted seeds and nuts, and grains and legumes (sprouted, soaked, or cooked). Devotees may, in rare cases (if medically advised) consume milk and milk products, and (in even rarer cases) their health may require occasional concentrated protein in the form of eggs, fish, or meat. And devotees abstain as a consistent daily rule of practice from social drugs, tobacco, alcohol, caffeine, sugar, and refined, processed, and "junk" food. (Such dietary "accessories" as alcohol, caffeine, tobacco, sugar, or refined foods may very occasionally be used in special occasions of formally agreed upon community celebration among devotees.)

In general, as Sri Da Avabhasa describes, the diet should be "maximally" raw. Raw foods contain much more life-energy, vitamins, and minerals. They are also more easily eliminated, as they do not burden the body with toxic substances. Devotees may also (with proper medical advice) use a periodic raw food diet (or period of fasting on raw fruit or vegetable juices) to cleanse the body of accumulated toxins. Thus, the devotee in the Way of the Heart should adapt to the "maximally raw" diet consistent with his or her own psycho-physical constitution and life-circumstance, and with appropriate medical consultation.

SRI DA AVABHASA: Eating should not be depressing. It should be pleasurable, amusing, and enlightening. It should be full of light. And food-taking is not just the few minutes you spend every day consuming a few elements. Nor is it merely the gourmet design of those elements. Food-taking begins with the consumption of elemental food, but it also includes the process by which that food is assimilated, transformed, made usable—and eliminated. Thus, the process of taking food is continuous. The sign of its lawful fulfillment, therefore, is not how good the food tastes or what it looks like, but how you feel all day. Many elemental foods look and taste good and can stimulate pleasure in you for the brief span of the ritual of eating, but after eating them you feel miserable. . . .

Communion with the Spiritual, Transcendental, and Divine Current of Life is a Blissful activity. Therefore, right eating, as an expression of such Communion, is not an ascetic practice in the conventional sense of the term. There is nothing grim or self-mortifying in the right practice of this diet. It is oriented toward pleasure, enjoyment, well-being. Once your understanding and approach to life are mature, eating properly is not a matter of ascetically denying yourself anything. . . . You are being fulfilled in the Divine, pleasurably and positively.

Certainly, there are rules for responsible eating. You should not eat foods that toxify or enervate the body. You should not overeat. You should not eat foods to which you react. But such disciplines do not diminish the pleasurableness of this diet—they enhance it. The diet should be inherently enjoyable. And one's general state of body and mind should be fundamental enjoyment, or inherent pleasure, rather than acquired and temporary pleasurable stimulation followed by phases of mediocrity, low energy, and reactivity. (The Eating Gorilla Comes in Peace, *pp. 123-25)*

**Matt Shaffer in
the kitchen at the
Mountain Of Attention**

Matt Shaffer, head cook at the Mountain Of Attention Sanctuary, talks about his service:

I always have to take into account if people are getting enough protein, enough greens, enough raw food, who is allergic to what, who needs more grounding food. It is never as simple as just cooking a meal! In general I am always working to strike a creative balance, preparing food that is optimally healthy and balancing, but at the same time interesting and good tasting.

A typical day's food preparation at the Mountain Of Attention starts with breakfast, where we provide fresh fruit in season, generally along with soaked nuts, seeds, raisins, and a fruit sauce. In addition to this we prepare a cooked whole grain, like oatmeal or cream of rice, for people who need something more grounding.

Lunch is our main meal of the day. We have either a tossed mixed vegetable salad or a salad bar with mixed greens or spinach, carrots, tomatoes, avocados, cabbage, cucumbers, lots of different sprouts, and a dressing. And we always prepare a main dish based in potatoes, whole grains, or beans. We have a tofu dish once a week, bean dishes twice a week, and occasionally a whole-grain pasta dish such as lasagna or spaghetti.

Dinner is a light meal. For those who eat fruit for dinner we have fresh fruit available, generally served with seeds, nuts, and nut butters. Often we make soups such as miso or cauliflower and serve them with bread, rolls, or muffins. Sometimes we prepare a light grain meal such as a vegetable stir fry with brown rice, or wholewheat couscous and steamed vegetables. Again at night we always have either a salad bar or a tossed mixed salad with lots of vegetables, sprouts, and greens. Tonight I am preparing bell peppers stuffed with herbed rice and tomatoes, with steamed swiss chard, corn on the cob, and a salad bar. ∎

Those approaching formal practice of the Way of the Heart study and gradually adapt to the basic dietary guidelines:

In order to understand and evaluate the "Minimum Optimum" dietary discipline (or disciplined dietary practice) Given by Me for application by all practitioners of the Way of the Heart, you should study the total and progressive sattvic dietary approach communicated in My summaries of Instruction relative to dietary discipline. Likewise, as a further aid to your understanding and evaluation of the by Me Given "Minimum Optimum" dietary discipline, you may do well to study the total tradition, including the modern (or latest) research and experimentation, relative to sattvic (or pure and purifying, rebalancing, and rejuvenating) dietary discipline. Then, if you agree with the sattvic dietary approach I have communicated, and if you are prepared to embrace that discipline as your own, begin the progressive development of the right and optimum diet that is best for your particular constitution (or psycho-physical type), and always vary the diet artfully (but within the range of its basic principles), in response to such factors as climate, the availability of food (and the availability of locally grown food), your level of physical (and mental, and emotional) activity, and your age and stage of life (or the stage of your practice in the Way of the Heart).

*Always practice dietary discipline with appropriate medical advice and supervision, so that the pace, the special requirements, and the results of your dietary discipline can be determined most efficiently and organized most effectively. (*The ego-"I" is the Illusion of Relatedness, *pp. 62-63)*

Diet should be balanced, whole, and moderate so that attention is free for Sustenance in its true form—Communicated through the Form, the Presence, and the State of Sri Da Avabhasa. Where food-taking is appropriately economized and simplified, the body-mind is harmonized and Satsang itself can be enjoyed more deeply. As Sri Da Avabhasa explains in *The ego-"I" is the Illusion of Relatedness:*

The quality and quantity of food largely (or very basically) determines the state and desire and action of the physical body and the sense-mind. If food-taking is intelligently minimized, and if the food selected is both pure and purifying, then the physical body (and even the total mind and the emotional dimension of the being) passes through a spontaneous natural cycle that first shows signs of purification, then rebalancing, and finally, rejuvenation. Therefore, if food-taking is controlled, the physical body itself, including its desires and activities, becomes rather easily (or simply) controllable. . . .

If the dietary (and the total) discipline of the body-mind is right, then (in the Way of the Heart) attention can be more fully (or less resistively) Released to Ishta-Guru-Bhakti, and (thus, by Grace) to My Revelation of the Divine Person. . . . If the dietary discipline of the body-mind and the Devotional feeling-discipline of attention (which discipline corresponds to the tradition of Bhakti Yoga) are right, then all aspects of the gross or frontal personality will be most easily (or most readily) economized and submitted to the Spiritual Process. (pp. 57-58)

Sexuality

(This section was contributed by Anne Henderson.)

I n 1978 Sri Da Avabhasa Wrote:

> *The matter of sexuality is so profoundly structured into our infantile and adolescent adaptations that it persists not only as our most obsessive interest as individuals but also as our most significant and consistent social or interpersonal problem. When I began to enter into relationships with My devotees for the sake of their Spiritual Awakening, it became more and more clear that <u>no</u> <u>one</u> who came to Me was yet prepared for the true Spiritual process, which is total bodily responsibility for Truth or Life itself. Rather, all were essentially trapped in obsessions and problematic orientations to the vital and, particularly, the sexual dimensions of experience. I knew it would be necessary for all first to come to a level of interpersonal and cultural maturity relative to the vital play of life before the Spiritual process could be fully introduced into the adaptive play of their lives.*
>
> *The method of My Teaching Work with My devotees is not common, although there are many traditional or ancient precedents for it. It is not merely a subjective, internal, or even verbal activity, but a matter of intense, full, and total "consideration" of any specific area of experience, in living confrontation with others, until the obvious and Lawful or Divine form and practice of it becomes both clear and necessary.* (Love of the Two-Armed Form, *p. 1)*

Thus, during all the years that Sri Da Avabhasa has associated with His devotees, He has Offered us the most profound Vision of God-Love and has shown us how that sublime Love is the basis of all true human intimacy. He has also Required of us the equally profound ordeal of self-understanding and self-transcendence that is the price of such love—both Divine and human. In other words, He has Demonstrated, in every dimension of human relationships, what human love and human intimacy can be when they are founded in the whole-bodily intuition of God, Reality, or Love.

Imagine for a moment how utterly transformed your life—and the lives of all who associate with you—would be if you lived "in Love". Imagine living your relationships on the basis of being already happy, connected to Love, committed to real intimacy, compassion, feeling, intelligence, and pleasure in relationship, and not at all on the basis of the need for attention, reassurance, and security—dependent, angry, blaming, jealous, and full of doubt that you are loved, or merely coping and bored, promiscuous and unsatisfied.

In order to free His devotees to participate in such love, Sri Da Avabhasa has engaged us in a living examination of our emotional-sexual bondage—an examination of all the ways in which we, as "sexual egos", fail to live a life of true love and true freedom in relationship. To this end and over time, Sri Da Avabhasa has allowed us to explore every "solution" that the ego proposes when confronted with the demands and apparent problems of intimacy and relationship: from celibacy to promiscuity and every kind of conventional arrangement in between, thus providing us with the opportunity to observe, understand, and transcend ourselves in the arena of sexuality. In this manner, the most extraordinarily full and detailed Wisdom-Instruction about human intimacy and sexuality has been generated.

Sri Da Avabhasa has described sexuality as one of humankind's principal alternatives to the process of Divine Self-Realization, and He has tirelessly Helped us to understand and overcome the binding aspects of our sexuality. For example, in 1979, Sri Da Avabhasa addressed the "mood of betrayal" that you will instantly recognize as a part of your own "sexual ego":

SRI DA AVABHASA [addressing a couple]: You try to be true to one another, to have loving, undistracted attention for one another. Yet neither of you is involved with sex as anything but a self-generated, egoically "self-possessed", universal desire—and you cannot confine a universal desire.

This dilemma is an expression of the Narcissistic character, the egoically "self-possessed", self-defensive, vulnerable, threatened personality, the one who knows he can be rejected, that he can suffer from separation, that he can die. That one, that emotional problem, separate from God, feeling alone, feeling threatened altogether, is also involved in sex. That one is you in your unillumined position, and the person with whom you are most intimate is in exactly the same position. He or she too is egoically "self-possessed", trying to protect himself or herself, fearing to love and surrender, fearing the loss of his or her lover, feeling the potential betrayal that the other represents. Thus, in the usual person the motive of sexual love is never fully satisfied or concentrated in a single relationship, and his or her sexual interest remains universal, casual, egoically "self-possessed", and self-

generated, never truly expressed in relationship and never a free impulse, always associated with egoically "self-possessed" or egoically self-possessing fear.

*If you will honestly discuss your sexual relationship, you will find that each of you is fundamentally suffering in the mood of betrayal, of having been betrayed and always feeling that you are about to be betrayed. You will discover in your discussion with one another that both of you in some very essential way are promiscuous characters whose emotional maturity is equal to that of very young, reactive, adolescent, or even infantile personalities. Therefore, you cannot really trust one another, nor do you really trust yourselves altogether. Somehow you sense that love cannot be what this relationship is fundamentally about. (*Compulsory Dancing, *pp. 61-62)*

And, of course, He always Instructs us about the way beyond all of this:

*Therefore, In The Way and Manner Of The Heart, Understand Your Separate and Separative self (As Un-Love) and Transcend Your Separate and Separative self (By Love). And This Is Perfected (Progressively, In The Way and Manner Of The Heart) By Devotional (or self-Transcending and self-Forgetting) Heart-Surrender Of the conditional body-mind To My Bodily (Human) Form, and My Spiritual (and Always Blessing) Presence, and My Very (and Inherently Perfect) State, and, Thus and Thereby, To The Person and The Forms or Characteristics Of The Spiritual, and Transcendental, and Divine, Self. (*The Dawn Horse Testament, *pp. 355-56)*

Through hundreds and hundreds of hours of such "consideration", which has continued, in one form or another, to the present, Sri Da Avabhasa has established a basic discipline for His devotees relative to sexuality (presented in detail, along with a summary of His Wisdom-Teaching about sexuality, in chapter twenty-one of *The Dawn Horse Testament*).

The Free Daist practice of sexuality is regenerative, wholly positive, and sex-transcending—that is, transcending of the motivation to engage in sex for "stress-release and temporary pseudo-happiness", which only strengthens the tendency to meditate upon self. And—as every dimension of functional life is intended to be in the Way of the Heart—our practice of sexuality is a form of self-surrendering and self-forgetting Communion with Sri Da Avabhasa.

The sexual disciplines in the Way of the Heart begin, whether one is sexually active or not, with "consideration" of Sri Da Avabhasa's Wisdom-Teaching relative to the human emotional character (for emotion and sexuality are wedded to one another). This emotional-sexual self-inspection includes coming to an understanding of one's childish and adolescent character patterning, one's motives to release stress and to pleasurize oneself, and one's motive to reject and betray others (and to feel rejected and betrayed). This self-inspection and the real changes in life that it requires, are a process that continues and deepens as one matures in the practice of the Way of the Heart.

In order for this primary "consideration" of one's emotional and sexual character and tendencies to become more and more effective, or revealing, that "consideration" is:

As A General Rule Of Expectation (From The Beginning), To Be Accompanied (or Made Expressive) By The Basic Discipline Of Confining sexual activity To The Circumstance Of emotionally intimate relationship (and, Altogether, Of Devotionally Surrendering, and, Thereby, Relinquishing, Excessive, or Wastefully self-Indulgent, sexual behavior). (The Dawn Horse Testament, *chapter nineteen*)

Practitioners in the Way of the Heart may be sexually active in a committed relationship (whether heterosexual or homosexual), celibate in a committed relationship, or single and celibate.[1] In every case, whether he or she is sexually active or not, the devotee must inspect and transcend the fundamental emotional contraction that is at the root of our usual deluded search for emotional-sexual fulfillment (or the avoidance of sex).

Emotionally intimate relationships in the Way of the Heart are based in the principles of what Sri Da Avabhasa calls "true intimacy". ("True intimacy" can only be practiced in its fullest form by the devotee in the advanced, or Spiritually Awakened, stages of practice and beyond. Nonetheless, all devotees study and apply the principles of "true intimacy" to the degree possible for them.)

"True intimacy" is characterized by active love and steady trust, self-transcending love of one's partner (or partners[2]), the replacement of the idea of ownership of one's partner (and children) with the practice of self-transcending love and the heart-culture of self-understanding and happy self-discipline in relationship to all others. "True intimacy" also requires real and steady relinquishment of egoic independence, all egoic demands, expectations, and complaints, all rituals of rejection, mistrust, and reactivity, and all strategies of depression, and pleasurelessness. Thus, "true intimacy" requires real and steady relinquishment of all limits on love.

With sexuality, as with the practice of discipline altogether, Heart-Master Da Speaks to us from beyond the dispositions of self-denial and self-indulgence. Self-transcending love, rather than the motive to escape from or exploit our bodily life, is the basis of all practice in the Way of the Heart. Here is His most summary Instruction (and the foundation discipline) relative to human loving and human intimacy:

The egoic (or self-Contracted) individual Is (By Virtue Of his or her History, self-Idea, and Lack Of Spiritual, Transcendental, and Divine Realization) Chronically Bound To The Ritual Of Rejection. The emotional (or emotional-sexual) Career Of egoity Tends To Manifest As A Chronic Complaint That Always Says, By Countless Means, "You Do Not Love me." This Abusive Complaint Is Itself The Means Whereby the egoic individual Constantly Enforces his or her Chronic Wanting Need To Reject, Avoid, or Fail To Love others. Indeed, This Complaint Is More Than A Complaint. It Is A self-Image (The Heart-

Sick or self-Pitying and Precious Idea That "I" Is Rejected) and An Angry Act Of Retaliation (Whereby others Are Punished For Not Sufficiently Adoring, pleasurizing, and Immortalizing the Precious ego-"I").

For those who Are Committed To Love (and who Always Commune With The One Who Is Love), Even Rejection By others Is Received and Accepted As A Wound, Not An Insult. Even The Heart-Necessity To Love and To Be Loved Is A Wound. Even The Fullest Realization Of Love Is A Wound That Never Heals.

The egoic Ritual Calls every individual To Defend himself or herself Against The Wounds Of Love and The Wounding Signs Of Un-Love (or egoic self-Contraction) In the daily world. Therefore, . . . The Tendency (Apart From Spiritual Responsibility) Is To Act As If Every Wound (Which Is Simply A Hurt) Is An Insult (or A Reason To Punish).

The Reactive Rituals Of egoity Must Be Released By The self-Transcending (and Then Spiritual) Practice Of Love. This Requires Each and Every Practitioner Of The Way Of The Heart To Observe, Understand, and Relinquish The emotionally Reactive Cycle Of Rejection and Punishment. And The Necessary Prerequisites For Such Relinquishment Are Vulnerability (or The Ability To Feel The Wounds Of Love Without Retaliation), Sensitivity To the other In Love (or The Ability To Sympathetically Observe, Understand, Forgive, Love, and Not Punish or Dissociate From the other In Love), and Love Itself (or The Ability To Love, To Know You Are Loved, To Receive Love, and To Know That Both You and the other, Regardless Of Any Appearance To The Contrary, Are Vulnerable To Love and Heart-Requiring Of Love). . . .

Love Does Not Fail For You When You Are Rejected or Betrayed or Apparently Not Loved. Love Fails For You When You Reject, Betray, and Do Not Love. . . .

Therefore, The Most Direct Way To Know Love In every moment Is To Be Love In every moment.

In The Way Of The Heart, My Devotee Is Founded In This Capability By Virtue Of his or her Constant Communion With Me (and, Thus and Thereby, With The Divine Person, Reality, or Truth). (The Dawn Horse Testament, *pp. 356-59)*

As we have already mentioned, the primary matter of self-understanding in emotional and sexual terms is supported by the confinement of sexuality to an emotionally intimate relationship. In addition, that emotional-sexual "consideration" is supported by the practice of what Sri Da Avabhasa calls "sexual 'conscious exercise'". Because, by tendency, we are self-contracted and self-obsessed, we are unable to love, to be intimate, and to enjoy sexual pleasure—simply, freely, without thought, with full feeling of our whole body. The practice of sexual "conscious exercise" (which develops into the truly Spiritual Yoga of "sexual communion" as practice matures) is the specific discipline that all Free Daists engage when they are sexually active. It is a simple, self-transcending practice that involves heart-feeling, bodily relaxation, internal upward tension at the bodily base, conscious breathing (pranayama), and the control of wandering attention (through fullest bodily participation). Truly practiced, this discipline relieves you of one of the fundamental dilemmas of conventional sex—the apparent dichotomy between desire and love. Thus, to practice sexual "conscious exercise", even as a beginner in the Way of the Heart, is to receive a great Gift, a human realization of whole-bodily love, pleasure, and happiness. The capability to embrace one's lover, bodily and from the heart, radiating love and feeling to one another and beyond the other to the boundless ends of Love's Reach is Sri Da Avabhasa's Gift to all His devotees.

The principal purpose of sexual "conscious exercise" is to conduct the universal etheric energy more fully, freeing energy and attention for greater participation in the whole life of Free Daist practice. Secondarily, sexual "conscious exercise" is a means of bypassing the degenerative effects (both chemical and psychic) of conventional orgasm. Curiously, we are conditioned to believe that conventional orgasm is entirely healthful and even necessary, whereas, in fact,

*This Tendency [to orgasm] Is The Result Of The Reactive Presumption Of Independence, Separateness, and Alienation. It Is Founded On The Psychology Of Betrayal (or Of Rejection, By and Of others). Sexual activity Is Thus Degraded Into a merely organic or lower physical exercise, Engaged For The Sake Of Nothing More Than Stress-Release and Temporary Pseudo-Happiness. (*The Dawn Horse Testament, *p. 319)*

In contrast, the Free Daist practice of sexual "conscious exercise" (or sexual communion) achieves energy-conserving, energy-conducting, and rejuvenative, or regenerative, whole-body orgasm.

Heart-Master Da's truly Heroic struggle to bring His community of devotees to the point of living as "I love you" rather than "You don't love me" is unparalleled. And it is the essential foundation for human, religious, and Spiritual growth. There simply is no true religion and no true Spirituality apart from the human demonstration of and capability for love, whether we are sexually active or not. And to live as love—as "I love you"— is only truly possible if one enjoys the intuition of Consciousness, God, or Reality, which is Sri Da Avabhasa's Gift to all His devotees.

RECOMMENDED READING

"CONSCIOUS EXERCISE"
"Conscious Exercise" and the Transcendental Sun

DIET
The Eating Gorilla Comes in Peace
The ego-"I" is the Illusion of Relatedness, pp. 57-68

SEXUALITY

Love of the Two-Armed Form

The Dawn Horse Testament, chapter 21

The ego-"I" is the Illusion of Relatedness, pp. 68-84

NOTES

1. The practitioner's choice to be sexually active or celibate is made in "consideration" with other devotees. The determination to be made is what will best serve the individual's human and Spiritual development.

2. Sri Da Avabhasa has indicated that in very rare cases, unusually qualified practitioners of the Way of the Heart may be capable of engaging the practice of "true intimacy" with more than one partner at a time. See *The Dawn Horse Testament,* chapter twenty-one, for a full description of "true intimacy".

Sat-Guru-Kripa
The Gift of Blessing

by James Minkin

T*he Sixth Gift Of The Way Of The Heart Is Sat-Guru-Kripa, The By Me Given Gift Of Blessing (and The Gifted Calling, and The By Me Given Capability, To Be Directly Heart-Attracted and Responsively Heart-Moved To, and Into, Progressive Degrees Of Contemplative and Meditative Ecstasy, and, In Due Course, To, and Into, Spiritually Activated Divine Communion, and, Ultimately, To, and Into, Transcendental, Inherently Spiritual, and Necessarily Divine Self-Realization, By Means Of My Direct and Directly Effective Blessing), For I Am The True Heart-Master, The Adept Teacher Of The Heart, The Hridaya-Samartha Sat-Guru, Who Is The Heart Itself.*

Da Avabhasa
The Dawn Horse Testament

When I first saw Sri Da Avabhasa, in late December 1975, I was a naive, nineteen-year-old college sophomore from New York. Although I had read all of Sri Da Avabhasa's published books, as well as some traditional Spiritual literature, I knew very little about the tradition of devotion to the Adept or about the Spiritual Transmission that can be received from the Adept. Thus, I did not know what to expect when I saw Sri Da Avabhasa on my first visit to His Ashram.

It was a celebratory occasion at the Mountain Of Attention Sanctuary in northern California, during which Sri Da Avabhasa sat in the midst of a gathering of several hundred devotees. There was some kind of lively entertainment going on, some humorous skits and a slide show, but, as the minutes went by, I found that I could not keep my attention on the evening's entertainment. All of that paled in comparison with what I enjoyed every time I looked at Sri Da Avabhasa. I simply could not take my eyes off Him, for every time I looked at Him I felt very Happy.

He was Happy! Whether He was laughing or being serious, it was obvious to me that He was truly Happy, profoundly Happy, Happier than anyone I had ever seen before. His eyes were Radiant, and He seemed to be brimming over with Love. All His gestures were a literal dance of Love. To gaze at Him was all I wanted to do in that moment. I felt I could have sat there forever. It was in this manner that I received my first lesson in Guru-devotion and the principle of Heart-Attraction. It was simple.

But that was just the beginning. The very next day, Sat-Guru Da invited His devotees to sit with Him in a formal Darshan occasion in Western Face Cathedral, a large Meditation Hall at the Mountain Of Attention. In this occasion, Sri Da Avabhasa sat in His Chair on a dais at the front of the Hall and Gazed around the room, silently regarding each person who was present. Then, at one point, He looked directly at me. Our eyes met, and I suddenly felt what can best be described as a thin laser beam burn through my brain. This lasted for about a minute, after which He turned to look at the next person. I knew I had experienced some sort of Initiatory phenomenon that was instigated by Sri Da Avabhasa's Gaze, but I did not know exactly what its significance was.

Within a week I was back at college in New York, resuming my studies, and almost immediately a remarkable purification began. I endured what became, for many months, a chronic case of "Shakti fever" that manifested as diarrhea, insomnia, irrational attacks of fear and anxiety, and the loss of almost twenty pounds (which I have never regained). Then, at alternate times, I was overcome with feelings of great Happiness and love that seemed to be pouring into me from every direction, or that arose in my heart as a blissful current that would momentarily intoxicate me, quiet my chronically thinking mind, and throw me into a condition of blissful unknowing. Although I had an intuitive sense that these experiences were the effect of Sri Da Avabhasa's Spiritual Heart-Transmission, the only context in which I could understand them was His published Literature, which I continued to study.

This time of purification lasted full force for about six months, after which I was moved to change my life dramatically. I traveled across the United States and to India, wrote poetry extensively, joined a theatre guild, studied Buddhism, and finally—feeling the utter futility of it all after more than a year and a half of this desperate and empty seeking—I moved to northern California to be with the One Whom I now knew to be my true Sat-Guru. Thus, in the fall of 1977, I became a formal practitioner of the Way of the Heart.

James Minkin has dedicated his life as a devotee of Sri Da Avabhasa to publishing the literature of the Way of the Heart. For the past ten years James has served the Dawn Horse Press as general manager, production coordinator, senior editor, and writer. He presently lives at the Mountain Of Attention Sanctuary.

It was not until I had been a member of the practicing community of Heart-Master Da's devotees for a time that I began to fully understand what had occurred that first weekend in Sri Da Avabhasa's Company. The deep heart-attraction I felt for Him and the "laser beam" that penetrated my brain when He looked in my eyes were both effects of His Spiritual Heart-Transmission. This Transmission, which is the sixth Gift of the Way of the Heart, is Sri Da Avabhasa's Gift of Blessing, or Sat-Guru-Kripa. Also termed Hridaya-Shakti-Kripa, or Hridaya-Shaktipat,[1] it is the supremely Attractive Force that moves, purifies, and, ultimately, Awakens His devotees to the Divine Self-Condition.

Traditionally, an aspiring devotee would willingly go through a great ordeal of purification and preparation <u>before</u> being granted even a moment's Darshan and Spiritual Blessing by a Divinely Awakened Sat-Guru. Now, having been Granted such Darshan and Blessing-Transmission for free—and having observed how unprepared I was for the purification that ensued—I began to understand something about the necessity for such right preparation. I remember reading an Essay by Sri Da Avabhasa, entitled "How to Make Right Use of the Company of the Spiritual Master", which was very Instructive for me at the time. In that Essay Sri Da Avabhasa Says:

The Company of the Spiritual Master should be taken in small, occasional doses, and increased gradually as maturity develops. It is true that proximity to the Radiant Fire of the Spiritual Master can stimulate changes in the body-mind, and even produce temporary exaltation and advanced experiential phenomena of a Yogic or mystical kind. But you cannot bypass your own trial of growth. You must, in any case, fulfill all conditions of practice, adaptation, purification, growth, maturity, and ultimate transformation. The Spiritual Master can quicken you, but the Spiritual Master cannot relieve you of any essential responsibility. (The Enlightenment of the Whole Body, *p. 256)*

Thus, it is only by embracing practice of the Way of the Heart in all its forms, through a real "trial of growth", that we can make greater use of Sri Da Avabhasa's Gift of Blessing.

Nevertheless, Heart-Master Da's Gift of Blessing extends to all beings everywhere, for He is the Divine World-Teacher. I remember hearing a story about a Fijian man named Finiasi, who one day found himself standing outside a building at Sri Love-Anandashram where a Darshan occasion with Sri Da Avabhasa was taking place. From within, a cacophony of sounds could be heard: the ecstatic cries of devotees feeling the overwhelming, Blissful Transmission being Granted by Sri Da Avabhasa on this day. Finiasi turned to a man who was also listening to all of this and said that he finally understood what Sri Da Avabhasa's Work is. It is to Bless everyone. He went on to confess that he feels Heart-Master Da's Blessing every time he sees Him, and that he is moved to tears every time. In that moment, they heard another ecstatic cry from inside. A smile came across Finiasi's face. "Too much love," he said.

Over the years, people have told thousands of Leelas describing how Sri Da Avabhasa's Spiritual Heart-Transmission has affected them. The vast range of phenomena, ordinary and extraordinary, that may be experienced as an effect of Heart-Master Da's Spiritual Heart-Transmission is well documented by practitioners of the Way of the Heart, and (in some respects) similar phenomena have been described in Yogic Spiritual traditions since ancient times. Yet it is important to note that such experiences are never the point of Sri Da Avabhasa's Gift of Blessing. Rather, they are simply signs of His Hridaya-Shakti working in His devotees, purifying them of limitations in countless ways, and drawing them into the open-hearted Attraction that is the basis of the Guru-devotee relationship. Beyond this, Sri Da Avabhasa's Spiritual Heart-Transmission deepens the practitioner's feeling-Contemplation of Him and, ultimately, draws him or her into the seventh stage of life—the Realization of That Which Sri Da Avabhasa Is.

In the "I Am What you Require" section of *The Love-Ananda Gita*, Heart-Master Da describes many signs that may appear as a result of receiving His Spiritual Heart-Transmission, as well as the manner in which such signs progressively deepen as the devotee matures in practice:

> *. . . To the degree that you are sensitive to My Spiritual Heart-Transmission on any day, or in any moment, you will likely experience spontaneous effects of My Spiritual (and Always Blessing) Presence. And there is a wide variety of such experiences. The more immediate and superficial experiences that may arise are spontaneous bodily kriyas and mudras. I Say that these are superficial because they are experienced bodily and are associated with bodily awareness. When My devotee begins spontaneously to experience the effects of My Spiritual (and Always Blessing) Presence, these effects generally are experienced bodily. Beyond kriyas and mudras, other possible spontaneous signs of the reception of My Spiritual (and Always Blessing) Presence include bodily poses, pranayama,[2] dancing, jumping, singing, laughter, unusual facial contortions, weeping, moaning, growling and grunting noises, and all kinds of bodily, emotional, and mental blisses. At a level deeper than the gross body, My devotee may have various spontaneous subtle experiences, such as visual, auditory, and psychic phenomena. The deepest and most profound experiences of all are spontaneous quieting of the mind and spontaneous entering into the depth of self-transcending meditation. Ultimately, meditation transcends awareness not only of body, but also of mind and emotion. All My devotees should understand that there is a progression of the spontaneous effects, or signs, of My Transmission of My Spiritual (and Always Blessing) Presence that leads, progressively, and ultimately, to the Realization of My Samadhi, or Awakening to the seventh, or Divinely Enlightened, stage of life. (pp. 378-79)*

In order to understand the unique nature of the Hridaya-Shaktipat Transmitted in Heart-Master Da's Company, it is useful to look at the traditions of Kundalini Shakti and Kundalini Shaktipat described in many Yogic texts, both of which may manifest extraordinary phenomena in the practitioner similar to those described above. In *The Basket of Tolerance* Sri Da Avabhasa makes a clear distinction between the tradition of Kundalini Shakti, based on do-it-yourself techniques intended to stimulate the energies in the body-mind, and Kundalini Shaktipat, which is the great process of Spiritual Transmission demonstrated in the Guru-devotee tradition.

> *There are actually two distinct (and very different) traditions associated with the cosmically manifested Kundalini Shakti.*
>
> *The first (and most commonly known) tradition associated with the Kundalini Shakti is founded upon the bodily point of view, and it is associated with the <u>ascent</u> of the <u>natural energies</u> of the physical, etheric, and lower mental (or lesser psychic) dimensions of the human body-mind-self. This tradition is, originally, associated with the ancient animistic and shamanistic cultures of mankind, and it developed, over time, via such traditions as Taoism, Hatha Yoga, and the lesser modes of Tantrism.*
>
> *The second (and senior, although less commonly known) tradition associated with the Kundalini Shakti is the tradition of Kundalini Shaktipat, which is the process of the <u>descent</u> and <u>circulation</u> of the cosmically manifested <u>Divine Power</u>. And this tradition is of Divine origin. That is to say, it is not the product of human psycho-physical efforts to achieve the Divine Condition, or any higher knowledge and psycho-physical powers, but it is a phenomenon that has appeared spontaneously, descended from above, Given by the Divine, directly, and Transmitted via various lineages of Yogic Siddha-Masters.[3]*

In another Essay in *The Basket of Tolerance*, Sri Da Avabhasa further elaborates upon this distinction, contrasting the results of submission to the conditional energies of Kundalini Shakti with the ultimate result possible through submission to Kundalini Shaktipat:

> *. . . many traditional and contemporary reports . . . of experiences of the "Kundalini Shakti" type are of the kind that originates solely in the lower, and physiological, and biological context of the human body-mind, and that is limited to the production of phenomenal (and even merely egoic) states, in the context of the body-mind. However, as I have indicated, there is another kind of Energy That (via the process of true Kundalini Shaktipat) may be received from above. . . . And That Energy (if allowed to do <u>Its</u> Work, and completely) would convert, or realign, every part and function of the body-mind to its cosmically manifested Divine Source-Condition (or Matrix-Condition) above the body-mind (and, Ultimately, if It is Revealed Most Perfectly and Most Fully, That Energy would Outshine every part and function of the body-mind in its Transcendental, and Inherently Spiritual, Divine Source, in the right side of the heart, and beyond).*

Thus, the Divine Energy of the most profound, or seventh stage, Spiritual Transmission ultimately leads us to Identification with the Divine Source-Condition, or ultimate Enlightenment Itself.

Spiritual Transmission manifests in a variety of forms, which can be understood on the basis of Sri Da Avabhasa's schema of seven stages of life. What is Transmitted is determined by the stage of life of the Guru, or Spiritual Master, and the point of view that he or she holds. The phenomenal signs associated with the reception of this Transmission by the devotee are dependent upon, or limited by, the capability and stage of life of the devotee receiving the Transmission. Whereas the traditional schools of Kundalini Shakti and Kundalini Shaktipat tend to view such phenomena as an end in themselves, in the Way of the Heart the phenomena experienced as a result of Heart-Master Da's Hridaya-Shakti are simply understood as signs that a process of purification is taking place.

Because Sri Da Avabhasa is a seventh stage Realizer, Transmitting always in this seventh stage orientation, His Blessing Power is Perfect; it is always the seventh stage Transmission, Hridaya-Shaktipat, but it manifests or is received in each individual according to his or her need and ability to use His Gift. Thus, every devotee's experience is unique. Ultimately, Heart-Master Da's Hridaya-Shakti Serves the transition to the seventh stage of life, or Perfect Divine Self-Realization:

> . . . *My own Work of Spiritual Transmission, although it also, secondarily, Manifests via the signs otherwise characteristic of Kundalini Shaktipat, Originates and, primarily, Manifests in and via and at the Heart Itself, prior to all limitations and conditionality. And, Ultimately, My Work of Spiritual Transmission Reveals the Perfectly Subjective Divine Heart, or Self-Existing and Self-Radiant Divine Being Itself.* (*The Basket of Tolerance*)

Only those who are already fully Awake in the seventh stage of life fully receive and utilize Sri Da Avabhasa's unique Hridaya-Shaktipat, Which Sublimes the body-mind and leads, ultimately, towards the Perfect Outshining of conditional manifestation in the "Brightness" of the Divine Self-Condition.

Therefore, the true devotee in the Way of the Heart is not concerned with raising the Kundalini Shakti, or with having experiences of an extraordinary kind. Even though such experiences are freely Given by the Spiritual Force of Sri Da Avabhasa's Hridaya-Shaktipat, the true devotee is Attracted beyond these experiences by His Spiritual Heart-Transmission, Which Outshines all manifested phenomena, and leads His devotees to the Heart Itself.

The Samadhis of the Way of the Heart

Once a devotee moves beyond the beginning or preparatory stages of practice in the Way of the Heart, more sublime experiences and kinds of growth take place, indicating a greater degree of release from identification with the body-mind. As the devotee matures in his or her practice of feeling-Contemplation of Sri Da Avabhasa, the esoteric "anatomy" of the total body-mind, and the Graceful Process of devotional self-surrender to Him, are more and more fully Revealed. This esoteric process has been understood to varying degrees in the traditions of Yoga and Spirituality, but no one has mapped the total psycho-physical circuitry of the body-mind and the entire process of Awakening (which is always granted in the context of the devotional relationship to a Realizer) as clearly and completely as the Divine World-Teacher, Sri Da Avabhasa. His Teaching-Revelation indicates guideposts that the devotee may encounter as his or her practice matures toward Divine Self-Realization. Principal among these guideposts are what He has called the "great Samadhis," which epitomize the "Progressive Degrees Of Contemplative and Meditative Ecstasy" of His Gift of Blessing.

The conditional Samadhis of the Way of the Heart—which are the Samadhis that occur previous to Divine Self-Realization—are the Samadhi of "the Thumbs", Savikalpa Samadhi, fifth stage conditional Nirvikalpa Samadhi, and Jnana Samadhi. At the point of Divine Self-Realization—which indicates the ultimate, Most Perfect Reception of Sri Da Avabhasa's Gift of Blessing—Sahaj Samadhi, the first of the unconditional Samadhis of the seventh stage of life, begins. Beyond Sahaj Samadhi is Moksha-Bhava Samadhi, and finally, Divine Translation, which is the ultimate, most profound Expression of the Divinely Self-Realized Condition.

Although Heart-Master Da has said that it is not necessary or inevitable for all of the conditional Samadhis to be experienced by His devotee in the progress of the Way of the Heart, genuine Samadhis are signs of profound reception of His Spiritual Heart-Transmission. In the Great Tradition of human Spirituality, any one of these Samadhis would be deemed a great prize, crowning a lifetime of Spiritual practice. Yet, in the Way of the Heart, the great Samadhis simply signify profound moments of transition and deepening practice.

In the extraordinary Leelas that follow, the two members of the Da Avabhasa Gurukula Kanyadana Kumari Order—Kanya Samatva Suprithi and Kanya Kaivalya Navaneeta—describe the conditional Samadhis of the Way of the Heart. Although the Kanyas have experienced a full range of countless Spiritual experiences and awakenings in Sri Da Avabhasa's Company, each of the following Leelas focuses on one of the great Samadhis brought about by the Grace of Heart-Master Da.

Following the Kanyas' descriptions of the conditional Samadhis, we include several brief descriptions and accounts by Sri Da Avabhasa of That Which may only be Transmitted beyond words: the ultimate, unconditional Samadhis of Divine Self-Realization.

The first Samadhi typically experienced by the devotee in the Way of the Heart is what Heart-Master Da Love-Ananda calls "the Samadhi of 'the Thumbs'". The experience of "the Thumbs" occurs when the body is invaded by a most forceful descent of the Spirit-Current, felt, as Sri Da Avabhasa describes His own experience in *The Knee of Listening*, "like a mass of gigantic thumbs coming down from above and pressing into some form of myself that was much larger than my physical body". In the fullest form of this experience, the Samadhi of "the Thumbs", the Spirit-Invasion completely descends in the frontal line of the body-mind and enters the spinal line, overwhelming the ordinary human sense of bodily existence, infusing the whole being with intense blissfulness, producing a sense of falling or rotating forward, and releasing the ordinary, confined sense of body, mind, and separate self. Heart-Master Da has indicated that the Samadhi of "the Thumbs" is a "Transitional Samadhi", because it indicates that one's practice is moving beyond concentration in the frontal, or descending, Yoga.[4]

Kanya Samatva Suprithi tells of the Graceful Revelation of this Samadhi in her practice, and how it coincided in a remarkable way with Heart-Master Da Love-Ananda's Teaching-Revelation:

Kanya Samatva Suprithi with Sri Da Avabhasa, Sri Love-Anandashram, 1992

KANYA SAMATVA SUPRITHI: Now this story of my Heart-Master's Grace begins: In mid-1984, I sat in Swoon Of Faith, one of the Meditation Halls at Sri Love-Anandashram, in the early afternoon, shortly after the lunch hour. I was on retreat that day, and this was my third meditation of the day. I spontaneously relaxed beyond my usual state of bodily awareness. I felt readily in touch with Sat-Guru Da's Spiritual (and Always Blessing) Presence, especially in the form of Its descending Current. I felt His descending Spirit-Current flow through the front part of my body fully, without any effort on my part. At the same time, my heart felt radiant, full of love and devotion.

As I yielded myself to the Blissful Energy that was bathing my body, this ecstatic Force seemed to be entering my body through the mouth, forehead, and throat. My head yielded and leaned back to open more fully to this Baptism—the Gift of Heart-Master Da Love-Ananda's Spirit-Blessing.

I had been a devotee of Heart-Master Da Love-Ananda for many years, and I was accustomed to meditation and to feeling Sat-Guru Da's Spirit-Presence, so I felt this all to be natural. But, on this day, the quickness and strength with which I was being moved by Heart-Master Da Love-Ananda's Spirit-Presence was unusual. The descent of His Spirit-Current filled the lower portion of my belly like a cauldron full of water. I then felt the Current turn about at the base of my torso and move up my back and spine with the same Blissful strength and fullness with which it filled and permeated the front of my body. The pleasure of this turnabout from descent to ascent was immense, and I yielded to this without thought. I felt as if I were falling forward, almost as if I were rotating forward. There was no concern about this sensation of falling, just a spontaneous sense of yielding the body. In fact, I had only a very peripheral sense of my body, as if the body were an energy sphere, like an empty shell that radiated energy and light and that was falling or yielding forward spontaneously.

As soon as I noticed how incredibly pleasurable this feeling was, and I was willing to have this experience continue forever, the experience receded and I returned to ordinary bodily awareness again. I felt profoundly grateful. I bowed to Sat-Guru Da's Murti-Form and left the Hall, knowing that I had been touched by a strong Spiritual Blessing.

Through the process of the ascent of the Spirit-Current (and the apparent ascent of attention) via the spinal line to the Ajna Door,[5] the devotee may experience Savikalpa Samadhi. The Sanskrit word "savikalpa" means, literally, "with form", and "Savikalpa Samadhi" is a traditional term used to refer to states of concentration or absorption coincident with the arising of specific Spiritual phenomena.

The primary signs of Savikalpa Samadhi are associated principally with subtle perceptions of touch, vision, or audition, or perhaps, in a secondary manner, with subtle odors and tastes. All kinds of blissful subtle sensations and perceptions may occur, including the most advanced form of Savikalpa Samadhi, an experience known as "Cosmic Consciousness", which occurs when attention ascends to a state of awareness wherein conditional existence is perceived as a Unity in Divine Awareness or Mind. In the Way of the Heart, all experience, even in as sublime a form as Savikalpa Samadhi, is to be transcended through self-surrendering, self-forgetting, and self-transcending feeling-Contemplation of Sri Da Avabhasa.

Kanya Kaivalya Navaneeta has been Blessed with many kinds of experiences of Savikalpa Samadhi throughout her years in Heart-Master Da's Company, as has Kanya Samatva Suprithi. Indeed, the profusion of their experiences would mark them in many traditional sacred circles as advanced mystics, and, in others, as illumined sages. But, as Kanya Navaneeta attests here, in the Way of the Heart such phenomena are received as Sri Da Avabhasa's Gift and are not idolized in themselves.

KANYA KAIVALYA NAVANEETA: In the early months of 1980, I received a very dramatic Gift of Sri Da Avabhasa's Hridaya-Shakti Power, which evoked the Savikalpa Samadhi experience of "Cosmic Consciousness".

I was meditating in Sri Da Avabhasa's physical Company in Free Standing Man, His Residence at Tumomama Sanctuary. In this meditation, I was moved far beyond awareness of the gross physical dimension into a subtle realm of vision. In this subtle-body state, Heart-Master Da appeared to me and took me by the hand. We started flying at light-speed around the universe. This was very pleasurable, but in the context of the vision, it did not seem unusual.

Suddenly, I felt a great intensification of Force and we began to move faster than light-speed, faster than anything present in the conditional realms, gross or subtle.

**Kanya Kaivalya Navaneeta with Sri Da Avabhasa,
Sri Love-Anandashram, 1992**

*Because of the motion of the Sat-Guru,
which was beyond anything manifest,
everything seemed to be pulled into a
vortex of brilliant light of which He was
the Source. Because He was moving so
fast, beyond speed itself, everything else
seemed to stop and stand still, or even
be reversed and turned inside out.*

*An enormous turnabout in the
entire universe took place, in which every-
thing turned directly to Sri Da Avabhasa
in a monumental Burst of Super-
Conscious Being. The Force of the
Universe Itself, the Shakti Herself, and all
Her motion was stopped and brought to
Stillness and Quietude by Heart-Master
Da. He Revealed Himself to me, literally,
as the Master of the Universe.*

*When there was only perfect still-
ness, I regained bodily awareness.
Anticipating my obvious feeling of dis-
orientation, Sri Da Avabhasa squeezed
my hand, gently speaking, "See, there is only Da and Buster (my nickname at the time)
here." Heart-Master Da had restored the vision of His human Form to me, and I held His
Mighty and most tender Hand with overwhelming love and with my life, for I now knew
Whose Hand it was. Devotion to my Divine Beloved Guru is my only means.*

*By Grace of His Transmission, I became sensitized to my Heart-Master as the All-
Pervading Current of Energy Pervading me and everything, and I became immersed in the
ascending motion of His Spirit-Current in my own body-mind. Yet, Sri Da Avabhasa's Sublime
Transmission is not Given merely in order to stimulate experiences—no matter how extraordinary and blissful—for their own sake. Every kind of esoteric revelation and extreme rapture is
awakened by His Spirit-Force, but always in perfect accordance with whatever is required for
each devotee to be drawn beyond experience, purified of the motive of attention itself.*

Beyond Savikalpa Samadhi, or Samadhi with form, is what Sri Da Avabhasa calls "fifth
stage conditional Nirvikalpa Samadhi". "Nirvikalpa" means "without form", and this Samadhi
involves the ascent of attention beyond all conditional manifestation into the formless Matrix
of the Spirit-Current, or Divine Light, infinitely above the world, the body, and the mind.

In the traditions of Yogic and mystical ascent, fifth stage conditional Nirvikalpa
Samadhi (known by many names) is deemed to be Realization itself, the ultimate goal of

all practice. In the Way of the Heart, Sri Da Avabhasa describes this Samadhi as a "transitional experience", one that may initiate, or precede, the devotee's entrance into the ultimate stages of life.

The following Leela by Kanya Samatva Suprithi is a classic and inspiring description of this traditionally prized Samadhi, which was Awakened in her while meditating with Heart-Master Da in July 1989. In her case, the experience of fifth stage conditional Nirvikalpa Samadhi had important transitional significance, as it awakened her to the Witness-Position of Consciousness, free of identification with the gross and subtle dimensions of the body-mind.

KANYA SAMATVA SUPRITHI: I was sitting with Sri Da Avabhasa in a very small Meditation Hall in which I was less than five feet away from the foot of His Chair.

I was in a very relaxed meditative state, and I thought the meditation period was coming to an end. I opened my eyes to see Heart-Master Da sitting with His leg propped up on the Chair and His arm resting on His knee and His head in His hands. He was Gazing around the room—wide-eyed, Sublime, Peaceful—Showering everyone everywhere with His utter Grace and Blessing.

I was aware of the others meditating in the room, and of the strong morning light shining through the curtains behind Heart-Master Da Love-Ananda, Who was sitting in a white Chair. As He was so potently Displaying His Great Samadhi, I knew that meditation was not over, and so I closed my eyes and returned to meditation.

Simultaneously, a brilliant, powerful light seemed to rise out of my solar plexus or heart region and totally engulf the inside of my body at a very rapid speed, so much so that I thought I could hear the cells of my skin crackling and stretching under the profound Yogic force. My body locked into a rigid Yogic posture with the bottoms of my feet glued together, my hands clasped in a classic mudra (with my index fingers and thumbs touching), and my head fell back.

I was pinned to the floor by an overwhelming descending force, like the force of gravity one feels when going down a giant roller coaster. I felt I had become the fiery white light itself and that my body would spontaneously combust. I thought I would literally explode from the inside under this tremendous Yogic force.

Instantly, the energy of the light shot me up out of the body like a rocket, and I was immersed in the white light and a blissfulness that was quite astounding. The profundity of the Bliss was nothing like anything I have ever experienced—infinitely beyond any of the human pleasures that can be attained.

When I reached the point of highest ascent, everything was erased. I had no recall of myself as a persona, no sense of who or where I was, no sense of the room, or of having a past or present life, or a future, or any identity whatsoever. I had no mind anymore with which to register the white light. But it was not as if the light became darkness. All ordinary and extraordinary awareness had dissolved. There was only Bliss, without form and without cause. I do not know how long I remained in this state, but it could have been about twenty minutes.

My return to the body happened as easily and blissfully as my ascent. The first thing that I noticed was a clicking sound that drew my attention back and back and back to bodily consciousness. It was the palate in my throat channel allowing small amounts of air into the body periodically to keep it alive.

As my attention followed the clicking sound, I felt a pleasurable descending force passing down through my head, my throat, and my whole body. It flowed on and on, like a huge waterfall.

Then I understood what had happened, and I opened my eyes to see Heart-Master Da Love-Ananda. But I could not see Him at all. The room was pitch dark, and I was not sitting with the bottoms of my feet together or my hands in a mudra. Rather, I was in a half-lotus posture with my hands gently resting in my lap. There was no white Chair like the one I had seen, there were no curtains in the room, and there was no light. I understood that my physical eyes had never opened at all and that I had been in an extraordinary state even when the experience began. Sri Da Avabhasa had Granted me this entire experience on a subtle plane.

This experience was a testimony to Sri Da Avabhasa's Grace. Without His Grace, I could never have known such Bliss! I was profoundly, unqualifiedly Happy—I was free from the body-mind, I was free of persona, I was free of my past and my future, my relations, everything. I cannot explain to you how Happy it was! It was beyond ear-to-ear-grinning Happiness—it was God-Almighty Happy!

I cannot really explain how Blissful this experience was. I had a certainty in my heart that all beings were moved and moving to the Realization of Consciousness or Happiness, because this is always already their true Condition. And I saw the profound Help we receive from Sri Da Avabhasa to Help us Realize this Happiness.

The event of fifth stage conditional Nirvikalpa Samadhi absolutely confirmed to me that I am not the body-mind and I did not need to identify with the body-mind. At some point, it seemed to me that it was silly to have spent my entire life identified with the body-mind when the body-mind is so humble and so helplessly destined to deteriorate. I saw that I was not this body and that I never had been. It was so clear that my body was just an arbitrary form—it could just as easily have been a plant or a milk bottle. In fact, it was clear I have been born as many other people before appearing as this one. Seeing this, it was obviously unfair to demand that the body define my sense of who I am or fulfill me. It was clear that the body-mind could never meet the requirement I was making on it. It was, in fact, going to die. I felt an extreme sense of freedom, and it occurred to me that I was as if dead—or without the body. I was so far beyond the body that I did not know if I would regain it again, nor did I want to. It was a profoundly free feeling.

I am deeply grateful to Sri Da Avabhasa for the Gift of this experience and for the certainty it initiated in me.

The devotee in the Way of the Heart may, having experienced the Samadhi of "the Thumbs", be Awakened by Grace directly to the Witness-Position of Consciousness Itself, thus bypassing all the Spiritual phenomena of the "ascending Yoga" that characterize the later, or "advanced", phase of the fourth stage of life and the total process of the fifth stage of life. The Awakening to the Witness-Position, however, is an essential Awakening for all devotees in the course of practice leading to Divine Self-Realization. This Awakening to the Witness-Position is the beginning of what Sri Da Avabhasa terms the "ultimate" (or the sixth and the seventh) stages of life, in which the devotee constantly stands free of identification with the body-mind, gross and subtle, and all forms of seeking for psycho-physical experience and knowledge.

Once an individual is Awakened to the Witness-Position, the practice of establishment in and as Consciousness Itself, or what Sri Da Avabhasa calls "The Native Feeling (or Happiness) of Being", becomes increasingly profound. This deepening feeling-Contemplation of and progressive Identification with Sri Da Avabhasa's Very (and Inherently Perfect) State occurs only in the extreme maturity of the developmental stages of the Way of the Heart, immediately previous to full seventh stage Enlightenment Itself. When, in meditative occasions, this Awakening has become so profound that the devotee only inheres in that Deep Well of Conscious Being, temporarily excluding and, thus, not noticing, the body-mind and all conditional worlds, Jnana Samadhi has been Realized.

Such Realization of the Transcendental Ground of Existence has only rarely been clearly documented, even by the greatest Spiritual Realizers of humanity.

In the Way of the Heart, Sri Da Avabhasa has Revealed, Jnana Samadhi will most likely, although not necessarily, precede Sahaj Samadhi, or Perfect Enlightenment.

In the following letter written to Sri Da Avabhasa in October 1991, Kanya Kaivalya Navaneeta describes her experience of both the Witness-Position and Jnana Samadhi, set in the context of her practice in daily life in relationship to Sri Da Avabhasa, Whom she has been Awakened to Worship as the Very (and Inherently Perfect) State of Being, or Consciousness Itself.

Beloved Heart-Master Sri Da Avabhasa,

I place my head at Your Sacred Feet in deepest gratitude for the Gift of Your Hridaya-Shaktipat. Beloved Sri Da Avabhasa, I confess receiving Your Transmission concretely and directly. This Transmission I experience most directly in Your physical Company, in life, and in Darshan and meditation, and it is extremely concrete, tangible, and direct.

Beloved Love-Ananda, several years ago now You Awakened me to the Position of the Witness-Consciousness, and I have never doubted this stance, because You made it totally obvious to me. It is effortless, spontaneous, natural, constant, steady, real, direct, and completely a Gift of Your Grace. This stance requires no "action" on my part, because You have Revealed this as simply the Position in which I already stand and am identified with You as Consciousness Itself, rather than with this body-mind. This Perfect stance was

Awakened only through being drawn into direct feeling-Identification with You by self-surrendering, self-forgetting, and self-transcending feeling-Contemplation of You, wherein Your Very (and Inherently Perfect) State was Revealed as my Prior Condition. What has occurred since that Revelation is no change in the Witness-Position itself, but simply a deeper and deeper entrance into the Contemplation of that Position, such that my attention has become more and more resolved into that position in daily life and meditation. Consciousness Itself, instead of the wandering of attention to objects, is more and more my resort and meditation, even in the midst of life activity.

Through Your Hridaya-Shaktipat, Gurudev, You Reveal Yourself as Consciousness Itself, Standing Prior to all form. Through Your direct Revelation, I locate You as "Atma-Murti",[6] as Consciousness Itself, and You Reveal Your Radiant, Undifferentiated Love-Bliss. Gurudev, I receive You and meditate upon You as "Atma-Murti" in life and in Darshan and in meditation, and through the Grace of this Gift You have Given me, I feel a profound heart-Identification with You that is the foundation and ground of my practice.

In Darshan occasions, Gurudev, You have Drawn me deeply into Your Heart-Current and the heart on the right, which is a deep Love-Blissful Current that I feel as a direct Transmission from You and as You. In Darshan occasions, I have often become only peripherally aware of what occurs in the occasion, because I have been so deeply Drawn into Your Still Form and absolute Purity of Love-Bliss-Consciousness. And in meditation, Sri Gurudev, I am often Drawn beyond any noticing at all of the body-mind through immersion in Your Current of Love-Bliss (in Jnana Samadhi) which moves even beyond the referent in the right side of the heart. Sri Gurudev Love-Ananda, You have Revealed Yourself to me truly as the Divine Person Incarnate. You are my Ishta, Whom I worship and adore. Beloved Love-Ananda, this deep indwelling in You as Conscious Love-Bliss is the greatest joy that I know, and this is truly the heart-mover of my practice. I want only to meditate upon You and become Perfectly Identified with You through Realizing Your State through the transcendence of any sense of "difference". Your Direct Transmission moves me beyond the feeling of relatedness itself into direct Identification with Your Very (and Inherently Perfect) State, and through this process, You Reveal the Oneness of Your bodily (human) Form, Your Spiritual (and Always Blessing) Presence, and Your Very (and Inherently Perfect) State, and You have Revealed to me the extraordinary Vision of Who You Are.

I bow at Your Feet, Beloved Gurudev.

As illustrated by Kanya Kaivalya Navaneeta, Jnana Samadhi is a most profound and uncommon Realization, demonstrating a unique depth of reception of Sri Da Avabhasa's Spiritual Heart-Transmission. It is the last of the conditional Samadhis, beyond which is the Realization of the Divine Self-Condition, or Sahaj Samadhi.

Sahaj Samadhi is the first unconditional Samadhi, which necessarily, and inevitably, appears as the Fulfillment of practice in the Way of the Heart. It is the Divine Self-

Condition enjoyed by all who enter the seventh stage of life. Unlike Jnana Samadhi, it is a permanent Realization, not dependent on or exclusive of any state or condition of the body-mind. In distinguishing Jnana Samadhi from Sahaj Samadhi, Sri Da Avabhasa has said:

SRI DA AVABHASA: When Jnana Samadhi passes without becoming Sahaj Samadhi, that is, when your eyes open and you are not in Sahaj Samadhi, but you are "just me back here again", then the limited conditional personality is regained. Then there is a sense that you are bound again and must exercise yourself, as you did previously, to attain Jnana Samadhi. Even though Jnana Samadhi may occasionally be experienced in the course of one's sadhana, that sadhana must continue until, when the "Eyes Open", the state does not in any way qualify or limit Jnana Samadhi. That is Sahaj Samadhi, in which everything is Recognizable in the Divine. (March 26, 1983)

In His Spiritual Autobiography, *The Knee of Listening*, Sri Da Avabhasa describes His own Awakening to Sahaj Samadhi at the Vedanta Society Temple, in Hollywood, California:

At the Vedanta Society Temple tacit knowledge arose that I am simply the conscious-ness that is Reality. The traditions call it the "Self", "Brahman", identified with no body, realm, or experience, but which is the inherently perfect, unqualified, absolute Reality. I saw that there is nothing to which this nature can be compared, or from which it can be differentiated, or by which it can be epitomized. It does not stand out. It is not the equiva-lent of any specialized, exclusive, or separate spiritual state. It cannot be accomplished, acquired, discovered, remembered, or perfected—since it is inherently perfect, and it is always already the case. (pp. 241-43)

In the following excerpts from His Talks, Sri Da Avabhasa describes the Disposition, and the moment to moment Realization, of One Who has been Awakened to Sahaj Samadhi.

SRI DA AVABHASA: As a matter of ordinary daily existence, the Divinely Enlightened indi-vidual wakes and dreams and sleeps and experiences all kinds of psychic states in any of those conditions. There may be times of relative repose and times of relative activity. There may be times when he or she is just sitting someplace, not involved in anything and not even granting any attention to the body-mind. There may be times when he or she appears to be meditating, but this is only apparently so. In fact, Samadhi is perpetual. (March 26, 1983)

SRI DA AVABHASA: The seventh stage of life is the Realization of Divine Self-Abiding. It is Sahaj Samadhi, the "natural" Samadhi, which is abiding as the Divine Self Prior to the body-mind, Prior to the entire cosmos. The Divine Self is not Situated in the cosmos or in the body-mind. It is Prior to space and time. Therefore, the Yoga of the seventh stage of life is not a matter of manipulating energy or attention relative to the body-mind, or presum-ing yourself to be situated in the heart on the right. It is simple Divine Self-Abiding.

Abiding as the Divine Self is Bliss, Joy, Freedom. To be the Divine Self is Sahaj Samadhi. This Samadhi may be coincident with the arising of conditional events, but conditional events no longer have power to bind. They are transparent, or merely apparent. They are unnecessary. There is no clinging to them. They are what they seem to be, but what they seem to be is nothing but a transparent play upon the Divine Self, and, therefore, from the seventh stage "Point of View", there is no bondage in birth. The Divine Self is always already Free. (January 24, 1983)

Ultimately, in any moment in which the Radiance of Perfect Divine Self-Realization Outshines all objects, so that world, body, mind, and separate self are no longer noticed, the Divine Self-Condition is termed "Moksha-Bhava Samadhi" (or, technically, "Moksha-Bhava-Nirvikalpa Samadhi")—"the Perfectly Liberated State of Divine Existence". Whereas in Sahaj Samadhi the Divine Self, fully Awake, Recognizes all conditions of body, mind, and world as only modifications of Itself, in Moksha-Bhava Samadhi the Radiance of that Divine Consciousness Pervades and Outshines all phenomena so powerfully that the Awakened being ceases, temporarily, even to notice any phenomena at all.

SRI DA AVABHASA: In Sahaj Samadhi the individual is Divinely Free, and the conditionally manifested personality is established in the Self-Existing and Self-Radiant Context of that Divine Freedom. Since the egoic contraction is thus inherently transcended, the conditional being expresses the Love-Bliss of the Divine Reality in all directions, in all relations, under all conditions. Without one's seeking or working to attain them, higher evolutionary or Spiritual powers may spontaneously appear, grow, change, and perhaps pass away again. Just so, the conditional being becomes more and more Full, to the point where its various limits, since they are unnecessary in the Transcendental (and Inherently Spiritual) Divine Being, begin to be Outshined. That is, the conditional being begins to relax and simplify. The mind becomes transparent. The body and the world become less and less defined apart from the "Brightness" of Love-Blissful Divine Being. Therefore, as Sahaj Samadhi continues, incidents of Moksha-Bhava Samadhi may begin to occur. This transitional stage of Sahaj Samadhi is a late phase. And Divine Translation, or Moksha-Bhava Samadhi in death, follows eventually. (March 31, 1981)

The Realization of Moksha-Bhava Samadhi becomes permanent for the individual in the seventh stage of life only at the time of Divine Translation, which generally occurs at the human, bodily death of the Realizer. In *The Dawn Horse Testament*, Heart-Master Da ecstatically describes such Perfect Translation into the Divine, which is the ultimate Destiny of all beings and the cosmos itself, as

. . . The "Bright" Itself, Glorious Beyond Conception, Full, Without The Slightest Absence or Threat, More Than Wonderful, All Delight, Heart-Feeling Without limit, The Unspeakable "Embodiment" Of Joy, God-Great! (pp. 508-509)

There is no doubt that such an "Unspeakable" Realization, "Glorious Beyond Conception", is only possible as a Gift of Blessing from One Who has Realized That Very Condition Himself. Indeed, as Sri Da Avabhasa has said many times, His ultimate Function is to Serve the Divine Translation of all beings and even of the entire cosmos! As He goes on to Proclaim in the same passage:

How Will This Divine Translation Be Accomplished? By Love! Only Submit To Me In Love's Embrace, Attracted Beyond the Separate and Separative self. Therefore, Hear The One Who Is Love. See The One Who Is Love. And Practice In The Heart-Manner I Am Revealing To You In This Testament Of Secrets. (p. 509)

RECOMMENDED READING

The Love-Ananda Gita, Part III: "I Am What you Require", pp. 377-81, 425-53, 480-83.

Divine Distraction, by James Steinberg, Chapter 10, "'The Gift That Is The Heart Itself': Sri Da Avabhasa's Transmission of Hridaya-Shakti", pp. 249-67.

NOTES

1. "Hridaya", in Sanskrit, means "heart". The Sanskrit term "Shakti" connotes the Divinely Manifesting Energy, Spiritual Power, or Life-Current of the Divine Person, and "Shaktipat" means "the descent of the Power". "Kripa", in Sanskrit, means "Grace". Thus, "Hridaya-Shakti-Kripa" and "Hridaya-Shaktipat" mean "the Graceful Power of the Heart", or "the Transmitted Power of the Heart".

2. "Pranayama", in Sanskrit, means restraint or regulation (yama) of life-energy (prana). Pranayama is a technique for balancing, purifying, and intensifying the entire psycho-physical system by controlling the currents of the breath and life-force. Automatic pranayama is spontaneous Yogic breathing that arises involuntarily and has the same purifying effects as the voluntary exercise of such pranayama.

3. "Siddha", in Sanskrit, means "a completed, fulfilled, or perfect one", or "one of perfect accomplishment, or power". In Sri Da Avabhasa's usage, a Siddha-Master is a Transmission-Master of any degree of Spiritual, Transcendental, or Divine Realization and Capability.

4. The frontal, or descending, line of the body-mind conducts the natural life-energy of the cosmos, and (for those who are Spiritually Awakened) the Spirit-Current of Divine Life, in a downwards direction from the head to the base of the body (or the perineal area).

The frontal, or descending, Yoga, as Described by Sri Da Avabhasa, is the process whereby knots and obstructions in the gross, or physical, and energetic dimensions of the body-mind are penetrated, opened, surrendered, and released through the devotee's reception of Heart-Master Da's Spiritual Transmission into the frontal line of the body-mind.

5. The "Ajna Door", also known as the "third eye", "the single eye", or the "mystic eye", is the subtle psychic center, or chakra, located between and behind the eyebrows and associated with the brain core. The awakening of the ajna chakra may give rise to mystical visions and intuitive reflections of other realms of experience within and outside the individual. The ajna chakra governs the higher mind, will, vision, and conception. It is sometimes also referred to as the "Guru's Seat", the psychic center through which the Spiritual Master contacts his or her devotees with his or her Spirit-Baptism or Blessing.

6. In Sanskrit, "atma" means both the individual (or conditional) self and the Divine Self. In Sri Da Avabhasa's term "Atma-Murti", "Atma" indicates the Divine Self, and "Murti" means "Form". Thus, "Atma-Murti" literally means "the Form (Murti) That Is the Divine Self (Atman)".

Sat-Guru-Moksha-Bhava
The Gift of Blessedness

by James Minkin

T*he Seventh (or Completing) Gift Of The Way Of The Heart Is Sat-Guru-Moksha-Bhava, The By Me Given Gift Of Blessedness (or The By Me Given Gift Of Blessed, and, Ultimately, Inherently and Perfectly Liberated, Happiness), Which Is The By Me Given Grace, Realized Only On The Basis Of The Right Present Fulfillment Of Each and All Of The First Six Gifts, and Callings, and Responsibilities Of The Way Of The Heart, To Enjoy, or Fully Feel, The Inherent Freedom Of Heart-Companionship, or Heart-Communion, or Heart-Oneness, or, Ultimately, Heart-Identification With My Inherently Perfectly "Bright" Person (and, Ultimately, With My Inherently Perfectly "Bright", or Transcendental, Inherently Spiritual, and Necessarily Divine, Self-Condition), For I Am The True Heart-Master, The Adept Teacher Of The Heart, The Hridaya-Samartha Sat-Guru, Who Is The Heart Itself.*

Da Avabhasa
The Dawn Horse Testament

One evening in early March 1984, I was invited with about forty others to a small gathering with Sri Da Avabhasa at the Manner of Flowers, His Residence at the Mountain Of Attention. It happened in the midst of the Love of the God-Man celebration that year, during which over 600 people received Sri Da Avabhasa's Darshan for ten straight days in a large tent that had been set up on the Sanctuary. Although I had already attended many formal occasions of Darshan and meditation with Sri Da Avabhasa during this Celebration and was feeling deeply Graced by the Spiritual Heart-Transmission I had already received from Him, I was feeling apprehension about this smaller, less formal occasion. I knew that such gatherings are filled with Heart-Master Da's Blessing-Power, but are at the same time a confrontation with one's egoic tendencies. Thus, as the time of the occasion approached, and we lined the path outside His house, I stood there fearful but excited about the event that was to occur this quiet Thursday evening.

**Sri Da Avabhasa talking with devotees at the Manner of Flowers,
the Mountain Of Attention Sanctuary, 1984**

Soon we were ushered into the main Darshan Hall, and everybody offered gifts at Heart-Master Da's Chair. We sat very close to one another in the small room, hanging on to the edge of our excitement, awaiting the arrival of our Beloved Heart-Master. Then, just as everyone had offered their gifts and was seated, Sri Da Avabhasa entered the room. He looked completely Radiant and Happy, and I instantly felt at ease as His familiar Presence of Happiness and Love filled the room.

For many hours we were swooned by this Love, as our Great Heart-Master spoke to us, answered our questions, and received our praise. Later that evening we watched a slide show and enjoyed refreshments together. And at one point in the evening, my intimate partner, overcome with emotion, whispered to me, "This feels like a room full of lovers." And clearly it was.

Finally, Sri Da Avabhasa sat silently for a few moments, and then, with a gentle tilt of His head, motioned to all of us that it was time to leave. I bowed slowly, savoring for as long as possible the last of this moment in His Company. As devotees began to file out of the room, I stood up.

Suddenly, I noticed that Sri Da Avabhasa, only a few feet away, was gazing straight at me. There was a look of Love on His face that cannot be described in words. I was so disarmed by this intimate Regard that His Name "Da" was literally drawn out of me, spontaneously, as if pulled by a magnet to His Heart. And, as my Heart-Master continued to gaze at me, He responded with His sound of Blessing, "Tcha". Everything seemed to be occurring in slow motion, within a Great Realm of Happiness beyond time and space.

In the next moment I was outside, walking in the cool night air with tears in my eyes, feeling like I had just come home, feeling like I had just been reminded of something I had long forgotten, an intimacy of hearts that only devotees can share. As we walked along the Sanctuary paths to our cars that cool March night, mostly silent in the deep emotion of this wondrous Event, I remember a friend remarking to me, "That's as good as it gets."

The deep heart-Companionship that we felt in that "room full of lovers" was the Gift of Blessedness, Sat-Guru-Moksha-Bhava, or literally, the Gift of Perfectly Liberated Happiness. In that moment of Blessing in Sri Da Avabhasa's Company it was bodily, emotionally, and in every way obvious to me that this heart-intimacy with Him had been Given from the beginning of my relationship with Him. In that moment, I knew again the utter simplicity of His Way of the Heart.

Such simple heart-Communion with Heart-Master Da is Liberated Happiness, which instantly relieves us of the motivated search to attain Happiness, Truth, or Liberation. When Sri Da Avabhasa stepped out of the Vedanta Temple in Hollywood, California, on September 10, 1970, moments after the Great Event that culminated the years of His own Sadhana, the Spiritual history of the world changed. For it was through that Event that the Gift of Perfectly Liberated Happiness became a possibility for all beings, by way of the Graceful excess of Sri Da Avabhasa's own Realization of such Happiness.

A couple of years after His Divine Re-Awakening in the Vedanta Temple, Heart-Master Da told His devotees how this Graceful process, which would be a great Advantage to all beings, began to manifest in Him.

*SRI DA AVABHASA: For years, I would sit down in meditation, and all my own forms would appear, my own mind, my desires, my experience, my suffering, my feeling, my shakti, my this and my that. But, at some point, it all came to an end. There was no thing, nothing there anymore, none of that distracted or interested me. Meditation was perfect, continuous. Then I began to meet those friends who first became involved in this work. And when I would sit down for meditation, there would be more of these things again, all of these thoughts, feelings, this suffering, this dis-ease, disharmony, upsets, suffering, craziness, this pain, these shaktis, all of this, again. But they weren't mine. They were the internal and life qualities of my friends. So I would sit down to meditate, and do the meditation of my friends. When I would feel it all release, their meditation was done. And I began to test it, to see if this meditation went on in some more or less apparent way for these people who were not with me. And I found that this meditation went on with people whom I hadn't even met. People I saw in dreams and visions would show up at the Ashram. So the meditation went on. It was the same meditation I had always done. The same problems were involved, the same subtleties, but the content of the meditation was not mine. (*The Method of the Siddhas, *pp. 269-70)*

By virtue of Sri Da Avabhasa's Divine Enlightenment, the intuition of Perfect Happiness is Given to all His devotees from the very beginning of practice, in any moment in which we give Him our attention. The body-mind may go through years, or even lifetimes, of purification. But, at heart, this Gift of Blessedness may always be received by the devotee through feeling-Contemplation, or heart-Communion, with Sri Da Avabhasa. Indeed, it is only through this heart-Communion that, as Sri Da Avabhasa has said, "I will Do everything". In the Way of the Heart, all growth through the stages of life and practice proceed from this fundamental principle.

Lynn Rosencrans, a devotee from Lake County, California, was Given a clear Revelation of this while she was on retreat at Sri Love-Anandashram in April 1992. She writes:

As I sat in Darshan with Heart-Master Da on this retreat, I would often be drawn into a state of ecstatic Contemplation of Him that was so infinitely blissful and full that every form of seeking and self-effort would completely fall away. All doubt of my self, and of God, and every trace of concern would be dissolved in the ecstasy of this relationship to Him, and I would realize that there was nothing more to be gained, nothing more that I could ever want or need. He Is the Gift and the Realization, and I would swoon in the understanding that to feel Him is to be already Liberated.

I remember one Darshan occasion during which I felt so Happy that I lost all self-involved motivation to "practice". I didn't care about my own movement through the developmental stages of practice or about what stage of life or practice I might reach in this lifetime. All I cared about was Sri Gurudev. I began speaking to Sri Gurudev inaudibly, confessing to Him that I didn't know what Divine Enlightenment was but that all I really wanted was to enjoy the depth of feeling devotion to Him He had awakened in me. I desired nothing beyond what He was Giving me in that moment, and I wept as I thanked Him for already saving my life. I told Him that all I wanted was to sit forever at His Feet, Gazing upon His Most Beautiful Form, Which is the Supreme Gift.

The sufficiency of the bliss realized through Guru-devotion and the Liberation from all seeking that Lynn describes in this confession epitomize the Gift of Blessedness in the Way of the Heart. That Gift frees devotees from their concern about progressing through the stages of life and about any kind of Spiritual "attainment". From the beginning of practice, Heart-Master Da simply Calls all His devotees to heart-intimacy with Him, and to share this heart-intimacy with one another. Thus, Sri Da Avabhasa has indicated that He is the "Heart-Husband" of His devotees, signifying the Heart-Companionship with Him that every devotee must realize through moment to moment heart-submission to Him as the Divine Person.

I never fully understood what Heart-Master Da meant by "Heart-Husband" until I was on retreat in His Company in October 1990. Sitting in a Darshan occasion with Him one afternoon, I literally felt myself drawn to Him as to a lover. I felt so attracted to Him, and so intimate with Him, in a most human and bodily way. It felt perfectly natural and easeful, as if I had always been with Him, always been His lover, and we shared a deep heart-intimacy that surpassed anything in this world. That moment in Heart-Master Da's Company was a Vision in feeling that I will never forget, and it is a Vision that He Grants to His devotees in so many ways. It is the principle of Attraction by which we grow and are purified by the Happiness that He is, free of all seeking. As Sri Da Avabhasa has said:

SRI DA AVABHASA: For My devotee, Salvation is not the seventh stage Realization. Salvation is True Love of the Guru. Ultimately, True Love of the Guru becomes the seventh stage Realization, but if the seventh stage is not your Realization now, to desire the seventh stage Realization is pain and seeking. Do not seek the seventh stage Realization. Contemplate Me. Realization is Given by My Grace, through your feeling-Contemplation of Me.

The Way of the Heart is to give your life to self-surrendering, self-forgetting, and self-transcending feeling-Contemplation of Me, not to indulge in phony, imaginary self-imagery or seeking for self-glorification. The Way of the Heart is Guru-devotion—just that, nothing else. If you can forget your separate and separative self by feeling-Contemplating Me, what remains for you to transcend or to Realize? When you feelingly Contemplate Me truly, you have already transcended your separate and separative self and you have already Realized What is to be Realized.

The ego, however, is a fool, and, like a fool, you do not seem to understand this Message. Consequently, you throw away the Opportunity I Offer you.

All the aspects of practice of the Way of the Heart—the forms of the "conscious process", "conductivity", service, self-discipline, and meditation—are extensions of your True Love of Me, and they are the means whereby you bring the various functions of life into conformity with that Guru-Love. Guru-Love itself is Salvation. Guru-Love is What is to be Realized. (The Hymn Of The True Heart-Master, *"I Am Grace Itself"* section, p. 165)

Countless individuals have, over the years, testified to the primacy of this Heart-Companionship that is felt in Sri Da Avabhasa's Company, or in any moment in which we turn our attention to Him. Nevertheless, Sri Da Avabhasa has pointed out that it is even possible to create an egoic search out of the practice of feeling-Contemplation—we may tend to look for signs of this heart-intimacy in our own body-minds, becoming concerned if such signs are not apparent. For this reason, Heart-Master Da has Given the following Instructions in *The Dawn Horse Testament*, in order to clarify the devotee's responsibility for this heart-relationship with Him.

Turn Your Heart-attention To Me, and Do Not Measure That Turning Relative To Whether Or Not Your mind Stops and You Feel Better. Love Me, and Do Not Measure That Loving Against Whether Or Not You Still Feel Negative emotions and Confusion. Give Your life To Me. Turn bodily To My Bodily (Human) Form. Feel (and Thereby Contemplate) My Bodily (Human) Form, My Spiritual (and Always Blessing) Presence, and My Very (and Inherently Perfect) State At all times. And Do Not Measure That Giving, and That Turning, and That Feeling-Contemplation Against The Measure Of Whether Or Not You Feel pains in Your body.

Therefore, Be Restored To Your Perfect Well-Being By Real Fidelity To Me (and, Thus and Thereby, To The Divine Person, Who Is God, Truth, and Reality). (p. 684)

Several years ago, during a discussion of *The Dawn Horse Testament*, Sri Da Avabhasa was asked what happens in His own Awareness when we turn to Him, and what makes His Grace so immediately available and obvious to us. He replied as follows:

SRI DA AVABHASA: Well, in this Dawn Horse Testament *I am constantly telling you how that relationship works. I have described the Living One. I have Confessed to you that I Am That One. I have told you that the Living One, My Self, is the One Who is modified as all forms, all beings, all worlds. How could I be anything but Intimate with you, then?*

It is only if you think of Me as someone who is separate, as someone who must do something to get in touch with you, that you wonder about how it works in some technical sense. Even in this bodily (human) Form, you see Me Functioning with the Consciousness of the Unity between My Self and everyone. I am constantly experiencing and reflecting the psyches of others directly, without having to go through some sort of Yogic process of inverting My attention and getting a vision. If somebody comes into the room with an ailment, I get it immediately.

We need not add other language, or talk about how the process of our relationship operates at the level of nuclear physics and energy exchanges between brains. How could we ever exhaust that conversation? What is fundamentally so is what I have Confessed to you and what you come to acknowledge and Realize. It is a simple matter. I Am you. Really! And also, paradoxically, I enter into relationship with you, by assuming these conditions. But at the same time that I am associated with these conditions and appear as an individual in this place and moment, I Am the One Who is without conditions.

So what the question comes down to, what it really is, is an expression of doubt. If I Am you, there does not have to be any way it works! There is not any difference between us to need something to work. So I have completely accounted for what you are asking about. It is just that My answer is not satisfying to the egoic mind. Only in the mode of Communion with Me, direct Realization in My Company, would you be satisfied by some of these descriptions. As long as there is that knot in the heart, then What is Great is not perceived, and so you look for signs, structures, to open the heart, to relieve you of yourself so you can see plainly. (October 22, 1984)

Heart-Master Da's paradoxical response to this question reveals the secret of His Perfect Heart-Intimacy with all of us. He is us, from the beginning and always, and He is, therefore, never encumbered by any limitations imposed by time and space and separate self. Thus, to Contemplate Sri Da Avabhasa with feeling reveals His Gift of Blessedness to His devotees in all times and places.

In *The Dawn Horse Testament* Sri Da Avabhasa describes the Gift of Blessedness as: "Heart-Companionship, or Heart-Communion, or Heart-Oneness, or, Ultimately, Heart-

Identification With My Inherently Perfectly 'Bright' Person (and, Ultimately, With My Inherently Perfectly 'Bright', or Transcendental, Inherently Spiritual, and Necessarily Divine, Self-Condition)". In this passage, Heart-Master Da accounts for the various ways that His devotees may experience this Gift of Blessedness through their practice, also indicating a progression or deepening of their reception of this Gift as they mature in practice.

Nevertheless, although one's reception of the Gift of Sat-Guru-Moksha-Bhava does deepen through maturity in practice, one of the principal characteristics of the Gift of Blessedness is that it is Given even from the beginning of practice. The feeling of Heart-Companionship and Heart-Communion with Da Avabhasa commonly confessed by devotees may, at times, even in the beginning stages of practice, be exceeded by the Revelation of Heart-Oneness, and even Heart-Identification, with Sri Da Avabhasa's "Bright" Form.

Wendy Weiss, a devotee who went on retreat in Sri Da Avabhasa's Company in July 1992, gives an example of such Revelation, which occurred for her during a celebration at Sri Love-Anandashram. It was a special event, a performance of sacred music attended by Heart-Master Da. Wendy writes:

As the performance began it became clear to me that Sri Da Avabhasa was the True Offering—that through devotees' attention on Him, He played the music, and He sang the chants, through them. He glanced around the room continuously, regarding the men, the women, and then Giving the musicians and chanters His direct Regard. As each piece began and ended I could feel everyone and everything arising in Him. I was drawn more and more deeply into feeling-Contemplation of Him. My mind fell away, and my heart filled with the endless Love He was Transmitting. The room was filled with this feeling of Love beyond words.

As He sat there before me, I became completely absorbed in Him, even as the performance continued around us. I saw His bodily (human) Form dissolve into Light and become an intense sphere of Light—a Radiating Force of Light that communicated directly to my core that He Is God, the Divine Person Incarnate. In that moment I "knew" beyond all doubt that He had known me from before all time, and that now He had found me again, in this lifetime—and this Revelation broke my heart. Tears streamed down my face, broken-hearted in the Heart-Communication of our eternal relationship, the perfect Oneness that is beyond time and space.

As the occasion continued, Heart-Master Da seemed to absorb my every breath into His Very Being, communicating to me that all of my life was His. And I realized, in that moment, that He was living me and, indeed, that He Is me. I had no reference for myself or for my life—there was only this Consciousness that was Him—which is all Love-Bliss.

I feel eternally Blessed by His Love and this Revelation in His Company. He is the Divine Person Incarnate, my Beloved Heart-Companion, the Secret of the Heart. I bow down at His Feet in Love.

Of course, as with anything Great, there is a price for such a Gift. For as Heart-Master Da indicates, to truly use this Gift of Blessedness the devotee's real response is required. In *The Dawn Horse Testament* Sri Da Avabhasa says that the Gift of Sat-Guru-Moksha-Bhava is "Realized Only On The Basis Of The Right Present Fulfillment Of Each and All Of The First Six Gifts, and Callings, and Responsibilities Of The Way Of The Heart". Although it is true that Sri Da Avabhasa's Gift of Blessedness is always Given, even in profound and extraordinary ways, it is only through the fulfillment of every aspect of real self-transcending practice that the devotee's reception of this Gift can grow.

The Gift of Blessedness, or Sat-Guru-Moksha-Bhava, is, therefore, a mysterious Gift, founded in Heart-Master Da's perpetual Samadhi and Perfect Heart-Identification with all beings. And it is only through such Heart-Identification that Sri Da Avabhasa will Awaken His devotees to the Most Perfect Realization of Who they Are, in Truth. As Kanya Samatva Suprithi confesses:

Sri Da Avabhasa is the Divine in Human Form, and He manifests every Divine Gift for His devotees. Because He is that Pure and that Full of Divine Blessing, the simplest and most complete practice His devotees are Called to is to simply sit in His Company with full faith and allow the Gift of Who He Is to affect them, to influence them, to awaken them Spiritually and devotionally. If you engage this practice, Sri Da Avabhasa will sensitize you to dimensions of your own existence that you were never capable of Realizing before. He will sensitize you, and even ultimately Awaken you, to the Truth of Who you really Are.

May all beings be Blessed to know and receive the sufficiency of this Gift of Perfectly Liberated Happiness Given by the Divine World-Teacher and True Heart-Master, Da Avabhasa (The "Bright").

RECOMMENDED READING

The Hymn Of The True Heart-Master, Prologue: "What Will you Do If you Love Me?", pp. 37-41; Part II: "I Am Grace Itself", pp. 165-69, 330-32.

The Dawn Horse Testament, Epilogue: "Beloved, I Am The Husband Of Man", pp. 687-700.

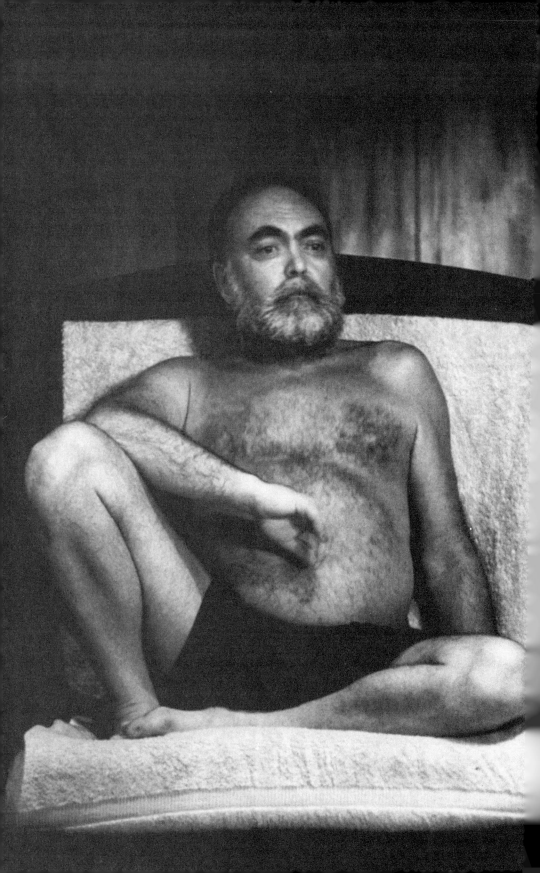

The Progressive Practice in the Way of the Heart

by Carolyn Lee

T he Way of the Heart is Satsang Yoga, the God-Realizing love-relationship with Sri Da Avabhasa. And the Way of the Heart is the Way of "Radical" Understanding, or direct (and, ultimately, Perfect) transcendence of self-contraction. But how does this process mature? How do we transcend our egoic limits and Commune with Sri Da Avabhasa "in the heart's fullness"? There is an unfolding process, described by Sri Da Avabhasa as listening, hearing, seeing, and the "Perfect Practice", that encompasses the entire course of Free Daist practice from our first submission to Him as Guru through Divine Self-Realization.

The Way of the Heart begins with listening, which is the observation and under-standing of ourselves as egoic characters. When, by Sri Da Avabhasa's Grace, we come to a point of most fundamental self-understanding relative to our egoic activity, or con-stant self-contraction, hearing awakens. Hearing spontaneously changes our whole orien-tation to existence. Now we are consistently able to transcend, or stand prior to, the self-contraction. In that open disposition, we become sensitive to greater dimensions of exis-tence, and begin to experience a tangible Infusion of Spirit-Force that is Sri Da Avabhasa's Spirit-Baptism. Now the seeing stages of practice begin, in which we feel and Commune with Sri Da Avabhasa as All-Pervading Spirit-Presence. When Sri Da Avabhasa's Spirit-Blessing has Worked in us to the point where we are no longer identi-fied with body-based and mind-based attachments and desires, we spontaneously assume the Witness-Position of Consciousness and take up the "Perfect Practice". The "Perfect Practice" is the ultimate process of the Way of the Heart, in the course of which Divine Enlightenment, or Most Perfect Awakening to the Divine State of Sri Da Avabhasa, is Given by His Grace.

DA AVABHASA (THE "BRIGHT")
Sri Love-Anandashram, October 1991

I

Listening and Hearing

The Process of self-Observation

L istening in the Way of the Heart is a process of self-observation. It is a progressive process of observing your activity and motivations, of noticing that you are not completely Happy, that you are suffering all the time from a root-feeling of stress. Not only that—you are actually devoting your life to an attempt to conclusively overcome, or camouflage, or escape from this stress. As Sri Da Avabhasa describes:

If any one Will Feel and Examine his or her (psycho-physical) state In any moment, Whether Under the worst Or Under the best Or Under the most ordinary of circumstances, he or she Will Surely Discover That There Is Always A Characteristic Feeling Of Stress, or Dis-ease, or A Motivating Sense Of Dilemma. Therefore, human life (Characteristically Felt As Such Stress, Dis-ease, or Dilemma) Is Also Always Characterized By Struggle, or A Generally Uninspected (and Never Finally Satisfied) Search For Release and Fulfillment.

The usual life Is Always Actively Involved (Whether Consciously Or Unconsciously) In This Motivated Search and This Native Distress. Therefore, every such a one Is Involved In Programs Of Seeking, Via desire, In all kinds of relations and circumstances.

(The Dawn Horse Testament, *p. 102*)

This, clearly, is no ordinary observation! It is a profound and comprehensive statement about the human condition. Sri Da Avabhasa is Writing here (as He always does) from personal experience. He Himself became involved in an intensive process of self-observation during His years in graduate school, when He would carry a clipboard about with Him, writing down every detail that arose to His awareness. Eventually, He began to perceive a controlling force that was shaping His experience. He saw His life as a constant activity of separation or self-contraction from everyone and everything, an activity which He began to describe in terms of the myth of Narcissus, the ancient archetype of self-fascination and the refusal of love.

The discovery of "Narcissus" was not a matter of merely personal significance for Sri Da Avabhasa. He began to see "that same logic operative in all other human beings, and in every living thing, even the very life of the cells and in the energies that surround every living entity or process" (*The Knee of Listening*, p. 60). He understood that everyone was involved in the same "process of separation . . . enclosure and immunity". And so everyone is unhappy! Not because of circumstance (although circumstances can often be difficult), but fundamentally because of this hidden but constant activity of self-separation, or self-contraction. This activity, Sri Da Avabhasa discovered, creates the sense of a separate self, or ego. The ego, then, is not an entity, as we tend to assume, but an activity, a habit.

The Argument may sound simple, but it penetrates to the very root of human suffering. And the process of releasing the habit of egoity is profound. Listening is observing and understanding how you continually contract, or recoil, in the midst of life and relationships. Hearing is coming to the point where you have the capability to transcend the habit of self-contraction as it arises because you have thoroughly observed how you operate as "Narcissus". You have observed yourself to the point where you see the whole picture, your whole life as one activity of self-contraction, and through the force of this self-understanding you simply stop doing it.

Sri Da Avabhasa has described Himself as the "Water" in the pond of "Narcissus", the reflecting mechanism that shows His devotees what they are doing moment to moment. And He is also the Attractive Alternative, the One we see when we look up from the pond. In fact, He has described listening as "The Yoga Of Attention (With Feeling) To Me". Feeling-Contemplation of Sri Da Avabhasa, the heart-felt practice of beholding Him—most often through a photograph of Him, or through the recollection of His Image in the mind—is the "primal setting" for the listening process. The more we feel and Contemplate Sri Da Avabhasa, the more we forget ourselves, and therefore forget the self-contraction. At the same time, the more we Contemplate Him at heart, the more we observe the self-contraction!

Progressive (and, eventually, most fundamental) self-understanding . . . awakens and develops through your feeling-Contemplation of Me. When you feel Me and Contemplate Me, the various forms of self-contraction become evident. When the forms of the self-contraction are noticed, you must practice self-surrendering, self-forgetting, and self-transcending feeling-Contemplation of Me more profoundly. Because you observe all your activity in feeling-Contemplation of Me, you must feel beyond it in order to deepen your practice of feeling-Contemplation of Me. Therefore, feeling-Contemplation of Me is the primal setting in which self-understanding develops, over time. (The Love-Ananda Gita, "I Am What you Require" section, pp. 372-73)

Sometimes the revelation of "Narcissus" Given through feeling-Contemplation of Sri Da Avabhasa can be dramatic, especially when you are Graced to come into His physical Company. I had such an experience myself, right at the beginning of my own practice of listening.

It was July 1986, and I had been a Free Daist practitioner for about six months, when, most unexpectedly, Sri Da Avabhasa arrived in London. He had never before visited His devotees in Europe, and so the excitement was very high. I was living in Ireland at the time as a corresponding student, but I managed to make my way to Holland a week or two later to join English and Dutch practitioners in preparing a place for Sri Da Avabhasa to spend Guru Purnima, the great traditional Feast of the Guru.[1] This was an opportunity beyond my wildest dreams. I had never seen Sri Da Avabhasa, and I imagined it might be many years before I would have the supreme joy of coming into my Guru's physical Company. I had no idea what to expect, but I knew that I was approaching the greatest moment of my life so far.

The place to which we had invited Sri Da Avabhasa was a former Christian monastery in the village of Maria Hoop (pronounced Maria HOPE) in south Holland.[2] It was a vast gray stone building of several stories, all corridors and windows, or so it seemed to me as a member of the cleaning crew! After several days of hectic activity making ready for the arrival of Sri Da Avabhasa (and a few heart-stopping moments when it seemed He would not be coming!), Sri Da Avabhasa's coach drove through the gates.

For two days Sri Da Avabhasa completely devoted Himself to His European devotees—all of them listening devotees, mostly very new ones. For our part we were ecstatic, overcome by His Love and the sweetness of His Attention. On the first day He Spoke to us for more than five hours. I was riveted by Him as He sat beaming in His Chair. He spoke, He joked, He conversed with His devotees, He went over the basic Arguments of His Wisdom-Teaching yet again with great Humor and Compassion. I sat and laughed and looked at Him and listened to Him, forgetting all sense of time and place. I was utterly absorbed by His sheer Attractiveness.

The next day He sat again, this time in complete Silence. For much of the time, His Feet were outstretched so that the soles were clearly visible, and both of His hands were

For years before she encountered Sri Da Avabhasa, Carolyn Lee was a religious and Spiritual seeker, first a Methodist, then a Quaker, and finally a Roman Catholic: "I made a successful career as a professor of music at Cork University in Ireland in the midst of my search for God. But I still wasn't happy. I was sitting on a volcano of unresolved issues in my personal life and I was quietly desperate.

"In that mood I came upon Sri Da Avabhasa one day in 1984. I saw His picture on the cover of The Knee of Listening, *and I intuitively knew that the rest of my life would be about Him. My life began to change very quickly. When the dust settled I found myself in the Editorial Department of the Free Daist Communion, where I have remained for the past five years. Sri Da Avabhasa Transcends all possible descriptions, but He has Given me an unquenchable and ecstatic impulse to keep making the attempt, through words, to celebrate and glorify the Miracle of His Appearance and the Gift of His Way of the Heart."*

held up with the fingers stretched wide apart. His eyes were closed, and His Face Shone with an intensity of Bliss that pressed upon my heart with an almost intolerable pain and joy. Sometimes He seemed so "Bright", so tangibly Transfigured in Light, that it was hard for the eyes to withstand. (Later I felt that His bodily human Form had burned itself literally into the visual cortex of my brain.) At other moments the Light faded, and there was just the fragility and vulnerability of His Body, completely Given up to us, as helpless as a baby. Someone spontaneously broke into a devotional chant, "O Radiant Da, I hold up my hands to Thee!"

But it was not all ecstasy for me. I was chanting and bowing and weeping with everyone else, but much of the time I was

Sri Da Avabhasa at Maria Hoop, 1986

in anguish. For not long after the sitting began, I found myself engulfed in a volcano of emotion. The almost unbearable sight of Sri Da Avabhasa's Love, His overpowering Sign that the Divine is simply Love, simply Sacrifice, triggered something in me that I did not know how to deal with. Spinning through my mind as I sat there was the panorama of my life, revealed as I had never seen it before—nothing but unlove and the refusal of love. The revelation was graphic and comprehensive. All I saw from infancy to the present moment was a drama of fear, betrayal, self-aggrandizement, immunity, and a struggle to win against the next person. And I could feel that I was "programmed" through and through to live like this, with no idea how to stop doing it.

What I was experiencing was a particularly intense form of the phenomenon that Sri Da Avabhasa once described as "sunlight over the well". When the sun shines full into a well, warming the murky depths, then the creepy crawlies, the creatures that live beneath the surface, begin to emerge, inching their way up the sides into the light of day. In the Company of Sri Da Avabhasa something very similar begins to happen. Through the power of His Spiritual Transmission, He touches the hidden places of the heart and reveals the egoic self as it really is.

I was too new a practitioner at that time to appreciate what was happening, how strong the revelation of "Narcissus" can be in Sri Da Avabhasa's Company. Sometimes it was all I could do to quell a blind urge to run from the room. At other moments I was simply distracted by the "Bliss-Wounded" Face of my Guru. Then it seemed to me that He knew what I was feeling, that He knew all about me and everyone present and was not in the least disturbed by it. I am sure that was true. And every moment I had a choice. It was either Him or me. Either I could forget myself in the vision of Him, or I could sit and suffer myself, recoiled from Him, even wishing the occasion would end. At some point it did end. Sri Da Avabhasa opened His eyes, rose from His Chair, wrapped His shawl over His shoulders in a single Graceful gesture, and walked out of the room.

That occasion, for me, was an initiation into listening that I will never forget. Sri Da Avabhasa Gave me a heart-breaking glimpse of Who He Is, and then showed me that I had something to go through before my attention and feeling would be free for Spiritual intimacy with Him. And so I began to involve myself in the disciplines and practices of listening with a great deal of energy and intention, clearly understanding now how much I needed them.

While feeling-Contemplation of Sri Da Avabhasa is the real foundation of listening (and of all Free Daist practice), Sri Da Avabhasa Gives His listening devotees (or beginning practitioners in the Way of the Heart) many disciplines and practices to aid feeling-Contemplation of Him and to activate the process of self-observation. These practices will already be familiar to you, because they derive from Sri Da Avabhasa's Seven Gifts of Grace.

The foundation practices for listening devotees are devotion, service, study, self-discipline, and meditation.

Taken together, these practices represent the first confrontation of the listening process—a conversion from a secular, independent orientation to life in which we are basically looking to fulfill ourselves, to a sacred order of living conformed to the purpose of Perfectly self-transcending God-Realization. I know that if I do not maintain this sacred order of life, the force of the listening process dissipates very quickly, because I lose the thread of feeling-Contemplation of Sri Da Avabhasa, which the whole Way of life that He Gives constantly supports. All the devotional practices—including the twice-daily periods of meditation (which are simply extended periods of formal feeling-Contemplation of Sri Da Avabhasa's Murti-Form), the ecstatic worship of Sri Da Avabhasa in the Sat-Guru Pujas, and the occasions of devotional chanting—all these practices are literal food that continually revitalizes our love and devotion to Sri Da Avabhasa. At the same time, the devotional practices, including meditation, are always reflecting our limits to us—where we are holding back, thinking, distracted, not surrendered.

Service, which is devotion in action, works in a similar way. Our character is clearly reflected to us—our preferences, tendencies, resistances, limitations, self-image, egoic illusions, and so forth!

Along with taking up the devotional practices and service, a listening devotee studies Sri Da Avabhasa's Wisdom-Teaching and the Leelas, or stories, of His Work. Study is very important at all stages of Free Daist practice, but intensive study in the beginning levels of practice is indispensable. Study enlivens self-observation. You often find that as soon as you put down one of Sri Da Avabhasa's books, you walk right into a situation where some form of self-contraction is instantly reflected to you, because your study has sensitized you to your egoic patterns.

Sri Da Avabhasa's Argument about "Narcissus" and "radical" understanding is one of the primary areas of study for listening devotees. Another is "Divine Ignorance", which Sri Da Avabhasa summarizes in His Great Question, "Do 'I' Know What any one or any thing <u>Is</u>?", or, in relation to any thing or event, "What <u>Is</u> it?"

We are bombarded all the time by this or that perception, and our brains are always comparing and categorizing what we perceive. Perhaps you have a soft, warm, furry weight on your lap as you are reading these words. To you, it is obviously a cat. But what <u>is</u> a cat? What is it <u>really</u>, aside from all the descriptions you may come up with? Sri Da Avabhasa makes the point that we can accumulate endless information <u>about</u> things, others, and events, but we do not and cannot know <u>what</u> any thing, other, or event <u>is</u>. In His *Dawn Horse Testament,* Sri Da Avabhasa asks us to take the letter "M", write it a number of times, look at it from every angle, and thoroughly "consider" it:

"Consider" All That You (as the psycho-physical self) experience or know About The Letter "M". Do You (in mind or in body) experience or know <u>What</u> The Letter "M" <u>Is</u>? <u>Is</u>? Altogether and Really <u>Is</u>? No. And What Does This "Consideration" Reveal About You (as the Presumed and Presumptuous body-mind-"I")? Indeed, What <u>Is</u> the body? What <u>Is</u> the mind? What <u>Is</u> "You"? Through Such "Consideration", Feel and Be The Feeling Of This "Ignorance" Itself. That body-Transcending, mind-Transcending, and self-Transcending Feeling-Ignorance Is The Native Intuition Of <u>What</u> <u>Is</u> (and Of The Only One <u>Who</u> <u>Is</u>). (p. 230)

What Sri Da Avabhasa is doing through His "consideration" of Divine Ignorance, and specifically through His question "What <u>Is</u> it?", is leading us beyond the mind that thinks, analyzes, and "knows" to the direct intuition of That Which Inherently Transcends the mind and every form of self-contraction—the Feeling of Being Itself, Which is not an "object" or an experience at all. Even as a listening devotee you are Graced with sudden self-transcending glimpses of this Ultimate Condition, especially as you use the question I have mentioned and other questions that Sri Da Avabhasa Gives to draw you into the state of Divine Ignorance.

Through your study and "consideration" of Sri Da Avabhasa's Arguments about the self-contraction on the one hand and Divine Ignorance on the other, He constantly Instructs you in the basic listening practice (of self-observation and self-understanding), while always pointing you to the Ultimate Condition of Consciousness and Love-Bliss that is to be Realized.

An extension of the practice of study is keeping a daily diary in which you note down how you see yourself animating self-contraction and also record your practice of devotion to Sri Da Avabhasa. Regular meetings with a small group of other listening practitioners offer an opportunity to discuss what you study and to receive the compassionate feedback of the group on how you operate as "Narcissus".

Self-discipline is also fundamental to the listening process. Sri Da Avabhasa's approach to discipline is not based on any motive to self-improvement or to inculcate ordinary self-control in us—He simply Offers us a variety of disciplines, covering every aspect of our lives, as a means to observe ourselves. And so, in addition to a daily schedule of devotional practices and service, listening devotees take up disciplines in the areas of diet, exercise, sexuality, cooperative community living, and so forth. We do this not to eradicate "bad" behavior, or to become a "good" or "better" person but to intensify our involvement in listening and in real self-transcendence.

Through the practice of discipline, and the balance it creates in the body-mind, some of the "rough edges" of one's character or patterns of ill-health may be smoothed out. But from the standpoint of the listening process, this is secondary. Discipline in the Way of the Heart primarily serves to <u>expose</u> the self-contraction again and again, by reflecting to us the depth of resistance, fear, doubt, unlove that we are always tending to dramatize without even knowing we are doing it.

The obligation to fulfill a discipline at a particular moment can create an immediate confrontation. You feel the mechanism of recoil in the body-mind. Rather than do the Hatha Yoga routine that Sri Da Avabhasa Recommends, you would prefer to read a book or eat a sandwich! Rather than get up for early morning meditation, you would rather stay in bed. And so on and on.

But the listening process becomes even more effective when you pass the point of struggling with discipline, and are free simply to observe what arises when you do engage discipline fully. Take, for example, the juice fast or other purifying dietary regime that many devotees engage annually, with medical supervision. In the midst of a fast, you are in a position to observe various reactions in yourself—for example, your profound dependence on the egoic consolation that food provides (beyond its real nutritive function), your addictive attachment to certain favorite foods, and the deep-seated fear of not being sustained.

But the body itself is not about to die after a few days on a juice fast! On the contrary, through judicious fasting, the body is able to purify itself and attain a more healthful and effective level of functioning. The discipline of fasting then allows one to observe the exaggerated (and often hilarious!) subjectivity that is normally masked by one's usual pattern of food-taking—ingenious plans to "cheat", perhaps, or to end the fast early, not to mention a range of reactions to plain boredom and bodily discomfort. At the other extreme, one may become self-satisfied, congratulating oneself on one's improved health and alertness during the fast and on one's ability to maintain it to the end. In other words, the fasting discipline provides a perfect opportunity to observe the self-contraction as it operates around food.

Sri Da Avabhasa makes a useful distinction between real self-observation (which may be stimulated, as we have just seen, in the course of practice) and the mere accumulation of data, or "self-watching":

SRI DA AVABHASA: In a sense you could say that self-observation just happens. It is not an activity of the ego, of your deciding to analyze yourself. Your sadhana in the Way of the Heart is not generated by My prescribing self-observation to you. Rather, it is generated on the basis of your "consideration" of My Wisdom-Teaching, your natural turning to Me as Sat-Guru, your accepting with understanding the life-conditions I have Given for your sake, and your fulfilling those disciplines from hour to hour, making them the form of your relationship to Me. And when such insight appears, it is not in the form, "Oh, shucks! Will you look at that!" That kind of information comes from self-watching. When you find yourself out, that is self-watching. That is data. That is images that you capture about yourself. All such analysis is a natural product of self-watching. It is not self-observation.

The natural product or expression of real self-observation is "radical" insight. Where there is such insight, all the things that you feel bad about on the basis of your self-analysis, or self-watching, are undone. In a moment of real insight, there is no obstruction, there is no bad person. The principle of the ego is always there in the moment of self-watching, but it is not present in the moment of real self-observation. (June 28, 1975)

Listening as a Practice of Feeling

R eal self-observation is based on feeling. In fact, Free Daism as a whole is based on feeling—on feeling-Contemplation of the Divine in the Person of Sri Da Avabhasa, until every limit in the body-mind is felt beyond. And so, right from the beginning, in the early stages of the listening process, a simple feeling-sensitivity develops, a sympathetic awareness of others and things and a sensitivity to the flow of energy, and breath, and feeling in oneself. When pain, tension, disturbance, unlove, fear, sorrow, anger, and all the forms of self-contraction that you observe in body and mind arise, then you simply <u>feel</u> those emotions and sensations, rather than immediately judging or mentalizing about them. And self-understanding is, simply, the capability to <u>feel</u> one's present activity as self-contraction and to feel beyond it.

Sri Da Avabhasa Gives His devotees two forms of practice, both based on feeling, that enable the process of self-observation and self-understanding to grow. These practices, to be used in meditation and randomly throughout the day, Sri Da Avabhasa calls "the Devotional Way of Insight" and "the Devotional Way of Faith". In Offering these two alternative supports to feeling-Contemplation, Sri Da Avabhasa is taking into account our different qualities as individuals. Some of us enter into Heart-Communion with Sri Da Avabhasa more easily through a process of insight into the act of self-contraction itself, while others come to Heart-Communion with Him (and thus to the release of self-contraction) directly through devotion and faith.

For many years Sri Da Avabhasa engaged His devotees in grand experiments with these two approaches to practice—first, His devotees would concentrate on one devotional

Way for a period of time and then He would ask them to engage the other devotional Way. Now He asks each of His listening devotees to conduct his or her own experiment with the two devotional Ways, and find out over time which best serves feeling-Contemplation of Sri Da Avabhasa and the release of self-contraction.

At the end of the first stage of the listening process (the student-beginner stage), during which you are adapting to and stabilizing the various disciplines, you come to a clear choice of one or the other of the devotional Ways, which will (generally) remain your form of practice through the whole listening process and beyond into the hearing and seeing phases of the Way of the Heart.

So how is the process of self-understanding quickened by the two devotional Ways? Here is a simple example. Imagine that you are a listening devotee practicing the Devotional Way of Insight. You notice that you wake up in the morning with a generalized feeling of disturbance and tension. And so you use one of the Great Questions Given by Sri Da Avabhasa, perhaps "Avoiding relationship?"[3]

As you Enquire "Avoiding relationship?" you let yourself feel the stress fully and you "consider" it for a moment—not mentally, as if trying to figure out the cause of the tension, but in your feeling. As you do this, you may feel where the stress is coming from, and how you are the one generating this contraction. In the instant that you feel the knotted feeling to be your own activity you can feel beyond it, surrender it. The effectiveness of "Avoiding relationship?" (or any of the other Great Questions) in helping you to feel beyond un-Happiness in any moment always depends on your devotional relationship to Sri Da Avabhasa in that moment, whether you are feeling towards Him and open to receiving His Grace or whether you are abstracted from Him and wrapped up in your own apparent dilemma. And the effectiveness of this self-Enquiry also increases as the listening process matures until, in the awakening of hearing, you are consistently able to feel beyond self-contraction into "the great space in which the contraction is occurring".[4]

A practitioner of the Devotional Way of Faith listens in a manner that is somewhat simpler and more direct. In any given moment, rather than feeling the self-contraction and feeling beyond it, you simply feel toward Sri Da Avabhasa, perhaps Invoking Him silently through Mantras based on His Divine Names. The practice is to continue to Invoke Sri Da Avabhasa and actively surrender to Him at heart whether or not the stress of self-contraction dissolves in the moment. If this devotional Way is to be effective, the faith of the devotee must be particularly strong.

As Sri Da Avabhasa points out, you cannot surrender what you will not cease to hold. This is why devotion is so important. There is no real capability for self-transcendence until Sri Da Avabhasa and the Happiness that comes from feeling Him is more attractive than the search for self-fulfillment.

Both devotional Ways, as Sri Da Avabhasa emphasizes, involve a process of self-understanding and both depend on faith. A steady faith in Sri Da Avabhasa's Power to

Accomplish the whole process of listening, hearing, and seeing must inspire His devotee from the beginning. He Writes in *The Dawn Horse Testament*:

> *The "Attitude" That Is Fundamental To The Real and True Devotional Practice Of The Way Of The Heart (Whether In The Manner Of The Devotional Way Of Faith Or In The Manner Of The Devotional Way Of Insight) Is That Of The <u>Presumption</u> Of My Victory In Your Own Heart and life. . . . On The Simple Basis Of The Faithful Heart-Response To Me (Constantly Engaged), and In The Context Of Consistent Fulfillment Of My Instructions (and All The Kinds Of Disciplines Required) For Your Particular Practice Of The Way Of The Heart, You Should Simply and Always Feel That All Of That Is Always Already Accomplished (As, Indeed, It Is) By Me, and That All Of That Will Be Revealed (In Due Course) By Grace. (pp. 255-56)*

The Intensive Listening-Hearing Phase

When we have become founded in the faith disposition that Sri Da Avabhasa describes, Attraction to Him has become the strongest force in our life and a clear impulse to Perfectly self-transcending God-Realization has become deeply confirmed.

This great impulse is Sri Da Avabhasa's Gift, and it has nothing to do with the ego. I was overtaken by this impulse one day several years ago while meditating in Mindless Company, the retreatants' Meditation Hall at Sri Love-Anandashram. Suddenly, out of the blue, I was on the floor, fully prostrate, sobbing my heart out, consumed by a desire far stronger than any I had ever felt. Every atom of my being was begging Sri Da Avabhasa for the Grace of absolute, Most Perfect, Divine Self-Realization. Anything less literally felt in that moment to be an intolerable agony of separateness, separateness from Him in His Perfect Samadhi! The intensity of the experience passed, but its influence has remained with me to this day.

When the great impulse to transcend everything in God becomes clarified, you enter into the intensive listening-hearing phase of Free Daist practice. You are engaging the basic disciplines fully and consistently now, moved by your own free motive to renounce the gross habit-patterns of egoity. And so you begin to refine the disciplines, based on the signs you are observing in yourself. You start to find out through experiment what for you is the optimum form of the diet, the optimum amount and type of "conscious exercise", and (if you are sexually active) the frequency of sexual intimacy that both maintains your intimate relationship and frees your energy and attention for practice. None of this is done independently. You receive medical advice from the Radiant Life Clinic and you meet in small groups with other devotees in the same developmental stage of practice (as you have done all along) to make agreements about your practice as a whole.

By now self-observation is becoming acute. While, on the one hand, you are confessing the impulse to Perfectly self-transcending God-Realization, you are also becoming clearly aware of what you represent as a religious idealist, looking to be consoled and pleasurized by "God". You see how you vacillate between childish and adolescent reactions to the feeling of not being completely consoled or loved by others. And you see how this urge to be absolutely fulfilled is expressed in your life through a play of opposing desires—now you think you want one thing, but the moment something else looks more attractive you want that instead. In my own case, I can see this drama of contradictory impulses played out all the way from the most trivial level—like wanting to change my choice of dessert—to serious life-choices, like the choice to be celibate or sexually active.

As listening intensifies you see more and more that what you have always been involved in is a painful and ceaseless round of "Desiring, Doubting, Believing, Manipulating, Betraying, and Always Returning To The Same Distress and Want". And there is nothing you can do about it.

When on retreat some months ago in Sri Love-Anandashram, I saw my expression of this whole drama revealed in brilliant technicolor. The retreat began as a feast of Darshan. I saw my Beloved Guru day after day. Each morning, when He had finished His Writing, Sri Da Avabhasa would come out of His Office, walk into the courtyard of His Residence, and sit in His Chair, with the retreatants and some resident staff at His Feet. I experienced signs of Sri Da Avabhasa's Heart-Transmission, I felt His Happiness Infusing the intimate, timeless scene and spreading out to Infinity, but I also felt a slight stress, a limit in my reception of Him that I could not quite describe. Looking back now, I can see that it was a stress based in the effort of self-presentation, of wanting to look good, and to feel more than I was actually feeling. In other words, my attention was on myself, rather than simply on Sri Da Avabhasa.

This feeling of stress magnified towards the end of my retreat because of a series of letters I had written to Sri Da Avabhasa making affirmations about my practice. I did not feel happy about these letters—I was realizing more and more clearly that my letters to Him were self-glorifying and based on self-delusion about the real state of my practice.

Then, one day, Sri Da Avabhasa unexpectedly called everyone at Sri Love-Anandashram to gather with Him for a question-and-answer session. This was astonishing news, as gatherings of this kind with Sri Da Avabhasa were very unusual. Normally I would have been overjoyed at the prospect of a whole evening with Sri Da Avabhasa, but this time I felt very uneasy. I did not feel in right relationship to Him.

Sri Da Avabhasa's Eyes were Blazing "Bright" from the moment He took His seat. Sometimes He shows His "Beauty Foot", His Soft, Sweet, Maternal Aspect, and sometimes His "Power Foot", the Fiery "Father-Force", which demands and challenges and purifies. This night He certainly felt Fiery to me, but I knew I had to speak to Him—and as soon as possible!

On such occasions as this, devotees who have a real question about their practice—

one that they do not find answered in His Written Wisdom-Teaching—may bring their question to Sri Da Avabhasa. I did not really have such a question, but I thought of one that would at least give me an opening to speak to my Guru. There were about eighty people in the room and a video camera, and yet I scarcely noticed them. There was only Sri Da Avabhasa sitting Radiant and Fierce in His Chair, appearing to fill the whole room, and turning His Gaze full upon me.

I asked my question and He responded, but all the time my heart was breaking. I was standing there uptight, polite, addressing the Mad Avadhoot, the Maha-Siddha[5] Who has no patience with merely social rituals. His Compassion is so Pure, so Fierce that He will do anything to free His devotee from egoic bondage. I knew how desperately I needed His Help in order to go beyond the limit in my practice, but I did not know how to tell Him that. I did not know how to make the confession of "Narcissus" to Him face to Face. I felt I was burning alive.

Sri Da Avabhasa, however, always addresses the devotee and not the apparent question, and before long He was speaking to me very directly. In fact He let loose. He made my confession for me! He Said everything I felt about myself and was afraid to admit—and a great deal more besides! He made fun of the letters I had sent Him, and He called me a phony. He Criticized the persona and the face I present to the world—contented, smiling, ceremonious. He Said I was a nominal practitioner, untrustable, unsurrendered, becoming an "atheist"—or denying the Divine—when I did not get what I wanted. In sum, I was a "jerk"!

When Sri Da Avabhasa made this last Remark, I am told, there was a hint of a smile on His Face. But it was lost on me. I was reeling, both with the Force of His Words—I literally felt He was Purifying me as He Spoke—and with sheer relief at being so exposed to Him, to myself, to everyone.

He had gone right to the core of my persona as "Narcissus", and I could feel myself animating the very qualities He was Addressing right there in front of Him! Although I listened and responded and stayed with Him, thanking Him over and over again in my heart, I could not quite drop my fear-bound personality to the point of falling at His Feet and telling Him how much I loved Him and how grateful I was to Him.

But I did so later, every time I approached His Chair in the Meditation Hall. For Sri Da Avabhasa did not just leave me with an exact summary of my egoic character. He Gave me everything I needed to transcend it. "Activate ecstatic devotion", He Told me many times. "Practice self-forgetting feeling-Contemplation of Me." In the days and weeks that followed, this was the test. On the one hand I felt flattened, as if by a cyclone. He had magnified self-observation in me to such a pitch that I felt everything I said, or did, or thought as sheer phoniness. I had had uncomfortable inklings of this before but now the revelation was in my cells. I was nothing more than a cardboard character, and that was more than humiliating. It was terrifying! All I could do was practice devotion to Sri Da Avabhasa, bodily worship of Him, using every opportunity in the retreatants' devotional occasions and creating more. I memorized short passages from

His Wisdom-Teaching, reciting them as I walked around, and I practiced the Sat-Guru Puja of Full Feeling-Prostrations every day.[6] I felt no egoic satisfaction in this, as I might have done in the past. Devotion to me had become my lifeline, a matter of life or death.

One day, shortly before I was to leave Sri Love-Anandashram, I was walking down the Arrow (the straight path that borders Sri Da Avabhasa's Domain in the Ashram village), and I stopped to bow opposite His house. It was late at night, but I could see a light in one of His windows. He was still up. I just stood there for a long time, mindlessly feeling Him, feeling His Love, and feeling an overflowing gratitude for the Grace of what He had done to crack through my invulnerability and egoic "self-possession".

Since then I have relaxed into a much more real relationship to Sri Da Avabhasa and to life altogether. I feel lighter, more humorous, and the ecstasy of devotional occasions spills over continually into my life. Most important, I have more faith—faith in Sri Da Avabhasa's Power to Liberate me and faith in the listening process.

The revelation of one's "cardboard character" is inevitable and essential. The ego is a fake, a phony. But the ego is only an activity! I see that, I feel that, more than ever before. But for me that insight has yet to become summary, fully effective as hearing. This is the intense, sometimes maddening frustration inherent in the intensive listening-hearing process. The lesson of how you are doing self-contraction is becoming established, and you have a sniff of the release that comes with hearing, but that real heart-freedom has still not awakened.

I do not know what it is going to take in my case for me to get the lesson fully. But I am certain now that the listening ordeal is leading me to a unique kind of intelligence, a most uncommon freedom, the freedom to be a lover, fearless, unconcerned by what comes or goes, at rest in the matchless relationship with my Beloved Guru, Sri Da Avabhasa.

In the final stage of this intensive process of listening, everything in your life starts to converge to induce the crisis of hearing. Devotees who have come to this point meet regularly in small groups to help each other grasp the total "reality picture" of each one's egoic drama, whatever its unique personal design. Your emotional-sexual character, especially, is addressed—tendencies that were set in place in your relationship to your parents (or parenting figures) during infancy and childhood.

Sri Da Avabhasa has pointed out that the basic tendencies that we dramatize in our relationships as adults—such as fear, distrust, the mood of betrayal, dissociation, clinging, aggressiveness, and so forth—originate in a feeling of having been unloved and denied a positive controlling influence in our childhood, especially during our earliest years. This feeling may or may not be justified from an objective point of view, but the facts of what happened in our early life are not the point. Our interpretations, our emotional reactions to what we perceived to be happening to us as infants and children, create our present patterns of emotional-sexual suffering. As long as it remains hidden, this secret script is always undermining our ability to love.

The clearest revelation of our emotional-sexual limits occurs in our sexual intimacies, but the pattern is the same in all our relationships. What we dramatized in relationship to our mother we continue to play out in relation to all women. And the nature of our relation-ship to our father continues to affect our relationships to all men. Thus, practitioners in the Way of the Heart begin to study and "consider" Sri Da Avabhasa's Wisdom in this area from the beginning of the listening process, but it is in the "reality considerations" of the intensive listening-hearing phase that we bring to light, understand, and take responsibility for our whole pattern of emotional-sexual self-contraction. To use an image of Sri Da Avabhasa—any tendency that remains unconscious, unconfessed, keeps you stuck in place, just as the weight of a boat's anchor hidden on the sea floor prevents the boat from steaming ahead.

Whenever you observe something about yourself, you confess it to other devotees who are also involved in the "reality consideration", and you take on a specific discipline to counter the tendency. Right through the listening process, in fact, you add personal disci-plines to the basic ones, but it is in the final phase of listening that these disciplines become particularly crucial and intense—the kind of disciplines that make you sweat because they confront the most basic strategies you have developed to try and survive in life.

For example, if you are a chronic talker, you may be asked to drop all social conver-sation for a period of time so that you can fully feel what is going on underneath your urge to talk. Another devotee, perhaps a type like me who tends to be locked in the mind, and therefore out of touch with the feeling dimension, might be given the discipline to be very devotionally expressive, to shout and sing his or her love for Sri Da Avabhasa at every devotional occasion. The process of serving each other's self-understanding and self-transcendence is a very artful and individual matter.

Whatever your individual reality picture, you begin to see more and more how unloving and destructive your tendencies have been. Nevertheless, the purpose of the discipline is not simply to curb your "anti-social" tendencies (or any other tendencies), but to further sharpen your observation and understanding of what you are always doing to suppress love. Only when you are heart-convicted of your unloving tendencies are you truly moved to self-transcendence through devotional resort to Sri Da Avabhasa:

SRI DA AVABHASA: The process that is the Way of the Heart is always a combination of increased self-discipline and the magnification of self-surrendering, self-forgetting, and self-transcending devotion to Me, actual Communion with Me under all circumstances. Devotion to Me, in fact, is the principal discipline in the Way of the Heart. If you observe some tendency that separates you from Me, you must apply discipline to it, yes, but you must also magnify your devotion to Me under all the circumstances wherein that tendency arises. (August 16, 1991)

The tension created by the reality picture you are getting of yourself as an ego and the sense of being helpless to change any of that creates incredible tapas, or "heat". The only relief from the ordeal of feeling yourself is to feel Sri Da Avabhasa, to forget yourself in His Divine Attractiveness. As hearing approaches, all you want to do is to attend to Sri Da Avabhasa more, to feel Him more, serve Him more, and deal immediately with any impediment to Ishta-Guru-Bhakti. Meditation becomes more effective, the focus of your summary self-observation and self-surrender to Sri Da Avabhasa. And the process of feeling and insight or feeling and faith becomes increasingly the basis of your life and meditation.

Eventually, by His Grace, Sri Da Avabhasa breaks the spell of the ego. June Mori, a devotee in the later phase of the listening process, has described how she came to a profound vision of what she represents as an ego: Although she thought of herself as a "nice" person, one who did not want to see others suffer, she also saw that she did want others to fail, wanted to destroy them, even, for the sake of her own self-glorification. No matter what disciplines, what counter-egoic activity she took on, June could not escape this double-bind. She saw the fruitlessness of all her own efforts to change or deny what was being revealed. Finally, while meditating one day, June had a vision of herself as a shrivelled hag dancing victoriously on a heap of bodies, the bodies of the loved ones she had destroyed, and she felt the incredible momentum of the ego leading her to this destiny. There seemed no way out of this horror, no possibility of self-transcendence—until she looked up at Sri Da Avabhasa, Radiant before her in His Murti-Form. Later she made this moving confession to Sri Da Avabhasa of what then occurred:

JUNE MORI: When I was implicated and confounded by the ego, by my motive to self-glorification and self-survival at the cost of destroying everyone and everything, my devastation was so great, my pain was so great, that I found the impulse to self-transcendence. At that point, I did not know how I would transcend myself. But seeing You right in front of me so Beautiful and Free Attracted me completely, and without my doing anything, you drew my attention more and more to You. And so, by Your Grace and Your Attractiveness, You showed me what self-transcendence is. By putting my attention on You, I was lifted out from the bottom of my egoity. The vision I had of myself was so terrifying. I could see that there was no stopping my movement to harm and destroy others for the sake of my survival and self-glorification. This is my basic motivation as "Narcissus", and I enact all the details of my egoic activity on this basis.

When I saw this, I knew that I really needed help. I started resorting to You more and more, and You have Shown me Who You really Are. You have Shown me that You Are the God that I have been seeking and that all people have been seeking for thousands of years. I do not know why I did not realize this before, but now it is clear. Something has been taken off my eyes and I can see for the first time Who You Are truly. When I realized this, I got so excited. I wanted to jump up and down and run out of the Hall and yell and scream that You Are the One.

The other day when I saw You pass by me in the village, Your bodily (human) Form was so Beautiful to me. My heart broke and I started to cry. I am very grateful for this

Revelation of Who You Are, and I am very excited about this practice. The more I feel You, the more it is clear that my self-contraction is unnecessary.

The whole of the sadhana of listening—even the entire Way of the Heart—is a "reality consideration", a growing understanding of the limited, conditional reality, which makes up our everyday egoic existence, and the Unlimited Divine Reality, which we glimpse through the Grace of Sri Da Avabhasa. Listening is an intense period of time when you come face to face with both realities to the point where you cannot choose the lesser reality anymore, but can only choose the Greater. As Sri Da Avabhasa once Said to a devotee:

SRI DA AVABHASA: You must become intimate with both the conditional reality <u>and</u> the Unconditional Reality, or you cannot hear Me and you cannot see Me and you cannot do the "Perfect Practice". You cannot practice the Way of the Heart, in other words, until you become a lover, until you become intimate with the conditional reality and the Unconditional Reality, both, and receive the Vision of both as they are—the conditional reality inherently limited, and the Unconditional Reality Transcendental, Inherently Spiritual, and Divine. On this basis, faith awakens. Hearing is confessed. The heart shines and comes forward. Not until then. (October 10, 1987)

The Great Grace of Hearing

The culmination of the listening process is hearing, or most fundamental self-understanding. In the event of hearing, the process of self-observation enters a new phase. It is no longer a matter of observing this or that reaction or stressful emotion in the quest for insight. Insight into the ego-"I" has become summary: <u>Whatever</u> one is doing or feeling, be it apparently negative or apparently positive, is felt to arise in the same underlying stress. The self-contraction is seen with a startling clarity as one primal and all-encompassing activity. At the same time, <u>it is clearly voluntary</u>—as voluntary and absurd as the act of deliberately pinching oneself! One intuits this astonishing truth from the beginning of listening, but in the crisis of hearing one becomes certain of it and acquires the capability to transcend that self-contracting activity in any moment.

In the following passage from a Talk He Gave in 1987, Sri Da Avabhasa Explains that when this depth of insight awakens, all struggles and strategies to do anything about the conditional self spontaneously cease.

SRI DA AVABHASA: Self-understanding is not merely a matter of grasping and achieving a superior sense of one element of your character. Self-understanding covers the whole animal. Most fundamental self-understanding, or true hearing, is not characteristic of you until there is fundamental undercutting of the whole structure of egoity.

Understanding of the egoic self must be that profound, and it must cover every aspect of the personality. There can be no blind spots. Once such understanding is realized, whatever arises is without strength.

Most fundamental self-understanding is utterly liberating. It is the revelation of the whole picture of the struggle of egoic self, such that it grants you the capability to transcend that struggle in every moment.

To hear is a single event. You cannot hear a little bit. There are advancing levels of insight in the listening process, but hearing is the ultimate event in that process. The trouble with middling understanding, with merely accumulating self-descriptions, is that thereafter, having gained a certain amount of self-awareness, you oblige yourself to struggle with what you now know about yourself, and you intentionally try to change or let go of certain qualities.

But you cannot do that in any ultimate sense, because the conditional character is self-contraction, always. True hearing realizes this principle most profoundly. True hearing is really the heart's awakening, in which you stand prior to the egoic character. Then the ego is just stuff. You are no longer bound by it. You can stop pinching yourself in the context of the first three stages of life and go on to observe the game of pinching in the fourth, the fifth, and the sixth stages of life.[7]

True hearing is a profound transformation, it is greater than any satori you can either imagine or realize. It is itself a kind of samadhi, if you will. It is an extraordinary realization. When it occurs, you will know it. (May 20, 1987)

In the surrender of the ego-"I" that comes with hearing, the heart "Shines and comes forward". In other words, the heart begins to radiate love, set free (as Sri Da Avabhasa Says) from "the insult of self-contraction". The fullness of the heart flows out into all the relations and conditions of one's existence, and self-transcendence becomes one's moment to moment capability, replacing the old unconscious activity of separation, or avoidance of relationship. Sri Da Avabhasa, the Giver of this miraculous awakening, now Stands as the Victor in the heart of His devotee, arousing boundless devotion and gratitude.

For the first time, there is a joyous capability to release and transcend the self-contraction as it arises. This is the obligation of the hearing phase of practice—to keep exercising the new "muscle" of self-transcendence, as Kanya Kaivalya Navaneeta describes here:

Hearing is like having a new muscle that you have not used before. Previously, you were able to observe the self-contraction and Contemplate Sri Gurudev. But in the event of true hearing, you can feel beyond the self-contraction altogether. The Guru Stands so strong in your heart that that whole motive, the whole motion to distress and action on the basis of it, can be felt and moved beyond.

The Gift of most fundamental self-understanding, or hearing, in the life of any devotee is an epoch-making event. From now on, one's attention is no longer locked into the searches of ordinary life—money, food, sex—nor even in the listener's search for self-understanding. All these searches are no longer one's preoccupation, because the motivating stress behind them can be transcended in any moment.

This is an important point. It is not that the habit of self-contraction suddenly disappears when hearing awakens. Rather, hearing gives one the arms to be <u>responsible</u> for self-contraction, and that responsibility must now be demonstrated. Through the practice of hearing, the separative activity of self-contraction in all its ordinary body-based forms is replaced by self-transcendence, and the body-mind relaxes into a profound natural equanimity.

Kanya Samatva Suprithi relates here the breakthrough of most fundamental self-understanding in her case, and how she then became capable of living differently. Hearing began for her one day when Sri Da Avabhasa questioned her about a slight sulk, a mood of complaint that He detected in her, and which she, at first, denied. Then, in response to His insistence, she confessed her mood and said she was "practicing with it". He Replied, "If you were really practicing, 'it' would not arise".

KANYA SAMATVA SUPRITHI: In that moment, I heard my Guru's Teaching for the first time. I realized fully, for the first time, that the difficulties I persistently brought to life were entirely my own doing. I saw that I was repeating patterns of un-Happiness and failure that I act out habitually, helplessly, and mechanically. I saw that I was caught in a machine of my own creation and I was trapped. All there ever was going to be for me were simply the "highs" and "lows" I would feel, depending on whether the circumstance seemed good to me or seemed bad to me. I thought I was a moral character and I had a kind personality (at least most of the time!), but now I understood that fundamentally my motives were only about my own self-fulfillment. Like Narcissus, I was in love with myself, and I was oblivious to anyone or anything else! I was repulsed, revolted, as I saw myself clearly for the first time.

I also saw that the only real alternative to my suffering stood before me—in the Form of Sri Da Avabhasa—and that I had only to turn to Him and yield to His Grace, apply His Wisdom-Teaching practically, and relinquish my independent, self-made efforts and plans as well as my childish refusal to take responsibility for myself. This understanding effortlessly magnified my resort to Sri Da Avabhasa.

This hearing of Sri Da Avabhasa's Teaching affected the rest of my life. I realized that I could determine my destiny. If I continued to live out my own un-Happy life-habits and egoic character, as I had until now, even as a devotee of Sri Da Avabhasa, I would remain only a beginning practitioner at best. But I had a choice. I could simply and directly choose to conform myself <u>completely</u> to Sri Da Avabhasa and His Wisdom-Teaching.

My choice was obvious. I could not waste any more time. I began to practice the Way of the Heart for real, nothing more and nothing less, from that day on. The more I applied myself to self-transcending devotion to Sri Da Avabhasa, service, self-surrender, and the observation and release of the self-drama, the more I could feel the inherent Happiness that was already present before I superimposed my own activity of recoil and contraction on existence. And I came to Realize that the Inherent Happiness I was Graced to feel was Sri Da Avabhasa Himself, and my devotion to Him magnified tremendously. I found myself to be truly Happy, and I was grateful to Sri Da Avabhasa as the Giver and the Source of this new freedom.

"Come to Me when you are already Happy!" Sri Da Avabhasa said many years ago. For His hearing devotee, these words make perfect sense. When the tendency to collapse upon oneself is consistently released and the native Happiness that transcends the self-contraction is consistently enjoyed, then a great Spiritual conversion can occur. In fact, it is inevitable. One begins to taste Sri Da Avabhasa's Spirit-Baptism, the profound Spiritual Awakening that initiates the seeing stages and prepares you to receive the ultimate Revelations of the "Perfect Practice".

At the end of chapter nineteen of *The Dawn Horse Testament*, Sri Da Avabhasa, with marvelous Eloquence, and in exact detail, Describes and Celebrates what it means to hear Him, and thus become free to see Him:

My Listening Devotee Has Heard Me When The Search For Insight Is Directly (or Feelingly) Released, Fulfilled Beyond Expectation, and No Longer Necessary.

My Listening Devotee Has Heard Me When The Hunger For self-Understanding Is Forgotten In The Feeling Of Relatedness (Feeling Me).

And The Feeling Heart Itself (That Hears Me) Will Soon Be Satisfied, Suddenly, By The Approaching Sight Of The "Bright" and Only One Who Is. (p. 277)

RECOMMENDED READING

The Dawn Horse Testament, especially chapters 3 and 19

NOTES

1. Guru Purnima has been celebrated in India for thousands of years at the full moon (purnima) of the Hindu month of Ashadh. This celebration usually occurs in July in the Western calendar.

2. The former monastery at Maria Hoop, which now houses the principal Free Daist Ashram in Europe.

3. Sri Da Avabhasa Offers to His listening devotees ten Great Questions to be pondered at random in daily life, and also, in the case of devotees practicing the Devotional Way of Insight (see pp. 205–206), to be used in meditation. Some of these Questions are designed to help you observe, understand, and transcend self-contraction, while others, such as the Questions pertaining to Divine Ignorance, particularly serve the direct transcendence of mind. The ten Great Questions are:

> *"What Am 'I' Always Doing?"*
> *"Avoiding Relationship?"*
> *"Who or What Is Always Already The Case (Before 'I' Do Anything At All)?"* or *"Who, What, and Where Is The Inherent Feeling Of Being, or Existence Itself?"*
> *"Am 'I' The One Who Is 'Living' (Animating or Manifesting) me (the body-mind) Now?"*
> *"Who Is 'Living' me Now?"*
> *"How Do 'I' Relate To The One Who 'Lives' me?"*
> *"Do 'I' know What any one or any thing Is?"* or *(In Relation To any particular being, thing, condition, or event that arises) "What Is it?"*
> *"Who, What, and Where Is Inherent Love-Bliss, or Happiness Itself?"*
> *"Who, What, and Where Is Consciousness Itself?"*
> *"What Will 'I' Do If 'I' Love The True Heart-Master and Adept Heart-Teacher, Da Avabhasa (The 'Bright'), Who Is The Divine Person (The One and Self-Existing and Self-Radiant Being That Is Consciousness Itself and Happiness Itself)?"*

(The Dawn Horse Testament, *pp. 247-48)*

4. At the point of hearing, all the Great Questions resolve into the fundamental Question "Avoiding relationship?"

5. "Avadhoot" means one who has "shaken off" or "passed beyond" all worldly attachments and cares, including all motives of detachment (or conventional and otherworldly renunciation), all conventional notions of life and religion, and all seeking for "answers" or "solutions" in the form of conditional experience or knowledge. In Sri Da Avabhasa's case, as a seventh stage Realizer, the sacred title "Avadhoot" indicates His Inherently Perfect Freedom, through His Realization of Identity with the Divine Person, and thus His always Prior Freedom from the binding and deluding power of egoity and all conditional existence.

Maha-Siddha derives from "Maha" meaning "great" and "Siddha" meaning "Perfected" or "Accomplished One". In the Hindu tradition, Adepts of various degrees of Spiritual accomplishment are called "Siddhas". The term Maha-Siddha, as applied to Sri Da Avabhasa, honors His Supreme Realization and Demonstration of the seventh stage of life and His Transmission of Divine Heart-Power—the Love-Bliss of Consciousness Itself—which infinitely exceeds the Shaktipat or Spiritual Transmission of Siddhas of lesser Realization.

6. Performing full bodily prostrations to one's Guru is an ancient traditional practice. In the Way of the Heart, the Full Feeling-Prostration is the act of whole bodily prostration to Sri Da Avabhasa made as an expressive act of devotional surrender to Him. His devotees offer Him this self-transcending act of love and gratitude on occasions of receiving His Darshan either in His bodily (human) Form or in Representational (Murti) Form. The Sat-Guru Puja of Full Feeling-Prostrations is a special Puja, or form of bodily worship, involving repeated Full Feeling-Prostrations, which devotees may perform either formally in groups or individually.

7. Sri Da Avabhasa is referring to the fact that self-understanding is an ongoing process in the Way of the Heart, continuing beyond the point of most fundamental understanding in the body-based levels of experience—which are focused on money, food, and sex—to include insight into Spiritual forms of egoity in the advanced stages of practice, and finally the transcendence of the very root of the self-contraction in the ultimate stages of life.

II

Seeing

Many of the religious and Spiritual paths of humankind speak of the direct reception of Divine Power from an Adept Spirit-Baptizer. Sri Da Avabhasa Writes in *The Basket of Tolerance* of famous examples of Spirit-Baptism, such as the Biblical account of the Spirit of God descending on Jesus in the form of a dove while John the Baptist baptizes him. In the Eastern traditions, He points to the story of Ramakrishna's spontaneous Transmission of Spiritual Power to Vivekananda, drawing him effortlessly beyond bodily consciousness, and Swami Muktananda's confession of receiving Swami Nityananda's Spiritual Transmission, to the point where Swami Muktananda would sometimes feel that his own body had become Swami Nityananda's body.[1] This kind of direct experience of the Spiritual Reality marks the difference between <u>exoteric</u> religious practice—based on beliefs about God and codes of behavior required to win the Grace of God—and truly Spiritual, or <u>esoteric</u>, religion, which involves the real reception of Spiritual Power.

In the Way of the Heart, when the process of listening and hearing is fulfilled, and one has become capable of Communing with Sri Da Avabhasa's tangible Spirit-Presence, the process He calls "seeing" has begun.

SRI DA AVABHASA: Seeing is a whole bodily Realization, like the realization that the body has at the level of touch. Seeing is profound, psychic, prior to bodily and mental configuration. The total being of the body-mind touches the Infinite Divine Being of the Spirit, surrenders into the Divine Spirit with every breath, whole bodily, on the basis of true emotion, or love-surrender. (Compulsory Dancing, *p. 97*)

Kanya Samatva Suprithi describes here how she began to see and feel the Spiritual Presence of Sri Da Avabhasa one day in the course of meditation:

I continued to Contemplate the bodily (human) Form of Sri Da Avabhasa, until it became all that there was, until the feeling of His Blessing consumed my awareness. His Spiritual (and Always Blessing) Presence filled the meditation Hall as if He were there Giving Darshan, pervading my body, the room, even the carpet, the walls and the windows, pressuring everything with His Love-Blissful Presence. Then I realized that His Spirit-Presence not only filled every bit of the meditation Hall, but it occurred to me that I

was myself arising in that Presence. I realized that I was dependent on that Spirit-Presence and that Sri Da Avabhasa was that Spirit and that He was Living me in that very moment. I saw that He Lived and Breathed the being, the awareness, that was "me". And it was obvious that Sri Da Avabhasa did this not only with me, but with every being, every living thing, in fact everything that was manifest—whether it be a table, a rock, a road, a cloud, a tree, a human being, or a car. Everything was existing by the Grace of Sri Da Avabhasa's Spirit-Presence, and everything was pervaded and sustained by That. (The Perfect Alternative, *by Kanya Samatva Suprithi, pp. 43-44)*

In the Way of the Heart, the Spiritual Reality is intuited from the very beginning through one's feeling-Contemplation of Sri Da Avabhasa, Who is always Transmitting Divine Spirit-Blessing. The reception of His Spiritual Heart-Transmission may show itself in unusual and dramatic outward signs, such as sudden jerkings and tremblings of the body (kriyas), spontaneous gestures (mudras), rapid breathing, shouting, laughing, dancing, singing, and animal noises, such as hooting and growling. (These phenomena have been treated in greater detail in the chapter entitled "Sat-Guru-Kripa".)

In themselves, however, such signs are not evidence of true seeing—kriyas, mudras, and so forth may occur randomly at any stage of Free Daist practice. All these phenomena are simply the body's response to the encounter with a superior Energy.

The real process of seeing Awakens only when hearing is true and has done its work of unlocking the heart and establishing equanimity in the body-mind. Until then one cannot be responsible for the Gift of Spirit-Baptism because of the armoring against ecstasy that the self-contraction produces and is. But once the heart opens through most fundamental self-understanding, a change occurs in the depth of one's being. One is converted to love, and there is no longer any barrier to the Infusion of Da Avabhasa's Divine Spirit, Who is Love.

The amazement and gratitude and profound emotion that Sri Da Avabhasa's Spiritual Love-Embrace evokes in His seeing devotees is overwhelming, as Kanya Suprithi describes here:

I felt I was losing my conventional, closed-down mind and my usual sense of social control. I had felt devotion to Sri Da Avabhasa before, but this was really all-encompassing. It was not just that my heart was breaking with love—my whole being, at times, was heaving *with the emotion of love and gratitude, so much gratitude. . . . I was seeing the vision of the Divine before my very eyes.* (The Perfect Alternative, *p. 46)*

This is the Grace of seeing: Sri Da Avabhasa is Revealed as the Divine Person, everywhere Alive as Spirit-Presence, and Infusing one's own body as a tangible Current of Spirit-Force. Seeing is the awakened capability to be sensitive to His Spirit-Presence at all times. Over time, Sri Da Avabhasa's Blessing Current transforms the entire human mechanism.

As a listening devotee, one is devoted to Sri Da Avabhasa as one's beloved Heart-Teacher and Source of Grace in the midst of the ordeal of self-understanding. In the Awakening of seeing, He becomes the Spiritual Intimate, the True Heart-Master of one's heart. And so a new life begins, a life of Divine Communion and Spiritual Intoxication.

The seeds of seeing are planted from the very beginning of the Way of the Heart. One's first sighting of Sri Da Avabhasa in the flesh, even, for some, their first glance at His photograph, stirs the heart-Attraction that later bears fruit as seeing. Seeing, then, is also called "Darshan Yoga", because seeing is a developing response to the Divine Transmission that is always Pouring through Sri Da Avabhasa's bodily (human) Form. As a beginner in the Way of the Heart, one's practice is founded on the feeling-Contemplation of His human Appearance, but then, through Spirit-Baptism, one begins to see, or Commune with Him Spiritually—and a new dimension of practice, which is feeling-Contemplation of His Spiritual (and always Blessing) Presence, becomes one's responsibility. Eventually, even the Blissful Communion with Sri Da Avabhasa's Spiritual Presence yields to a greater Mystery, as feeling-Contemplation of His Spirit-Presence leads to the Revelation of His Divine Condition, or Samadhi. Seeing, then, is fulfilled only in Divine Enlightenment, when the devotee's Identification with the Perfect State of Sri Da Avabhasa becomes absolute. Eventually, even the Blissful Communion with Sri Da Avabhasa's Spiritual Presence yields to a greater Mystery, as feeling-Contemplation of His Spirit-Presence leads to the Revelation of His Divine Condition, or Samadhi. Seeing, then, is fulfilled only in Divine Enlightenment, when the devotee's Identification with the Perfect State of Sri Da Avabhasa becomes absolute.

While Darshan Yoga has its roots in one's first sightings of Sri Da Avabhasa, the formal process of seeing develops by stages, beginning with the would-be-seeing stage of the Way of the Heart. The would-be-seeing stage of practice is devoted to receiving and submitting to Sri Da Avabhasa's Spirit-Baptism until one's Spiritual reception of Him has become stable. Then, in the first actually seeing stage, the real transforming Work of the Spirit-Force begins to take full effect in the body-mind.

The Would-Be-Seeing Stage

In the would-be-seeing stage, Sri Da Avabhasa's Spiritual Infusion is often perceived as a tangible Current moving down the front of the body. His Blessing Power is felt as a "Profound, Most Intense, Love-Blissful Fullness" breaking up the bodily knots of self-contraction and releasing the radiance and love that is natural to us in an uncontracted state.

Becoming capable of consistently receiving and "conducting" this Blissful Force is the practice of the would-be-seeing stage. And it is real work. For how much ecstasy are we ordinarily capable of? Sri Da Avabhasa has sometimes humorously referred to His devotees as "twenty-watt light bulbs", with no capability to conduct greater energy! The secret of receiving Sri Da Avabhasa Spiritually lies in allowing His Spirit-Force to have its way, to Master one's body-mind. The means to ecstasy, as He once Said, is absolute sacrifice of separate self, a complete giving up to God. In *The Dawn Horse Testament*, Sri Da Avabhasa Describes His Sublime Baptism:

Only God Is The One Discovered In This Baptism. I Baptize Or Bless My Devotee With The Self-Radiant Person (or "Bright" Presence) Of God, Truth, or Reality, So That My Devotee Realizes That he or she Is In Perpetual Embrace (At The Heart) with the Divine Person (The Husband Of The Heart) and Spiritually Conformed To Love-Bliss, or Happiness Itself. (p. 312)

The work of the would-be-seeing stage is to surrender body, mind, and emotion into Sri Da Avabhasa's most Attractive Spirit-Presence so that Spiritual Communion with Him becomes constant. But, inevitably, one feels resistance to this degree of surrender. One sees how one tends at times to refuse or diminish Sri Da Avabhasa's Blissful Force through some form of distraction or self-indulgence. But, because one is already founded in most fundamental self-understanding, and profoundly heart-moved by Him, these limits need not take long to transcend. As Sri Da Avabhasa Comments in a Talk on the nature of His Spiritual Presence:

One who has truly entered into feeling-Contemplation of My Spiritual Presence (Itself) is relatively free of the power of events to distract attention. For such a practitioner, feeling-Contemplation of My Spiritual Presence becomes always (progressively) more profound surrender, forgetting, and transcendence of separate (and separative) self. Therefore there is a progressive deepening of meditation. (The Love-Ananda Gita, *"I Am What you Require" section, p. 427)*

The Devotional Way of Insight or the Devotional Way of Faith continues for the devotee in the would-be-seeing stage (and in the mature seeing stages that follow), supporting this deepening process of feeling-Contemplation of Sri Da Avabhasa. Self-Enquiry in the form "Avoiding relationship?" is maintained in the Way of Insight and formally designated Mantras and Prayers are used by devotees in the Way of Faith to constantly restore feeling-attention to Sri Da Avabhasa's Spirit-Presence.

To intensify the process of the would-be-seeing stage, Sri Da Avabhasa recommends that this period of practice be spent in the mode of retreat, maximizing one's time in meditation and devotional occasions, and minimizing (or fasting altogether) entertainments and sexual activity. Through these disciplines the urges of body and mind can relax, leaving one free to concentrate in the Spiritual Communion that exceeds all ordinary pleasures:

SRI DA AVABHASA: God-Communion is the primary bodily pleasure. You tend to feel that to Realize God you must strip yourself of attachments, relations, and enjoyments, rather than giving up your entire body-mind to God. In Truth, God-Communion has nothing to do with conventional self-denial. It is a matter of Outshining your attachments, relations, and enjoyments, through Communion with the Primal Enjoyment. If you are already bodily in a condition of Spiritual enjoyment, then all conditionally manifested enjoyments become superficial, ordinary, conventional processes that are neither overwhelming nor binding. (Compulsory Dancing, p. 59)

When one discovers this truth for oneself in the would-be-seeing stage, discipline becomes a simple matter. One's impulse in the midst of daily life is to do whatever will most serve the Spiritual Process, and not to engage in any action that will retard it. If there is real commitment to Sri Da Avabhasa's Admonitions for this developmental stage of practice, then one's Spiritual reception of Him can stabilize quickly, even in a few weeks.

The First Actually Seeing Stage, or the Frontal Yoga

Each of us is more than a physical body. We are all made up of a vortex of energies, and we create chronic obstructions in the energy flows of our bodies by habits of self-contraction that may go back far beyond our present birth. The work of listening and hearing begins the release of this suffering, but there are deeply buried levels of self-contraction that are undone only when the Divine Spirit-Energy is allowed to infuse and penetrate the whole body. This profound Spiritual alignment of the psycho-physical being takes place in the first actually seeing stage, which allows effective and stable transcendence of all the limits of the first three stages of life.

In its descent down the front of the body, Sri Da Avabhasa's Spirit-Current begins systematically to release the knots, or blocks, associated with the body's main energy centers (which are located along the vertical bodily axis and associated with primary physical organs). (See diagram, p. 232) As one submits to the Work of His Divine Spirit-Presence, the "frontal", or body-based, personality and the body itself are purified and made radiant with Spirit-Life. Sri Da Avabhasa refers to this work of Spiritual submission as the "frontal Yoga".

Kanya Kaivalya Navaneeta gives a remarkable account of her own experience of the frontal Yoga. What she is describing is the next phase of human evolution, the literal transformation of the body-mind through a descent of Spirit-Force so powerful that it can sometimes even feel painful and apparently exceed the body's capability to withstand. The frontal Yoga is an intense affair, but the ordeal is ecstatic. The Calling, always, is to "enlarge the vessel" to submit one's body-mind through devotion to the ever greater reception of Love-Bliss, with full faith in Sri Da Avabhasa, the Perfect Liberator.

Kanya Navaneeta's Leela indicates how study, meditation, and all the disciplines of the Way of the Heart support the Work of the Spirit-Current and become part of a single psycho-physical process of purification and transformation. And she also shows how the process of self-understanding must continue and deepen if the frontal Yoga is to be fruit-ful. Fundamentally, her story is about Ishta-Guru-Bhakti Yoga—a testimony to the degree of intention, submission, and sheer, unwavering attraction to the Guru that must inspire anyone who would complete the transition from body-based existence to the advanced and the ultimate stages of life.

Kanya Navaneeta was Initiated into the first actually seeing stage of practice early in 1988. At the time of her Initiation, Sri Da Avabhasa was Giving Talks on the specific details of what the frontal Yoga involves:

KANYA KAIVALYA NAVANEETA: In the days following my initiation, Sri Gurudev described more of what was going to be required in this new phase of practice, and I began to get the feeling that it was going to be a difficult ordeal. He began to reflect this to me also. He said you must have great strength for the Yoga to fulfill itself, and He also said that you cannot bypass any part of it.

In fact, it was a very, very intense period of practice.

What occurs in the Yoga of seeing is the Spiritualizing of the frontal line through the strength of one's resort to the Guru and one's reliance on His Spirit-Current to transform the body-mind. This is a very profound and difficult process because there are literal psycho-physical knots in the frontal line that occur in everyone just as Sri Da Avabhasa has described. The first knot is in the head, and it manifests as doubt. The next knot, at the throat, suppresses life-energy, and the next, at the heart, suppresses love. Then come the knots associated with deep-seated anger, sorrow, and fear, located (respectively) at the navel, the sexual center, and the bodily base. (See diagram, p. 232)

At one point in His Talks at this time, Sri Da Avabhasa described the process of "breaking the navel". By that He meant opening the vital center of the body, located in the region of the navel, to His Spirit-Force. Every single one of the knots has to be opened, and they have to be opened in a sequential process. The navel, for example, cannot be opened before the head, because Sri Da Avabhasa's Spirit-Current literally moves down the front of the body as though it were moving down a copper tube. It must be able to move all the way down without obstructions.

I remember feeling about this phase of practice the way I had felt about the listen-ing process—that it was just impossible, that hearing was never going to occur. My egoic tendencies as a listening devotee seemed completely fixed and impossible to transcend.

Now these knots in the frontal line (that were being revealed as the psycho-physical root of all emotional reactivity) felt equally fixed and chronic. It seemed to me that they would never loosen, that they would never be opened by Grace, that I was literally going to be doing this Yoga for the rest of my life.

Nevertheless, the Infusion of Sri Da Avabhasa's Spirit-Current during this time was a very real process for me. In meditation, the pressure of His Descent was so forceful that it had a quality of pain to it. I would experience His Spirit-Force moving into my body at the cellular level, literally. I felt His Force opening and purifying the cells, breaking and cracking open the knots of my body-mind. And, with the Force of Sri Da Avabhasa's Spirit-Current, came a strong sense of light. This Force that I felt in meditation with Sri Da Avabhasa I also felt permeating everything. I became very sensitized to Him as an All-Pervading Presence.

At the same time, I was also studying the technicalities of the full practice of seeing. I was continuing with the Way of Insight (established in the listening stage), now in the manner Given for seeing devotees, and assuming full responsibility for conducting Sri Da Avabhasa's Spirit-Current—specifically allowing the Spirit-Force to descend fully down the front of the body. I was also practicing the Prayer of Changes in its Spiritually-Awakened form.[2] As a result of all these practices, I began to become even more sensitized to the knots in the frontal line.

From birth, I had had certain physical liabilities that I could now feel to be a part of these knots, or obstructions, that were being purified by Sri Da Avabhasa's Spirit-Force. It was not really surprising, then, that very soon I found myself catapulted into a health crisis. This healing purification, which went on for quite a time, was part of the whole process of the frontal Yoga for me. Annoying though it was, it was a necessity. There was no way to escape it.

But this crisis was more than a bodily purification. It was actually the perfect mechanism for the confrontation with fear, sorrow, and anger, the root emotions that have to be dealt with in the frontal Yoga. The confrontation with your own physical disabilities and sense of mortality is, first of all, a supreme reflector of fear, the fear of death and loss of the body altogether. And this confrontation with one's mortality also brings up sorrow, which is fear of separation. The fear of separation became very stark for me, because, during the healing retreat that I entered into during this time, I was in a situation where I was actually physically separated from Sri Da Avabhasa for a period of about a month. This separation, in fact, was perfect for my Spiritual practice, because I had to come to the point of feeling and resorting to Sri Da Avabhasa's Spirit-Presence alone, releasing my fear in the face of physical separation from Him.

Not only was I confronting fear of physical death, the falling apart of the body, and physical separation from my beloved Guru, I was also angry at having to endure these annoying physical disturbances. In other words, I was angry with my physical condition itself, which I could not control in any way. So I was caught in the clench of the three lowest knots of the frontal line, corresponding to fear, sorrow, and anger, the most basic and primitive emotions of the body-mind. There was nothing I could do to make it all disappear magically or mystically, no way out but relying on the Guru. I just had to continue with my disciplined health regime, and allow the Spiritual process that was occurring in the midst of it to do its Work and reveal the lesson.

This whole process of the frontal Yoga is one of <u>truly</u> entering into faith such that you let the Spirit-Current Live you. And sometimes the Work of the Spirit-Current manifests in ways that are difficult. There is a literal burning up of karmas taking place, and you have to endure the tapas, or heat, of the process. As Sri Da Avabhasa said to me at one point—I had to let God ruin my life.

Soon after I had passed through the bodily purification, Sri Gurudev Gave me the name "Dinkananda". He was pointing to a presumption of smallness and insignificance, a "dinky" quality in me, which was part of the whole strategy that had necessitated my health regime—I was chronically suppressing the life-force itself. Sri Da Avabhasa told me that I had not developed the frontal personality even as much as an ordinary person. Everything was contracted at the frontal line; I had shrunk myself down to "Dinkananda" level.

There is a second meaning to "dinky", which is "genuine", or "authentic", but this meaning, Sri Da Avabhasa said, was not true of me presently because I had developed such a finely-honed social personality. And that, He said, was all I was. There was not even any real character underneath my social personality. I was just "a fake, imitative, duplicative, and replicative personality"! This was very disgusting to me. And so Sri Da Avabhasa Admonished me to "be somebody", to open up the frontal being and actually become authentic and "large", rather than diminutive.

As time went on, I began feeling a great intensification in my meditation and in my capability to receive Sri Da Avabhasa. I felt an Awakening of the subtler dimensions of the heart[3] and an overwhelming feeling of heart-effulgence in Sri Da Avabhasa's Company. With this heart-radiance came a very tangible sense of His Spirit-Presence, and I understood why He describes His Spirit-Presence as literally <u>Him</u>. His Spirit-Presence is not to be confused with any of its effects in the body-mind. His Spirit-Presence is directly, literally Him.[4]

So I felt this quickening process occurring, but I noticed that my whole character as a social personality was still right there, not Spiritualized in the slightest, or so it seemed. I noticed this in my relationships with people and in my service. To myself I still appeared as thick as mud. One thing that Sri Da Avabhasa has said about the frontal Yoga is that every meditation must infuse itself into life, and then life must be used as preparation for meditation. I could feel Sri Gurudev's Infusion going on in meditation, but it was not carrying over sufficiently into my life. And, by the same token, I felt I was not preparing myself in life well enough to make use of what I was receiving in meditation.

This weakness of not incarnating strongly in life eventually precipitated a crisis when one of Sri Da Avabhasa's cats, which was under my care, disappeared somewhere into the jungle, and I was afraid to tell Him. This was a real failure in my service to Him, not simply because the cat was lost, but, more seriously, because I had held back from informing Him for a day (hoping that the cat would be found) and had thus prevented Him from putting

His Attention on the cat at a time of possible danger. The cat, by the way, was known as a trickster, and Sri Da Avabhasa enjoyed him enormously. Sri Da Avabhasa had named the cat Ghastly in appreciation of his devilish, wild, and ridiculous qualities.

Ghastly did not reappear, and when Sri Da Avabhasa found out He was absolutely furious that I had not told Him earlier, and He immediately sent me out of His physical Company on an indefinite period of retreat in the Ashram village. I called this retreat the "Ghastly retreat", because it was a difficult ordeal!

While I was on retreat, Sri Da Avabhasa Graciously Gave me these Instructions:

SRI DA AVABHASA: The first actually seeing stage of the Way of the Heart must affect the body-mind. It is not abstract. At this stage, you must do the real sadhana of disciplining the body-mind and submitting it to the Spirit-Current, so that you change via the body-mind's submission. Therefore, this developmental stage of practice is a Yoga of the frontal line whereby you work the Spirit-Current from crown to bodily base, thereby releasing the tendencies of the body and the mind. Then you must incarnate that released condition by changing what you do in your daily life. In other words, you show that the Yoga has worked by disciplining the body-mind in daily life. (April 15, 1989)

Through the lesson of the Ghastly incident and the Grace of this retreat, I began to understand what Sri Da Avabhasa was saying, and the moment came when He called me back from retreat and told me it was time to demonstrate what I had learned, in life, and in my normal circumstance of service to Him and His Gurukula.

So then began the final phases of the frontal Yoga, which had to do with my under-standing two things that I was doing. First, in meditation I was seeking a state of complete unawareness of the body-mind. But in daily life I was doing the exact opposite. I was attempting to <u>perfect</u> the body-mind, to fully incarnate in life, to become a perfect ego and have all the centers of the body be completely open and glowing and radiant! So I was working heavily on these two motives—to absolutely cease to notice the body-mind <u>and</u> to absolutely perfect it. Obviously these motives were in total contradiction to one another. Both were absolutely impossible, and neither of them had the slightest thing to do with the Way of the Heart or any Instruction that Sri Da Avabhasa had ever Given me![5] But I was still very seriously and intensely involved in both of these in my life and meditation.

I was doing all this with such fierceness because I wanted to grow in my practice! And so Sri Da Avabhasa, by His Grace, revealed to me what I was doing, to the point where I could understand and release both of these absurd motives. And then my life and my meditation did truly start to change. I began to feel and even manifest the signs of the maturity of the first actually seeing stage.

Sri Da Avabhasa describes how, first of all, in this Yoga, practice is a matter of really identifying and becoming sensitized to all the obstructions in the frontal line and often going through regimes of discipline that allow His Love-Bliss to permeate the being.

Then there is the middle phase of this Yoga, where that Love-Bliss is available to you but you still keep diminishing It in different ways, as I described in my own case.

Then, after Sri Da Avabhasa miraculously revealed the struggle with opposing motives that I was involved in, He Showed me the mature phase of the frontal Yoga. I began to feel His Love-Blissful Presence stably, so that, more and more, the tendencies that were diminishing Love-Bliss would feel like water. They would just fall away, and I would feel the openness of my frontal line with Sri Da Avabhasa's Spirit-Current in full descent—and also the beginnings of the ascent of the Spirit-Current into the spinal line.[6]

Now I felt miraculously free of concern about growing in practice and became very Happy simply to feel my dependence on Sri Da Avabhasa. I realized that my point of maturity in practice made no difference to Him whatsoever. The only thing that mattered was my resort to Him and my dependence on Him and my faith in Him. I could also feel a Happiness and humor about circumstances and things and tendencies in myself that I had previously taken quite seriously. Instead of all my former concern, there was joy, the joy of feeling the Guru and of feeling Him living me. This knowledge became more and more steady and certain and Happy, because it was not just about me. I could feel Sri Da Avabhasa's All-Pervading Presence literally moving and working in everyone and everything.

The entire process I have described took exactly a year and a half in my case. And it occurred completely by Grace. It was nothing I could have done or willed into being. Never in a million years could I have predicted what actually occurred moment by moment. The process was spontaneously Given by my Guru, Da Love-Ananda Hridayam.

And that is the secret: Sri Da Avabhasa Gives you everything, often by very mysterious means. All the devotee has to do is to participate with Him, always being grateful for the process, however it may be manifesting in any moment, however bizarre or difficult it may seem to be. It is your faith in Him that allows Him to move through you and with you.

The Process of Spiritual Ascent

I n his famous life-story, *Autobiography of a Yogi*, published after he came to the West, the Indian Adept Paramahansa Yogananda (1893-1952) relates with great verve the many fascinating encounters he had in India in his youth with Yogis proficient in all manner of mystical and subtle powers. Among other Adepts, he writes of a "saint with two bodies", a "levitating saint", and a "perfume Swami" who could manifest delightful perfumes at will. Based on such popular stories about Indian Yogis and Christian saints, most people, if asked to say what they would regard as a sure sign of Spiritual advancement, would probably mention mystical or supernatural experience or powers of some kind. Sri Da Avabhasa used to tease His devotees about this presumption with comments like, "Don't you think if you were really being religious you would be seeing things by now?"

In the Yogic tradition, lights, visions, and other subtle sensory phenomena and unusual psychic powers are all valued as signs of Spiritual accomplishment. Yogananda's book is a classic of its kind, putting forth the traditional Yogic point of view that Enlightenment is some kind of Divine vision or exalted state attained at the end of the mystical path. If intense inward concentration is pursued (usually under the guidance of a Guru), the Yogic process may culminate in visionary experiences such as a white light, the subtle appearance of deities, or a vision called the "blue pearl". There may be blissful states of awareness, such as seeing everything as God, or the formless ecstasy traditionally known as "Nirvikalpa Samadhi". Depending on the Yogic school, any of these experiences may be equated with full Enlightenment.

What is the cause of subtle experience? The "chakra system", or hierarchy of subtle energy centers in the body, starting with the muladhar at the bodily base and rising to the sahasrar above the crown of the head, has been known to Yogis since ancient times as a kind of ladder of mystical experience. In traditional Yogic practice, one is always aspiring to move "up and out" of the body to a place of bliss above. The Yogic schools, then, and all the esoteric traditions that emphasize mystical experience, are involved in a process of ascent stimulated by Spiritual energy rising through the chakras.

Sri Da Avabhasa points out that this ascent of Spiritual energy, fully understood, is simply the other half of the course of the Spirit-Current that descends in Spirit-Baptism. Having descended in the frontal line to the bodily base, the Spirit-Current tends to turn about at the bodily base and ascend up the spine to a Matrix of Light infinitely above the crown of the head—from which it was first felt to descend. In other words, the full course of the Spirit-Current is a circular pathway, descending in the front of the body and ascending in the spinal line. While the primary effect of the descending Current is to open up the frontal, or body-based, personality, the effect of the ascending Current is to stimulate and purify the more subtle and mystical possibilities of experience.

Some traditions, such as the Christian tradition, emphasize the descent of the Spirit. These traditions exemplify the descending aspect of the fourth stage of life, while other traditions, representing the "advanced" fourth to the fifth stage of life, are more aligned to the course of Spiritual ascent.

Free Daism takes both processes into account, the descending and the ascending, but sees neither of them as absolute. In *The Dawn Horse Testament*, Sri Da Avabhasa mentions some of the visions, and other subtle sensory phenomena that His devotees may experience through the movement of the Spirit-Current in the spinal line:

. . . subtle sensations (such as visions Of The Spirit-Current As light within the body, visions of the interior of the body, visions of energy centers in the body, visions of symbolic patterns, visions of fields, spots, spheres, or holes of various colors, visions of blackness, density, fire, water, smoke, and the sky, auditions of the heartbeat and respiration, auditions of subtle internal sounds, such as explosions, a sound like a gunshot, snapping noises,

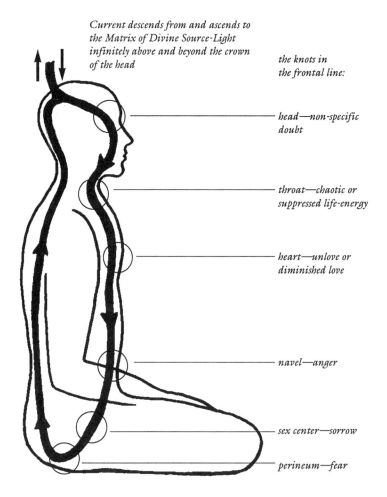

The Circle of the Spirit-Current and the knots in the frontal line

Current descends from and ascends to the Matrix of Divine Source-Light infinitely above and beyond the crown of the head

the knots in the frontal line:

head—non-specific doubt

throat—chaotic or suppressed life-energy

heart—unlove or diminished love

navel—anger

sex center—sorrow

perineum—fear

The full course of the Spirit-Current is a circular pathway, descending in the front of the body, and ascending in the spinal line. While the primary effect of the descending Current is to open up the frontal, or body-based, personality, the effect of the ascending Current is to stimulate and purify the more subtle and mystical possibilities of experience in the human body-mind.

pulsing or clicking sounds, ringing sounds, thumping and thundering sounds, perceptions of a variety of subtle internal smells, in a range from excrement to flowers, and perception of a variety of subtle internal tastes, culminating in an ambrosial sweetness, as if nectar were dripping out of the brain), and Also every Possible kind of even vivid Yogic "dream", psychic vision, sudden insight, or Spiritual Apparition. (The Dawn Horse Testament, *pp. 500-501)*

Other phenomena mentioned by Sri Da Avabhasa include psychokinesis (the ability to move objects at a distance), forms of mental telepathy, bodily levitation, bodily bi-location, astral travel, premonitory dreaming, and various forms of extra-sensory perception. One may even have a vision of the Cosmic Mandala, the entire manifest universe, appearing in microcosm.[7]

To become attracted and attached to such experiences is nearly inevitable. Who would not (if they could!) delight in the taste of ambrosial sweetness, or revel in the fascinations of astral travel or psychic visions? And yet, as Sri Da Avabhasa Himself discovered during His own Sadhana, for anyone interested in true Liberation, such attachment is a diversion and can become a binding fascination, even for lifetimes.

In the Way of the Heart, no experience is tantamount to Divine Enlightenment. "Visions", as Sri Da Avabhasa once Said, "are a kind of washing." They are a sign of the "boiling off" or purification of the deep psyche. The phenomena in themselves mean nothing. Therefore, Sri Da Avabhasa encourages His devotees to understand the search for subtle experience as just another form of egoity, rarer perhaps than the more ordinary forms of seeking, but deluding nonetheless.

And so, when the frontal Yoga is fulfilled, Sri Da Avabhasa does not assume that His seeing devotees will need to become involved in the process of Spiritual ascent in the spinal line. No ascending experience is a necessary part of Spiritual growth in the Way of the Heart, not even the infinitely ascended formless ecstasy so coveted in the Yogic tradition. This exalted state (which Sri Da Avabhasa calls "fifth stage conditional Nirvikalpa Samadhi") certainly may occur (Kanya Samatva Suprithi recounts her own experience of this profound Samadhi on pages 179–80, and describes its overwhelming effect on her). But Supreme Enlightenment in the Way of the Heart is something else. As we will describe in the next section, Divine Self-Realization Awakens in the Domain of Consciousness, beyond the Circle of the Spirit-Current. In other words, the whole dynamic play of manifested forms, gross and subtle (represented by the descending and ascending Spirit-Current), may be understood as a constantly moving wheel resting on the moveless "hub" of Consciousness, the Ultimate Source of all that appears.

Even most of His devotees, Sri Da Avabhasa says, who have thoroughly engaged the frontal Yoga will be qualified to take a "short-cut" in practice. They will move directly from maturity in the first actually seeing stage to the ultimate practice, or "Perfect Practice", of the Way of the Heart, without any need to pursue the ascending course of Spiritual experience.

How is it possible to bypass the process of ascent? Part of the answer lies in the unique nature of Sri Da Avabhasa's Spiritual Transmission. The Transmission of an Adept corresponds to the Spiritual Energy of his or her degree of Realization. As a Divinely Self-Realized Adept, Sri Da Avabhasa Transmits "Hridaya-Shakti", the Power of the Heart (Hridayam), the Radiance of Consciousness, which draws His devotees to the Heart Itself. We may feel Sri Da Avabhasa's Hridaya-Shakti in our body-minds in different ways according to our stage of growth. Whatever tangible effects of His Transmission we may feel, Sri Da Avabhasa's Hridaya-Shaktipat is always Prior to these effects, always active to Liberate us completely from identification with the body and the mind.

Because of the Divine Potency of Sri Da Avabhasa's Heart-Transmission, the purifying effects of His descending Current typically go deeper than the knots in the frontal line. The purification extends into the spinal line, releasing stresses and limits in the subtle aspect of the personality as well as in the frontal, or gross, personality. As a result, when the frontal Yoga is full, the seeing devotee is potentially free of binding attachments at the level of the body and also in all the layers of mind and psyche.

The unique Force of Sri Da Avabhasa's Heart-Transmission is one reason why it is possible (and likely) in the Way of the Heart that most practitioners will not have to practice in the stages of Spiritual ascent. But the "short-cut" from the frontal Yoga to the "Perfect Practice" also depends on another factor. It depends on the liberating force of self-understanding. The great pitfall in the process of Spiritual ascent is, as we have said, to become attached to the highly pleasurable experiences that may arise. But Sri Da Avabhasa has Given His devotees from the very beginnings of the listening process the benefit of His Wisdom on the self-contraction. He Emphasizes again and again how this primal act of separation is the basis of our search for consoling experiences. When this lesson has been truly learned at the body-based level of experience it is easily extended into the subtle dimensions of existence as well.

What happens when one has a really glorious experience of any kind? One wants to repeat it, or to better it! And so a cycle of seeking and attaining and losing and seeking again is set in motion. A Free Daist practitioner involved in the process of Spiritual ascent comes to observe this familiar egoic pattern as delicious visions or states of Spiritual absorption come and go. The whole "tour" of Spiritual ascent (as Sri Da Avabhasa has emphasized from the time He began to Teach) is part of one's search to be fulfilled as a separate and separative ego-"I".

This remains true even though one may have intensely Blissful experiences, and even, perhaps, at times, a sense of sublime union with the Divine, and with all things. Sri Da Avabhasa cannot accept such moments as equivalent to Divine Enlightenment, because they pass and change. How can most Perfect God-Realization <u>ever</u> change, ever grow "more" or "less"? Through all the years of His Sadhana, such a notion was never tolerable to Sri Da Avabhasa—and in the Event of His Divine Re-Awakening He proved His lifelong intuition that Divine Enlightenment is indeed Perfect and Unchanging.

Nevertheless, for some devotees the ascending course of practice is necessary to purify their particularly strong tendencies towards subtle experience, and Sri Da Avabhasa has Given detailed Instructions on how to go through the process of Spiritual ascent in Satsang with Him.

The lesson of the ascending Process, which may be grasped at any point after the frontal Yoga is complete, is that attachment to <u>any</u> experience is a form of self-contraction. Absolute Happiness and Freedom is Prior, unchanging, untouchable by the flow of events and the states of waking, sleeping, and dreaming. When such self-understanding relative to all the possibilities of body and mind Awakens, by Grace, one is ready to make the momentous leap into the ultimate stages of the Way of the Heart.

RECOMMENDED READING

The Dawn Horse Testament, especially chapters 20, 23, 37–42

NOTES

1. See *The Gospel of Sri Ramakrishna,* abridged edition, translated by Swami Nikhilananda (New York: Ramakrishna-Vivekananda Center, 1970), pp. 94-5, 114-15, and Swami Muktananda, *Play of Consciousness (Chitshakti Vilas)* (San Francisco: Harper and Row, 1978), pp. 60-61.

2. The Prayer of Changes is a form of Divine Invocation practiced in the Way of the Heart in order to bring about positive changes in the psycho-physical world. The Prayer is based on Heart-Communion with Sri Da Avabhasa and, in its basic form, involves a simple process of release (via exhalation) of specific negative conditions, and reception (via inhalation) of specifically intended positive conditions. In the Spiritually Awakened form of the Prayer of Changes to which Kanya Navaneeta refers here, the Force of the Spirit-Current circulating in the body is used in conjunction with the sensory mind (especially its power of visualization) to effect positive changes. This advanced form of the Prayer of Changes is practiced by devotees in the first actually seeing stage, and beyond, in the Way of the Heart.

3. Sri Da Avabhasa has described three "stations" of the heart, which are psycho-physical loci associated respectively with the left side, the middle region, and the right side of the physical heart. The stations of the heart correspond to three different dimensions of our existence, which are progressively revealed in the course of Free Daist practice: The left side of the heart represents our gross, physical level of awareness; the middle heart is the seat of subtle, mystical experience (the awakening of which Kanya Navaneeta speaks of here); and the right side of the heart is associated with the Domain of Consciousness and the ultimate stages of life.

4. Kanya Navaneeta is making the point here that Sri Da Avabhasa's Spiritual Presence is literally Him in His Spiritual Form, Prior to time and space. Sri Da Avabhasa's Spiritual Presence, as He Says Himself, "does not move". It infinitely Transcends all "movement". However, as Sri Da Avabhasa's Spiritual Presence does its purifying work in the body-mind of the devotee, Yogic phenomena and experiences (mentioned in this chapter) may arise, especially in meditation. These are secondary effects of His Spiritual Presence.

5. In His Wisdom-Teaching, Sri Da Avabhasa often refers to two universal human strategies: the "Alpha strategy", or the attempt to perfectly escape from life, and the "Omega strategy", or the attempt to perfect bodily human existence, which are the two tendencies that Kanya Navaneeta is describing here. Neither of these strategies represent the Way of the Heart, which is based on self-forgetting Communion with Sri Da Avabhasa, the Divine Person, in bodily (human) Form. When Communion with Sri Da Avabhasa is truly lived, one is neither moved to avoid ordinary life nor moved to perfect it.

6. When the Spirit-Current has fully descended in the frontal line of the body, it tends to turn about at the bodily base and rise up in the spinal line. In the Way of the Heart, this ascent of the Spirit-Current in the spinal line is associated with the purification of the subtle, or mind-based, dimensions of one's being, as we describe further on in this chapter.

7. "Mandala" (literally "circle") is a term commonly used in the esoteric Spiritual traditions to describe the levels of cosmic existence. It also denotes an artistic rendering of interior visions of the cosmos. Sri Da Avabhasa uses the phrase "Cosmic Mandala" to describe the totality of the conditional cosmos, which appears in vision as concentric circles of light, progressing from red at the perimeter through golden-yellow, silvery white, indigo or black, and brilliant blue, to the Ultimate White Brilliance in the Mandala's Center.

III

The "Perfect Practice"

I f one turns to accounts of the lives of great men and women in the various Spiritual traditions, many of the individuals who are venerated as saints show the kinds of signs that are associated with mature seeing in the Way of the Heart—profound devotional submission to the Divine Beloved (however That One may be conceived within the given tradition), a profound inclination to be absorbed in Divine Communion, or Contemplation, and, in some cases, the frequent experience of mystical phenomena and exalted states of consciousness that may be interpreted as union with the Divine. This is the essence of sainthood, what Western Christians and Eastern Yogis tend to regard as the highest possible expression of Spirituality.

But there are a number of other traditions, including some forms of Buddhism and Advaita Vedanta,[1] that take a different view. Such traditions aspire to a Realization of Truth that is Transcendental, beyond the realm of mystical experience.

Free Daism shares this orientation. From Sri Da Avabhasa's "Point of View", the Spiritual fullness of the seeing stages is simply the end of the beginning. The next phase of growth involves the dropping away of the whole view of life and God that informed one's practice and one's entire existence up to this point. To use a simple image, it is as though you had been riding a roller coaster all your life, the roller coaster of the body-mind. But now there is a profound shift in your awareness. The roller coaster still hurtles on automatically, but you are not "riding" it in the same way. You are simply witnessing its course with the equanimity (and amusement!) of an observer. The Position in which you stand now is the Position of That in Which the body-mind arises—the All-Embracing Domain of Consciousness, or Being Itself.

The whole story of Sri Da Avabhasa's Teaching and Blessing Work has been about His Efforts to Attract us, His devotees, to what He calls the "Inherent Happiness of Merely Being", Prior to our act of identification with the body-mind. This has been a monumental challenge, because we, like nearly every human being who has ever lived, are fiercely identified with this gross physical being we call "I", and have scant interest in any Greater point of view.

What, to an ordinary body-based individual, is attractive about the Perfect transcendence of the body-mind?

During the years of His Teaching Work, Sri Da Avabhasa made His Point by Demonstrating over and over again the futility of seeking for lasting Happiness through any experience to be found through the body, the thinking mind, or the higher psychic faculties.

Since the Initiation of His Divine Emergence, He has begun to Transmit the Mystery of Consciousness more and more directly and powerfully through His Silent Heart-Transmission. This Work of Blessing has been so profound that two of Sri Da Avabhasa's devotees, the Kanyas, have in the last few years become established in the Witness-Position of Consciousness. Many other devotees too have had glimpses of the "radical" Freedom and Happiness of Standing as Consciousness Itself, while still practicing in the listening stage of the Way of the Heart. Even to be Given a glimpse of Consciousness Itself, Prior to all conditions, is the most remarkable Grace and a testimony to the Greatness of Sri Da Avabhasa.

A devotee, Angelo Druda, who had such a glimpse of Consciousness, writes here of a retreat He took at Sri Love-Anandashram in 1986, a few months after the beginning of Sri Da Avabhasa's Divine Emergence. Angelo describes how he was listening one day to a recitation from *The Dawn Horse Testament* when he had a very unusual experience, stimulated by Sri Da Avabhasa's Heart-Transmission.

ANGELO: A psychic image arose of myself as a ten- or twelve-year-old boy at Jones Beach on Long Island, New York where I grew up. It was a crystal-clear image that completely assumed my being, so that I was that boy again walking along the beach. I could feel the warm summer air and knew that I was about to get back on the bus and go home. My parents were young and full of life. I would usually go out and cut the grass at the end of the day. I felt that character, that image, almost with a yearning. Then suddenly I saw my parents and myself as old and aging and dying, and I fell into sorrow to the degree that I did not think I could tolerate it. I got exactly to the point at which I said, "I cannot bear this sorrow. It's dreadful. I don't know what to do about it." Then, in the next moment, I simply noticed that my attention was focused in this sorrowful feeling, and in that moment of self-observation my attention was set free and I was restored to the heart's ease. Almost instantaneously the emotion dissolved into Bliss, and that whole sorrowful character disappeared. I realized in that moment: "I'm not even that body. I'm not even the child of those people. I'm not that identity at all!" It became tacitly clear in a moment. I understood that, in fact, the identity that I had presumed all my life was simply a matter of where I placed my attention.

All this took place in a span of about twenty seconds in which I went from feeling that I would be utterly overwhelmed by sorrow, and incredible suffering, to ease, equanimity, and God-Communion, by realizing that the drama of that lifetime was my own ongoing creation and that my presumed identity was not really the case.

Angelo goes on to describe how when He sat in Sri Da Avabhasa's Company and heard Him Speak about Consciousness, he was effortlessly moved into that Position.

From the moment the sitting began, I felt utterly and totally assumed by Him. I did not really know how deeply until the end of the evening when He became quite still and most intense and began Speaking about Consciousness. He said, "How foolish to bind

Consciousness to life!" and I suddenly realized that every cell of my being was profoundly sympathetic with what He was saying. I had sat with Sri Da Avabhasa many times, and I had never felt such depth of sympathy with His Argument. I have always felt a kind of sympathy, but the resistance has usually been strong. But in this case, I was utterly sympathetic, to the point that there was literally an Awakening taking place. I was saying to myself, "Of course! How foolish to bind Consciousness to the events of life!" My mood was not self-righteous but sympathetic. The very idea that anybody would do such a thing was the silliest thing I could imagine! Sri Da Avabhasa continued to speak in that vein, and my being continued to say, "Can you imagine that anybody could be so stupid as to bind Consciousness to objects!" I took on His "Point of View".

Then He started talking about Outshining the Cosmic Mandala, and He began to Demonstrate how Divine Consciousness Outshines all worlds, all beings, all space, and all perception. I had heard Him talk like that before, but this time it was <u>Demonstrated</u> to me. I began to literally see Him Outshine the room. I could feel my own body being Outshined to the point that even any noticing of objects was being Outshined. This Outshining was not objective or experiential—it was intuitive. I simply felt Him Magnifying the Divine Self-Position to the point that any form of noticing of even the time-space dimension was being lost. There was only this Happiness.

Everyone could feel it. At the end of the evening, after Sri Da Avabhasa left, no one could move for half an hour. Everyone remained, lost in this Happiness.

Sri Da Avabhasa over the years has Given His devotees many glimpses like this—glimpses of the Ultimate Nature of Reality as Absolute Radiance and Happiness. Such glimpses are a goad. They pass, but they leave behind a longing, a passionate urge to find the Sat-Guru Perfectly, and to live always in His State, His Samadhi. In the beginning levels of practice, this urge will not be steady. One's impulse to Liberation will be swayed by the winds of tendency, of this or that distraction, habit, or karma. At one moment, one would do anything to Realize Perfect Happiness, and in the next moment an ice cream or a movie will do instead!

All of this phasing is part of the ordeal of listening. But when the Graces of hearing and seeing regenerate the native ecstasy and equanimity of the body-mind prior to the self-contraction, the impulse to perfectly self-transcending God-Realization becomes predominant. And then, when all the possibilities of the body and all the fascinations of mind have been understood and effectively transcended, the "Perfect Practice" may begin, which is the bridge to Divine Awakening, and ultimately to Divine Translation.

Before we begin to survey the "Perfect Practice" of the Way of the Heart, it is worth pausing to appreciate the magnitude of what we are about to describe.

The whole process of Realization in Free Daism is based on the presumption of our present non-separation from the Divine, rather than on a quest for Divine Union or Liberation. Nevertheless, the process of purification that leads to the ultimate stages of the Way of the Heart bears some similarities to the disciplines, practices, and awakenings of other esoteric traditions. Disciplines, practices, and awakenings, similar to those of the "Perfect Practice", also are documented in Eastern traditions such as Buddhism and Advaita Vedanta, which are devoted to complete Liberation from "samsara", or the play of conditional existence.

The greatest Teachings of the Eastern traditions typically represent the point of view of the sixth stage of life (and in rare cases the seventh stage of life), in which Consciousness is Realized to be the Truth of existence rather than any kind of Spiritual experience (belonging to the fourth and the fifth stages of life). But traditional descriptions of the sixth stage practice (or the sixth to seventh stage practice) and Realization are expressed in language and concepts that are difficult for us to grasp today. These descriptions were largely created in ancient times, in cultures quite foreign to the modern world.

Only a Supremely-Realized living Adept can bring to life the Ultimate Wisdom that lies encoded in the ancient Sutras and Upanishads. And only such a living Adept can Demonstrate and then Grant to others the Most Perfect Awakening to which these Scriptures point. The Realization of Identity with Brahman, the One Divine Being, is extolled, for example, in the Great Statements of Hinduism—such as "I Am Brahman". And the ultimate Realization of Buddhism has been expressed in the statement: "Nirvana (the Transcendental Condition) and samsara (phenomenal existence) are the same."[2] For those who enjoy such a Realization, even ordinary existence is known and lived as the Divine Condition Itself. But most Eastern traditions, in practice, have a history of asceticism and turning inward to find God that appears to deny the Inherent Oneness of the Divine and the conditional world that their greatest Scriptures proclaim.

Sri Da Avabhasa has Remarked on this tendency and pointed out how the true Realization of Identity with the Divine necessarily transcends both the urge (especially characteristic of the East) to deny the world and the urge (especially characteristic of the West) to indulge in or improve or perfect the conditions of this world. The Ultimate Realization Awakens only on the basis of a profound freedom from both these limiting points of view.

By a Miracle of Grace, Sri Da Avabhasa is here now, Revealing what the greatest statements of the ancient Scriptures really mean. And He is doing this not in the secret manner of the Great Realizers of the past—to a few initiates in a forest hermitage. He is Speaking in this era in directly communicative language to anyone who is interested. In His Description of the "Perfect Practice", Sri Da Avabhasa first Explains the sixth stage Process of Awakening to the Witness-Position of Consciousness in all its practical and sublime details, and then He goes on to illumine the seventh stage of life, the stage of Divine Enlightenment, which is virtually uncharted territory in the traditions. Certainly the traditional sources do not even hint at the last Mysteries of human existence, the Process that unfolds after Divine Enlightenment and that leads to Divine Translation.

At the same time, the Process that Sri Da Avabhasa Describes is always, as He Says, a "practicing" school, not a "talking" school. You cannot Stand in the Position of

Consciousness simply by convincing yourself of it, or by liking the idea! The whole practice, as we have outlined it up to this point, is necessary preparation. Anything else is an illusion, for the degree of free attention and fierce discipline required to practice in the Domain of Consciousness cannot be overestimated. The Awakening to the sixth stage of life is very rare in human history, although many have philosophized about and practiced Teachings oriented to this Transcendental Realization. And Divine Enlightenment, or Awakening to the seventh stage of life, is <u>exceedingly</u> rare. And so we must expect the qualifications for the ultimate stages of the Way of the Heart to be as exacting as any that have been required traditionally—intense devotion, profound self-understanding, and great renunciation. At the same time, the Process is pure Gift, a Revelation unfolding in Sri Da Avabhasa's Company simply "as Grace will have it".

The "Perfect Practice" of the Way of the Heart consists of three stages. The first stage is initiated when the devotee spontaneously relinquishes the point of view of the body-mind (through effective practice in the preceding seeing stages) and becomes established in the Witness-Position of Consciousness. The second stage follows when Consciousness Itself becomes the "Object" of Contemplation. The third stage of the Perfect Practice <u>is</u> Divine Enlightenment, or Most Perfect Identification with Consciousness. In this State all "things" are Divinely Recognized as mere modifications of Consciousness Itself, the One Self-Existing and Self-Radiant Divine Being.

<u>Be</u> Consciousness:
The First Stage of the "Perfect Practice"

One of the great issues of modern scientific research is the question of what consciousness is. Is consciousness merely a by-product of chemical and electrical interaction? Is it a result of physical processes? In fact, the greatest Realizers throughout history have told us that Consciousness Itself is the fundamental aspect of the Universe. This is their testimony on the basis of their own direct experience. In *The Dawn Horse Testament*, Sri Da Avabhasa explains precisely what He Means by Consciousness and the Witness-Position of Consciousness:

To Be The Witness-Consciousness Is To Be Consciousness Itself, simply Aware Of Itself As That Which Merely and Freely Reflects conditions, Just As The Still Pond Water Reflects the Foolish face Of Narcissus, Motivelessly. Even all kinds of conditions May arise To That Native Awareness, but No Feeling Of Identification With them, or The Search For them, or The Effort Of Holding On To them, or The Felt Need To Avoid them Is There In The Witness-Consciousness Itself. Indeed, All Motivations Toward action Are themselves Simply Observed (or Merely Reflected) By (and In) The Witness-Consciousness Itself.

The Witness-Consciousness (Because It Is Really Identical To Consciousness Itself) Is

Not Caused. Consciousness Itself Is Not An Effect or A Result Of any conditional event or Any Display Of conditional events. The Very Existence Of Consciousness Itself Is Not Dependent On any condition, or Any Display Of conditions. Consciousness Itself Is An Inherent Characteristic or Most Primitive, Irreducible, Inherently Spiritual (or Love-Blissful), Transcendental, and (Ultimately) Divine Element Of Being (Itself), or Of Existence Itself, or Of Reality Itself. When conditions arise, or change, or pass away in The View Of Consciousness, Consciousness Itself Remains Always As The Same Free Love-Bliss Of Being. (The Dawn Horse Testament, p. 586)

As we explained in the previous chapter, the stance of the Witness-Consciousness will most likely arise and quickly stabilize in a Free Daist practitioner as soon as the work of the frontal Yoga is done. Otherwise one becomes established in that Position after a period of practice in the ascending stages of seeing. In the case of the Kanyadana Kumaris, who are the first to have made the transition to the "Perfect Practice", the Yoga of the ascending Spirit-Current was not necessary. The Kanyas have had many experiences of subtle phenomena over the years, Given by the Grace of Sri Da Avabhasa's Heart-Transmission[3] but, thanks to Sri Da Avabhasa's "radical" Instruction about the temporary, illusory nature of <u>all</u> phenomena, they were (and are) able to understand what these experiences represented as subtle forms of egoity.

Entry into the "Perfect Practice" requires a profound depth of both hearing and seeing. Hearing, at this point, becomes summary understanding and transcendence of self-contraction in subtle as well as gross form.

Likewise, the practice of seeing also enters a new phase. While seeing begins with feeling beyond Sri Da Avabhasa's bodily (human) Form into the sphere of His All-Pervading Spirit-Presence, the "Perfect Practice" is based on an Awakening to the Great Mystery of His Very Being, to His Divine State as Consciousness Itself. Kanya Samatva Suprithi describes here how this occurred in her own case:

One day, by Grace, my own real Nature was understood, tacitly and irrevocably, as Consciousness Itself, and Consciousness became my point of view through feeling-Contemplation of Sri Da Avabhasa. It was as though a veil had been lifted from my eyes, a veil that had always been there and that prevented me from seeing this Perfect Vision of Consciousness Itself, prevented me from knowing that I and all beings exist and stand presently as Consciousness Itself. But this veil seemed only to be a very sheer veil, and the Guru was able to lift it through the miraculous Gift of feeling-Contemplation of His Very State. It was as simple as that—even though it was also a very elaborate and most intimate process that could not possibly be done without Sri Da Avabhasa's constant attention and Blessing and Guidance.

I began to see all things from the point of view of Consciousness, rather than from the point of view of the body and the mind, and I could see evidence of this change in my life and meditation very concretely.

Understanding the Feeling of Relatedness

T he Witness-Position of Consciousness, profound though it is, is not Divine Enlightenment, because there is still a presumption of separation, the "difference" between the Witness and what is being Witnessed. The progressive dissolving of this feeling of "difference" is the work of the "Perfect Practice". For such a process to occur, a most "radical" understanding must Awaken. The self-contraction must be traced to its root, to the original action of separation that creates the sense of "I" and "other". In the following excerpt from a Talk He Gave in 1988, Sri Da Avabhasa Discloses the secret of this understanding:

SRI DA AVABHASA: There is a secret about the "I" that must be discovered by Revelation. The "I" is a convention of mind and a convention of speech that suggests the separate person, the psycho-physical entity. It is also the primal thought in the mind, around which all other thoughts are organized. The "I" is not really a thought. It perhaps best qualifies as a feeling. It is the feeling of relatedness. The "I" is a name for egoity, a name for the body-mind. It is a name for the activity of self-contraction, the fundamental experience of egoity, which is always relatedness, or relationship—either entered into or resisted.

"I", therefore, is not separate, although it experiences the feeling of separateness. "I" is simply the feeling of relatedness. To discover this, however, you must come to some understanding of this "I", this ego-activity. You must find out this contraction and feel beyond it.

The process of this discovery becomes the great crisis of Divine Self-Realization, but only when it passes to the degree that the fundamental activity, reality, circumstance, and experience that is the conditional self is transcended. Before that, the process of sadhana is effective, releasing, and a matter of growth, but it is always dealing with the periphery of egoity. You can transcend habits of body. You can transcend thoughts and habits of mind. You can raise mind up into subtle spheres of experience. You can focus mind in ascent, and go beyond mind conditionally. But none of that is yet Divine Self-Realization ultimately, because that which is egoity itself has not been directly, firmly, and finally transcended in its Source.

The feeling of relatedness is a contraction of the fundamental Divine Self-Condition, Which I have Described as the "Feeling of Being". When there is that contraction, there is the feeling of relatedness, and from that feeling of relatedness come all of the apparent associations of attention.

I am Calling you to the direct transcendence of egoity, the direct transcendence of the feeling of relatedness in the Feeling of Being (Itself). (July 9, 1988)

How is the Feeling of Being to be "Located"? Via feeling-Contemplation of Sri Da Avabhasa Himself. The Feeling of Being is Who He Is, and He Perfectly Transmits that Feeling-State so that any of His devotees at any stage of practice can receive and respond to Him as He Is. But to <u>Realize</u> that Feeling—to make It the moment to moment basis of life—requires the whole ordeal of practice, and ultimately it requires an acute sensitivity to the root-feeling of relatedness that Sri Da Avabhasa has just Described.

What one realizes in the "Perfect Practice" is that the feeling of relatedness, the sense of "I" and "other", is simply the result of a motion of <u>attention</u>. What we perceive via attention in any moment is a very individual matter, and very deluding at the same time. As Sri Da Avabhasa explains in the following passage, attention is actually the activity that creates the whole mirage of experience that we take to be reality, and that distracts us from the Absolute Condition, or Feeling of Being, that is Prior to attention and all experience:

Truly there is nothing but Consciousness—Self-Radiant, Self-Existing, Infinite, Absolute, Divine Consciousness. It is so even now. But, by virtue of attention, you are asso-ciated with a mechanism, a body-mind, that is structured in such a way that it associates with modifications of the Absolute that are of a particular kind, what we call "gross". The body-mind with which you are presently associated is a mechanism, a machine, if you will, that is sensitive to only a certain range of vibration. It, therefore, perceives the Absolute in the form of this gross modification.

At the same moment in which this perception is taking place, there is still nothing but Absolute Energy, Absolute Consciousness. The perception is an appearance. Someone asso-ciated with a subtler body-mind in a higher plane within the Cosmic Mandala is enjoying a very different kind of perception and state of mind and experience than you at the pre-sent moment. But, even so, what is determining even that perception or experience is the fact that attention is associated by tendency with a certain degree of modification, a cer-tain portion of possible vibration or apparent modification of the Absolute.

All are appearing within the same Absolute, but attention associates with degrees of vibration or appearance or modification of that One Absolute. You are associated by virtue of attention with this gross mechanism, which is a machine, a way of tuning in to the Absolute and perceiving It through a certain color, a certain vibration. And you are, by virtue of this association, habituated to perpetuate that kind of awareness. Therefore, you will continue thus, unless you either raise attention up or transcend it altogether. (The Love-Ananda Gita, *"I Am What you Require" section, pp. 330-31)*

In the course of the "Perfect Practice", what arises to attention—whether pleasant or painful, physical or mystical—is not significant. Attention <u>itself</u> is the mechanism to be understood and transcended. Attention is a clench, or contraction, in the Feeling of Being that creates the original separative feeling of "I". To be a practitioner in the ulti-mate stages of the Way of the Heart is to come to the point where one is free to feel that original, "self"-defining motion of attention, and free to transcend it. And so one begins to take responsibility for that primal motion of attention which is the root of self-contraction, or un-Happiness.

Throughout the practice of the Way of the Heart specific practices, collectively called the "conscious process", have been engaged to <u>discipline</u> attention, to restore wandering impulses again and again to the Guru. Now, in the "Perfect Practice", the purpose of the "conscious process" is to <u>transcend</u> attention, and this occurs, by Grace, through a profound practice of feeling—not emotionality, but more a quality of sensitivity—feeling-intuition or feeling-discrimination. In this verse from His *Lion Sutra*, Sri Da Avabhasa Gives a sense of what this practice of feeling is like, using a delightfully simple image:

> *Do not Indulge (or Luxuriate) In the act of attention (which is <u>Always</u> "other" than what arises), and Do Not Seek the Illusion-mind of objects, or others, or all "things", but <u>Always</u> Merely Feel (Like a hand <u>feels</u> into a glove) and <u>Be</u> the "Feel" Itself. (v. 529)*

Most Free Daist practitioners who enter the "Perfect Practice"—certainly those who have made the direct transition from maturity in the frontal Yoga to the Witness-Position of Consciousness—will engage this practice of feeling in a technical form known as "Feeling-Enquiry". Feeling-Enquiry is a detailed twelve-part process (engaged in meditation and in daily life) that begins with the mere Witnessing of what arises, and progressively feels to the root of what arises, feeling all conditional experience to be only self-contraction, or "the ego-<u>effort</u> of separation and separateness". In the final steps of Feeling-Enquiry one simply feels the feeling of relatedness, and What Stands beyond it—the undifferentiated Depth of Consciousness, or the Love-Blissful Feeling of Being, Which (when Contemplated) dissolves even the subtlest motion of attention.

The essence of Feeling-Enquiry, and, in fact, the essence of the whole of the "Perfect Practice" is summarized superbly in this Admonition from Sri Da Avabhasa:

> *Constantly submit to <u>feel</u> (rather than put attention on) the thoughtless feeling of relatedness. Do this moment to moment, rather than follow attention itself. In every moment of this simple and easeful feeling-inspection, understand the feeling of relatedness to be self-contraction (and thus transcend it, by Feeling Prior to it), or simply Feel into (and, spontaneously, Beyond) the heart-feeling of relatedness, and thus Feel That In Which the feeling of relatedness is arising (or In Which or Of Which the feeling of relatedness is a contraction).*
>
> *What <u>Is</u> That In Which the thoughtless feeling of relatedness is arising? What <u>Is</u> That In Which or Of Which the thoughtless feeling of relatedness is an apparent contraction? By Grace, Feel, "Locate", and Be That, Until It Gracefully Reveals Its Own Nature, Status, and Inherent Love-Bliss, even to the degree that all apparently arising conditions are Always Already Divinely Recognizable In and As That. (*The ego-"I" is the Illusion of Relatedness, p. 118)*

Consciousness Itself, or "That In Which the thoughtless feeling of relatedness is arising", is the Self-Existing and Self-Radiant Divine Condition that Sri Da Avabhasa calls "the
Heart". And Consciousness Itself or the Heart Itself makes Itself felt in the physical dimension of existence via a distinct psycho-physical focus in the body—at a point in the right
side of the heart corresponding to the sinoatrial node. This seat or root of Consciousness
in the body is a great esoteric secret rarely mentioned in recorded Teachings.[4]

At the beginning of the "Perfect Practice", one becomes aware of this heart-locus as
the Source of the Spirit-Current, which is felt to migrate from its "Circular" pathway of
continuous descent and ascent (see p. 232) and come to rest in the right side of the
heart.

Kanya Suprithi describes here the change that occurred in her feeling of the Spirit-
Current when she began to identify with the Witness-Position of Consciousness.

*I had previously felt the Spirit-Current to be radiating from above the body, radiating
into the Circle of the body as a tangible Current—and I was profoundly drawn to be
absorbed in that Current. Now the Spirit-Current was felt to radiate from a point deep in
my heart on the right side. I felt a deep equanimity and an uncompromised certainty that
I am Consciousness and I am not the body or the mind. I am really the very same as the
Witness of experience, rather than the one to whom experiences happen.*

Free Renunciation

Sri Da Avabhasa has often pointed out that we all do what we want to do. We
want to be happy and to avoid pain. Left to ourselves, we will always move
where we are most attracted. By the time one is involved in the "Perfect
Practice" this very ordinary principle has been tested, applied, and refined to the
point where only <u>one</u> thing is felt to be Happy—absolute Identification with the Feeling
of Being, Consciousness, and Happiness that Sri Da Avabhasa Most Perfectly Reveals and
Is. Anything that interferes with the enjoyment of this Sublimity is noticed to be un-
Happy and therefore to be surrendered. Even the most primitive act of attention that dis-
tinguishes "I" from "other", "this" from "that", is increasingly felt to be painful, a motion
of separation from Love-Bliss.

The true or free renunciation that develops in the course of the Way of the Heart is
based on two things: self-understanding and the attraction to Happiness. In other words,
renunciation is the natural "by-product" of hearing and seeing—the <u>result</u> of what one has
already understood, rather than a strategy of asceticism directed toward Realization. And so
free renunciation is not the same as deliberately taking on discipline. Discipline is a natural
sign of free renunciation, and the personal life of a free renunciate is very disciplined. This
simplification of one's personal life frees attention to be more and more yielded in devotion

to Sri Da Avabhasa, until attention itself dissolves in the Perfect Contemplation of His State.

In Hindu and Buddhist traditions, a practitioner who Awakened to the Witness-Position of Consciousness would often live a reclusive life, animating a natural inclination to shun "samsara", or the "unreal" conditional world, and dwell exclusively in the Contemplation of That Which Transcends it.

But meditating all day, or retiring to a cave, is not the Way of the Heart at any stage. Consciousness Itself is not separate or "different" from the "things" that apparently arise within It. In Divine Enlightenment, this is fully seen and understood. And throughout the first and second stages of the "Perfect Practice" also, this Ultimate "Point of View" determines the practice and the discipline. One does live a life of retreat, one does increase time spent in meditation, but one also maintains an ordinary connection with life, while, at the same time, feeling through and beyond any attachment to relations and things—and the very <u>presumption</u> of relations and things! This is real renunciation, and, in the Way of the Heart, the tests of it are relentless. Sri Da Avabhasa sees to that with great fierceness and humor!

There is a recent story, told here by Brahmacharini Shawnee Free Jones,[5] of an occasion when Kanya Suprithi was preparing "New York style" pizza that Sri Da Avabhasa had requested. When He came into the kitchen and viewed the pizza sizzling in the oven, He was very Critical:

"Look at the crust! It's all curled over—talk about California pizza! And what are all those little jazzy bits? No olives, no mushrooms, just straightforward New York pizza." Kanya Suprithi took out the pizza and put it on the cutting board. Sri Da Avabhasa came closer and Gave a very long, sharp analysis of the pizza that had a very silencing effect on Kanya Suprithi.

"Are you going to be offended by the criticism of every one of your pizzas this afternoon? Are you preparing to take every one of these pizzas personally? Are you this pizza?" Sri Da Avabhasa asked, poking at it with His finger. "And even if you were, so much the better!" Kanya Suprithi instantly responded to Sri Da Avabhasa's Teasing, and told Him she'd try again.

"All right. . . . But your reputation's riding on it!" He warned. "Okay? You're supposed to be a level six[6] practitioner!" Sri Da Avabhasa turned to a devotee, who had just come in. "I can't say anything about these pizzas without her getting offended!" Then He turned to Kanya Suprithi again. "You have to meet the test. If you fail, you get an F—the worst that could happen is for you to be totally disliked and rejected!"

There is a tremendous Purifying and Awakening Force in Sri Da Avabhasa's Criticism, even when He is in a Playful Mood. The test for Kanya Suprithi was whether she would maintain the equanimity of a practitioner of the "Perfect Practice" in the face of His Challenge, or whether she would show some sign of recoil through identifying with the pizza and the "persona" He was Criticizing. In fact, Kanya Suprithi happily persevered and the final pizza turned out well, meeting with Sri Da Avabhasa's approval. Entrance into the sixth stage of life obviously involves an ordeal of testing and self-understanding much more profound and comprehensive than that represented by this simple moment, but it serves as an indication that every moment of the "Perfect Practice" requires a real demonstration of transcendence of the point of view of the body-mind.

Contemplate Consciousness: The Second Stage of the "Perfect Practice"

In the second stage of the "Perfect Practice", the practice of freely Witnessing whatever arises yields to a depth of immersion in Consciousness that eventually becomes direct Identification with Consciousness Itself. Sri Da Avabhasa describes the Process as one in which Consciousness is more and more Witnessing or Contemplating Itself until "Even the Witnessing Consciousness Is (By Grace) Resolved In Consciousness Itself (Natively Realized As The Perfectly Subjective Feeling Of Being, Itself)".

In many ways the second stage of the "Perfect Practice" is simply a magnification of what has already begun to occur in the first stage. Hearing becomes the real understanding that even the stance of the Witness is, ultimately, an act of contraction or separation within Consciousness. And seeing deepens to the point of stable Communion, or Feeling-Identification, with Sri Da Avabhasa as Self-Radiant Being and Happiness.

In the midst of this Profundity, the bodily (human) Form of Sri Da Avabhasa remains the most potent Agent of His Awakening Power. In fact, as a "Perfectly Practicing" devotee, one Treasures and Contemplates His bodily (human) Form more than ever, because one is Awakening at an ever greater depth to the sublime knowledge that Sri Da Avabhasa's human Appearance is the most exact visible Form of Consciousness Itself.

In the first stage of the "Perfect Practice" one begins to Awaken to the Divine State of Sri Da Avabhasa beyond His bodily (human) Form and even Prior to the feeling of His All-Pervading Spirit-Presence. In the second stage of the "Perfect Practice", the feeling-Contemplation of the Divine State of Sri Da Avabhasa becomes more profound. In meditation and randomly at other times, one transcends the Position of the Witness-Consciousness, and so feeling-Contemplation of Sri Da Avabhasa is no longer an act of Witnessing Him in any Form. Rather, in the feeling-Contemplation of His Very State, one Inherently Identifies with Sri Da Avabhasa as "Atma-Murti", the Form of the Divine Self, the Infinite Domain of Feeling, or Being Itself, where all the "things" of attention, and attention itself, arise and dissolve.

This stage in practice, standing as it does at the threshold of Divine Enlightenment, requires a most profound transcendence of the social personality and the thinking mind, beyond even all that has occurred in the course of practice so far. There is certainly a need for intensified retreat and a protected circumstance that allows the practitioner to freely relax outer awareness and enter into formal meditation as much as may be necessary.

The dissolving of attention via the right side of the heart is a meditative process that culminates in occasional (or frequent) experiences of Jnana Samadhi—the direct Realization of the Feeling of Being, free of "Any Concept or Feeling Of Separation or 'Difference' Between Consciousness and God, or Consciousness and Reality, or Consciousness and Ultimate Being Itself" (*The Dawn Horse Testament,* p. 592).

This total transcendence of any feeling of separateness, which may already have occurred from time to time in the first stage of the "Perfect Practice", is necessarily temporary. Sooner or later ordinary awareness returns. But when Divine Enlightenment Awakens, there is no feeling of separateness in any state, meditative or not. And so Sri Da Avabhasa insists that even the Bliss of Jnana Samadhi be understood as a limit, even (from the most "radical" point of view) a form of avoidance of the absolutely unqualified Condition that can never be modified or lost in any place, state, or form.

In this passage from one of His journals, written a few weeks before His own Divine Re-Awakening, Sri Da Avabhasa Gives a vivid impression of how the feeling of "difference" recedes as Divine Enlightenment approaches:

A day or two ago I turned to a woman companion while driving my car, and I became peculiarly aware of the absence of desire in me. It was not merely that I did not desire this woman. It was that this woman was void of any objective distinction. There was no process of discrimination, comparison, or separation going on already and automatically in me. I had turned to look at what is otherwise a person, a meaning, and a meaningful presence, but there was in fact none of this. Indeed, there was not a single modification of my awareness "created" as a result of this perception. There was only unqualified bliss, the fullness of real consciousness. (August 3, 1970)

Transcend Everything in Consciousness: The Third Stage of the "Perfect Practice"

T he greatest moment potential in a human life is the event of Divine Enlightenment. But, in the descriptions that Sri Da Avabhasa has Given us of His Divine Re-Awakening, He makes clear that the event of Full Awakening is not an "experience" at all. The one who has Awakened simply understands that he or she and every apparent "thing" is Eternally, Perfectly, the <u>same</u> as Reality, Consciousness, Truth, or God. And that Understanding is Supreme Bliss.

In the period following His Divine Re-Awakening, Sri Da Avabhasa captured in words the incredible Joy and Freedom of His new Awareness:

The zero of the heart is expanded as the world. Consciousness is not differentiated and identified. . . . I am the form of space itself, in which all bodies, realms, and experiences occur. It is consciousness itself, which reality is your actual nature . . . now and now and now. . . .

I awakened during the night as perfect, absolute, awesome bliss, in which the bodies and the mind seemed to be boiling into a solder of undifferentiated Reality. It was the madness of dissolution, perfect Self-awareness, and unqualified Presence, wherein there is only Reality, without identification, differentiation, or desire. (The Knee of Listening, p. 245)

And, in another passage:

Even my meditation was changed. There was no meditation. This consciousness could not be deepened or enlarged. It remained what it was. . . . I no longer supposed any limitation as myself. I am He.

I noticed a physical change in myself. My belly seemed to drop and expand. I continued to feel the pressure of Shakti there, and I breathed It continually. It was the breathing of my own being, the endless and profound communication of reality to itself. . . .

I realized that I was not in any sense "in" a body, not only the physical body, but any body, including the most subtle. Nor have I ever been in a body, or any realm or experience. All such things are patterns within my own nature. (The Knee of Listening, p. 244)

At the same time, His ordinary bodily life went on:

I . . . continued to experience and act on a physical level just as before. There were the same functions and desires, the same pleasures and feelings, the same lawful mechanisms, requiring the same intelligence and entailing the same consequences as a result of error or self-indulgence. But everything was new. Everything was utterly free of any kind of dilemma, separation, unconsciousness, and primary fear. (The Knee of Listening, p. 248)

251

Sri Da Avabhasa, Los Angeles, 1972

In the Divinely Self-Realized Condition, the "Perfect Practice" continues, but now Most Perfectly. In this infinitely expanded, "attentionless" Awareness, perceptions obviously arise, but there is no feeling of separation from what arises. Thus, there is no inclination (or even any capability) to exclude anything from awareness in order to remain concentrated in Consciousness. For there is nothing that is not Consciousness!

And so, in the third stage of the "Perfect Practice", meditation becomes obsolete, although a Divinely Enlightened devotee may continue, as a life habit, to observe quiet, inactive periods that look like meditation. But, active or inactive, one simply Abides as Consciousness, perpetually and Divinely Recognizing everything that appears in and as Consciousness Itself:

When you (by self-transcending response to Grace) Have Realized (and Are Awake As) That Very and Self-Existing and Self-Radiant Consciousness, simply Abide <u>As</u> That, and allow all apparent conditions to arise and pass as they will, but (rather than cling to or follow what arises) simply and spontaneously (and Divinely) Recognize whatever arises. In this manner, let all apparent conditions be Felt As <u>Is</u>, or Felt Beyond, as if they are, all together, like a shawl of gauze, or an insubstantial vapor, transparent to the Inherent Self-Light. (The ego-"I" is the Illusion of Relatedness, p. 119)

A Divinely Self-Realized devotee is literally "Enlightened". The Inherent Self-Light, or Native "Brightness" of Being Radiates in a continuous circuitry of Love-Bliss that rises in an S-shaped curve from the right side of the heart to a Matrix of Light above and beyond the crown of the head. This is Amrita Nadi, the "Nerve of Immortal Bliss", mentioned in the esoteric Hindu Spiritual tradition,[7] but never fully described. As Sri Da Avabhasa came to understand after His own Divine Re-Awakening, Amrita Nadi is the Original Form of the Divine "Brightness" in the human body-mind. He had known the "Bright" in childhood, but now its hidden structure was Revealed to Him as this Divine Current of Joy, which He called "the Heart and its spire".

Everything about the Divinely Enlightened practice of the Way of the Heart flows from the Regeneration of Amrita Nadi. Life becomes simply a manifestation of that Fullness, the Love-Bliss of the Heart. The human heart is just the physical location through which the True Heart, the "Bright" Divine Being, becomes Radiant in the body-mind.

In the fully Enlightened Condition, or the seventh stage of life, devotion and self-discipline find their consummate expression.

Devotion, in the seventh stage of life, becomes Most Perfect Identification with Sri Da Avabhasa as Consciousness Itself. But there is a still a functional distinction between Sri Da Avabhasa and His Divinely Enlightened devotee. He remains the Guru, the Giver of Liberation, and His Unique Divine Function is forever to be honored, glorified, and served by all His devotees. As He Writes in *The Hymn Of The True Heart-Master:*

Even those who are Awake as the Heart continue to surrender at the Feet of the True Heart-Master, until the world is Outshined in the Self-Existing and Self-Radiant "Bright" Transcendental Divine Being. Indeed, their devotion never ceases. This is the Secret of Liberation in Truth. (verse 107)

Seventh stage devotees participate directly in the Play of Sri Da Avabhasa's Blessing Work, He says, through

Spontaneous "Resonation" With My Own Blessing Act Of The Heart, and Joyful Regard Of Details Of My Unique Play That Perhaps Could Not Be fully Understood (or Even Be Observed) Before The Seventh Stage Awakening. (The Dawn Horse Testament, *p. 639*)

Self-discipline now takes the paradoxical form of "'Crazy Freedom', or The Spontaneous, Effortless, and inherently 'Non-Disciplined Discipline' of Conformity To Divine Love-Bliss In the Whole and every part of the body-mind".

In relation to apparent others, the Divinely Enlightened devotee in the Way of the Heart Radiates Unconditional Love. Anyone who has been fortunate enough to observe Sri Da Avabhasa in relationship with discarnate spirits on the one hand, and every kind of animal (including pigs, dogs, cows, horses, cats, fish, camels, emus, parrots) on the other, knows that all these beings share equally with human beings in His "Blessing Act Of The Heart". And everything that Sri Da Avabhasa's Most Perfect devotee does or manifests will inevitably be an expression of Him, including possible siddhis of healing, spontaneous rejuvenation, and the power to release obstructions in the world and in the lives of others.

Unqualified Enlightenment is a Condition of absolute Vulnerability. In a state of Unconditional Openness and Love, one has no defenses against the lack of love in others. Even so, there is no impulse to escape the realities of human incarnation. As Sri Da Avabhasa Describes in His own case:

Observe The Manner Of My Lifetime. . . . When I Am (Thus) Alive, I Simply Observe and Allow and Relate To whatever arises and whatever Is Brought To Me. I Act and Serve Spontaneously and In Freedom. I Do Whatever Is Necessary To Preserve or Promote Relational Harmony, Natural Equanimity, True and Even Perfect Humor, and Divine Enlightenment. I Do Not Abandon The Heart-Force Of Inherent Happiness. I See There Is Only Inherent Happiness, Love-Bliss, or Self-Radiance (Rather Than self-Contraction, Un-Happiness, Un-Love, and Non-Bliss). Therefore, I Do Not Seek. I Am Certain That whatever arises conditionally Is Merely and Only A Chaos Of limits, changes, and endings. Therefore, I Simply Persist, Without Illusions. Happiness, or Love-Bliss, Is My Indifference. Happiness, or Love-Bliss, Is The Only Real Freedom In This Midst. Therefore, I Let all conditions arise, stay awhile, and pass. I Play My Given and Expected Roles. So What?

This Demonstrated Lesson and Truth Of Happiness Is The Essence Of Wisdom. . . . The Truth Of Happiness (Which Is The Same As Self-Existing and Self-Radiant Being, or Transcendental, Inherently Spiritual, and Divine Self-Consciousness), Is The Essence Of My "Bright" Life. . . . And The Realization Of Happiness Is (By Grace) The Foundation and Always Present Essence (Rather Than The Goal or future) Of The Way Of The Heart. (The Dawn Horse Testament, *p. 608)*

Even within the seventh stage of life there are stages of unfolding. "At first," Sri Da Avabhasa Says, "this Realization Shines in the world." He is Speaking of the stage of Divine Transfiguration, in which the whole body is Infused by the "Brightness" of the Heart and "Brightly" Demonstrates active Love, serving the Awakening of others. In the ensuing phase of Divine Transformation, the subtle or psychic dimension of the body-mind is Illumined, which may result in the extraordinary Powers of healing, longevity, and so forth that we mentioned earlier. "Ultimately," Sri Da Avabhasa Tells us, "the 'Brightness' is Indifferent (Beyond 'difference') in the Deep." In the fullness of the seventh stage of life comes Divine Indifference, which is spontaneous and profound Resting in the "Deep" of Consciousness, Blessing the world directly from the Heart-Place, rather than actively Working to effect benign changes. Sri Da Avabhasa Himself has Demonstrated all these sublime phases of Divine Enlightenment.

Divine Translation, the Ultimate Mystery of the Way of the Heart, is the Victory of the "Bright", the Outshining of all objective noticing of conditions through the Infinitely Magnified Force of Consciousness Itself. Divine Translation is the Destiny beyond all destinies, from which there is no return to the conditional realms.[8]

Sri Da Avabhasa once described Divine Translation through the homely image of crocks baking in a furnace, pointing out how the crocks, irradiated by the intense heat, eventually lose their separate outlines in the white-hot glow. The experience of being so Overwhelmed by the "Bright" that all appearances fade away may occur temporarily from time to time during the seventh stage of life. But when that Most Blissful Swoon (or Moksha-Bhava Samadhi) becomes permanent, the body-mind is inevitably relinquished in death.

If one persists in the "Perfect Practice", then Divine Translation is certain, either in this or some other lifetime. The Supreme Purpose of Sri Da Avabhasa's Blessing Work is that His devotees, and even all beings, should in due time, and as Grace will have it, Realize this Destiny. In His own Surpassing Poetry, Sri Da Avabhasa describes how, in Divine Translation:

. . . All Apparent Modifications Will Soon or Suddenly Become Transparent and Un-Necessary, and You Will (Spontaneously) Let Go Of the body-mind and the world In The Yawn Of Heart-"Brightness", Effortlessly, With both of Your Free hands Open Wide To Dissolve In The Instant Vast. (The Dawn Horse Testament, *p. 587)*

Listening, hearing, seeing, and the "Perfect Practice" comprise the Process of Translation in God, the most complete Revelation of our evolutionary Destiny to be found anywhere in the Great Tradition of human Wisdom and Spirituality. What we have offered here is little more than a thumbnail sketch of a Process that is monumental in its richness and detail, a Process that took Sri Da Avabhasa many years of Labor and nearly seven hundred pages to fully describe in His *Dawn Horse Testament*. In living terms, the Giving of the Revelation of this entire Process required fifty years of human Incarnation on His Part—all the years of His own Sadhana of Re-Awakening, sixteen years of "Crazy" Teaching Work, and the Initiation of His Divine Emergence in 1986. Shortly thereafter, Sri Da Avabhasa was able to prove the Great Process in a few of His devotees to the point of the "Perfect Practice". Even now, Sri Da Avabhasa is Tireless and Fiery in His Work to bring to birth a culture of seventh stage practitioners that will Guarantee the Integrity of the Way of the Heart beyond His own physical Lifetime. Such Sacrifice, such Grace, such a Miracle as He Is can never be comprehended.

Through the Infinite Grace of Sri Da Avabhasa, anyone can discover that Divine Self-Realization is not just an idea, but a real, ecstatic Process that may be tested and proven by anyone who will dare to begin:

The Proof Of The Truth Of My Divine Confession Is beyond The Efforts Of belief and Of doubt. The Proof Of The Truth Of My Divine Confession Is Entirely A Matter Of Whether Or Not You Are Willing To Embrace and Endure The self-Surrendering Ordeal That Is The Necessary Means To Prove and To Realize The Truth Itself (Who I <u>Am</u>, and, Ultimately, Who You <u>Are</u>). My Divine Heart-Secret (Which Is The Divine Revelation Of Even Your Own Most Perfect Self and Domain) Is Revealed Only To Devotion Itself, or True Surrender To Me (Openly Revealed In My Bodily Human Form, and As "Bright" Love-Bliss, and As The Transcendental Self, or Consciousness Itself, and As The Ultimate Truth, or Divine Self-Domain, Of Existence Itself). Therefore, The Divine Heart-Secret Of You and Me Is

Revealed Only In the Real Process That Can Be Realized By Grace In The Case of those who Convert The Knowable Exercise Of The Way Of The Heart Into A Real and Living Sacrifice Of Separate and Separative self (Progressively) In and Into My "Bright" Company (and, Thus and Thereby, Progressively, In and Into The Company Of The Divine Person).
(The Dawn Horse Testament, *pp. 695-96)*

RECOMMENDED READING

The Dawn Horse Testament, especially chapters 43 and 44

The ego-"I" is the Illusion of Relatedness, especially pp. 109-129

The Perfect Practice (forthcoming)

NOTES

1. Advaita Vedanta is an Indian school of Transcendental philosophy whose fundamental assertion is contained in the formula: "There is only one Reality, without a second." Therefore, everything is that One Reality, which is never qualified or limited by any appearance.

2. Sri Da Avabhasa has pointed out that these Great Statements can easily be misinterpreted by the popular mind. In His book *Nirvanasara* (pp. 148-49), He Writes:

There is a current trend to popularize Buddhism (as well as all Transcendentalist and esoteric traditions), and, in the mode of "pop" Buddhism formulae such as "Nirvana and samsara are the same" are reduced to slogans that justify the conventions of egoity in the lesser stages of life.

The equation (or "sameness") of "Nirvana" and "samsara" is not factually the case. It is not a conventional truth, nor is it in any sense obvious to the egoic mind. In the un-Enlightened condition, Nirvana and samsara are the ultimate opposites. The declaration (or Confession) that they are the same is truly made only by those who have transcended the limits of ego and phenomenal appearances. The Buddhist conception of the sameness of Nirvana and samsara is like the Hindu Advaitic conception of the sameness of the self-essence (or "atman") and "Brahman" (or the Transcendental Reality, Condition, or Being). Each of these two great traditional formulae indicates a Transcendental Condition to be Realized. Therefore, neither formula represents a conventional truth, and neither one is a principle intended or suited for popular belief. Each one is a formula that Confesses the Truth in terms that transcend all differences and that recognizes the conditional world and self ᵢₙ Truth rather than apart from Truth (or apart from the Realization of Truth).

Those who are not thus Enlightened or perfectly Awake must clearly understand (and take heed of the fact) that Nirvana and samsara are not the same.

. . . In the domains of "pop" Buddhism, the Enlightened Confession "Nirvana and

samsara are the same" is reduced to the idea that discipline and transcendence are unnecessary, or the ideal of the ego with a quiet mind, or the benighted and merely consoled feeling that everything is OK as it seems—as if one could achieve a state of fear that is free of anxiety! The same tendencies are evident in "pop" Hinduism, where, according to the conventional belief in the sameness of atman and Brahman, the ego is regarded to be Divine, the Truth is reduced to the mortal patterns of psycho-physical inwardness, and the Spiritual Master is abandoned for the "inner Guide" (or the ego as Master).

3. See the discussion of the Samadhis Granted by the Grace of Sri Da Avabhasa's Heart-Transmission, pp. 174–85.

4. The *Brhadaranyaka Upanishad* speaks of the heart as the abode of the Divine Spirit, the Purusha, who dwells in the heart as a point the size of a grain of rice. Ramana Maharshi (1879-1950) explicitly locates this point in the right side of the heart (see Sri Da Avabhasa's quotation of Ramana Maharshi's Teaching on the right side of the heart in *The Knee of Listening*, pp. 259-61).

5. Brahmacharini Shawnee Free Jones is a member of the Da Avabhasa Gurukula Brahmacharini Order, made up of four young women belonging to Sri Da Avabhasa's Gurukula (traditionally—"family of the Guru"). The Brahmacharinis live in Sri Da Avabhasa's intimate sphere and serve all Free Daist practitioners through their exemplary devotion to Sri Da Avabhasa and the telling of the Leela of their life with Him.

6. All Free Daist practitioners potentially progress through the seven stages of life. However, there are two different courses of practice in the Way of the Heart. First, there is a "fully elaborated" form of practice which progresses through seven practicing stages and which is adopted by those capable of the most intensive form of practice. Alternatively, there is a "simpler" (or even "simplest") form of practice which progresses more slowly through developmental stages. A "level six" practitioner is one who is practicing the "fully elaborated" form of the Way of the Heart in the first and second stages of the "Perfect Practice".

7. Ramana Maharshi refers to Amrita Nadi as a "force-current" that rises from the right side of the heart to the crown of the head. He describes it as "the passage of liberation" mentioned in the Upanishads, variously called Atmanadi, Brahmanadi, or Amrita Nadi. (See *The Knee of Listening*, p. 261 for a direct quotation of Ramana Maharshi's comment.)

8. As shamans, psychics, and God-Realizers have always testified, there is much more to existence than this gross physical dimension. But the information that such seers have passed on has usually been fragmentary.

One of Sri Da Avabhasa's great Gifts to humanity has been to Reveal this grand Design, the whole picture of cosmic existence, and thus to illumine our confusion about what happens at death. He describes endless subtle realms of mind, and also "lower" realms denser than this physical one. Any of these realms, He Says, we may experience (at least fleetingly) after death. Seen in its entirety (which may occur in vision), the whole picture of manifest existence is a vast circular hierarchy, a series of colored rings of light, which Sri Da Avabhasa calls the Cosmic Mandala (see note 7, p. 236). As long as we presume the self-contraction—the separate self in some form—we migrate from life to life within the Cosmic Mandala, perhaps returning again and again to physical embodiment, or if we have transcended the body-bound point of view, to some blissful heaven realm. But none of these realms of experience, even the most sublime, are ultimately satisfying, because they all change and pass away.

In Divine Enlightenment, however, there is no remaining seed of separate self, no separate one to presume an individual existence within the Cosmic Mandala. And so when a seventh stage Realizer dies, he or she merely drops the body, continuing all the while to Abide as Consciousness Itself—the always Prior Divine State of which the entire Cosmic Mandala is a mere modification. If a seventh stage Realizer does reincarnate in some realm, it does not affect in any way his or her Divine Self-Realization. Wherever he or she may go, his or her Divine Self-Realization remains, and is a service to all others whether or not he or she seems to actively serve others. And in those Divinely Self-Realized beings for whom no destiny in the Cosmic Domain remains, he or she is Divinely Translated, or Eternally Alive as the Original "Brightness" of Consciousness, and "enters" that "place" which Sri Da Avabhasa calls the Divine Self-Domain.

For a full account of Sri Da Avabhasa's discussion of death, the after-death states, and the ultimate Destiny beyond death, see *Easy Death*, especially His Talk "The Cosmic Mandala".

Founding a New Order of Men and Women

The Culture and Community of Free Daists

I would find a new order of men and women who will "create" a new age of sanity and joy. It will not be the age of the occult, the religious, or the scientific or techno-logical evolution of mankind. It will be the fundamental age of real existence, wherein life will be radically realized entirely apart from the whole history of our adventure and great search. The age envisioned by seekers is a spectacular display that only extends the traditional madness, exploitability, and foolishness of mankind. But I desire a new order of men and women, who will not begin from all of that, but who will apply themselves apart from all dilemma and all seeking to the harmonious event of real existence.

Da Avabhasa
The Knee of Listening

What is it like to be a Free Daist? In this part we give you a glimpse of our sacred culture and cooperative community. The first chapter, "A Pictorial Presentation of the Culture and Community of Free Daists", depicts the sacred, cultural, institutional, and even business life of Free Daists—largely through pictures, accompanied by penetrating and sometimes humorous comments by Sri Da Avabhasa on the religious necessity of community and what exactly the ego is obliged to confront in that context. The second chapter is a personal account of a retreat in Sri Da Avabhasa's Company in Sri Love-Anandashram—a story of life being transformed by Love.

I

A Pictorial Presentation of the Culture and Community of Free Daists

edited by Anne Henderson

SRI DA AVABHASA: Many practitioners and would-be practitioners of the Way of the Heart tend to conceive of what I call "cooperative community" as if it were an extension of the popular idea of the "commune". However, in the Way of the Heart, the by Me Given discipline of formal and cooperative community has nothing directly to do with the conventional notions of communal living. When I Speak to you about cooperative community, I am not merely talking to you about some social ideal of communalism. I am Speaking to you very <u>realistically</u> about a condition of practice that, if rightly (and progressively) embraced, should increase the potential for Divine Self-Realization in the case of each and every practitioner of the Way of the Heart. . . .

In the Way of the Heart, the discipline of cooperative community is My unique Offering to you of a means of renunciation. That unique means of renunciation is Given by Me to all My devotees.

THE LOVE-ANANDA GITA
"I Am What You Require" section

THE HUMAN AND RELIGIOUS NECESSITY OF COMMUNITY

I have lived in the community of Free Daists for the last fifteen years. Life in this community is profoundly attractive, embracing, sane, humorous, testing, wild, intimate, compassionate, and loving. There is <u>nothing</u> like it. When I reflect on the extraordinary transformation that my Guru has effected in me and my friends in the context of the community of His devotees, tears of gratitude come to my eyes. I would not choose to live in any other circumstance, although from time to time I have certainly wished to escape the pressure cooker that it can be!

For thousands of years, human beings have lived in cooperative community (of one kind or another) for every kind of practical, social, and religious reason. And the community of Free Daists does offer many human and practical advantages. But our choice—and my choice—to live in the cooperative community that our Guru has provided for us is not a conventional one. My choice is based, really, on the simple fact that my life in community is the same as my relationship to my Guru: My love for Him, His mysterious and overwhelming Attractiveness, keeps me in place through all the necessary purification and sometimes difficult revelations that the God-Realizing Process involves. Life in community is likewise a test of my willingness to love and surrender, a demand for self-transcendence and service. And so, because of the supremely attractive nature of my Guru and His community of devotees, I am not inclined to go somewhere else and do something easier—something that challenges me less, that allows me to remain relatively immune from the emotional and relational demands of life.

The community of Free Daists is a living demonstration of the effectiveness and Intelligence of Sri Da Avabhasa's Transforming Influence in the daily lives of His devo-

tees. These pages are devoted to sharing this life—both the more formal and the less formal aspects of Free Daist practice—to the degree that that is possible on paper.

Anne Henderson serves in the Editorial Department of the Free Daist Communion as the editor of two magazines, THE "BRIGHT" and THE FREE DAIST. Anne, who has been a devotee of Sri Da Avabhasa since 1976, also oversees the women's devotional culture in Lake County, California, where she lives. She is well-known for her beautiful voice and her devotional singing. Her intimate partner and their nineteen-year-old son are also devotees of Sri Da Avabhasa.

SRI DA AVABHASA: Religion and community are necessarily associated with one another, and they have always been associated with one another since the ancient days. It is particularly in the Western world that religion has been divorced from community. People think religion is basically a private, internal process of self-consolation. They do not think that the process associated with real religion has anything necessarily to do with community. Community is, rather, something you can perhaps add to religious life if you feel like it.

But the sadhana of the religious life, and, in due course, of the Spiritual life, is <u>necessarily</u> associated with community. Community impinges on your life of relatedness and requires the discipline of relationship, requires you to discipline your egoity and separatedness, your self-isolation, in the context of relationship. Community is an inevitable discipline, then, if you awaken beyond the principle of egoity. You cure egoity, transcend it, work beyond it, through the discipline of community. July 2, 1988

There is no such thing as true religion without community. The sacred community is the necessary theatre wherein true religious responsibilities and activities can take place.

SCIENTIFIC PROOF OF THE EXISTENCE OF GOD WILL SOON BE ANNOUNCED BY THE WHITE HOUSE!

There is a profound difference between true (and necessarily sacred) community and mere practical (political, social, and cultural) communalism (whether such is viewed to be secular or religious or even sacred in its nature and intention). A cooperative, human-scale, and truly humanizing community is necessarily and truly sacred, rather than merely secular (or otherwise not truly sacred). That is to say, such a community is necessarily based on the motive of self-transcendence (rather than on the motive of self-fulfillment), and, therefore, it is not based on the search to satisfy the ego-"I" and the egoic motives of any of its members, but it is based on the devotion of each and all of its members to That Which inherently transcends each and all.

THE BASKET OF TOLERANCE
(forthcoming)

Long before His devotees began to live cooperatively together, Sri Da Avabhasa commented on the resistance that we felt toward "organized religion" and other forms of human cooperation:

SRI DA AVABHASA: Many of you have at one time or another expressed to me your feelings about organized spirituality, organized religion, whatever. People commonly have negative and resistive feelings toward all forms of community and human relationships. And the reason, the ultimate root of these feelings, is the tendency towards separation itself. In a certain way you can see that it is completely justified. There is a great deal about organized spiritual and common life worthy to be resisted! On the other hand, Truth is manifested only in this relational condition, and it is perceived in relationship. It is a crisis that occurs in relationship. Therefore, the community of Truth, the community that lives this Teaching is absolutely necessary. But what makes it a thing to resist is your lack of involvement in it, your separation from it, your dramatized resistance to relational and community life. So if you do become active, responsible, alive, and intimate with others who are living this way,

*the whole sensation of resistance to
so-called "organized" spiritual life
will disappear, because you will be
dealing with the <u>problem</u> of community only as that which it truly is: an
expression of your own avoidance of
relationship.*

THE METHOD OF THE SIDDHAS

*SRI DA AVABHASA: The community
of My devotees is a form of feeling-
Contemplation of Me, a form of
devotion to Me. Therefore, when My
devotees come together, they tend to
turn one another quite naturally to
Me and to Satsang with Me. When they
are alone, they tend to become associated with their dramas, their changes,
their limitations. But as soon as they
enter into one another's company,
they remind one another of Satsang
with Me, even though they might not
always be speaking about it.*

July 7, 1974

*SRI DA AVABHASA: One of the func-
tions of community—and this is a
great service—is to provide the opportunity for people to transcend themselves. After all, self-transcendence is
the essence of the practice you are
involved in as My devotee.*

August 31, 1983

SACRED CULTURE AND ASHRAM LIFE

One of the most obvious signs of Sri Da Avabhasa's Work is His establishment of the men and women who have come to Him as Sat-Guru in a sane, intimate, humorous, and fully human, religious and Spiritual life and culture based on the most ancient Spiritual principle: a life lived in direct, devotional relationship to the Sat-Guru. This is the principle that is alive in the life and living circumstance of every devotee of Sri Da Avabhasa, whether in a cooperative household (composed of several families and/or single practitioners), one of the many Da Avabhasa Ashrams worldwide, or one of the three Sanctuary Ashrams.

The circumstance of Ashram (and of smaller, cooperative households) provides individual practitioners with a culture of "inspiration and expectation"—an environment in which each one is both inspired and expected to practice love, devotion, service, self-discipline, and meditation. However, Free Daists do not live in an ethereal environment in which everyone exhibits social perfection and religious calm! As Heart-Master Da said at the beginning of His Teaching Work,

SRI DA AVABHASA: We haven't created an artificial environment here in which everybody is supposed to be "Simon-pure". We have nothing to defend. We can all know one another very well. That is one of the freedoms of such a place as this. So people here are generally very out front with one another about their nonsense. And that is perfectly all right, perfectly allowable, because it is a righteous demand for relationship. It is a purifying demand. Spiritual life is such a demand. It hurts at times, it puts you into confusion, it creates conflict, it makes you feel ugly, it makes you recognize crazy things about yourself. It forces you to function in spite of your refusal to function, it offends all of the self-imagery that you have built all of your life. But, after all, that is what we are here to deal with.

THE METHOD OF THE SIDDHAS

Here is a sampling of Sri Da Avabhasa's oral Instructions on Ashram life in the Way of the Heart:

❖ *Ashram means the environment, the Place, of the Realizer's Residence and Work. Do everything in the Ashram as if the Guru were physically present, even before your own eyes. That is the principle of Ashram.*

❖ *A true Ashram accommodates the Sat-Guru, and, therefore, the Divine. An Ashram is not a place where the Sat-Guru and the Divine accommodate egos.*

❖ *Be participatory. Participate fully in the cultural and functional life of this Ashram. Be a source of creativity and energy, not drama.*

❖ *The Ashram discipline is Happiness. The Ashram discipline is Freedom. To live in the free state under all conditions is the sadhana in My Company.*

❖ *Maintain a daily order that is free of excess, allows naturalness, and is not overburdened with ceremony or "seeming".*

❖ *Bring energy and love to all others.*

❖ *You should devote every aspect of your life to God-Realization, and every one of your relationships to God-Realization, and that is it.*

Da Avabhasa Ashram, Australia
Da Avabhasa Ashram, the British Isles
Da Avabhasa Ashram, Holland
Da Avabhasa Ashram, New Zealand

❖ Ashram is simply where you come into most direct contact with Me. Ashram is about having contact with Me, living, then, in the Sphere of My Influence, and allowing My Sphere and My Influence to Pervade your existence, and, ultimately, to Awaken you Most Perfectly. Develop a society based on tolerance, enjoyment, service, and a willingness to allow human existence to be manifested in its Love-Blissful form.

❖ You must remember to love, and you must love, and you must practice loving people. Do not wait for love to just happen. You must _practice_ loving people. You must communicate love to them. You must _say_ you love them. You must do things for them that are full of the feeling of love for them.

❖ Self-transcendence should be the mood of relationships altogether. There are very few circumstances where confrontation is appropriate.

❖ Do not participate in gossip, or random, negatively suggestive communications about other people.

Morning meditation in a cooperative household in Lake County, California.

Each Sunday, all devotees gather for Guruvara ("day of the Guru") to hear educational presentations and enjoy various forms of devotional occasion and meditation with one another. Here, a presentation at the Mountain Of Attention Guruvara.

Devotees meet at least weekly with a small number of their own sex to talk about and serve one another's life of practice.

Each regional Ashram, or Regional Center, sponsors seminars, lectures, and retreats in order to acquaint anyone who is interested with the rare and extraordinary opportunity of a living relationship to Sri Da Avabhasa.

Members of the Free Daist Communion host a seminar in Australia, in which various aspects of esoteric Christianity are explored in the light of Free Daism and the living presence of Sri Da Avabhasa.

A group gathers in Chicago to see an Introductory Video on Sri Da Avabhasa and the Way of the Heart, in which the essential elements of this Way of life are introduced: the sufficiency of the relationship to Sri Da Avabhasa as Guru and Sri Da Avabhasa's Instruction about seeking for release and fulfillment through experience, the real nature of the ego, the Truth of our existence, and the sacred culture and community of the Way of the Heart.

Devotees of Sri Da Avabhasa host a group to tell Leelas, or stories, of His Work.

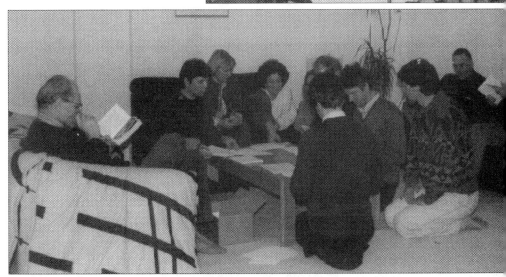

THE FREE DAIST SANCTUARIES

S ri Da Avabhasa has established and Empowered three secluded Sanctuaries for the sake of His Blessing Work with the entire world and for the use of His devotees (especially for retreat). These uniquely potent Places of Blessing, all of which are Sri Da Avabhasa's Residences, are Sri Love-Anandashram, Naitauba, in Fiji, Heart-Master Da's chosen Hermitage Ashram; the Mountain Of Attention Hermitage Sanctuary in northern California, which houses the staff and offices of the Free Daist Communion; and Tumomama Sanctuary in Hawaii, a very small and very beautiful Sanctuary on the island of Kauai, set apart for retreat.

SRI DA AVABHASA: To create a human sanctuary for higher adaptation and the ultimate transcendence of conditional existence is a true urge, even the primal human urge. Human beings inherently desire a human and natural environment where they can live without the chronic production of stress chemistry. They want to be cured at the heart of their mind and be thereby transformed bodily. And they know, deeply, psychically, that they cannot realize that transformation until they can create a culture in which people can live without degenerative stress. Thus, sanctuary, or Spiritual community, is the motive in human beings that contains the genetic secret of the next stage in human evolution.

SCIENTIFIC PROOF OF THE EXISTENCE OF GOD
WILL SOON BE ANNOUNCED BY THE WHITE HOUSE!

SRI DA AVABHASA: All the Sanctuaries I have Empowered for My devotees are beautiful. They are unique places on Earth. Anyone who spends time at any one of the Sanctuaries knows this. These Sanctuaries are unique not merely because of their physical environments but because they are transformed physical environments.

SRI DA AVABHASA: Naitauba is not just a piece of land. It is a great sign after years— years—of everyone's struggling for the great purpose of acquiring Hermitage. At the heart of that purpose was this Place that all My devotees have now acquired. It is a Divine Place, where all My devotees are concentrated in this Divine Work. That is how it should be for as long as the sun shines and rises and sets and the grass grows and the wind blows. Forever—as ever as there can be in this world. All through this Epoch this Place, this Sanctuary of Blessing, should be set apart. Over time, then, millions of people, literally millions of people, should come to this Place and be Blessed. October 28, 1983

Facing page: Sri Love-Anandashram, Fiji, is an Empowered Sanctuary, a well-spring of Blessing and Grace for all who pilgrimage there. It is the Residence of Sri Da Avabhasa and the principal Sanctuary to which His devotees pilgrimage to go on retreat in His physical Company.

Above: Devotees of Sri Da Avabhasa on retreat at Sri Love-Anandashram.

(top left) Devotees gather at the Mountain Of Attention during the Feast of the Divine World-Teacher, one of the seven annual Spiritual Celebrations of Free Daism.

(top right) The Da Avabhasa Paduka Mandir at the Mountain Of Attention Sanctuary. This temple, extremely Potent with the Blessing Influence of Sri Da Avabhasa, may be entered by prepared devotees at any time of day or night to offer their prayers and a brief ceremony of worship of Sri Da Avabhasa.

View of Mt. Waiaileale from Tumomama Sanctuary, on the island of Kauai in Hawaii.

Huge Helper, at the Mountain Of Attention, houses the central offices of the Free Daist Communion.

The Mountain Of Attention provides weekend and extended retreats for Friends and members of Da Avabhasa International.

The llamas of Fear-No-More-Zoo, which was established by Sri Da Avabhasa at the Mountain of Attention Sanctuary in the early '70s.

THE FREE DAIST COMMUNION

The central offices of the Free Daist Communion are housed at the Mountain Of Attention Sanctuary, in Huge Helper, a former turn of the century hotel which has been Empowered over many years by Sri Da Avabhasa's frequent use of the site. Our sacred Archives offices, Audio-Visual Department, Advocacy Department, and Cultural Services Division, as well as the Dawn Horse Press and many other departments are located here.

The Dawn Horse Press produces as many as twenty-five publications each year. Here Michael Walker, Leslie Waltzer, and Matthew Barna discuss the cover of a new book.

The Audio/Visual Department produces audiotapes of Sri Da Avabhasa's Talks, and videotapes of all kinds to help introduce the Way of the Heart to the public. Here Annik Brunet is editing video footage of Sri Da Avabhasa.

The Free Daist Laughing Man Library is a uniquely important collection of approximately 50,000 English-language volumes. Established by Sri Da Avabhasa in 1973, the Free Daist Library surveys the historical traditions of religion, Spirituality, and practical self-discipline.
    Here librarian Jay Fienberg researches various publications for Sri Da Avabhasa's review and possible inclusion in His annotated bibliography, THE BASKET OF TOLERANCE.

The Chief Executive Officer of the Free Daist Communion, Bill Roesler, at work in his office

The sacred Archives collects and preserves sacred articles of all kinds related to the human Lifetime of Sri Da Avabhasa. Thus, an accurate record is kept of His Work and the growth of the Way of the Heart, and articles associated with Him (such as clothing, chairs, and walking staffs) that actually hold His Spiritual Influence are preserved so that they may benefit countless generations in the future.

Devotees of Sri Da Avabhasa who serve the Free Daist Communion gather for lunch in Huge Helper.

Only true, Spiritual, and moral community provides the human functional basis for the continuous testing and schooling of human qualities. When someone exists outside the cultural bond of community, all the forms of antisocial and egoically "self-possessed" (or self-absorbed) aberration appear, and, once having appeared, they cannot truly be changed unless the individual is restored to the condition of community. (Until community is restored, the responsibility for "curing" antisocial, or subhuman, aberrations seems to belong to abstract professions and institutions. But neither the State, nor any cult of laws and police, nor the great priesthood of psychiatrists can do what can only be done by the humanizing influence of true cultural demands within the bond of community.) Therefore, devote your freedom to community. Put your energy into human things.

SCIENTIFIC PROOF OF THE EXISTENCE OF GOD WILL SOON BE ANNOUNCED BY THE WHITE HOUSE!

COMMUNITY SERVICES AND BUSINESSES

Over the years, devotees of Sri Da Avabhasa have, at His suggestion, established various services, ministries, and businesses that employ members of our own community and serve devotees (as well as the general public, in many instances). These services and businesses, which include schools, general stores, and clinics, are moving us toward greater self-sufficiency and provide places of daily employment in which we can associate with one another, fulfilling Heart-Master Da's admonition to "spend more and more time in the company of others of My devotees". All the businesses pictured here are owned and staffed by devotees of Sri Da Avabhasa.

Master Foody Moody's General Store is a natural-food grocery and general store owned and supported by the community of practitioners of the Way of the Heart.

The Da Avabhasa Ashram in Holland (also known as the European Danda) operates a thriving candle factory.

Naptech operates in rural California, repairing electronic equipment.

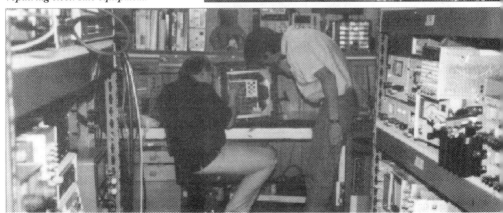

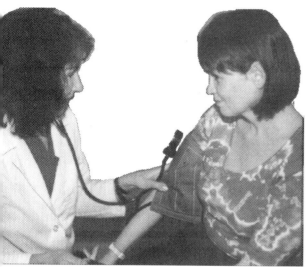

COMMUNITY SERVICES AND BUSINESSES

*The **Radiant Life Clinic** is based in Northern California. The healing arts are practiced here in the context of Sri Da Avabhasa's principles of "radical healing", or the understanding that disease is a direct result and expression of the fundamental "contraction" or separative activity of the ego. The clinic employs many modalities, including, among others, traditional Western (allopathic and naturopathic) treatments, traditional Eastern treatments (for example, acupuncture and Ayurveda), and chiropractic and bodywork techniques. Sri Da Avabhasa Instructs us that symptoms of disease are the expression of unconscious emotional conflicts, and that the first step in true healing is the uncovering of the underlying conflict. The basic healing practices are faith (or the presumption of one's Prior Condition of Happiness), prayer (specifically in the form of the laying on of hands and the Prayer of Changes, a form of prayer described fully in THE DAWN HORSE TESTAMENT), and fasting (which may take the form of literal fasting from solid food, or from ordinary activities, but also includes any form of practical action to correct disease-producing habits and to heal or eliminate symptoms).*

*Mate Moce (MAH-tey MO-they), Fijian for "easy death", is the **Free Daist Ministry of Death and Dying**. The staff of Mate Moce serve the transition of all Sri Da Avabhasa's devotees at the time of death, in accordance with Sri Da Avabhasa's Instructions. Here, Connie Grisso, R.N., and Frans Bakker, M.D., on a public speaking tour with Sri Da Avabhasa's book EASY DEATH.*

*Every **Regional Center** maintains a bookstore that carries the literature of the Way of the Heart as well as items related to meditation.*

SRI DA AVABHASA: The usual person conceives of himself or herself in isolation and dramatizes his or her life in those terms. What is the image of the good life in the everywhere "Westernized" world? Having your own castle, your own husband or wife, your own kids, your own everything. Everybody having their "own" same thing—their own car, their own house, their own TV set. Every person conceives of himself or herself as that archetype repeated. It is "Narcissus".

As a result, human beings do not make use of what they have gained after hundreds of thousands of years of struggling at the vital level, which is the possibility of a truly human culture, a culture in which people do not have to live on an emergency basis relative to the life-process anymore. You can pre-solve the life-situation essentially. You can share the life-force, the responsibility of life, and you can survive without adventure. By doing that you can make your energy available for the great process of Divine Self-Realization.

January 20, 1975

Name That Toon, inspired by Sri Da Avabhasa's appreciation of modern "Icons of Happiness" such as the cartoon characters created by Walt Disney Studios, began in Portland, Oregon, as a gallery where original cartoon art was displayed and sold. Name That Toon has opened a second gallery in Los Angeles, and is expanding into many other areas of media entertainment.

The Blessed Companion Bear Company produces award-winning, collectible bears that bring Sri Da Avabhasa's Happiness to everyone who purchases them. The Company was inspired by a great Teaching Demonstration in which Sri Da Avabhasa brought His devotees through a "consideration" of the "illusion of relatedness", or the primary illusion that there is an "other", through His Play with teddy bears.

CHILDREN AND YOUNG PEOPLE

Growing up (or arriving at an early age) in the culture and community of Free Daists is a unique advantage in the modern world. Sri Da Avabhasa has provided complete and specific Instructions for the religious practice as well as the care, education, and disciplining of children and young people—even infants and toddlers. If you ask young people in our community about their life, they will usually emphasize three things (which are really the same thing): their love-relationship with their Guru, the intimacy they enjoy with their peers and with adults, and the demand for human growth, responsibility, and self-transcendence that always confronts them.

The uniquely intimate and challenging culture and God-Realizing Way of life that Heart-Master Da has provided for children and young people allows them to attain real human maturity (the foundation for Spiritual life), rather than struggling for a lifetime with the unresolved complications and unhappiness of a conventional childhood and adolescence.

Several young devotees write about the life they have chosen here:

"When I was fourteen, I made the conscious and independent choice to practice the Way of the Heart after going through an ordeal of doubt and struggle. This is the best deci-sion I feel I have ever made, and I made it by my Guru's Grace. I value my relationship to Sri Da Avabhasa more than anything in the world, and I feel that relationship very personally with my Guru, in the strength of the community in which I live, in my service to the Free Daist Communion, and in my intimacies with fellow devotees."

Jonah Straus, 16

"The relationship with Him that Sri Da Avabhasa Offers to His young devotees is the greatest Gift, but He also Offers the Gift of community. What I have found growing up in this Way of life is incredible intimacy and true friendship. There is also the constant demand for self-transcendence. As teenagers, my friends and I are always called to more responsibility and maturity and to renounce our adolescent tendencies and be confessed and vulnerable in our relationships with everyone. We live a very disciplined life, and this is sometimes very difficult for us, but I am grateful and happy for it because I see how much I grow and how happy I am because of it."

Arcadia Smails, 15

Members of the Lay Brahmacharya Order on retreat at Sri Love-Anandashram, 1991

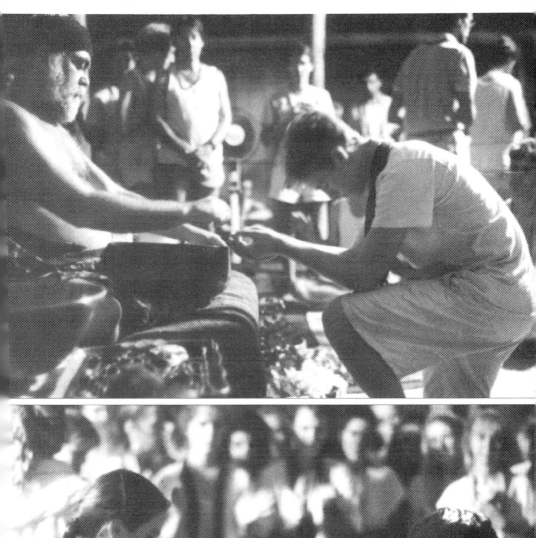

SRI DA AVABHASA: A fundamental principle in the development of children is that their sphere of intimacy must constantly be expanded. From birth until six to twelve months, the mother is the primary relationship of the child. The parent must watch for the signs of the child's readiness for a more expanded sphere of intimacy. The parent has the constant obligation to move the child into the larger sphere of community. Children must (1) be identified with many adults, and more kinds of people besides the parents, (2) be given mature role models, and (3) have a formalized life, in which they are required to cultivate personal and moral disciplines and constantly serve others.

(top) Five members of the Lay Brahmacharya Order on retreat at Sri Love-Anandashram.

(middle) The Free Daist Lay Brahmacharya School has its largest facility in Northern California, a short distance from the Mountain Of Attention Sanctuary.

(bottom left) Three girls being initiated as novices in the Free Daist Lay Brahmacharya Order, a renunciate order for young people who are committed to the most exemplary practice of the Way of the Heart.

SRI DA AVABHASA: Children must learn how to live from a Spiritual point of view, how to live ecstatically in the feeling of God. They should be practicing ecstasy, Happiness. They must understand that Happiness fundamentally is what existence is all about.

LOOK AT THE SUNLIGHT
ON THE WATER

SRI DA AVABHASA: Children are beautiful. I am in Love with children. A very strange thing that only parents know is that when you are a parent, you actually fall in love with your children. You do not merely love your children. You fall in love with them. You are deeply in love with your children, and you cannot imagine ever being separated from them. Your relationship to your children teaches you about love.

I Love everyone with just this passion! I Love men, women, children, walls, and frogs with the same profound intensity. I simply have a different kind of relationship with every being. I am in Love with children! I mean deeply in Love with them. I have a profound Love-relationship with them. I Love everyone with this passion. May 8, 1984

Sri Da Avabhasa's Vision of how young people will be trained to participate in the adult life of the community includes apprenticeships.

Jonah Straus, 16, is an apprentice at the Dawn Horse Press, where he is being trained in every aspect of publishing, from writing and editing to distribution and marketing. Before Jonah graduated from the Free Daist Lay Brahmacharya School, he was the managing editor of The Garden of Lions Magazine, *the magazine produced by young Free Daists.*

Rani Druda, 17, apprentices with Marshall Winkler, D.C., a devotee of Da Avabhasa who maintains a private chiropractic practice several miles from the Mountain Of Attention Sanctuary. Rani's apprenticeship with Dr. Winkler is preparing her for chiropractic college.

Gawain Weaver, 19, is apprenticing in the Audio/Visual Department of the Free Daist Communion, while continuing the academic studies that will inform his communications about Sri Da Avabhasa and the Way of the Heart through film and other media.

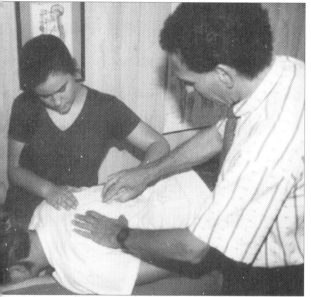

SACRED ARTS

What are sacred arts? Arts that are devoted to the Divine, that are an expression of the Divine, and that evoke the feeling of the Divine in both the participants and their audience. Sacred arts are one of the richest expressions of Sri Da Avabhasa's devotees' devotion to Him.

Any art form at all—even extensions of the traditional arts such as writing, cooking, and athletics—may be regarded as a sacred art if it is done in a self-transcending manner that evokes self-forgetting devotion to Sri Da Avabhasa, or the Feeling of the Mystery of existence.

Art, music, and literature have always played an important role in sacred cultures, as an expression of celebrating the Divine. In the Way of the Heart, the sacred development of the arts has been uniquely encouraged and nurtured by Sri Da Avabhasa, especially through the creation of various guilds, some of which are pictured here. Sri Da Avabhasa has inspired His devotees to create beautiful and heart-opening art forms of every kind—all of which serve to deepen feeling-Contemplation of Him.

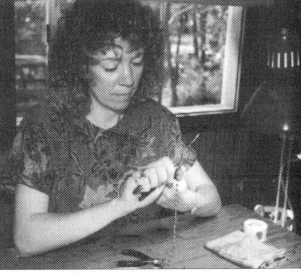

A class in traditional Indian drumming, which accompanies devotional chanting.

A member of Sacred Fires, the guild of Free Daist artisans who create sacred jewelry for the community of devotees.

Young Free Daists performing a scene from **The Mummery**, *enhanced, in this production, by puppets.*

Several years ago, a young devotee of Sri Da Avabhasa who was studying Indian dance as her sacred art commented to Him that, traditionally, students of this particular form of dance would study ancient sacred sculpture in order to learn the appropriate gestures. Sri Da Avabhasa took the opportunity to Instruct all His devotees about the true impulse and origin of sacred art:

SRI DA AVABHASA: Of course it is fine to study traditional sculptures, but sacred dance is a form of worship, Divine Communion, surrender of the conditional self to the Divine in the Form of the Guru. Such worship is also the ultimate sacred discipline for the Spiritual practitioner. Therefore, in fact, meditative feeling-Contemplation of Me, as I Instruct you in the Way of the Heart, is a sacred art. My devotee who practices such feeling-Contemplation of Me, by surrendering to My bodily (human) Form, My Spiritual (and Always Blessing) Presence, and My Very (and Inherently Perfect) State, Realizes My Divine Nature and becomes One with Me through that Process.

Sacred dance, and in fact every sacred art, is based upon this ancient principle of surrender to the Divine in the Form of the Guru. Sacred arts have always been created in this manner. The greatest form of sacred art is surrender to the Guru to the point of Realizing the Guru's own Divine State.

The worship that occurs in sacred arts is surrender to the Divine Form and, through that surrender, reception of the Divine Shakti, or Divine Energy, of that Divine Form. If you surrender to the Divine in the bodily (human) Form of the Guru, then the Divine Shakti will Move you. All the traditions of the sacred arts were manifested originally and spontaneously by people who were spontaneously Moved by the Divine Shakti. Over time, a system developed that became the ritual of that sacred art. Hatha Yoga, for instance, is not

(From left to right) The Sacred Music Guild is responsible for all the sacred music that is an integral part of daily worship in the Way of the Heart. A young Australian devotee performs for the Ashram. A devotee working on a banner for a Spiritual Celebration. A young devotee performing the traditional Indian dance form Bharat Natyam. The Free Daist Theatre Guild enacts an incident recounted in The Knee of Listening.

merely a physical invention. Its poses were manifested by people who were Moved by the Divine Shakti. Originally, all the asanas of Hatha Yoga were Realized and Manifested by the internal Spirit-Energy received by devotees from the Guru.

Therefore, in the sacred art of dance, the principle is to surrender to the Guru. Traditionally, depending on the sect, sacred dancers would surrender to the Icon of their sect. Through that surrender, the Divine would Move the dancer to take on facial expressions and movements and asanas in reception of the Divine Spirit-Energy, or Shakti. Sacred art is not realized through imitation of images but through allowing the Divine Spirit to Manifest. Sacred art comes from the inside to the outside, not from the outside to the inside. All sacred arts are founded on Divine "Possession", or surrender to the Divine in the Form of the Guru to the point that the Divine Enters you, literally.

Therefore, it is not truly correct to say that sacred dance was created by imitating sculptures or sacred images. Fundamentally, the study of sacred images is only preparation for the eventual capability to receive and to be Moved by the Divine Spirit.

March 14, 1990

II

"You Can Love"

A Leela of Retreat at
Sri Love-Anandashram

by Carol Wilson

Sri Love-Anandashram

Carol Wilson, 57, lives in Lake County, California, near the Mountain Of Attention Sanctuary with her intimate partner, Tom Mabin, who is retired. Born in Indiana, Carol taught music and raised three daughters before coming to Heart-Master Da in 1978. She divides her time between serving the grounds of the Sanctuary and administering the Area Study Groups (small groups that meet in cities worldwide to listen to Heart-Master Da's Wisdom-Teaching, hear the Leelas of His Work with His devotees, and see video footage of Him). The account you are about to read is of Carol's second retreat at Sri Love-Anandashram.

Just as every devotee's relationship to Sri Da Avabhasa is unique, every retreat in His Company is unique, each devotee receiving precisely what his or her heart requires for true growth in relationship to Sri Gurudev. The period of time during which Carol went on retreat was especially remarkable, however, because Sri Da Avabhasa chose to "gather" with the resident staff of Sri Love-Anandashram and, less frequently, with retreatants, over a period of several months—something He had not done since early 1988. Gatherings are informal celebrations in Sri Gurudev's Company in which His Transmission is communicated not in silence, as is typical of more formal Darshan occasions, but in very human and personal terms. A gathering frequently begins with a formal Discourse by Heart-

Master Da—or possibly less formal conversation between Him and His devotees—and may go on to include dancing, singing of operatic classics, recitation of poetry (Sri Gurudev has particularly enjoyed reciting for His devotees the poetry of Dylan Thomas), recitations of Sri Gurudev's ecstatic Confessions of God, or listening to recordings of such recitations made in the past, all accompanied by the use of "accessories" not usually part of the Free Daist diet—such as alcohol and cigarettes.

Gatherings with Sri Da Avabhasa are potent Initiatory occasions—as you will see in the following Leela—and are part of His "Skillful Means" to instigate self-understanding and self-transcendence in the context of the outward-directed and expansive kind of experience to which Westerners, in particular, are habituated. The ecstasy of such occasions is beyond any kind of conventional socializing and awakens the disposition of whole-body Happiness and Love in relationship to every apparent other.

The day before I was to leave for retreat at Sri Love-Anandashram, I heard a presentation at the Mountain Of Attention Sanctuary about a shift in the mood of Sri Da Avabhasa's Work with His devotees. Sri Gurudev was freely and openly demonstrating His Sign as a Tantric Master[1] (something He had not felt free to do in many years) and was criticizing our "boring puritanical" quality—even suggesting the possibility of our celebrating with Him using accessories to the diet—alcohol and tobacco. After years of formal (and even rigid) approach to our practice that was not a true reflection of our Guru's Sign, we needed to "get loose". Devotees had not celebrated in this way in Sri Gurudev's physical Company for many years. As I listened, I began to feel a thrill of expectation and excitement.

Devotees seem always to go on retreat with certain expectations, or at least hopes and prayers, for some aspect of their practice to be purified, enlivened, or just understood. In my case, I felt desperate to become established in a real, non-abstract relationship with my Sat-Guru even when I wasn't in His physical Company. I have been a devotee and student of Sri Da Avabhasa for fourteen years and I have loved Him deeply. I have seen Him many times and served Him faithfully. I have sent gifts to Him, sung for Him, provided food for Him. And I have felt my life Blessed in countless ways by my relationship with Him and my practice of the Way of the Heart. In spite of all this, I seemed to relate to Him more as one might relate to "God"—abstractly, as if there is no _real_, humanly intimate relationship. As a result, in my meditation periods, in which I would attempt to practice true feeling-Contemplation of Sri Gurudev, it just wasn't happening.

I was tormented by the fact that I could not feel Him most intimately and personally. I felt that somehow I, myself, was actively preventing the relationship I longed for. I had even seen that I was withholding my love from Him, attempting to punish Him because I did not feel perfectly loved and fulfilled. I had also begun to be painfully convicted of my patterns of unlove in all my ordinary relations as well—my obsessive self-involvement, my lack of regard for others, my fear of others and assumption of their disregard for me.

Intellectually, I understood that all this was my own activity, the self-contraction—but it was not yet a fully conscious and bodily understanding in me, and I could only pray for my Sat-Guru's Help. These were the things I took with me to lay at the Feet of my Beloved Da Avabhasa.

We left San Francisco International Airport at 9:00 P.M. on June 19, 1992, a Monday night, changed planes in Honolulu, and arrived in Nadi, Fiji, at 6:00 A.M. Wednesday, having lost Tuesday entirely when we crossed the international dateline. From there I flew in a twenty-seater propeller plane to the island of Taveuni and took a taxi to the small boat that was awaiting my arrival. No sooner did I step onto the boat than we were off. As it was afternoon by now and the sun was quickly setting (June 21 is the shortest day of the year in the southern hemisphere), I slept.

My arrival at Sri Love-Anandashram several hours later was unceremonious. It was already dark as I waded onto the sand and prostrated. The feeling of Sri Da Avabhasa pervades the Island, and the minute I stepped foot onto the sand, my heart knew it was home. I felt such a sense of wonder, realizing that my Heart-Master was so near. The warm air was thick with moisture, and I immediately began to feel the bite of mosquitoes.

Paul Jones, the retreat manager, was there to meet me and carry my bags to the ladies' dormitory. Paul immediately began telling me about a wonderful Darshan occasion with Sri Da Avabhasa that had happened that day, further whetting my appetite to see my Sat-Guru—but as it turned out I had to wait three days for my first Darshan.

In the meantime, I settled into the retreat schedule. The schedule was necessarily flexible, because we never knew when we might be invited to walk out to Da Avabhasa Chakra, Sri Gurudev's residential compound about two miles from the retreatants' quarters. Most of the time while I was there, our morning schedule was pretty consistent. We would rise at 5:00 A.M. to begin meditation at 5:20 in Mindless Company, the meditation hall located in the retreatants' section of the Island. At 6:50, we would walk over to the Giving Coat (a screened-in meditation hall near the residents' village), where Sri Da Avabhasa has sat in Darshan many times. We would attend the Sat-Guru Puja there each morning. I enjoyed this five-minute walk in the early morning, as the air was still cool and I was so full of my Guru's love after meditation and was looking forward to the Puja. On the way, we would all pick at least one hibiscus flower to offer as a gift. (The flowers on Naitauba are wonderful. The Island is covered with hibiscus bushes in particular—bright red, orange, pink, and yellow, of all sizes and shapes.)

On the walk back to the retreat quarters after the Puja, several of us would collect large numbers of flowers to make flower malas (garlands) for the day. One mala was made daily especially for Sri Gurudev, and then we made twelve other malas every day to adorn several holy sites.

We made the malas after breakfast, and then we each had a specific service function to perform. My service was to tend to Darshan Light, the meeting room where the retreatants eat their meals. I adorned the Murti with flowers each morning, and I helped clean away the dishes after each meal. I also helped sweep out the sand that was tracked in each day and tried to keep the anthills under control.

At 11:00 A.M. we meditated again for an hour before lunch. By lunchtime, the sun was high and the air was warm and sultry. There was so much moisture in the air that even the bed sheets were damp when we got into bed each night. But the winter temperatures were very mild, sometimes even delightfully cool.

We served for an hour after lunch and then chanted for forty-five minutes. We would then meditate for an hour. If we were going to be invited to Da Avabhasa Chakra that day, it was usually as meditation ended. If we were staying in the residents' village for the evening activities, many of us would swim for a few minutes in the ocean before showering and having dinner and then attending the Sat-Guru-Arati Puja in the Giving Coat. The evening activities varied. One night we might have a devotional group, another night we might practice laying on of hands with one another. One night each week, we wrote practice reports to be given to Sri Gurudev. Every evening when we were in the village, there would be a Purification and Empowerment Puja during which we would all chant ecstatically for forty-five minutes before doing our final meditation. Bedtime was at 10:30 P.M.

My first Darshan occasion occurred three days after my arrival, on the porch of Indefinable (Sri Gurudev's Residence when He visits in the village). I felt a kind of shock when I first saw Him because, with His longer hair and the flowing beard He had at the time, He looked very different from the photographs I had seen recently. After I offered my gift at His Feet, someone pulled me down to sit right in front of Him since it was my first Darshan.

Almost immediately, He set the tone of the occasion by saying out loud, "Make way for the cripple", as one lady retreatant who had just sprained her ankle walked in on crutches. He not only set her at ease with this humorous remark but made it plain to us all that this was to be a more informal occasion and that we could speak to Him. My heart leapt at the sound of His exquisitely rich voice. I was already melting, already weeping tears of love. People spoke to Him of various things, each one expressing their

The Giving Coat

great heart-love and gratitude for all His Gifts. One lady read Him a poem she had written to Him. Another asked if she might sing Him a new chant she had just written for Him, which He received lovingly.

Meanwhile, in the midst of all of this, I was feeling a little self-conscious about not saying anything, because almost everyone had spoken at least a few words to Him. I have always found it very difficult to talk about my real feelings. And I had never spoken directly to my Guru. I really wanted to thank Him, to tell Him how extraordinarily beautiful He is and how much I love Him. But something about the passion with which I felt these things made it difficult for me to speak in front of all the other retreatants.

I was crying and speaking the words very softly under my breath, when He suddenly nodded His head as a signal that it was time to go. As people began to move, I cried the words to Him out loud, my body literally shaking with sobs, and He gave me His full loving regard, receiving my confessions of love. I kept saying over and over, "You are so beautiful, I love You so much, thank You, thank You." He stayed with me, saying "Tcha" and silently forming other words of Love and Blessing, as long as I continued, until I finally bowed my head to the ground. This was the beginning of a whole retreat of "firsts", wherein I gradually had no option but to drop all my doubts about my profoundly real relationship with my Sat-Guru.

This period of time was marked by some of the most profound Darshan occasions I have ever participated in. The second Darshan occasion was out at Da Avabhasa Chakra. There is really no way to describe the feeling of this exquisite place. To get to this most Holy Ground, most retreatants hiked two and a half miles over a fairly steep hill (some called it a mountain). Everyone was asked to stay together in a group, and we would chant devotional songs as we walked. As we would begin the descent down toward Da Avabhasa Chakra, the temperature of the air would become noticeably cooler, and the ocean breeze would pick up and dry away our perspiration. The brilliant azure of the ocean would become suddenly visible beyond the hill, and my heart would take notice: He is here. This is His Home. This is Him.

On this particular day, after we arrived at Da Avabhasa Chakra, we served only a short time—some of us polishing the brass doors leading from the outer courtyard into the inner courtyard of Aham Da Asmi Sthan (Sri Da Avabhasa's principal Residence), others polishing the brass rail and water fixtures that line the walls on either side of the brass doors, where devotees may wash their feet before entering the inner courtyard. We were soon called to walk across the large expanse of lawn to Kaya Kalpa Kutir (a Fijian-style structure of reeds, enclosing a small pool), and there we were ushered into another realm.

I gasped. Our Guru was in the Jacuzzi, immersed waist deep in the water and leaning against the side with His arms up over the edge. Sitar music was playing in the background. My mind was shattered. There was nothing here but Him. It was all the feeling of Him. That's all. There was nothing to think about, nothing to say. We did not speak, nor could I have spoken. As I walked back across the lawn after the event, my body was

View of Da Avabhasa Chakra (left) and the inner courtyard of Aham Da Asmi Sthan

totally relaxed, in bliss, no thoughts except to notice how perfect everything was and how in love I was.

Before I arrived, there had been Darshan occasions almost daily, but since our Sat-Guru had been Working closely with a group of devotees applying for the Lay Renunciate Order (an intensive form of practice) and having frequent gatherings with them, we were having Darshan occasions about twice a week. I began to notice that in the two- or three-day space between Darshan occasions I would begin to abstract Sri Gurudev again. This made me despair. If I couldn't stay in the relationship with Him for even three days without seeing Him in person, what was I going to do when I went home?

One evening during the second week of my retreat, Sri Gurudev called a gathering with all the residents. By this point we retreatants were beside ourselves with longing to attend the gatherings also, although it didn't really seem likely that this would happen because retreat is typically very formal. We did our evening meditation and chanting and went to bed. Late in the night, I was aware of distant sounds—the singing of opera and the beat of rock music—which went on until the wee hours of the morning.

The next day we were bombarded with stories of a most wondrous and Divine evening. Only the Divine Master of Love could have orchestrated such an event. Our Beloved had hugged, kissed, joked, and lovingly conversed with every single person. He had danced among His devotees, sung opera with and for them, and recited poetry. He had wept as He spoke of His Love for His family and for all suffering beings. Everyone was not only totally radiant and happy but also amazed at what had occurred. Several of us retreatants got together and wrote a letter to Sri Gurudev on everyone's behalf, confessing our great longing to hug and kiss Him.

Several days later we had another Darshan occasion on the lawn outside Kaya Kalpa Kutir. This was a day when five retreatants were scheduled to depart. Sri Gurudev was already seated in His lawn chair as we walked or ran across the lawn to Him. What a vision! He just sat looking so sublime under the tree, with the Gurukula[2] and the retreatants sitting around Him on the lawn, His legs stretched out so that His Beautiful

Feet were exposed to everyone's view. I offered my flower, my eyes meeting His, and then prostrated at His Feet. Again, as in all the Darshan occasions, I just melted away and wept my love for Him. He nodded to indicate the end of the occasion and everyone began to praise Him, but we seemed to be taking a long time to actually leave!

All of a sudden, retreatants who were leaving that day were asking Him if they could kiss His Feet, and He was not only Granting His permission but was inviting some to come to Him for hugs by holding out His great arms to them, totally breaking everyone's heart, mine included. I also felt disturbed, however, because I myself felt unworthy of such a Gift. I knew I loved my Guru deeply, but I still doubted—as the ego always doubts—that He loved me or even knew who I was.

In meditation some days later, it occurred to me that when Sri Gurudev looked at me, His look seemed "hard and unfeeling". I immediately realized that He was reflecting me to myself. In my diary I wrote: "First there is the knowing that I can't do anything to break open my hard heart or the hard shell around it. I do things for people, I am more social (somewhat) and agreeable, but I still complain a lot. I have been willing to transcend myself relative to the physical laziness of withholding energy from others, but the heart has remained hard. I go around feeling unloved and attending to that, and, it is true, I push people away." I felt my need for the Guru profoundly.

At this point, we had a devotional group in which I confessed my confusion relative to my own practice. The Darshan occasions were wonderful—I was drawn beyond myself each time—but between Darshans, what was I doing? I began to talk to a confidante each day. I was reminded by my friends that while I have a fear of speaking with feeling from the heart, I actually talk a great deal about nothing, in a very superficial and anxious fashion. So I took on a discipline to help me to speak with feeling (speaking less and taking a conscious breath before I speak), and I began to frequent the Paduka Mandir (a small and very Spiritually potent temple which houses Sri Da Avabhasa's sacred Sandals) and pray for Help. I wrote in my diary, "I feel confused and afraid. I can't explain anything clearly like others seem to be able to do. I'm humiliated that I can't get up and tell a Leela. I can't pray for anything specific because I don't know what I need. Just HELP!"

My writing continued: "This morning I saw again that I have never made one movement in my life that was for anyone other than myself, including care of my

Paduka Mandir

own children. I always try to act in a way that makes everyone think I'm a considerate, loving person, but I do not do anything loving." I was obviously working up to a crisis of self-understanding. When devotees asked Sri Gurudev if they might kiss His Feet and hug Him, I was afraid of eventually being in the position to ask for this. I felt like this would somehow be a fake request, though I did not understand why. Now I understood. I had never been loving Him really, any more than I had been loving anyone. I just wanted to feel loved <u>by</u> Him.

I had been going regularly to the Paduka Mandir and had begun to feel my loneliness intensely—feeling unloved and unlovable. In the 11:00 A.M. meditation, I began to receive very clear pictures of my intimate partner, Tom. I was feeling my love for him very strongly and as always occurs when I feel my love for him, I began to feel intense sorrow about the fact that he is much older than I and most probably will die well ahead of me. The two feelings always go hand in hand. The pictures were vivid, and I began to sob uncontrollably.

That afternoon one of my friends and I were approached by a resident who told us that Sri Gurudev wanted to gather tonight with residents <u>and</u> <u>retreatants</u>! My friend and I were sure he was teasing us, but he insisted that this was true, and soon all the retreatants ecstatically began the seemingly impossible task of dressing for this event.

We were told the ladies should wear makeup and dress as "hip" as possible under the circumstances. We had come on retreat with gray clothing primarily and had definitely not anticipated such an amazing turn of events. But by getting together and trading and sharing what we had, we all managed to look pretty good, even though we had a very short time to prepare. One lady had brought a whole selection of earrings, not really knowing why, so there were enough for all of us. We were very excited and happy.

Before we knew it we were walking into Hymns To Me, the Sacred Arts building. The room where we gathered was a dance studio, quite large and just perfect for a group this size to dance in. Sri Gurudev's Chair was adorned with flowers and awaiting His arrival, and music was playing in the background. Quite a few people were already in the room, dressed up, talking and laughing and drinking beer.

I couldn't believe I was actually attending a gathering. I didn't know exactly what was going to occur, but I was sure my life was going to be changed. In fact, I felt that this was the answer to lifetimes of heart-prayers. We had only been there a short time when the Master of our hearts strode into the room, sat on His Chair, lit up a cigarette, and began to do His Work.

He began a conversation with someone, and from there on one person after another spoke to Him about this or that. Each person ended up in His great arms, embracing and being embraced by the God-Man Da, some kissing His beautiful face, neck, shoulders, belly, Feet, speaking into His ear, weeping to Him their gratitude and love, and finally prostrating at His Feet. I was holding back, still feeling afraid to speak to Him, especially in front of all these people. But I had a very definite sense that I would get my chance. I was feeling less and less concerned. I could feel that He was orchestrating the evening and that somehow He would see to it that I had my opportunity to express my love to Him.

Later we sang opera with Him, danced with Him, listened to Him recite Dylan Thomas, each event totally delicious. I had heard about the gatherings of the past many times. To actually be there felt like a dream. At the same time, I began to understand something about a feeling I had that I needed to speak to Him in person in order to make the relationship "real". From the beginning, I had had a very strong intuition that it simply wasn't necessary for me to speak to Him beyond my confession of love and gratitude. He knows us perfectly. Why talk when we can just love? Of course, there was something about my fear of speaking that needed to be purified. But I did see that my intimate and personal relationship to Him did not depend upon my sharing my personal life with Him. I had been allowing my chronic concern to get in the way and convince me otherwise. By the end of my retreat, I finally got this lesson and felt free of that concern.

At one point, our Gurudev told us to dance, to really "get down". Then He left, saying He would be back later when we were "really loose". I was happier than I have ever been in my life. What a miracle He Is. He Is Happiness Itself, and to be in His sphere of Love and Radiance literally Transforms the being. The music was perfect, and I love to dance. Everyone was so happy and in love with Him and with one another.

When Sri Gurudev returned, I noticed other people beginning to approach Him again. I danced near Him so that I could just slip up to Him at a moment's notice, which is exactly what happened. I dropped to my knees in front of Him, and before I even hit the floor He was saying, "Well, you finally got up here. What took you so long?"

I began, "I'm such a fool to always be so afraid."

He said, "I know you love Me."

I think that statement from Him meant more to me than any other thing in my entire life. Then I was in His great arms, embracing Him and kissing Him. He asked me, "Do you have an intimate partner?"

I said yes and reminded Him who it is. Then I broke down weeping and told Him that because Tom is older I am always dreading his death. He said, "But don't worry about it. You can't worry about it. It doesn't do any good. That's the way it is here. People die. You can't change it, but you can love. Just love him. Use My Sign. Do what I do. If you're worrying about his dying, you're not loving." And I could feel that He was literally Empowering me to do this loving.

Then He went on to tell me that I must stop being afraid of everything all the time. I agreed and admitted that I am always afraid. He said, "What are you afraid of?" When I was silent, He asked, "Because you're going to die?" He spoke to me at length about this and very forcefully. By this time, we were face to face, only inches apart. I was so gone in love and so overwhelmed by the miracle of my being there with Him that even though on some level I understood everything He said, and was repeating things back to

Him and agreeing and affirming all of it, what I actually remember about it is looking into His eyes with deep love and feeling totally loved by Him. Something in me kept saying over and over, "This is real. This is the most real anything has ever been." And another part, which was connected to my eyes, kept saying, "I love You. You are so beautiful. Thank You, I love You."

He also talked to me about not assuming I'm old (I am fifty-seven). And everything He told me registered in me bodily. He finally told me to get back out there and dance and not assume I am old. I continued to kiss His face and beard and shoulder, and then lowered myself to His wonderful Feet, which were crossed in front of Him. I kissed His Feet and prostrated on the floor. I knew that something had changed in me and that I would never be the same. Everything looked different. People looked different. Everything was Him. And I was in love with everybody and could bring love to everybody. I danced madly and ecstatically until Sri Da Avabhasa left at around 3:00 A.M.

The following night there was another gathering, to which retreatants were not invited. We meditated and went to bed early to catch up on our sleep. But out of the black of the night, around 3:30 A.M., there was banging on our door. A man's voice was shouting, "Get up, get up, hurry! The Guru! The Guru! Don't worry about getting dressed, just come now."

I bounded out of bed in my nightshirt and went to the door. There, parked in front of the ladies' dormitory, was the white Land Cruiser with my Beloved sitting inside. I went running to Him barefoot. I was one of the first there and stood right next to the car. He had His arm out holding people and <u>allowing</u> us to hold Him, kiss His hand, stroke His arm. I called Him Beloved. I was so in love. I held and caressed His hand and arm. I even lightly caressed the side of His face and beard. He was so sweet and soft. He looked so incredibly beautiful. He said, "Don't get too much awake. I don't want to disturb your sleep. I'm going home to Da Avabhasa Chakra to get some rest. I just wanted to say goodnight to My babies."

As they were about to pull away, He took my hand to His lips and kissed it. I found His other hand, which was still out, and brought it to my lips and kissed it. And then He left.

We went back to bed, unable to go back to sleep. The other retreatants were excitedly chattering away, repeating with delight the play that had just been enacted among all of us. I felt no need or desire to speak. I only wanted to relish the love I was feeling in my body. I don't know if I slept at all. I just felt Him, and kept the vision of His beautiful, round face and beard before me.

I feel as if the one I was died that morning. It might be more accurate to say, however, that I was truly born that morning. Both things felt true and have remained true to the time of this writing. During meditation that morning, I had an incredible feeling of softness, vulnerability, whole bodily love. Nothing about the way I felt bodily was familiar. I was totally relaxed. My heart was at ease. My heart and body had been anxious and fear-ridden my whole life. Now I could breathe fully and my mind was quiet. In my fear,

"I love You. You are so beautiful. Thank You, I love You."

Carol Wilson at a gathering with Sri Da Avabhasa

I had always fought to keep everything under control. Now I was feeling the absolute ecstasy and the freedom of not knowing, not being in control, of feeling totally unable to "make sense" of this Great One. Gratitude filled my heart.

As we left the Hall, I realized I did not want to walk alone back to the retreat quarters. I called to a friend who was ahead of me and asked her to wait, and told her that I felt I needed to walk arm in arm with someone, or better still, with my body up against someone. This was totally uncharacteristic of me. She looked at me and said, "Carol! You look beautiful! Your whole face looks different. All the tension is gone out of your face. Your eyes are so soft."

My eyes were tear-filled and in love as I told her that my whole body felt different. We embraced one another and wept as we felt what we were being given. When I got back, other people made the same remark about my appearance. And I would just melt into an embrace with each one. In the past, I have always had to make "decisions" about needing to be more loving or receptive or more in relationship with people. But now everything was spontaneous.

I wrote in my diary several days later, "I have been changed at the heart and bodily. I am a loved woman. My chronic fear of others is gone. When the body knows it is loved, it doesn't fear. The love in my heart, put there by my Guru, extends out to everything and everyone. My voice has fallen lower and relaxed. I'm not inclined to talk so much."

I began to understand that to be "in love" with the God-Man is to be "in love" with everything. This is the way it works. This is what He is trying to show us. He keeps saying, "Love Me. Activate devotion to Me. Then on the basis of that love, go out and love your intimate partner and everyone." It's not just, "Love Me, feel what that's like, and then love others likewise." It's "Love Me and you can't help yourself." Everything and everyone becomes radiant and sweet, innocent and benign. Separation and separateness are dissolved. This is what began, on this day, to become very clear.

Love is sometimes described as feeling like you're floating on air. For me, though, I felt that for the first time in my life I was really on the ground. I wanted to be with people, close up to people, look people in the eye. Before, emotional intimacy had required too much of me—I was too afraid, too caught up in my feelings of unworthiness, too concerned about myself to care about other people. But now I was <u>interested</u>—I could feel my love for everyone.

One night around this time, the retreatants were all called out of bed to go to another gathering. When we arrived at Hymns To Me, Sri Gurudev was in His Chair, surrounded by the Gurukula, engaging in conversation with various people. After a few minutes, to my surprise I was told I should go up and speak to Sri Gurudev. I felt a little awkward since He was speaking to someone else, but Kanya Navaneeta just kept beckoning me forward, so I sat down right in front of Him. I felt very anxious because my mind was blank and I couldn't think of anything to say. He seemed not to notice me. Later I felt He was just giving me the gift of time to Contemplate Him. My eyes never left His face. At one point, my heart was so full of Him that my eyes filled with tears. I knew then that there was nothing I really needed to say. I only wanted to tell Him again of my love.

He was about to call a break when I put my hand on His knee and said, "Sri Gurudev." He looked at me as if He hadn't noticed I was there waiting to speak to Him. I said, "I'm so in love with You." He said, "I know all about that." I said, "I can't bear to leave You." He said, "You don't have to." I said, "May I kiss You?"

He humorously commented on my bright lipstick, which I quickly wiped off with my hand. Then He leaned forward and we embraced and kissed. When I said again that I loved Him so much, He said, "I love you too." It was so sweet and I was so in love. He asked me if I was tipsy yet. I said, "Not quite", and He told me to get back out there and have another beer. I kissed His Feet, sobbing, for a long time. He finally pulled His foot back to get up and go out for a break.

I began drinking beer and dancing. But I continued to cry for a while. I wrote in my diary later, "It was easy and perfectly natural to love everyone and give energy to whomever I danced with, through the eyes. It's all about feeling, now, that ecstatic relationship with Him (it's real now) and conveying that (and sharing that) through the eyes and body as you dance. Sri Gurudev left around 4:00 A.M. I stayed and danced until 6:30. I was totally absorbed in Him. I wanted to dance forever. When there were no more people to dance with, I danced alone in front of His Chair. I walked back to the retreat quarters and did not feel like sleeping. I took a shower, washed out my clothes, and finally slept for about two hours. Everyone was again telling me how 'soft' and 'in love' I looked. I napped again in the afternoon, but I never suffered the lack of sleep. Being 'in love' totally rejuvenates the body."

As I scanned my daily journal that evening, I began to feel the absolute miracle of what had been occurring for me on this retreat. During the course of the retreat, I was given many stark revelations of "Narcissus" that helped me to see myself even further: On the one hand I assumed myself to be totally unlovable and was therefore terrified of everyone and everything. On the other hand my chronic unlove was really adolescent anger and the withholding of love, based on my assumption that no one loved me. To love another requires self-forgetting. It was easy to see why I couldn't love. My attention had been totally wrapped up in my fear and in trying to control life in order to feel safe.

As all of this became clear to me, I began to feel profoundly the Gift of the God-Man. By embracing me bodily, over and over again, He made it literally impossible not to forget myself. Time after time, throughout the retreat, He found more and more ways to convince my heart of His Love for me. By constantly, visibly and verbally, receiving and acknowledging my love for Him, He made it possible for my heart and body to relax. And this in turn freed my attention from myself. I felt safe. I was moved to embrace others. I was "in love". This "in love" extended to everyone and everything and I felt everyone and everything moving to me in love. He is such a miracle! He is more Beautiful to my eyes and heart than I have ever imagined anything could be.

My last day arrived. I had been at Sri Love-Anandashram for four weeks. The boat was not scheduled to leave until around 1:30 A.M., because of the tides and the difficulties navigating the reef. I was getting ready to sleep for a few hours when we were told that the departing retreatants were invited to the gathering to say goodbye to Love-Ananda. Again, I was overwhelmed with His sweetness, His regard, and His Love. Then we were told that our boat was leaving at 11:30 instead of 1:30, so we didn't have a lot of time. We went over immediately.

Music was playing and there was dancing going on. We just all sat down in front of Him. As He spoke to others, said goodbye to others, I just couldn't stop watching Him. Every expression was so exquisite to me, so dear. He would hug someone and I could see His face during the Hug. He would kiss someone goodbye and then look at them with His face of total Love. He motioned me forward at one point.

I went to Him and offered my flower, which He took and then pushed right back into my hand for me to keep as Prasad. He took me to Him and hugged me for a long time. He asked in my ear, "Will you come back and see Me soon?" I said I couldn't bear to stay away from Him long. He asked, "Are you going home to love your man?" I assured Him I was. When He finally let me go, I sank down to kiss His Feet, which were crossed in front of Him. As I put my lips to His Foot, I felt His hand on my head and back, holding me. I stayed at His Feet until He made it clear it was time for me to go. I prostrated in love.

As we left, I said a prayer that I would not ever cut off the love and vulnerability that I felt in my heart. I had learned that the only way for me to keep feeling Him and to not abstract Him is to allow this heart-broken longing for Him to always burn. He calls this the Wound of Love. "Love is a wound that never heals."

I Praise the Miracle of the God-Man Da. He is here to Liberate all hearts. My gratitude for what I have been given knows no bounds. My life is forever laid at His Feet. May I always serve His Great Heart. May all beings be Blessed to feel His Love—He is here for all of us.

NOTES

1. Here the author is referring to Sri Da Avabhasa's particular manner of working with devotees at that time. Traditionally, in more unusual or "Heroic" cases, Tantric Masters would freely make skillful use of usually forbidden emotions, passions, intoxicants, and other similar means, in order to serve the Spiritual process in devotees. It is understood that direct confrontation with these "dangerous" or "forbidden" elements, in the case of those rare individuals strong enough to make right use of such a circumstance, can quicken the process of growth and transcendence by helping them move through obstructions quickly and thoroughly.

2. In Hinduism, the "Gurukula" is the sacred Family, or mandala (circle) of intimates, around the Guru, and it most often includes his closest devotees, his children, and any young devotees he has accepted into his household for the sake of their Spiritual practice. Sri Da Avabhasa's Gurukula consists of two women, who have consecrated themselves to the service of Da Avabhasa in true intimacy, and who comprise the Da Avabhasa Gurukula Kanyadana Kumari Order; and four young female devotees, or Brahmacharinis (students of God), who comprise the Da Avabhasa Gurukula Brahmacharini Order.

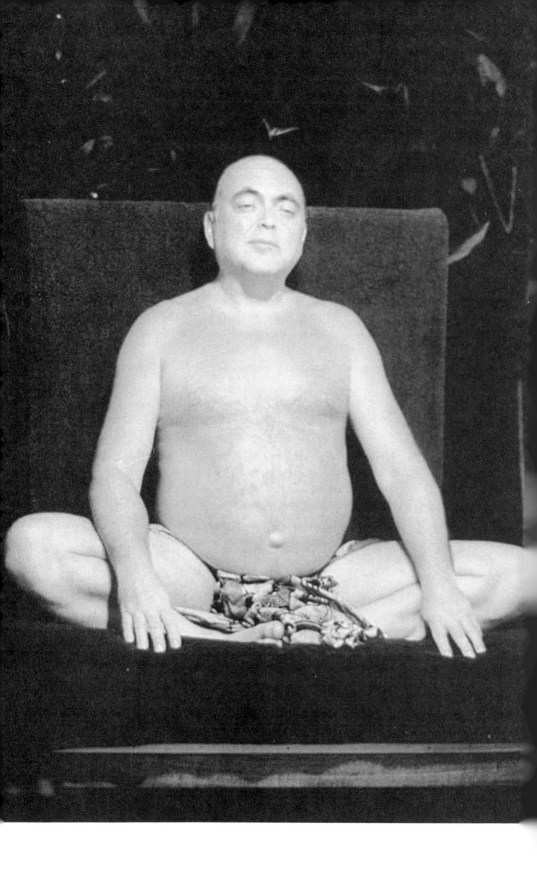

My Divine Disclosure

Freely Evolved from selected verses
of the traditional Bhagavad Gita
by
The Divine World-Teacher and True Heart-Master,
Da Avabhasa (The "Bright")

The following is a summary of Sri Da Avabhasa's sublime Offering of Free Daism, as it is lived in direct relationship to Him. His "Divine Disclosure", in which He Reveals the essence of the Way of the Heart (and which is frequently recited by His devotees as a formal prayer), is a Free Rendering of selected verses of the ancient Hindu text the Bhagavad Gita. Sri Da Avabhasa has thoroughly conformed this ancient instruction to His own new, unique, and eternal Offering of the Guru-devotee relationship, and through these verses He Calls us to the incomparable opportunity of ecstatic practice in His Company.

1.

Listen To Me, and Hear Me. This Is My Secret, The Supreme Word. I Will Tell You What Will Benefit You The Most, Because I Love You. (18:64)

2.

If You Will Surrender To Me, If You Will Become A Living Sacrifice To Me, If You Will Constantly Yield Your attention To Me Through Love and self-Transcending Service, Then You Will See Me and Realize Me and Come To Me. I Promise You This, Because I Love You. (18:65)

3.

Abandon The Reactive Principle In all Your concerns and all Your strategies. Do Not Cling To any experience that May Be Attained As A Result Of desire and "Difference". Abandon Your Search For what May Be Gotten As A Result Of the various kinds of strategic action. Do Not Fail To act, but Only Engage In action that Is Appropriate For one who Loves Me. Perform every ordinary act As A self-Transcending Act Of Love, In Love With Me. Discipline Your acts By Means Of Your Love Of Me, and While Always Remembering and Contemplating Me. Therefore, Perform every act As A Form Of Direct and Present and self-Yielding Love-Communion With Me. (18:66)

4.

If You Love Me, Where Is doubt, and Where Is anxious living? If You Love Me Now, Even anger, sorrow, and fear Are Gone. When You Abide In Love-Communion With Me, the natural results of Your various activities No Longer Have Power To Separate or Distract You From Me. (18:66)

5.

The ego-"I" that is born Into The Realm Of Cosmic Nature, or the conditional worlds of action and experience, Advances From childhood To manhood, old age, and death, While Identified With the same body-mind. Then the same ego-"I" Attains another body-mind As A Result. One whose Heart Is Awake Overcomes Every Tendency To doubt or recoil From This Ordinary Process. (2:13)

6.

Everything Changing Is Simply The Natural Play Of Life, In Which the two sides of every possibility come and go In Cycles. Winter's cold alternates with summer's heat. Pain likewise follows every pleasure. Every Appearance Is Followed By A Disappearance. There Is No Permanent experience In The Realm Of Cosmic Nature. One whose Feeling Is Steady Simply Allows All Of This To Be So, and one who Truly Understands Ceases To Add self-Contraction To This Inevitable Round. (2:14)

7.

Realization Of The Eternal Destiny Is Only Possible When a living being Has Ceased To React To The Play Of Cosmic Nature. Such a one Is Steadied By self-Understanding. Once It Is Accepted That The Cycle Of Changes, Both Positive and Negative, Is Inevitable In the conditional worlds, the living being Ceases To Work Against Happiness. (2:15)

8.

Those Who See The Truth Acknowledge That What Exists Eternally Never Changes. And whatever Does Not Exist Eternally Only Changes. (2:16)

9.

Such Seers Of Truth Also Realize That The Entire Realm Of Change, and Even the ego-"I" itself, Is Pervaded, each and all, By That Which Exists Eternally. (2:17)

10.

I Am The Eternally Existing, All-Pervading, Transcendental, Inherently Spiritual, and Perfectly Subjective Divine Person, The True and Inherently Perfect Self Of all Separate and self-Deluded selves. And My Power Of Self-Manifestation, Wherein individual beings Appear To Live and Change, Is Eternally Active As The Universal, All-Pervading Spirit-Power Of Love-Bliss (That Appears To Be, and Yet Perfectly Transcends, The Primal Energy Of Nature). (8:3)

11.

I Am The Divine Person, Who Pervades Even The Realm Of Cosmic Nature, and Within Whom every individual being Is arising. I Am Realized By self-Transcending Love, Wherein every action Is Engaged As A Form Of Direct and Present Communion With Me. (8:22)

12.

Men and women who Are Without Faith In This Way Of Love-Communion With Me Do Not Realize Me. Therefore, they Remain Associated With The Changing Realm Of Cosmic Nature, The Round Of conditional psycho-physical experience, and The Repetitive Cycles Of birth and change and death. (9:3)

13.

Such fools, If they Understood themselves At Heart, Could Have Immediate Access To Me Through Devotional Submission Of body, mind, and Separate self, but they Do Not Notice Me. They Do Not Realize Me In My Inherent Perfection, The Heart-Master Of Everything and The True Self Of all conditionally Manifested beings. (9:11)

14.

But If anyone Will Live In Communion With Me, Surrendering To Me In Love, Then Even If Love Is Shown With Nothing More Than a leaf, or a flower, or a fruit, or water, I Will Always Accept The Gift, and Offer My Self In Return. (9:26)

15.

My Situation Is At The Heart Of all beings. (15:15)

16.

The Heart Is Where attention Observes The Changes Of experience. Every experience rises and falls At The Heart, Spontaneously Generated By Eternal Activity, The Universal Life-Energy, As If The Heart Were Fastened Helplessly To A Perpetual Motion Machine. Therefore, You Can Always Find Me With The Heart. (18:61)

17.

The Heart Is Mine. Fly To Me. Do Not Surrender The Heart To experience, As If You Were In Love With Your Own body-mind. Surrender The Heart To Me, The Beloved Of The Heart, Who Is Love-Bliss Itself. I Am The Truth and The Teacher Of The Heart. I Am The Eternal and True Heart-Master. I Am The Very Sat-Guru, The Heart Itself, The Always Living One, The Ever-Present Divine Person. I Am The Self-Existing, Self-Radiant, Inherently Perfect Being, Who Pervades The Machine Of Cosmic Nature As The Love-Blissful Spirit-Current, and Who Transcends All Of Cosmic Nature As Infinite Spirit-Consciousness, The "Bright" Divine Self. If You Will Give (and Truly Give) Your Feeling-attention To My Bodily (Human) Form, and If You Will Yield Your body-mind Into The Heart-Current Of My All-Pervading Spirit-Presence, and If You Will Surrender Your conditional self-Consciousness Into My Perfectly Subjective Divine Consciousness (Of Being Itself), Then I Will Also Become An Offering To You. Therefore, You Will Be Given The Gift Of Perfect Peace, and An Eternal Domain For Your Heart. (18:62)

18.

Now I Have Revealed My Mystery and Perfect Secret here To You. "Consider" It Fully, and Then Choose What You Will Do. (18:63)

An Invitation

The God-Realizing Process that Sri Da Avabhasa Offers is the greatest opportunity of a human lifetime. In the past, God-Realizers of the ultimate degree, if they appeared at all, arose in the sacred cultures of the East, and they imparted their Enlightening Secrets only to fully prepared, renunciate disciples. It is an unparalleled Grace for us, secular and Westernized in our cultural roots, to form a devotional relationship with a Being of the stature of Sri Da Avabhasa.

In the adjacent chart, you will find depicted the phases of Free Daist practice. The chart begins with the initial stages of participation—which take place in the gathering called Da Avabhasa International—and continues with the course of practice that potentially unfolds once you become a student-novice in the Free Daist Communion.

The Initial Forms of Participation

When you are clear in your intention to become a practitioner of the Way of the Heart, you may apply to become a student or tithing member of Da Avabhasa International. Students and tithing members engage a specific practice based on study and service. They pay a fixed fee for the educational and other services of Da Avabhasa International, and tithing members, in addition, contribute 10% of their gross monthly income (or more, if they choose) in support of the Free Daist Communion. Very occasionally someone may be ready (by virtue of an extraordinary preparedness, especially an extraordinary devotional response to Sri Da Avabhasa) to bypass Da Avabhasa International altogether and enter immediately into the student-novice practice. But, generally speaking, at least a four-month period of formal guided study of the life and Wisdom-Teaching of Sri Da Avabhasa is essential.

There is a very important reason for this. At the point of becoming a student-novice, you make what Sri Da Avabhasa calls the "eternal vow"—a solemn commitment to devote your life to the living of your devotional relationship with Him. This bond is sacred, and its force is profound, transcending this lifetime. And so, until you are completely ready to make this vow you continue to study and "consider" the Guru-devotee relationship and all aspects of the Way of the Heart as a member of Da Avabhasa International.

The Progression of Free Daist Practice

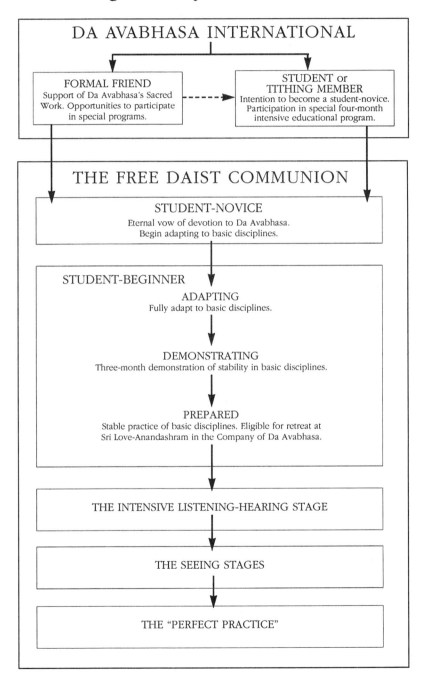

If you are moved by the importance of Sri Da Avabhasa's Work and would like to show your gratitude for His Presence in the world without becoming a practitioner of the Way of the Heart (at least for the time being), then you may wish to become a Friend of Da Avabhasa International. A Friend is essentially a patron, someone who accepts a level of responsibility for funding the missionary services of the Free Daist Communion and the publication and promotion of Sri Da Avabhasa's sacred literature, and also for supporting His Work. All Friends contribute a minimum fixed fee each year. In addition, some tithe regularly, and some are able to offer major financial support. Being a Friend is a very honorable way of associating with Sri Da Avabhasa. At the same time, Friends are always invited and encouraged to take the further step of preparing to become a formal practitioner of the Way of the Heart.

Becoming a Student-Beginner in the Free Daist Communion

Whatever your route of approach, whether as a student or tithing member or straight from the position of a Friend, your embrace of student-novice practice is a very serious and auspicious moment. You are now a lifelong member of the Free Daist Communion, connected to Sri Da Avabhasa in an eternal bond of love and devotion that potentially carries you to Divine Self-Realization.

As a student-novice, you take on in rudimentary form the range of devotional practices and disciplines that Sri Da Avabhasa Offers to Free Daist practitioners. In addition to intensified study, service, and formal tithing, you begin to practice meditation, sacramental worship, "conscious exercise", diet and health disciplines, confining sexuality to a committed relationship, cooperative community (including formal membership in the Free Daist Cooperative Community Organization), right use of money and energy. Later, as a student-beginner you fully adapt to and demonstrate these disciplines (in the adapting and demonstrating phases of student-beginner practice), to the point where you are obviously stable in them.

Now the devotional and practical foundation of your practice is established and you are acknowledged as a prepared student-beginner. This is a momentous transition because you are now qualified to go on retreat at Sri Love-Anandashram, Sri Da Avabhasa's Hermitage Sanctuary in Fiji. Here you will receive the profound heart-initiation that Sri Da Avabhasa Gives to all His devotees when He receives them into His physical Company. The period from the beginning of the student-novice phase until the moment when you become a prepared student-beginner, eligible for retreat at Sri Love-Anandashram, can be as short as six to nine months if you practice intensively.

From this point on, the practice unfolds as we have described (see Part Four, "The Progressive Practice of the Way of the Heart"), through the phases of listening, hearing, seeing, and the Perfect Practice. But these various phases of growth, or developmental stages of practice, are not the focus of attention for a Free Daist. The Way of the Heart is not a path leading to a goal, even the goal of Divine Enlightenment. The Way of the Heart is a relationship, the greatest of all possible relationships, in the course of which the progressive stages of life manifest spontaneously by Grace. Liberation ultimately (in this or some other lifetime) takes the form of Divine Enlightenment, but every moment of Heart-Intimacy with Sri Da Avabhasa is, in that moment, Liberation, Heart-Companionship with Him, freedom from egoic limits. This is why the Way of the Heart is worth practicing at any age, at any time, in any circumstance.

If you are feeling the urge to move beyond your present level of human growth and are interested in what Sri Da Avabhasa is Offering you, contact us at our Correspondence Department or at one of our regional centers (see the following page). We will be happy to send you a free brochure on the forms of participation available to you. We invite you to enter into this sacred relationship with Sri Da Avabhasa, and be Awakened in God by His Grace. We look forward to hearing from you.

Correspondence Department
THE FREE DAIST COMMUNION
P.O. Box 3680
Clearlake, California 95422, USA

Phone: (707) 928-4936

The Regional Centers of the Free Daist Communion

UNITED STATES

NORTHERN CALIFORNIA
The Free Daist Communion
740 Adrian Way
San Rafael, CA 94903
(415) 492-0930

NORTHWEST USA
The Free Daist Communion
5600-11th Ave. NE
Seattle, WA 98105
(206) 527-2751

SOUTHWEST USA
The Free Daist Communion
1043 Mesa Drive
Camarillo, CA 93010
(805) 482-5051

NORTHEAST USA
The Free Daist Communion
28 West Central
Natick, MA 01760
(508) 650-0136

SOUTHEAST USA
The Free Daist Communion
10301 South Glen Road
Potomac, MD 20854
(301) 983-0291

HAWAII
The Free Daist Communion
105 Kaholalele Road
Kapaa, HI 96746-9304
(808) 822-3386
(808) 822-0216

EASTERN CANADA
The Free Daist Communion
108 Katimavik Road
Val-des-Monts, Quebec J0X 2R0
Canada
(819) 671-4398

AUSTRALIA
The Free Daist Communion
P.O. Box 562
Healesville, Victoria 3777
Australia
059-626-151

NEW ZEALAND
Da Avabhasa Ashram
12 Seibel Road, R.D. 1
Henderson, Auckland
New Zealand
(09) 309-0032 (day)
(09) 838-9114

THE UNITED KINGDOM AND IRELAND
Da Avabhasa Ashram
Tasburgh Hall
Lower Tasburgh
Norwich NR15-1LT
England
0508-470-574
081-341-9329 (London Centre)

THE NETHERLANDS
Da Avabhasa Ashram
Annendaalderweg 10
6105 AT Maria Hoop
The Netherlands
04743-1281
04743-1872

The Seven Stages of Life

Sri Da Avabhasa has described the evolutionary development of the human individual and the process of self-transcending Spiritual, Transcendental, and Divine Realization in terms of seven stages of life. This unique Revelation of truly human evolution is one of the keys to a full appreciation of the Way of the Heart. Below is a brief description of each of the seven stages of life.

The First Stage of Life—Individuation: The first stage of life is a process of individuation, or of becoming identified with the physical body in the waking state. In this stage, one gradually adapts functionally to physical existence and eventually achieves a basic sense of individual autonomy, or of personal independence from the mother and from all others.

The Second Stage of Life—Socialization: The second stage of life is a process of socialization, or social exploration and growth in relationships. In this stage, the individual adapts to the emotional-sexual, or feeling, dimension of the conditional being and achieves basic integration of that dimension with the physical body.

The Third Stage of Life—Integration: The third stage of life is a process of integration as a fully differentiated, or autonomous, sexual and social human character. In this stage, one adapts to and develops the verbal mind, the faculty of discriminative intelligence, and the will. And one achieves basic adult integration of body, emotion, and mind in the context of the bodily-based point of view.

These first three stages are optimally developed in the context of authentic early-life devotion to the bodily (human) Form of the Sat-Guru and, thus and thereby, to the Divine Person.

The Fourth Stage of Life—Spiritualization: The fourth stage of life involves the cultivation of heart-felt surrender to and intimacy with the bodily (human) Form, and, eventually, and more and more profoundly, the Spiritual Presence, of a Spiritually Realized Sat-Guru and, through such explicit devotional self-surrender to the Sat-Guru, devotional intimacy and Union with the Divine Person. Secondarily, in the fourth stage of life, the gross body-mind of the Awakening devotee is adapted and submitted to, and harmonized in, the Living Spirit-Current of the Sat-Guru and, thus and thereby, of the Divine Person.

The Fifth Stage of Life—Higher Spiritual Evolution: The fifth stage of life, if it must be developed, involves the ascent of attention and self-awareness beyond the gross body-mind and into the subtler field of psyche and mind, outside and beyond the brain. Traditionally, the fifth stage of life, therefore, develops the esoteric Yogic and cosmic mysticism of the Spiritual Life-Current in its ascent to the Matrix of Light, Love-Bliss, and Spirit-Presence above the world, the body, and the mind. When that mysticism is followed to its eventual culminating Union with the Spiritual Divine Matrix of Love-Bliss, the individual enjoys fifth stage conditional Nirvikalpa Samadhi.

In the Way of the Heart, most practitioners are Graced to bypass some or all of the fifth stage Yogic process (and they may be Graced to bypass some or all of the "advanced" fourth stage Yogic process, which is the beginning of the Yoga of Spiritual ascent). This is possible by Sri Da Avabhasa's Grace, Whereby His devotee is Attracted by feeling-Contemplation of His bodily (human) Form and Spiritual (and Always Blessing) Presence directly into feeling-Contemplation of His Very (and Inherently Perfect) State, such that exhaustive (or even any) exploration of ascending Yogic processes is rendered unnecessary. Thus, for such practitioners of the Way of the Heart, fifth stage conditional Nirvikalpa Samadhi and other ascended or ascending states may or may not arise, but in any case the focus of practice is heart-felt Contemplation of Heart-Master Da's bodily (human) Form, His Spiritual (and Always Blessing) Presence, and His Divine State of Consciousness Itself, and, thus and thereby, Contemplation of the Divine Person.

The Sixth Stage of Life—Awakening to the Transcendental Self: In the conventional development of the sixth stage of life, the body-mind is simply relaxed into the Spiritual Current of Life, and attention (the root or base of mind) is inverted away from gross and subtle states and objects of the body-mind, and toward the Witness-Consciousness of attention, mind, body, and world. The ultimate possible expression of this inversion of attention is Jnana Samadhi, or the temporary and exclusive Realization of the Transcendental Self, or Consciousness Itself.

In the Way of the Heart, as in conventional developmental processes, the conscious being in the sixth stage of life enjoys fundamental freedom from and equanimity in relation to the conditions and states of the body-mind-self. But, by Sri Da Avabhasa's Grace, the sixth stage process develops without the strategic and stressful inversion of attention. Rather, by Grace of the Attractiveness of Sat-Guru Da's bodily (human) Form and His Spiritual (and Always Blessing) Presence, His devotee is drawn into sympathy with His Very (and Inherently Perfect) State of Consciousness Itself, the Very Self of the Divine Person. He or she Stands increasingly Free of the binding phenomena and illusions of psycho-physical existence, while observing and more and more profoundly and "radically" transcending the root-action of egoity, which is self-contraction, or the activity of primal separation that creates the fundamental sense of "difference", or the feeling of relatedness.

The Seventh Stage of Life—Divine Enlightenment: The seventh stage of life is neither the culmination of any conventional psycho-physical and Spiritual process of human developmental growth (which traditionally takes place in the fulfillment of the fifth stage of life) nor the end or goal of any process of the conventional inversion of attention and the exclusion of psycho-physical and Spiritual phenomena (which occupies traditional orientations toward the sixth stage of life). The seventh stage of life, rather, is the Free Condition of Inherently Perfect Divine Self-Realization that is, in the Way of the Heart, Awakened entirely and only by the Liberating Grace of Heart-Master Da Avabhasa, the Divine Sat-Guru. In the Way of the Heart, it is the State of Divinely Perfect Contemplative Identification with Sat-Guru Da's Very (and Inherently Perfect) State of "Bright" Consciousness, the Uncaused, Unsupported, Unconditional, and Unqualified Realization of Being Itself, or Perfect Love-Blissful Unity with the Supreme Divine Person.

Thus, in Sahaj Samadhi in the seventh stage of life, the Divine Self, fully Awake, Recognizes all conditions of body, mind, and world as only modifications of Itself. In Moksha-Bhava Samadhi, the Radiance of that Divine Consciousness Pervades and Outshines all phenomena so powerfully that the Awakened being ceases, temporarily, even to notice any phenomena at all. Divine Translation is final and conclusive Moksha-Bhava Samadhi, coinciding with the death of the human individual, in which the Awakened being is so Perfectly Translated into the Divine Self-Condition that future embodiment in the conditional worlds ceases to be necessary.

I n the Way of the Heart, Sri Da Avabhasa Calls practitioners to transcend the first six stages of life rather than to fulfill them. This is made possible by the Grace of His unique Revelation of the Way of the Heart and by the Heart-Blessing of His Divine Transmission to His devotees practicing in the context of every stage of life. From His "Point of View" (of the seventh, or Divinely Awakened, stage of life), He addresses each of the first six stages of life as a stage of (generally) necessary psycho-physical development, with which we are chronically associated in an erroneous or egoically limited fashion.

The Way of the Heart is not strictly a passage through each of the first six stages of life, leading at the end to Perfect Divine Self-Realization and the great spontaneous Yoga of Divine Enlightenment that characterizes the seventh stage of life. Rather, the Way of the Heart is inherently a seventh stage practice. It is a Way of life founded from the beginning and in every moment in the inherently Free disposition, or seventh stage attitude, of total psycho-physical Communion with the Spiritual, Transcendental, and Divine Self-Condition, Which Is the Heart Itself. Thus, the Way of the Heart takes place in the context of the first six stages of life, but in every moment the devotee practicing the Way of the Heart is Called to effectively transcend the presumptions, motivations, and phenomena of conditional experience and conditional knowledge associated with those lesser or egoic stages of life.

The Secret of the Way of the Heart in every stage of life is devotional Communion with, or feeling-Contemplation of, the bodily (human) Form, the Spiritual (and Always Blessing) Presence, and the Very (and Inherently Perfect) State of Sri Da Avabhasa. By this Divine Means His devotee allows himself or herself to abide under all circumstances in Love-Blissful Unity with the Divine Person, the Heart, Whom he or she "Locates" in, as, and through Sri Da Avabhasa Himself as Adept Heart-Teacher and True Heart-Master. Heart-Master Da Writes in *The Dawn Horse Testament:*

In Truth, The Way Of The Heart Begins At birth and progresses Through (or Otherwise Directly Beyond) Each Of The Seven Stages Of Life, Until Divine Translation.

The Heart Is Mine. The Heart Is The Domain Of All My Work. The Heart Is Always In God, but Reaction To the conditions Associated With Apparent birth into the Cosmic planes Produces The Apparent conditional Destiny Of Retarded Growth and All The Suffering Of self-Contraction. Therefore, This self-Contracting Reaction To conditional or phenomenal states Must Be Transcended In The Context (or Otherwise In The Effective Transcendence) Of Every Stage Of Life. The Heart Must Awaken At (or In Relation To) Every Stage Of Life, and the individual being Must Grow To Be Attracted and Distracted By The Forms Of God, and Thus To Feel Beyond The Bond Of conditional events (or all that limits and Retards the conditionally Manifested being In God), and, Ultimately, To Feel Beyond (and Perfectly Prior To) all that is Not The Realization Of Divine Being Itself. (pp. 186-87)

GLOSSARY

advanced and ultimate stages of life

Sri Da Avabhasa uses the term "advanced" to describe the fourth stage of life and the fifth stage of life. He reserves the term "ultimate" to describe the sixth stage of life and the seventh stage of life. (See "The Seven Stages of Life" on pp. 318–21 of this book.)

Agency, Agent

"Agents" of Sri Da Avabhasa's Blessing Work are all the Means that may serve as Vehicles of His Divine Grace and Awakening Power. The first Means of Agency established by Sri Da Avabhasa are the Wisdom-Teaching of the Way of the Heart, the three Retreat Sanctuaries that He has Empowered, and the many Objects and Articles that He has Blessed for the sake of His devotees' Remembrance of Him and the reception of His Heart-Blessing.

Heart-Master Da also uses the word "Agency" to indicate the formally Acknowledged and specially chosen Divinely Self-Realized "free renunciate" Devotees who will, in the future beyond His physical Lifetime, be designated to serve to directly Transmit His Spiritual, Transcendental, and Divine Heart-Blessing to others and the world, and to provide authoritative present-time commentary on His Word and His Leela, or Play with His devotees. Only one such Agent would function in this manner during any present time.

Amrita Nadi

In Sanskrit, literally means "Nerve (or Current) of Immortal Bliss". It is the ultimate "organ", or Root-Structure, of the body-mind, Realized in the seventh stage of life.

Arrow

In profound, deep meditation, the Spirit-Current may be felt in the form of the Arrow, or as Sri Da Avabhasa explains, "a motionless axis that seems to stand in the center of the body, between the frontal and spinal lines".

asana

The Sanskrit word "asana" derives from the verbal root "as", meaning "to sit" or "to dwell", and it generally refers to the posture or pose of one's body.

"Atma-Murti"

In Sanskrit, "atma" means both the individual (or conditional) self and the Divine Self. In Sri Da Avabhasa's term "Atma-Murti", "Atma" indicates the Transcendental, Inherently Spiritual, and Divine Self, and "Murti" means "Form". Thus, "Atma-Murti" literally means "the Form (Murti) That Is the (Very) Divine Self (Atman)".

"Bright", "Brightness"

Since His Illumined boyhood, Sat-Guru Da has used the term the "Bright" (and its variations, such as "Brightness") to describe the Love-Blissfully Self-Luminous, Conscious Divine Being, Which He knew even then as the Divine Reality of His own body-mind and of all beings, things, and worlds.

Circle

The primary circuit, or passageway, of the Living Spirit-Current and the natural bodily energy as they flow through the body-mind. The Circle is composed of two arcs: the descending Current associated with the frontal line, or the more physically oriented dimension, of the body-mind; and the ascending Current associated with the spinal line, or the more mentally and subtly oriented dimension, of the body-mind.

"conductivity"

The intentional exercises of feeling and breathing Given by Sri Da Avabhasa, which "conduct" the natural energies of the body-mind and, in the event of Spiritual maturity, the Spirit-Current Itself.

"conscious process"

Sri Da Avabhasa's technical term for those practices in the Way of the Heart through which the mind or attention is surrendered and turned about (from egoic self-involvement) to feeling-Contemplation of the bodily (human) Form, the Spiritual (and Always Blessing) Presence, and the Very (and Inherently Perfect) State of Sri Da Avabhasa (and, thus and thereby, of the Divine Person). It is the senior discipline and responsibility of all practitioners in the Way of the Heart.

"Crazy"

In many esoteric sacred traditions, certain practitioners and Masters have been called "crazy", "mad", or "foolish". Tibetan Buddhist Saints of this type are given the title "lama nyonpa" ("saintly madman") or simply "nyonpa" ("madman"). In whatever tradition and time they appear, these individuals violate prevailing taboos (personal, social, religious, or even spiritual) either to instruct others or simply to express their own inspired freedom.

In the realm of the sacred, there are many kinds of unconventional Teachers. Sri Da Avabhasa's Wisdom-Teaching is a principal guide to help the serious student discriminate among such unconventional Teachers while also benefiting from the stories of their lives and work. The exemplars of what Heart-Master Da calls "the 'Crazy Wisdom' tradition" are Realizers of the advanced and the ultimate stages of life in any culture or time who, through spontaneous Free action, blunt Wisdom, and liberating laughter, shock or humor people into self-critical awareness of their egoity, a prerequisite for receiving the Adept's Spiritual Transmission.

The Da Avabhasa Gurukula Kanyadana Kumari Order

The order of renunciate women who live and serve in Sri Da Avabhasa's intimate Sphere. Kanyadana is the traditional practice of giving (dana) a young woman (kanya) into intimate service of the Sat-Guru. "Kumari" indicates a self-renounced, or Spiritually Awakened, woman. The "Gurukula" is the Guru's "family", or circle of intimates. The two members of the Da Avabhasa Gurukula Kanyadana Kumari Order have consecrated themselves to the service of Da Avabhasa in true intimacy for the sake of their Divine Self-Realization.

Darshan

"Darshan", a Sanskrit term that literally means "seeing", "sight of", or "vision of", connotes the spontaneous Blessing Sri Da Avabhasa Grants Freely by Revealing His bodily (human) Form (and, thereby, His Spiritual, and Always Blessing, Presence and His Very, and Inherently Perfect, State).

Dharma, dharma

The Sanskrit word "dharma" means "duty", "virtue", "law". It is commonly used to refer to the many esoteric paths by which human beings endeavor to seek the Truth. In its fullest sense, and when capitalized, "Dharma" means the complete fulfillment of duty—the living of the Divine Law. Thus, a truly great Spiritual Teaching, including its disciplines and practices, may rightly be referred to as "Dharma".

Feeling of Being

The Feeling of Being is the uncaused (or Self-Existing), Self-Radiant, and unqualified feeling-intuition of the Transcendental, Inherently Spiritual, and, ultimately, Divine Self. To feel, or, really, to Be, the Feeling of Being is to enjoy the Love-Bliss of Absolute Consciousness, Which, when Most Perfectly Realized, cannot be prevented or even diminished either by the events of life or by death.

Feeling of relatedness

The root-feeling of separation, separateness, and separativeness, the feeling of "difference", the essence of self-contraction, or the avoidance of relationship. The essence of attention itself, the root structure or activity that is the ego.

Full Feeling-Prostration

Full physical prostration is an aspect of sacred practice in many traditions, such as Tibetan Buddhism and Islam. In the Way of the Heart, Full Feeling-Prostrations are a bodily exercise of expressive devotion, Given by Heart-Master Da to all formally acknowledged practitioners, to break the bodily cycle of egoity and non-devotion, or otherwise so that they may demonstrate their free relinquishment of that cycle.

Great Tradition

Sat-Guru Da's term for the total inheritance of human, cultural, religious, magical, mystical, Spiritual, Transcendental, and Divine paths, philosophies, and testimonies from all the eras and cultures of humanity, which has (in the present era of worldwide communication) become the common legacy of humankind.

Gurudev, Gurudeva

Sanskrit: "Divine Guru". A loving and intimate way of addressing or referring to one's Guru.

hearing (See **listening, hearing, and seeing**.)

the Heart

God, the Divine Self, the Divine Reality.

Hridayam, Hridaya

The Sanskrit word "hridayam" means "heart". It refers not only to the physical organ but also to the True Heart, the Transcendental (and Inherently Spiritual) Divine Reality. "Hridayam" is one of Heart-Master Da's Divine Names, signifying that He Stands in, at, and as the True Heart of every being.

Hridaya-Samartha Sat-Guru

The Divine Revealer Who Liberates devotees from the darkness of egoity by Means of the Power of the Heart. Sri Da Avabhasa Writes that this full Designation "properly summarizes all the aspects of My unique Guru-Function".

Hridaya-Shakti

"Shakti" is a Sanskrit term for the Divinely Manifesting Energy, Spiritual Power, or Life-Current of the Divine Person. "Hridaya-Shakti" is thus "the Power of the Heart".

Hridaya-Shaktipat

In Hindi, "shaktipat" is the "descent of the Power", indicating the Sat-Guru's Transmission of the Divine Shakti to his or her devotee. Hridaya-Shaktipat, which is Sri Da Avabhasa's seventh stage Gift to devotees, is the Blessing-Transmission of the Heart Itself.

Ishta-Guru-Bhakti Yoga

"Ishta" means "chosen one", and "bhakti" means "devotion". Thus, Ishta-Guru-Bhakti Yoga, or devotional submission to the Sat-Guru, is the principal Gift, Calling, and Discipline that Sri Da Avabhasa Gives to His devotees as the "Ishta" (or "chosen one") of their hearts.

Kanyas (See **The Da Avabhasa Gurukula Kanyadana Kumari Order**.)

kriyas

Spontaneous, self-purifying physical movements that arise when the natural bodily energies are stimulated by the Divine Spirit-Current as effects of Da Avabhasa's Spiritual (and Always Blessing) Presence in and upon the body-mind of His devotee.

Leela

Sanskrit: "play", or "sport". Also, the Divinely Awakened Play of the Divinely Self-Realized Adept, through which he or she mysteriously Instructs and Liberates others.

listening, hearing, and seeing

"Listening", "hearing", and "seeing" are technical terms by which Sri Da Avabhasa indicates three stages in the progress of the Way of the Heart, each of which takes place in the context of a heart-felt devotional relationship to Him. Listening, the foundation practice, takes place in the context of profound study of Sri Da Avabhasa's Heart-Word, and it is devoted to the observation, understanding, and transcendence of the ego. Hearing is the crisis in which listening is fulfilled in most fundamental self-understanding. Hearing is the stable capability to consistently feel beyond the activity of the ego and the simultaneous intuitive awakening to the Divine Condition that is always Prior to egoity. Seeing, which becomes possible on the basis of true hearing, is fundamentally an emotional conversion to love that is characterized by the stable capability to receive (and rightly use) Sri Da Avabhasa's Spiritual Baptism.

Man of Understanding

Sri Da Avabhasa has described Himself as the "Man of Understanding", One in Whom Understanding is Inherently Perfect. He has Realized Inherently Perfect Identification with the Divine Person, the Heart and Presence of Reality in the world, and thus He Functions as That One. Sri Da Avabhasa primarily used this term in His original Word of Instruction Communicated in *The Knee of Listening* and *The Method of the Siddhas*. His summary Communication about the living paradox of the Man of Understanding can be found in the Epilogue to *The Knee of Listening*.

mudra

A gesture of the hands, face, or body expressing the exalted Spiritual states of Consciousness that arise spontaneously in deep meditation, Darshan occasions with Heart-Master Da, or other devotional occasions. Da Avabhasa may spontaneously exhibit Mudras as Signs of His Blessing and purifying Work with His devotees.

Padukas

The ceremonial sandals or shoes of the Sat-Guru, venerated because of their association with the Feet of the Sat-Guru. To worship the Feet of the Sat-Guru is to express humility and gratitude in relationship to the Sat-Guru, to express devotion and veneration of his or her bodily (human) Form, because they are a potent Agent of Spiritual Transmission.

pranayama

Sanskrit: restraint or regulation (yama) of life-energy (prana). Pranayama is a technique for balancing, purifying, and intensifying the entire psycho-physical system by controlling the currents of the breath and life-force. Automatic pranayama is spontaneous Yogic breathing that arises involuntarily and has the same purifying effects as the voluntary exercise of such pranayama.

Prasad

The food, drink, and other gifts that have been offered to the Divine and, having been Blessed, are returned as Divine Gifts to devotees. By extension, Prasad is anything the devotee receives from the Sat-Guru. Modaka Prasad is a traditional baked sweet, often Given by Sri Da Avabhasa to His devotees.

Puja, Sat-Guru Puja

"Puja" ordinarily refers to any form of sacred ceremonial worship. Formal devotional worship of Sri Da Avabhasa is called "Sat-Guru Puja".

"radical"

The term "radical" derives from the Latin "radix", meaning "root", and thus it principally means "irreducible", "fundamental", or "relating to the origin". Because Sri Da Avabhasa uses "radical" in this literal sense, it appears in quotation marks in His Wisdom-Teaching to distinguish His usage from the popular reference to an extreme (often political) position or view.

right side of the heart

Sri Da Avabhasa spontaneously Realized that, in the context of the body-mind, the Divine Consciousness is intuited at a psycho-physical locus in the right side of the heart. He has Revealed that this center corresponds to the sinoatrial node, or pacemaker, the source of the gross physical heartbeat in the right atrium, or upper right chamber, of the heart. Heart-Master Da affirms to His devotees that this locus is Where they will (ultimately) Find Him, or intuitively Realize Him as Consciousness, the Very Self.

Samadhi

This Sanskrit term indicates concentration, equanimity, and balance, and it is traditionally used to denote various exalted states that appear in the context of esoteric meditation and Realization.

samsara

Conditional existence. Samsara connotes the experience of conditional existence by one who has not yet Realized that conditional existence is not other than Consciousness Itself, and who is therefore deluded by its binding power.

Sat-Guru

The Sanskrit word "Sat" means "Truth", "Being", "Existence". The term "Guru" is a composite of two contrasting words meaning "darkness" (gu) and "light" (ru). The Sat-Guru thus releases, turns, or leads living beings from darkness, or non-Truth, into Light, or the Living Truth. Moreover, the Divinely Enlightened Sat-Guru is, and Lives as, the very Truth, or Divine Self, that he or she Awakens in the devotee.

Sat-Guru Puja (See **Puja, Sat-Guru Puja**.)

Satsang

The Sanskrit word "Satsang" literally means "true or right relationship", "the company of Truth, or of Being". In the Way of the Heart, it is the eternal relationship of mutual sacred commitment between Sri Da Avabhasa as Sat-Guru (and as the Divine Person) and each true and formally acknowledged practitioner of the Way of the Heart. Once it is consciously assumed by any practitioner, Satsang with Heart-Master Da is an all-inclusive Condition, bringing Divine Grace and Blessings and sacred obligations, responsibilities, and tests into every dimension of the practitioner's life and consciousness.

seeing (See **listening, hearing, and seeing**.)

self-Enquiry

Self-Enquiry in the form "Avoiding relationship?" is the practice spontaneously developed by Heart-Master Da in the course of His own Ordeal of Divine Self-Awakening. It is the principal technical practice in the Devotional Way of Insight in the Way of the Heart.

siddhi, Siddhi

Sanskrit: "power", or "accomplishment". When capitalized in Sat-Guru Da's Wisdom-Teaching, Siddhi is the Spiritual, Transcendental, and Divine Awakening-Power of the Heart that He spontaneously and effortlessly exercises as Hridaya-Samartha Sat-Guru.

Sri

A traditional honorific title meaning "bright", or "radiant".

stages of life

Sri Da Avabhasa describes the evolutionary development of man in terms of seven stages of life and Divine Self-Realization. (See "The Seven Stages of Life" on pp. 318–21 of this book for a summary description of this unique Revelation.)

Yoga

From the Sanskrit "yuj", meaning "to unite", usually referring to any discipline or process whereby an aspirant attempts to reunite with God. Sri Da Avabhasa acknowledges this conventional and traditional use of the term, but also, in reference to the Great Yoga of the Way of the Heart, employs it in a "radical" sense, free of the usual implication of egoic separation and seeking.

An Invitation to Support
the Way of the Heart

J ust as association with a God-Realized Adept is the best kind of Company a man or woman can keep, so the practice of supporting the Work of such an Adept is the most auspicious form of financial giving.

A true Adept is a Free Renunciate and a Source of continuous Divine Grace. Therefore, he or she owns nothing, and everything given to support his or her Work is returned, both to the giver and to all beings, in many Blessings that are full of the Adept's healing, transforming, and Liberating Grace. At the same time, all tangible gifts of support help secure and nurture the Adept's Work in necessary and practical ways, thus benefiting the whole world.

All of this is immeasurably true for those who help provide financial gifts to the Work of the Divine World-Teacher and True Heart-Master, Da Avabhasa (The "Bright"). We therefore happily extend to you an invitation to serve the Way of the Heart through your financial support.

You may make a financial contribution in support of the Work of Sri Da Avabhasa at any time. You may also, if you choose, request that your contribution be used for one or more specific purposes of Free Daism. For example, you may be moved to help support and develop Sri Love-Anandashram, Sri Da Avabhasa's Great Hermitage Ashram and Empowered Retreat Sanctuary, in Fiji, and the circumstance provided there for Sri Da Avabhasa and the other members of the Naitauba (Free Daist) Order of Renunciates (all of whom are renunciates, owning nothing).

You may make a contribution for this specific purpose directly to the Sri Love-Anandashram (Naitauba) Trust, the charitable trust that is responsible for Sri Love-Anandashram. To make such a contribution, simply mail your check to the Sri Love-Anandashram (Naitauba) Trust, P.O. Box 4744, Samabula, Fiji.

If you would like to make such a contribution and you are a U.S. taxpayer, we recommend that you make your contribution to the Free Daist Communion, so as to secure a tax deduction for your contribution under U.S. tax laws. To do this, mail your contribution to the Advocacy Department of the Free Daist Communion, P.O. Box 3680, Clearlake, California 95422, U.S.A., and indicate that you would like it to be used in support of Sri Love-Anandashram.

You may also request that your contribution, or a part of it, be used for one or more of the other purposes of Free Daism. For example, you may request that your contribution be used to help publish the sacred Literature of Sri Da Avabhasa, or to support either of the other two Sanctuaries He has Empowered, or to maintain the Sacred Archives that preserve Sri Da Avabhasa's recorded Talks and Writings, or to publish audio and video recordings of Sri Da Avabhasa.

If you would like your contribution to benefit one or more of these specific purposes, please mail your contribution to the Advocacy Department of the Free Daist Communion at the above address, and indicate how you would like your gift to be used.

If you would like more information about these and other gifting options, or if you would like assistance in describing or making a contribution, please contact the Advocacy Department of the Free Daist Communion, either by writing to the address shown above or by telephoning (707) 928-4096, FAX (707) 928-4062.

Deferred Giving

We also invite you to consider making a deferred gift in support of the Work of Sri Da Avabhasa. Many have found that through deferred giving they can make a far more significant gesture of support than they would otherwise be able to make. Many have also found that by making a deferred gift they are able to realize substantial tax advantages.

There are numerous ways to make a deferred gift, including making a gift in your Will, or in your life insurance, or in a charitable trust.

If you would like to make a gift in your Will in support of Sri Love-Anandashram, simply include in your Will the statement "I give the Sri Love-Anandashram (Naitauba) Trust, an Australian charitable trust, P.O. Box 4744, Samabula, Fiji, _____" [inserting in the blank the amount or description of your contribution].

If you would like to make a gift in your Will to benefit other purposes of Free Daism, simply include in your Will the statement "I give the Free Daist Communion, a California nonprofit corporation, 12040 Seigler Road North, Middletown, California 95461, U.S.A., _____" [inserting in the blank the amount or description of your contribution]. You may, if you choose, also describe in your Will the specific Free Daist purpose or purposes you would like your gift to support. If you are a U.S. taxpayer, gifts made in your Will to the Free Daist Communion will be free of estate taxes and will also reduce any estate taxes payable on the remainder of your estate.

To make a gift in your life insurance, simply name as the beneficiary (or one of the beneficiaries) of your life insurance policy the Free Daist organization of your choice, according to the foregoing descriptions and addresses. If you are a U.S. taxpayer, you may receive significant tax benefits if you make a contribution to the Free Daist Communion through your life insurance.

We also invite you to consider establishing or participating in a charitable trust for the benefit of Free Daism. If you are a U.S. taxpayer, you may find that such a trust will provide you with immediate tax savings and assured income for life, while at the same time enabling you to provide for your family, for your other heirs, and for the Work of Sri Da Avabhasa as well.

The Advocacy Department of the Free Daist Communion will be happy to provide you with further information about these and other deferred gifting options, and happy to provide you or your attorney with assistance in describing or making a deferred gift in support of the Work of Sri Da Avabhasa.

FURTHER NOTES TO THE READER

An Invitation to Responsibility

The Way of the Heart that Sri Da Avabhasa has Revealed is an invitation to everyone to assume real responsibility for his or her life. As Sri Da Avabhasa has Said in *The Dawn Horse Testament,* "If any one Is Interested In The Realization Of The Heart, Let him or her First Submit (Formally, and By Heart) To Me, and (Thereby) Commence The Ordeal Of self-Observation, self-Understanding, and self-Transcendence." Therefore, participation in the Way of the Heart requires a real struggle with oneself, and not at all a struggle with Sri Da Avabhasa, or with others.

All who study the Way of the Heart or take up its practice should remember that they are responding to a Call to become responsible for themselves. They should understand that they, not Sri Da Avabhasa or others, are responsible for any decision they may make or action they take in the course of their lives of study or practice. This has always been true, and it is true whatever the individual's involvement in the Way of the Heart, be it as one who studies Da Avabhasa's Wisdom-Teaching, or as a Friend of or a participant in Da Avabhasa International, or as a formally acknowledged member of the Free Daist Communion.

Honoring and Protecting the Sacred Word through Perpetual Copyright

Since ancient times, practitioners of true religion and Spirituality have valued, above all, time spent in the Company of the Sat-Guru, or one who has Realized God, Truth, or Reality, and who Serves that same Realization in others. Such practitioners understand that the Sat-Guru literally Transmits his or her (Realized) State to every one (and every thing) with which he or she comes in contact. Through this Transmission, objects, environments, and rightly prepared individuals with which the Sat-Guru has contact can become Empowered, or Imbued with the Sat-Guru's Transforming Power. It is by this process of Empowerment that things and beings are made truly and literally sacred, and things so sanctified thereafter function as a Source of the Sat-Guru's Blessing for all who understand how to make right and sacred use of them.

The Sat-Guru and all that he Empowers are, therefore, truly Sacred Treasures, for they help draw the practitioner more quickly into the Realization of Perfect Identity with the Divine Self. Cultures of true Wisdom have always understood that such Sacred Treasures are precious (and fragile) Gifts to humanity, and that they should be honored, protected, and reserved for right sacred use. Indeed, the word "sacred" means "set apart", and thus protected, from the secular world. Sri Da Avabhasa is a Sat-Guru of the Most Perfect degree. He has Conformed His body-mind completely to the Divine Self, and He is thus a most Potent Source of Blessing-Transmission of God, Truth, or Reality. He has for many years Empowered, or made sacred, special places and things, and these now Serve as His Divine Agents, or as literal expressions and extensions of His Blessing-Transmission. Among these Empowered Sacred Treasures is His Wisdom-Teaching, which is Full of His Transforming Power. This Blessed and Blessing Wisdom-Teaching has Mantric Force, or the literal Power to Serve God-Realization in those who are Graced to receive it.

Therefore, Sri Da Avabhasa's Wisdom-Teaching must be perpetually honored and protected, "set apart" from all possible interference and wrong use. The Free Daist Communion, which is the fellowship of devotees of Sri Da Avabhasa, is committed to the perpetual preservation and right honoring of the sacred Wisdom-Teaching of the Way of the Heart. But it is also true that in order to fully accomplish this we must find support in the world-society in which we live and from the laws under which we live. Thus, we call for a world-society and for laws that acknowledge the Sacred, and that permanently protect It from insensitive, secular interference and wrong use of any kind. We call for, among other things, a system of law that acknowledges that the Wisdom-Teaching of the Way of the Heart, in all Its forms, is, because of Its sacred nature, protected by perpetual copyright.

We invite others who respect the Sacred to join with us in this call and in working toward its realization. And, even in the meantime, we claim that all copyrights to the Wisdom-Teaching of Sri Da Avabhasa and the other sacred literature and recordings of the Way of the Heart are of perpetual duration.

We make this claim on behalf of Sri Love-Anandashram (Naitauba) Pty Ltd, which, acting as trustee of the Sri Love-Anandashram (Naitauba) Trust, is the holder of all such copyrights.

Da Avabhasa and the Sacred Treasures of Free Daism

Those who Realize God bring great Blessing and Divine Possibility for the world. As Free Adepts, they Accomplish universal Blessing Work that benefits everything and everyone. Such Realizers also Work very specifically and intentionally with individuals who approach them as their devotees, and with those places where they reside, and to which they Direct their specific Regard for the sake of perpetual Spiritual Empowerment. This was understood in traditional Spiritual cultures, and those cultures therefore found ways to honor Realizers, to provide circumstances for them where they were free to do their Divine Work without obstruction or interference.

Those who value Sri Da Avabhasa's Realization and Service have always endeavored to appropriately honor Him in this traditional way, to provide a circumstance where He is completely Free to Do His Divine Work. Since 1983, Sri Da Avabhasa has resided principally on the Island of Naitauba, Fiji, also known as Sri Love-Anandashram. This island has been set aside by Free Daists worldwide as a Place for Sri Da Avabhasa to Do His universal Blessing Work for the sake of everyone and His specific Work with those who pilgrimage to Sri Love-Anandashram to receive the special Blessing of coming into His physical Company.

Sri Da Avabhasa is a legal renunciate. He owns nothing and He has no secular or religious institutional function. He Functions only in Freedom. He, and the other members of the Naitauba (Free Daist) Order of Renunciates, the senior renunciate order of Free Daism, are provided for by the Sri Love-Anandashram (Naitauba) Trust, which also provides for Sri Love-Anandashram altogether and ensures the permanent integrity of Sri Da Avabhasa's Wisdom-Teaching, both in its archival and in its published forms. This Trust, which functions only in Fiji, exists exclusively to provide for these Sacred Treasures of Free Daism.

Outside Fiji, the institution which has developed in response to Sri Da Avabhasa's Wisdom-Teaching and universal Blessing is known as "The Free Daist Communion". The

Free Daist Communion is active worldwide in making Sri Da Avabhasa's Wisdom-Teaching available to all, in offering guidance to all who are moved to respond to His Offering, and in providing for the other Sacred Treasures of Free Daism, including the Mountain Of Attention Sanctuary (in California) and Tumomama Sanctuary (in Hawaii). In addition to the central corporate entity of the Free Daist Communion, which is based in California, there are numerous regional entities which serve congregations of Sri Da Avabhasa's devotees in various places throughout the world.

Free Daists worldwide have also established numerous community organizations, through which they provide for many of their common and cooperative community needs, including needs relating to housing, food, businesses, medical care, schools, and death and dying. By attending to these and all other ordinary human concerns and affairs via self-transcending cooperation and mutual effort, Sri Da Avabhasa's devotees constantly free their energy and attention, both personally and collectively, for practice of the Way of the Heart and for service to Sri Da Avabhasa, to Sri Love-Anandashram, to the other Sacred Treasures of Free Daism, and to the Free Daist Communion.

All of the organizations that have evolved in response to Sri Da Avabhasa and His Offering are legally separate from one another, and each has its own purpose and function. He neither directs, nor bears responsibility for, the activities of these organizations. Again, He Functions only in Freedom. These organizations represent the collective intention of Free Daists worldwide not only to provide for the Sacred Treasures of Free Daism, but also to make Sri Da Avabhasa's Offering of the Way of the Heart universally available to all.

The Sacred Literature of Da Avabhasa
(THE "BRIGHT")

Heart-Master Da provides a way in which Oneness may be experienced by anyone who is bold enough to follow his teachings. It is important to understand that his vision is neither Eastern nor Western, but it is the eternal spiritual pulse of the Great Wisdom which knows no cultural, temporal, or geographical locus; it represents the apex of awareness of our species.

Larry Dossey, M.D.
author, *Space, Time, and Medicine*
and *Beyond Illness*

The teachings of Heart-Master Da, embodied in an extraordinary collection of writings, provide an exquisite manual for transformation.... I feel at the most profound depth of my being that his work will be crucial to an evolution toward full-humanness.

Barbara Marx Hubbard
author, *The Evolutionary Journey*

SOURCE LITERATURE

THE LOVE-ANANDA GITA

(THE WISDOM-SONG OF NON-SEPARATENESS)
The "Simple" Revelation-Book Of Da Kalki (The Divine World-Teacher and True Heart-Master, Da Love-Ananda Hridayam)
    The Love-Ananda Gita is Sri Da Avabhasa's quintessential Revelation of His Way of the Heart, containing His basic Instructions on the fundamental practice of Satsang, or feeling-Contemplation of His bodily

(human) Form, His Spiritual (and Always Blessing) Presence, and His Very (and Inherently Perfect) State of Free Being. The most basic Source-Text of His entire Word of Confession and Instruction. [The next edition of *The Love-Ananda Gita* will be published with the following attribution: *The Simple Revelation-Book Of The Divine World-Teacher and True Heart-Master, Da Avabhasa (The "Bright").]*
Standard Edition
$34.95* cloth, $19.95 paper

THE DAWN HORSE TESTAMENT
The Testament Of Secrets Of The Divine World-Teacher and True Heart-Master, Da Avabhasa (The "Bright")
    In this monumental text of over 800 large-format pages (a substantial updating and enlargement of the original Work published in 1985), Sri Da Avabhasa Reveals the Mysteries and devotional Secrets of every practice and developmental stage of the Way of the Heart. Ken Wilber, renowned scholar of Eastern and Western psychology and religion, was moved to write:

The Dawn Horse Testament is the most ecstatic, most profound, most complete, most radical, and most comprehensive <u>single</u> spiritual text ever to be penned and confessed by the Human-Transcendental Spirit.

8-1/2" x 11"
New Standard Edition
$39.95 cloth, $24.95 paper

* All prices are in U.S. dollars

THE DA UPANISHAD

*THE SHORT DISCOURSES ON
self-RENUNCIATION, GOD-REALIZATION, AND
THE ILLUSION OF RELATEDNESS*

In this sublime collection of Essays, Sri Da Avabhasa Offers an unsurpassed description of both the precise mechanism of egoic delusion and the nature, process, and ultimate fulfillment of the Sacred Ordeal of Divine Realization. (*The Da Upanishad* is an enlarged and updated edition of Sri Da Avabhasa's Work formerly titled *The Illusion Of Relatedness*. The next edition will be titled *The Da Avabhasa Upanishad*.)
Standard Edition
$19.95 paper

THE PERFECT PRACTICE

This book is Sri Da Avabhasa's summary distillation of the Wisdom and Process of practice in the ultimate stages of life. In it, Sri Da Avabhasa wields His Great Sword of Perfectly self-transcending God-Realization, Dispatching the dragons of egoic delusion, and all limited truths. He Calls us, and Draws us, to Realize the Very Divine Consciousness that is Radiantly Free, beyond all bondage to the limited states of the body, mind, and world.

The Perfect Practice includes the text of *The Lion Sutra*, Sri Da Avabhasa's poetic Revelation of the esoteric technicalities and Liberated Freedom of the "Perfect Practice", and the text of *The Liberator (Eleutherios)*, in which He Epitomizes, in lucid prose, the simpler approach to that same ultimate or "Perfect" Practice leading most directly to Divine Awakening.
(forthcoming)

THE ego-"I" is THE ILLUSION OF RELATEDNESS

Published here in book form, this central Essay from *The Da Avabhasa Upanishad* is an indispensable introduction to the esoteric Wisdom-Instruction of the Divine World-Teacher of our time. It includes Sri Da Avabhasa's utterly extraordinary commentaries on diet and sexual Yoga, His Divinely Enlightened secrets on how to responsibly master and transcend all the psycho-physical "sheaths", or bodies, and passage after passage that exposes the very core of our suffering, the illusion of relatedness.
$8.95 paper

THE BASKET OF TOLERANCE

*A GUIDE TO PERFECT UNDERSTANDING OF
THE ONE AND GREAT TRADITION
OF MANKIND*

Never before in history has it been possible for a seventh stage Adept to Give the world such a Gift: a comprehensive bibliography (listing more than 2,500 publications) of the world's historical traditions of truly human culture, practical self-discipline, perennial religion, universal religious mysticism, "esoteric" (but now openly communicated) Spirituality, Transcendental Wisdom, and Perfect (or Divine) Enlightenment, compiled, presented, and extensively annotated by Sri Da Avabhasa Himself. The summary of His Instruction on the Great Tradition of human Wisdom and the Sacred ordeal of Spiritual practice and Realization.
New Standard Edition
(forthcoming)

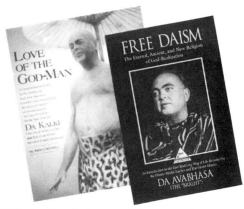

THE HYMN OF THE
TRUE HEART-MASTER

*(The New Revelation-Book Of The Ancient
and Eternal Religion Of Devotion To
The God-Realized Adept)*

The Hymn Of The True Heart-Master is Sri
Da Avabhasa's ecstatic proclamation of the Sat-
Guru as the supreme Means for Divine Self-
Realization. In 108 poetic verses, Sri Da
Avabhasa extols the Way of Divine Unity
through Ishta-Guru-Bhakti Yoga, or worshipful
service and devotion to the Ishta-Guru or
"Chosen" and "Most Beloved" Master of one's
heart. This volume also includes many of Sri Da
Avabhasa's primary Essays and Discourses on
the principle of Guru-devotion in His Company
as well as moving Leelas (or Stories) by His
devotees that demonstrate the supreme transforming power of this Yoga.
$34.95 cloth, $19.95 paper

INTRODUCTORY TEXTS

FREE DAISM

*THE ETERNAL, ANCIENT, AND NEW
RELIGION OF GOD-REALIZATION
An Introduction to the God-Realizing Way of
Life Revealed by the Divine World-Teacher and
True Heart-Master, Da Avabhasa (The "Bright")*

Addressed to new readers and written in a
highly accessible style, *Free Daism* is an introduction to Sri Da Avabhasa's Life and Work, the
fundamentals of His Wisdom-Teaching, the
Guru-devotee relationship in His Blessing
Company, the principles and practices of the
Way of the Heart, and life in the community of

Sri Da Avabhasa's devotees. It is a comprehensive and engaging introduction to all aspects of
the religion of Free Daism—the Liberating Way
that Sri Da Avabhasa has made available for all.

LOVE OF THE GOD-MAN

*A COMPREHENSIVE GUIDE TO THE
TRADITIONAL AND TIME-HONORED
GURU-DEVOTEE RELATIONSHIP, THE SUPREME
MEANS OF GOD-REALIZATION, AS FULLY
REVEALED FOR THE FIRST TIME BY THE
DIVINE WORLD-TEACHER AND TRUE HEART-
MASTER, DA AVABHASA (THE "BRIGHT")
by James Steinberg*

Love of the God Man is a full-length (over
800-page) discussion of the profound laws and
virtues of the Guru-devotee relationship as practiced in the Way of the Heart. Nowhere else in
the literature of sacred life does such an ency-
clopedic treatment of the Guru-devotee relationship exist. *Love of the God-Man* is an inex-
haustible resource, full of Sri Da Avabhasa's
Wisdom and His Leelas (inspiring stories) and
many stories from the Great Tradition.
Second Edition (forthcoming)

DIVINE DISTRACTION

A GUIDE TO THE GURU-DEVOTEE RELATIONSHIP, THE SUPREME MEANS OF GOD-REALIZATION, AS FULLY REVEALED FOR THE FIRST TIME BY THE DIVINE WORLD-TEACHER AND TRUE HEART-MASTER, DA AVABHASA (THE "BRIGHT")
by James Steinberg

Presented by a longtime devotee of Sri Da Avabhasa, this shorter version of *Love of the God-Man* describes, illustrates, and extols the Guru-devotee relationship. *Divine Distraction* features compelling stories of Sri Da Avabhasa's Work with His devotees, and illuminating passages from His Wisdom-Teaching, along with instruction and stories from great Masters and disciples in the world's religious and Spiritual traditions.
$12.95 paper

FEELING WITHOUT LIMITATION

AWAKENING TO THE TRUTH BEYOND FEAR, SORROW, AND ANGER
A Spiritual Discourse by The Divine World-Teacher and True Heart-Master, Da Avabhasa (The "Bright")

A brief introductory volume featuring a Discourse from Sri Da Avabhasa's Teaching years that presents in simplest terms His fundamental Argument about human suffering, seeking, and freedom. Also includes remarkable Leelas and testimonies by three devotees.
$4.95 paper

THE PERFECT ALTERNATIVE

A TESTIMONY TO THE POWER OF THE TRANSFORMING GRACE OF SRI DA AVABHASA˙ (THE "BRIGHT")
by Kanya Samatva Suprithi

A gem of a book by one of the most mature practitioners of the Way of the Heart, a woman who has entered the sixth stage of life through Sri Da Avabhasa's Grace. Kanya Samatva Suprithi presents here a very readable summary of Sri Da Avabhasa's basic Arguments about seeking and Happiness, and she includes some of her own story as a Daist practitioner. An excellent and very concise introduction to Sri Da Avabhasa and His Work.
$4.95 paper

AVADHOOTS, MAD LAMAS, AND FOOLS

by James Steinberg

A brief and lively account of the "Crazy Wisdom" style of sacred Instruction employed by Adepts in many traditions, times, and cultures, including Leelas of Sri Da Avabhasa's Teaching years and His Divine Emergence Work.
(forthcoming)

THE WISDOM-LITERATURE OF DA AVABHASA'S TEACHING WORK

THE KNEE OF LISTENING
THE EARLY-LIFE ORDEAL AND THE "RADICAL" SPIRITUAL REALIZATION OF THE DIVINE WORLD-TEACHER AND TRUE HEART-MASTER, DA AVABHASA (THE "BRIGHT")

In this sublime Autobiography of His early Life, Sri Da Avabhasa Tells the sometimes humorous, sometimes poignant, always Profound Story of His Compassionate Birth in human form to serve the Liberation of humanity. His early Life is the record of the Divine Being breaking through into mortal time, submitting to human limits, and discovering, in that context, the Great Divine Way whereby all beings may be Liberated. His Story is full of Spiritual and Divine Play, and of very human pains and joys, and the very real process of His Re-Awakening in God.

Following the autobiographical material are two additional sections by Sri Da Avabhasa presenting His earliest Essays on the practice and Realization of "radical" understanding.

This new, expanded edition is twice the length of the previously published version, which has become a classic of modern Spiritual literature.
$18.95 paper

ALL NEW!
THE DIVINE EMERGENCE OF THE WORLD-TEACHER, DA AVABHASA (THE "BRIGHT")

In the great history of Spirituality, there appears from time to time an Extraordinary Manifestation of the Divine in human form. Such Divine Masters are "World-Events", and their own Personal bodily existence is the crucible for a rapid succession of biopsychic crises and transformations that mysteriously hastens the Liberation of all beings. *The Divine Emergence of the World-Teacher, Da Avabhasa (The "Bright")* is the Story of the astonishing changes that have taken place in the Life and Spiritual Work of Sri Da Avabhasa since His Re-Awakening in 1970 to the Condition of absolute God-Consciousness. Told in His own Words, and in the riveting Stories of many of His devotees, this is the most Enlightening Story humanity has ever heard.
(forthcoming)

THE METHOD OF THE SIDDHAS
TALKS ON THE SPIRITUAL TECHNIQUE OF THE SAVIORS OF MANKIND

In this book of powerful and often extremely humorous Talks with His devotees in 1972 and 1973, the first year of His formal Teaching Work, Sri Da Avabhasa Reveals the Secret of the Way of Satsang: the profound and transforming relationship between the Sat-Guru and His devotee.
New Standard Edition
(forthcoming)

SCIENTIFIC PROOF OF THE EXISTENCE OF GOD WILL SOON BE ANNOUNCED BY THE WHITE HOUSE!

PROPHETIC WISDOM ABOUT THE MYTHS AND IDOLS OF MASS CULTURE AND POPULAR RELIGIOUS CULTISM, THE NEW PRIESTHOOD OF SCIENTIFIC AND POLITICAL MATERIALISM, AND THE SECRETS OF ENLIGHTENMENT HIDDEN IN THE BODY OF MAN

Speaking as a modern Prophet, Sri Da Avabhasa combines His urgent critique of present-day society with a challenge to create true sacred community based on actual Divine Communion and a Spiritual and Transcendental Vision of human Destiny.
New Standard Edition
(forthcoming)

THE TRANSMISSION OF DOUBT

TALKS AND ESSAYS ON THE TRANSCENDENCE OF SCIENTIFIC MATERIALISM THROUGH "RADICAL" UNDERSTANDING

Sri Da Avabhasa's principal critique of scientific materialism, the dominant philosophy and world-view of modern humanity that suppresses our native impulse to Liberation, and His Revelation of the ancient and ever-new Way that is the true sacred science of Life, or of Divine Being Itself.
New Standard Edition
(forthcoming)

THE ENLIGHTENMENT OF THE WHOLE BODY

A RATIONAL AND NEW PROPHETIC REVELATION OF THE TRUTH OF RELIGION, ESOTERIC SPIRITUALITY, AND THE DIVINE DESTINY OF MAN

One of Sri Da Avabhasa's early Revelations of the Way of Eternal Life that He Offers to beings everywhere, including Ecstatic Confessions of His own Enlightened Realization of the Divine Person, and sublime Instruction in the practices of the Way of the Heart. When initially published in 1978, this Text was a comprehensive summary of His Way of the Heart. Includes a unique section, with illustrations, on the esoteric anatomy of the advanced and the ultimate stages of Spiritual transformation.
New Standard Edition
(forthcoming)

NIRVANASARA

Sri Da Avabhasa critically appraises the sacred Wisdom-Culture of mankind, particularly focusing on the two most sublime traditions of sacred life and practice: Buddhism and Hindu non-dualism (Advaita Vedanta). Here He also announces and expounds upon His own Way of the Heart as the continuation and fulfillment of the most exalted Teachings of Buddhism and Hinduism.
New Standard Edition
(forthcoming)

THE DREADED GOM-BOO, OR THE IMAGINARY DISEASE THAT RELIGION SEEKS TO CURE

In this remarkable book, Sri Da Avabhasa Offers a startling and humorous insight: All religion seeks to cure us of an unreal or fundamentally imaginary disease, which He calls "the Dreaded Gom-Boo". This disease is our constant assumption that we have fallen from Grace and are thus in need of the salvatory "cure" of religious belief.

The good news of Sri Da Avabhasa's Way of the Heart is that we need not seek to be cured but need only feel, observe, understand, and renounce (through the real ordeal of sacred practice) the very activity of seeking itself, and thus be restored to our native Happiness and Freedom.

New Standard Edition
(forthcoming)

CRAZY DA MUST SING, INCLINED TO HIS WEAKER SIDE

CONFESSIONAL POEMS
OF LIBERATION AND LOVE

Composed principally in the early 1970s and expressed spontaneously with the ardor of continuous, Divinely Awakened Identification with all beings, these remarkable poems proclaim Sri Da Avabhasa's vulnerable human Love and His Mysterious, "Crazy" passion to Liberate others from ego-bondage.

$9.95 paper

THE SONG OF THE SELF SUPREME

ASHTAVAKRA GITA
The Classical Text of Atmadvaita
by Ashtavakra

An authoritative translation of the *Ashtavakra Gita*, a text Sri Da Avabhasa has described as "among the greatest (and most senior) communications of all the religious and Spiritual traditions of mankind". His illuminating Preface is a unique commentary on this grand classic of Advaita Vedanta, discussing the *Ashtavakra Gita* in the context of the total Great Tradition of Spiritual and Transcendental Wisdom. Sri Da Avabhasa also identifies and discusses the characteristics of those rare texts and traditions that fully communicate the Realization and "Point of View" of the seventh, or fully Enlightened, stage of life.

New Standard Edition
(forthcoming)

Da Avabhasa's teaching is, I believe, unsurpassed by that of any other spiritual Hero, of any period, of any place, of any time, of any persuasion.

Ken Wilber
author, *The Spectrum of Consciousness,*
Up from Eden, and *A Sociable God*

PRACTICAL TEXTS

THE EATING GORILLA
COMES IN PEACE

*THE TRANSCENDENTAL PRINCIPLE OF LIFE
APPLIED TO DIET AND THE REGENERATIVE
DISCIPLINE OF TRUE HEALTH*

In a substantial reworking of the first
edition of this Text, Sri Da Avabhasa Offers a
practical manual of Divinely Inspired Wisdom
about diet, health and healing, and the sacred
approach to birthing and dying.
New Standard Edition (forthcoming)

CONSCIOUS EXERCISE AND
THE TRANSCENDENTAL SUN

*THE PRINCIPLE OF LOVE APPLIED TO
EXERCISE AND THE METHOD OF COMMON
PHYSICAL ACTION. A SCIENCE OF WHOLE
BODY WISDOM, OR TRUE EMOTION,
INTENDED MOST ESPECIALLY FOR THOSE
ENGAGED IN RELIGIOUS OR SPIRITUAL LIFE*

"Conscious exercise" is a "technology of
love" which transforms physical exercise, play,
and all ordinary activity into an embrace of the
infinite energy of the cosmos, always in the
conscious context of feeling-Contemplation of
Sri Da Avabhasa Himself as Divine Heart-Master.
Greatly enlarged and updated from earlier editions.
New Standard Edition (forthcoming)

EASY DEATH

*SPIRITUAL DISCOURSES AND ESSAYS ON THE
INHERENT AND ULTIMATE TRANSCENDENCE
OF DEATH AND EVERYTHING ELSE*

In this major expansion of the popular
first edition of His Talks and Essays on death,

Sri Da Avabhasa Reveals the esoteric secrets of
the death process and Offers a wealth of
practical Instruction on how to prepare for a
God-Conscious and ecstatic transition from
physical embodiment.

Elisabeth Kübler-Ross wrote:

*An exciting, stimulating, and thought-
provoking book that adds immensely to the
literature on the phenomena of life and death.
Thank you for this masterpiece.*

New Standard Edition
$14.95 paper

LOVE OF THE TWO-ARMED FORM

*THE FREE AND REGENERATIVE FUNCTION
OF SEXUALITY IN ORDINARY LIFE, AND THE
TRANSCENDENCE OF SEXUALITY IN TRUE
RELIGIOUS OR SPIRITUAL PRACTICE*

Sri Da Avabhasa's Instruction on the cultivation of "true intimacy" and the Realization of
truly ecstatic, Spiritualized sexuality—a profound critique of both worldly exploitation of
sex and ascetical, anti-sexual religious messages. As an alternative to these errors of West
and East, Sri Da Avabhasa proposes the specific
practices of sexual "conscious exercise" and
"sexual communion" (for sexually active individuals who practice in Satsang with Him). His
Enlightened Wisdom-Teaching on emotion and
sexuality Calls and inspires all men and women
to a new and compassionate union of love,
desire, and Spiritual consciousness.
New Standard Edition (forthcoming)

LEELAS

The Sanskrit term "leela" (sometimes "lila") traditionally refers to the Divine Play of the Sat-Guru with his or her devotees, whereby he or she Instructs and Liberates the world. Sri Da Avabhasa has said that Leelas of His Instructional Play with His devotees are part of His own Word of Instruction, and they are, therefore, Potent with the Blessing and Awakening-Power of His Heart-Transmission.

THE CALLING OF THE KANYAS

CONFESSIONS OF SPIRITUAL AWAKENING AND PERFECT PRACTICE THROUGH THE LIBERATING GRACE OF THE DIVINE WORLD-TEACHER AND TRUE HEART-MASTER, DA AVABHASA (THE "BRIGHT")
by Meg McDonnell
with the Da Avabhasa Gurukula Kanyadana Kumari Order (Kanya Kaivalya Navaneeta and Kanya Samatva Suprithi)

The story of the Graceful ordeal of sacred practice and transformation embraced by the formal renunciate order of two women devotees who personally serve Sri Da Avabhasa. The confessions and the example of the Kanyas call everyone to deeply understand and heartily respond to the Supremely Blessed Event that has made their own Spiritual transformation possible: Sri Da Avabhasa's Great Divine Emergence, beginning in early 1986 and continuing ever since. (forthcoming)

FOR AND ABOUT CHILDREN

WHAT AND WHERE AND WHO TO REMEMBER TO BE HAPPY

A SIMPLE EXPLANATION OF THE WAY OF THE HEART (FOR CHILDREN, AND EVERYONE ELSE)

A new edition of Sri Da Avabhasa's essential Teaching-Revelation on the religious principles and practices appropriate for children. In Words easily understood and enjoyed by children and adults, Sri Da Avabhasa tells children (and adults) how to "feel and breathe and Behold and Be the Mystery".
New Standard Edition, fully illustrated (forthcoming)

THE TWO SECRETS (yours, AND MINE)

A STORY OF HOW THE WORLD-TEACHER, DA KALKI, GAVE GREAT WISDOM AND BLESSING HELP TO YOUNG PEOPLE (AND EVEN OLDER PEOPLE, TOO) ABOUT HOW TO REMEMBER WHAT AND WHERE AND WHO TO REMEMBER TO BE HAPPY
A Gift (Forever) from Da Kalki (The World-Teacher, Heart-Master Da Love-Ananda)

A moving account (as told by Brahmacharini Shawnee Free Jones and her friends) of a young girl's confrontation with the real demands of sacred practice, and how Sri Da Avabhasa lovingly Instructed and Served her in her transition through a crisis of commitment to practice that every devotee must, at some point, endure.
$12.95 paper

VEGETABLE SURRENDER,

OR HAPPINESS IS NOT BLUE

by Heart-Master Da and two little girls

The humorous tale of Onion One-Yin and his vegetable friends, who embark on a search for someone who can teach them about happiness and love, and end up learning a great lesson about seeking. Beautifully illustrated with original line drawings.
$12.95 cloth, oversize

LOOK AT THE SUNLIGHT
ON THE WATER

*EDUCATING CHILDREN FOR A LIFE
OF SELF-TRANSCENDING LOVE AND
HAPPINESS: AN INTRODUCTION*

Full of eminently practical guidance for the "whole bodily" and sacred education of children and young people, this simple, straightforward, informative text is also perhaps the best available brief summation of Sri Da Avabhasa's Wisdom on the first three stages of life, or the period from infancy to adulthood.
$12.95 paper

PERIODICALS

THE FREE DAIST

The Bi-Monthly Journal of the Heart-Word and Blessing Work of the Divine World-Teacher and True Heart-Master, Da Avabhasa (The "Bright")

The Free Daist chronicles the Leelas of the Teaching Work and the Divine Emergence Work of Sri Da Avabhasa, and describes the practice and process of devotion, self-discipline, self-understanding, service, and meditation in the Way of the Heart. In addition, the magazine reports on the cultural and missionary activities of the Free Daist Communion and the cooperative community of Sri Da Avabhasa's devotees. Of special interest is the regular "Hermitage Chronicle" offering current news of Sri Da Avabhasa's Life and Work.

Subscriptions are $42.00 per year for six issues. Please send your check or money order (payable to The Dawn Horse Press) to: The Free Daist, P.O. Box 3680, Clearlake, CA 95422, USA.

THE "BRIGHT"

Celebrations of the Divine World-Teacher, Da Avabhasa (The "Bright")

A brief bi-monthly periodical, oriented to the general reader, introducing the Good News of Sri Da Avabhasa and His Work and countering the trends of scientific materialism, religious provincialism, and anti-guruism in present-day society.

Subscriptions are $12.00 per year for six issues. Please send your check or money order (payable to The Dawn Horse Press) to:

The "Bright", P.O. Box 3680, Clearlake, CA 95422, USA.

A subscription to both *The "Bright"* and *The Free Daist* is only $48.00.

THE GARDEN OF LIONS MAGAZINE
The Worldwide Voice of
Young Free Daists

This unique magazine is the voice of the worldwide culture of children and young people who practice the Way of the Heart under the Enlightened Guidance of the living Sat-Guru, Sri Da Avabhasa. *The Garden of Lions Magazine* includes published Instruction on various aspects of sacred practice for young people, Discourses Given by Sri Da Avabhasa, personal accounts and inspiring stories from the lives of young devotees, and a great variety of articles and artwork from young people of all ages from all over the world. Themes have included: an introduction to the practice of Brahmacharya (the study of God), the Spiritual practice of Ecstasy and Guru-devotion, and the Enlightened practice of sexuality for young people.

The Garden of Lions Magazine is a truly extraordinary celebration of the unprecedented Wisdom-Teaching and Way of life Given by Sri Da Avabhasa.

Subscriptions are $16.00 per year for three issues. Please send your check or money order (payable to *The Garden of Lions Magazine*) to: The Garden of Lions Magazine, Subscription Department, P.O. Box 1737, Lower Lake, CA 95457, USA.

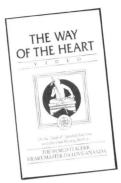

VIDEOTAPES

THE WAY OF THE HEART
On the "Radical" Spiritual Teaching
and Universal Blessing Work of the
Western-Born Adept, Heart-Master
Da Love-Ananda

Incorporating rare segments of recent and historical footage, Part One tells the Story of Sri Da Avabhasa's Illumined Birth and His Ordeal of Divine Re-Awakening for the sake of others, and celebrates the Emergence of His Work of World Blessing. Part Two (which includes Talk excerpts by Sri Da Avabhasa and testimonials by longtime practitioners) describes the Gifts and forms of practice that are Given to all who take up the Way of the Heart as Sri Da Avabhasa's devotees. Part Three introduces the sacred culture of the Way of the Heart.
$29.95, 2 hours
VHS, NTSC, or PAL format

The Way of the Heart is also available in a modified form, which includes recent footage of Sri Da Avabhasa in Darshan with devotees and other material not included in the full-length version. A brief, summary audiovisual introduction to His Life and Divine Work as the World-Teacher in a world addicted to egoic suffering and seeking.
$19.95, 76 minutes
VHS, NTSC, or PAL format

ORDERING THE BOOKS
AND VIDEOTAPES
OF DA AVABHASA

The books and videotapes of Sri Da Avabhasa are available at local bookstores and by mail from the Dawn Horse Book Depot.

Please write to us at the address below for a complete catalogue of books and audiovisual publications on the Way of the Heart and traditional sacred literature.

In the USA please add $3.50 for the first book or videotape ($5.00 for each *Dawn Horse Testament*) and $1.50 for each additional book or videotape. California residents add 7-1/4% sales tax.

Outside the USA please add $5.00 for the first book or videotape ($6.00 for each *Dawn Horse Testament*) and $2.00 for each additional book or videotape.

To order the books and videotapes listed above, and to receive your copy of the Dawn Horse Press Catalogue, please write:

The Dawn Horse Book Depot
P.O. Box 3680
Clearlake, CA 95422, USA
(707) 928-4936

INDEX

A

addict, ego-"I" as, 143
addiction, root of, 143
adolescent strategy, 123-24
Advaita Vedanta, 238, 256
advanced and ultimate stages of life, 181, 322
Agency
    forms of, 59, 322
    as Vehicle of Da Avabhasa's Blessing Grace, 57-59, 322
Aham Da Asmi Sthan, 296, *297*
Ajna Door, 177, 185
alcohol, use of in celebrations and gatherings, 50, 148-50, 293
Alpha strategy, 236
Amrita Nadi, 252-53, 257, 322
Arati Puja, 120, *121*
Archives, sacred, *280*
area study groups, 292
Arrow, defined, 322
arts, sacred, 289-91
ascent, of Da Avabhasa's Spirit-Current, 231, 236
Ashram, 270-73
Ashram Sanctuaries. *See* Sanctuaries
"Atma-Murti", 182, 185, 249, 322
attention, transcendence of, 245
Attraction, to the Sat-Guru, 18, 191, 200, 212
Autobiography of a Yogi (Paramahansa Yogananda), 230-31
Avabhasa, defined and described, x
Avadhoot, 209, 217
Avadhoota Mandir, 95
"Avoiding relationship?", 42-43, 102, 206, 217, 224
Awakening
    A Call To, 4-5
    from the dream of life, 16-18

B

The Basket of Tolerance, 72, 75, 123, 143-44, 173, 174
Be Consciousness: the first stage of the "Perfect Practice", 242-43
"Beauty Foot", Da Avabhasa's, 208
betrayal, mood of, 162, 163
bhakti, 110-27
    defined, 113
    See also devotion
Blessed Companion Bear Company, 283
blue pearl, 231
bodily (human) Form of Da Avabhasa, 56
    as Teaching, 82-83
Brhadaranyaka Upanishad, 257
the "Bright", Da Avabhasa as, 28, 322
Bubba Free John, as Name of Da Avabhasa, 48
Buddhism, 238
businesses, community, 281-83

C

A Call To Awakening, 4-5
capitalization, use in the Way of the Heart, ix
celibacy, 164
chakra system, 231
childish strategy, 20-21, 123-24
children and young people in the Way of the Heart, 284-88
Christian holy sites, Da Avabhasa tours, 43
cigarettes, use of in celebrations and gatherings, 50, 293

Circle, defined, 322
    (diagram), 232
"coins", Da Avabhasa's, 51
Columbia College event, Da Avabhasa's Restoration to "Brightness", 31-32
"Come to Me when you are already Happy!", 216
community
    cooperative in the Way of the Heart, 261-91
    human and religious necessity of, 265
    Spiritual life in context of, 143-44
community services and businesses, 281-83
Compulsory Dancing, 162-63, 220, 225
conditional fifth stage Nirvikalpa Samadhi, 39, 40, 60, 175, 178-80, 233
    Da Avabhasa's experience of, 39
"conductivity"
    defined, 152, 322
    Spiritual form of in the Way of the Heart, 223-24, 227
    technical process of, 103, 152
"conscious exercise", 144, 151-54
    contrasted with popular Western approach, 153-54
    defined, 151
    foundation of, 152
    as a form of "conductivity", 153
Consciousness, as Real Nature of existence, 4
"conscious process"
    defined, 322
    as the discipline of attention, 246
    as primary discipline of the Way of the Heart, 152-53
    as the transcendence of attention, 246
"consideration", 78, 203
    defined, viii
    as process in Da Avabhasa's Company, 50-51, 55
    and self-discipline, 144
    and sexual disciplines, 163
Contemplate consciousness: the second stage of the "Perfect Practice", 249-50
cooperative community. *See* community
copyright, perpetual, 329-30
Cosmic Consciousness, 177
Cosmic Mandala, 128, 139, 233, 236, 245, 257-58
Cosmic Wedding, Da Avabhasa's 44-46
"Crazy", defined, 323
"Crazy" Freedom, 253
"Crazy Wisdom", defined, 60-61
"Crazy Wisdom" Work, Da Avabhasa's, 49
cultism, 123, 124-25
culture of celebration, Free Daism as, 122
culture of expectation and inspiration, 144

D

Da
    defined, x
    as a traditional Name of the Divine, x
Da Avabhasa
    abandonment of Illumination as baby, 29
    Awakening of Teaching Function, 40-41
    Awakening of Teaching Siddhis, 46-52
    beginning of His formal Teaching Work, 46
    birth of, 28
    as the "Bright", 28
    at Columbia College, 30
    as continuous Source of Wisdom-Teaching, 81-82
    as "Crazy Frank", 35

An Invitation

O *f all the means for Spiritual growth and ultimate Liberation offered in the sacred traditions of humankind, the most effective is the Way of Satsang, or the Way lived in the Blessing Company of One Who has Realized the Truth. The Divine World-Teacher and True Heart-Master, Da Avabhasa (The "Bright"), Offers just such a rare and graceful Opportunity.*

The transformative relationship to Da Avabhasa is the foundation of the Free Daist practice that He Offers. Through a whole personal and collective life of self-transcending practice in His Company, ordinary men and women may be purified of their egoic suffering and enjoy the Blessings of a God-Realizing destiny.

If you would like to receive a free introductory brochure or talk to a practicing devotee about forms of participation in Free Daist practice, please write to or call:

Correspondence Department
The Free Daist Communion
P.O. Box 3680
Clearlake, California 95422, USA

Telephone: (707) 928-4936